Have Toddler Will Travel

Have Toddler Will Travel

SARAH TUCKER

HODDER
MOBIUS

First published in Great Britain in 2002 by Hodder and Stoughton
A division of Hodder Headline

4   6   8   10   9   7   5   3

A CIP catalogue record for this title is available from the British Library

0 340 81996 0

Typeset in Berkeley Book by Palimpsest Book Production,
Polmont, Stirlingshire
Printed and bound in Great Britain by
Mackays of Chatham plc, Chatham, Kent

Hodder and Stoughton
A division of Hodder Headline
338 Euston Road
London NW1 3BH

'Never go on trips with anyone you don't love'
Ernest Hemmingway.

I'd like to dedicate this book to Tom . . . who is sunshine, and to my husband Marco. All my love always.

Contents

PART TWO – **Toddler-friendly Travel**

Acknowledgements

To my round table of absolutely fabulous and supportive friends who every June turn up at Fredericks come rain, shine, bad traffic or better offers. I love you very much.

And to wonderful mums Sarah K, Emma D, Emma M, Emily and Rebecca, Claire B, Anna G and Pam G, who all had babies last year or when I had Tom – and will need this book some day soon. And not forgetting Jon L, Chris K, Robert T and Jonathan S, whose wives all had babies and are now finding the whole process rather bewildering (don't forget, it's your fault).

Very special thanks to Rowena Webb, Kerry Hood (and Emma!), Karen Sullivan and all at H&S who have been very supportive, enthusiastic and wonderful to work with. Thanks also to the excellent Eva at Hamleys, inspirational Lizzie at Baby Organix and especially Sarah Baldock and her team at Tesco. Thank you for your support Sarah. And to Fran for making me look how I would love to look everyday. Also to Nicola, who is an example to us all.

Foreword

Every mother's nightmare is travelling with a screaming two-year-old. It happened to me a few days ago. I carefully organised our return from a holiday in Italy for the middle of the day so that Ben (aged 23 1/2 months) would be at his best for the journey. Needless to say, there was a delay and we were left sitting on the tarmac for nearly an hour before take-off – by which time Ben was literally crawling up the inside of the aircraft. My efforts to restrain him were futile as he has extraordinary strength for one so small. By the time we did take off, his face was contorted with rage at being restrained and he shrieked for 10 minutes non-stop. At the other end, I bumped into a friend by the luggage carousel who commented on what a lovely looking child he was. Then it seemed to dawn on her that he might have been the source of the horrendous noise on the plane and her illusion of him as a cherubic looking angel was shattered.

Difficult as they may be as travelling companions, toddlers have a right to holidays too. Sarah's book does the nervous parent a great service in highlighting where their toddlers will be tolerated. There is nothing worse than staying in a hotel where they claim to welcome children and then insist on complete silence and pass on constant complaints to the embarrassed parents from other guests every five minutes. I have come across a few hotels that genuinely welcome toddlers over the years and have revisited these several times thereafter. My favourite child-friendly hotel is the Ballymaloe House in Co. Cork, Eire. Myrtle Allen, who owns the hotel, has around 20 grandchildren of her own and makes every small visitor feel like one of the family. Children have their own meal together in the evening with everything that they really like to eat on the menu, leaving the adults free to enjoy a quiet evening together later. If babysitters are required, they are procured from a local fishing village. In my experience, children behave much better in this environment. If they know that they are not welcome, they seem to vie with each other to attract attention – that is the sort of attention that you don't want.

Travelling makes an enormous impression on small children and can generate memories which will remain with them for the rest of their lives. When I was 21 months old, I travelled with my mother from London to Kenya to see my grandmother. This was in 1962 and the journey involved a stop at Rome and a stop at Cairo for refuelling. After many hours of travelling, we arrived at our destination, my mother exhausted and minus her lipstick which I had used to decorate the backs of the seats in front of us on the plane whilst she slept. I have vivid memories of my grandmother's cook in a purple fez, being pushed by the daughter of one of my grandmother's friends in a white wooden wheelbarrow, and being taken to a small zoo and meeting a baby rhino, a baby elephant and a zebra. These memories have been with me for the whole of my life. I can remember all my childhood holidays in great detail and I notice that my children are the same. They get enormously excited when I tell them where we are going and they want to know where it is on the map, how long it takes to get there and what sort of accomodation we will be staying in.

Travel is a great stimulation for a toddler. It provides new experiences in the form of things to look at, different smells, unusual tastes. I do hope that *Have Toddler Will Travel* will encourage more parents with young children to travel. Bon voyage!

Nicola Horlick, 2001

PART ONE

Which Holiday?

Are You Mad?

This is what my friends screamed when I told them that I wanted to travel with my toddler son, Thomas.

He was still only two years old, with a host of endearing – possibly alarming – toddler qualities: talkative (repeating verbatim every rude word at the most embarrassing times; in other words, public places); clumsy; accident prone; toddling like a robot on speed, all with the energy and sense of adventure of Indiana Jones, but without Jones' fear of snakes. To make matters worse, in a period of only months, he had managed to succumb to more known diseases than I have yet to catch in 36 years. Coughs, colds, allergies, infections – you name it, Thomas had it.

Toddlers, warned my patient GP, are more susceptible to illness than any other age group. And Thomas was undeniable proof of that theory. So what happened to my idyllic baby? Normal, it seems, but did I really want to travel with this bundle of fun?

Preparation was the answer, I mused. I would go to the library, bookshops and travel experts. I'd pick up armfuls of the many travel books out there claiming to have all the answers to travelling with children. And, I thought, hey, toddlers are children, are they not? So all those recommendations in books aimed at parents with young children, all those holiday brochures that so neatly line the shelves of the travel agents, with their inspiring advertisements for 'family-friendly' hotels, attractions, resorts and holidays . . . they would solve my predicament, right?

Wrong.

There is undoubtedly a wealth of information out there – all readily available from tourist offices, websites and glossy brochures – but I found most of it to be misleading. Don't get me wrong, the travel agents I approached as a mystery shopper were, in general, well informed. And websites such as www.family-travel.co.uk, www.mumsnet.com and www.travellingwithchildren.co.uk all proved excellent sources of information that parents of children of all ages (not just toddlers) can use to uncover the facts about the good resorts – and those that are downright ugly.

But much of the information provided was simply not relevant to small children. In fact, in the eyes of the travel industry, toddlers seem to be overlooked in the race to supply the best kids clubs and nursery facilities, neither of which is particularly relevant to a toddler's needs.

The definition and understanding of the phrase 'family-friendly' is as wide as it is vague. It was time to do my own research!

So, for the past 12 months I have travelled around the UK, meeting parents in health clubs, crèches, infant schools and nurseries, asking both children and their parents what they liked and disliked about their holidays. They explained what they wanted and needed (which were not necessarily the same thing), and what they perceived to be important and attractive to a family with a toddler or two in tow. They told me which countries proved to be the most toddler-friendly, which airlines and airports were most suited to travelling with toddlers, which hotel groups and tour operators provided the best value, and which mode of transport was preferred by parents and toddlers alike.

This research was conducted with over 1000 mums and dads of toddlers throughout the UK. In general, they almost all felt that the travel industry had yet to come to grips with the concept of toddlers, and that holidays for toddlers were not only almost impossible to find, but inaccurately marketed. One father summed it up by saying, 'It is still a rather grey area to some of the travel industry. It should be a black and white one.'

Lesson number one: Family-friendly does not mean toddler-friendly.

Toddlers are unique, or so it seems. From the almost sublime experience of travelling with a baby who does little more than sleep, feed and poo, a toddler is ridiculously difficult to control and entertain. Most parents find it difficult to keep a modicum of control in their own homes or at the local supermarket. And these, of course, are known territory to a toddler. So how can parents hope to keep the show on the road in environments unknown? And is there really any possibility of something called a 'family holiday'?

Parents who have travelled with their toddlers – either through necessity or in the desperate hope they could have a relaxing holiday together – all offered me the same advice: Don't. 'It is no holiday,' I was told. 'Family-friendly means cheap and nasty'; 'Sarah, you've got to realise you've downgraded by upsizing the family'; 'Leave them at home'; 'Don't even contemplate self-catering, because you will end up working harder on holiday than you ever do at home'. The warnings came thick and fast.

'Those resorts that target families are tatty around the edges, expensive and know you don't have any other options,' they advised. The 'they', of course, were the over 1000 parents who responded to my request for anecdotes and tips for travelling with one to four-year-olds. It was depressing.

So whatever you want to label it – extremely challenging, or a time when patience and compromise are the order of the day – it appears that travelling is no holiday when you have a toddler in tow.

But, there are some havens of toddler-friendliness. Some are in unexpected places, and others are with companies that don't even market their toddler-friendliness as a unique selling point. What's more, there are holiday companies and destinations that not only cater for this most challenging of age groups, but also remember that grown ups want to have fun and chill out, too.

3

And that's what this book is all about. We'll look at every aspect of preparation before a holiday, including helping to choose the break that will most suit you and your toddler, where the most successful holiday is likely to take place, how to get there, when you should go, what you should take and even the health precautions you should consider. Whether you are considering travelling independently, or with a tour operator package, camping or cruising, skiing or safariing, we'll look at the pros and cons of each, and help you to choose the holiday that is right for you. I've listed a huge number of addresses and websites for the operators, hotels, beaches, attractions and even car hire companies that parents have tried and recommended. In fact, you'll find everything here to make travelling with a toddler – well – easier.

We'll look closely at those countries that offer the most for families travelling with toddlers. Based on my extensive research, and the first-hand experiences of so many families interviewed for this book, this section delves into the fine details of each country, including the duration of the journey there, the local attractions, infrastructure, culture and points of interest for toddlers and parents alike. There are destinations to fit all tastes and budgets, from short-term breaks to long-haul holidays. Many of these countries may be off the beaten track, or places to which you had never considered travelling, but all have a lot to offer both for parents and toddlers alike. While in no way a comprehensive guide to what's available for toddlers around the world, this section acts as a useful introduction to countries that work for toddlers, based on the experiences of parents who have been there.

So what is a toddler-friendly holiday?

First of all, let's establish what exactly constitutes a toddler. For the purposes of this book, toddlers are children between the ages of one and four – no longer babies, but not really fully fledged children either. And as every parent of a toddler knows, they are in a class of their own when it comes to entertaining, travelling, and even getting through day-to-day life. That's the starting point, and the focus of this book. But do holidays need to be geared to cope with the demands of a toddler? You bet they do.

Holiday brochures that pitch themselves as 'family holidays' are not necessarily appropriate for families with toddlers. In the hundreds of holiday brochures I have examined over the past 12 months, the phrase most quoted was: 'plenty of fun for children of all ages'. Interestingly, however, the parents I interviewed all agreed on one thing – most holiday brochures are full of meaningless waffle. In fact, most of the resorts described as being suitable for families were simply not appropriate for families with toddlers. And the few that were suitable were only really ideal for families who didn't mind sharing their break with every other young family in the UK. So take 'family-friendly' resorts with a pinch of salt. They may be friendly to some families, but perhaps not to yours.

Of the 100 or so tour operators I approached with requests for information about facilities for toddlers, about 15 were able to deliver ideas, resorts and destinations that would provide the safety element, the fun aspects, the childcare and the kiddies club suitable for this age group. Many of the 'family-friendly packages' are aimed at children of four or five plus. So holiday brochures only tell you half the story. Before you book, through the net, a travel agent, or direct with a hotel or tour operator, make sure you establish the age group that needs to be catered for. Ask lots of questions, and get your answers in writing. If you want a holiday that is an experience to remember, you need to make sure you've got the facts straight, and that you know what to expect.

Which holiday?

The options are limitless, and it can be difficult to choose the holiday that will best suit you and your toddler's needs, particularly if you have other children to consider. Before planning a holiday with a toddler, there are a number of issues to contemplate. But one of the most important things you can do is to decide what you are looking for, and what every family members needs.

To help you along the way, I've detailed below a summary of the issues and experiences that parents and children most enjoyed – and disliked – about the holidays they've taken.

Toddlers liked . . .

According to the many four-year-olds with whom I spoke, the 10 'best bits' of holidays include the following.

1. Building sand castles on the beach
2. Playing ball on the beach
3. Burying daddy in the sand ('not mummy, as she may get hurt')
4. Playing with new friends – on the beach
5. The crabs/bits of broken wood/rock pools at the beach
6. Riding on a steam train (Thomas the Tank Engine or a close relation)
7. Watching the big fish (aquarium)
8. Face painting/dressing up (at kiddies clubs)
9. Seeing favourite cartoon character on flight TV
10. Spending more time with mummy and daddy

As you probably gathered, these are the things that children remember about their holidays, rather than those experiences that parents think they will remember. Sorry folks, but nothing about first time in a plane, or luxury resort in the Bahamas or the golden sands of the Seychelles, with a 24-hour maid service and 5-star treatment all the way.

Toddlers disliked . . .

The ten 'worst bits' of holidays were even more enlightening – for the parents of these toddlers, as well as for me!

1. Airports (hot, sticky, parents are 'cross' and 'distracted' – and its boring)
2. Not seeing enough of their parents
3. The sensation of being too hot/sticky (on flights/beaches/airports/anywhere)
4. Not being near or having the opportunity to go to a beach
5. Being left with someone they don't like (babysitter)
6. Older children (bullying/intimidation)
7. Losing a favourite toy
8. Being bored (long journeys in a car or plane)

9. Not having other similarly aged children to play (if parents
   are not about)
10. Having to go home

Airports seem to be a particular nightmare for parents and toddlers alike, so it's worth considering the options when booking your flight (see page 29). And long queues of traffic may be even worse – most toddlers I spoke to remember mummy and daddy being extremely cross . . .

So we know what toddlers want to do on their holidays, and what they want to have a little less of, but what about you? I asked parents the same questions.

Parents liked . . .
1. Seeing their children enjoy themselves on holiday
2. Value for money
3. The quality of childcare facilities – 'I' dotting and 'T' crossing. (everything from service into hotels to kiddie-club supervision)
4. Getting what they expected or more when they arrived (in other words, the brochure was accurate)
5. An excellent infrastructure on location (good roads, rail, accessibility to shops, beach, airport)
6. The airline they flew with (mainly a supportive cabin crew)
7. Friendly locals at chosen destination (culture, and the attitude to toddlers in restaurants and public places)
8. Access to a beach (ideally on beach rather than 'near' a beach, which can mean 10 miles away)
9. A 'safe' holiday or resort
10. A wide range of facilities (a variety of things for children as well as adults)

Parents disliked . . .
1. Having an unwell toddler, particularly if there is no medical help nearby
2. Poor weather – either too hot or too cold
3. Unfriendly locals

7

4. Big, busy airports (the smaller, local airports proved most popular; see page 33)
5. Flight delays (stressful)
6. Unsupportive cabin crew
7. Being surrounded by hundreds of other families in close proximity
8. Too much regimentation (kiddies clubs having fixed start and end times)
9. Lack of value for money ('everything is added on')
10. Long journeys to reach a destination, particularly after an exhausting flight (in other words, a seven-hour flight followed by a three-hour coach journey is not acceptable)

Most parents focused on the quality rather than the range of childcare facilities provided, and felt happiest when good healthcare was accessible (just in case!).

So it's important to know what both you and your toddler expect and want to get from your break away! If you set out on a hunt for a holiday with the knowledge of what will keep you and your toddler happy, you'll be much more likely to meet everyone's needs, and actually get a break in the process. Throughout this book I've considered the likes and dislikes of parents and toddlers and, in each section, outlined the basics – in other words, the elements and issues that are most likely to make and keep you all content.

Do you know what you want?

Holidays can be stressful times, and the longer the holiday, the more potential for stress. This is partly because everyone in the family is likely to be experiencing something new, whether it be spending a prolonged time away from nursery (in the case of toddlers), or learning how to balance the desire to explore with a child's need for the familiar (in the case of parents). Add to this a need for parents to relax and rejuvenate, along with a toddler's determination to be the centre of attention and entertained at all times, and you have a potentially explosive scenario.

Careful preparation and planning go a long way towards removing some of the stresses. This doesn't mean pre-booking and pre-planning every waking hour of your holiday, because a degree of flexibility is essential to make the experience workable. It does, however, mean considering your expectations, and planning in advance for potential pitfalls and problems. Ultimately, it means knowing what to expect. A little information and awareness goes a long way when you are travelling with toddlers in tow.

Consider how your toddlers will cope away from familiar friends and relations, who are doing familiar and favourite things back home. This is an important issue if you are travelling with a single child. If they are gregarious they will almost certainly find company en route. If, however, they are slower to build up contacts, consider choosing holidays where they'll have the time and space to make friends, at an easy pace with lots of opportunities. Good ideas include staying with another family, or choosing somewhere with a flexible kids club arrangement and organised activities. Will your child have the opportunity to make friends? Large groups of kids who all know each other can be a difficult nut for a toddler to crack, and arriving halfway through a holiday week, when the other children have already established friendships at kids clubs, can also be a problem.

So there are lots of elements to consider, quite apart from the obvious choice of holiday destination and mode of transport. This book is set out to help you decide what your toddler needs, and to anticipate and plan for problems before they can occur. Stress-free travelling with a toddler is certainly possible, but it takes a little advance legwork to get it right.

Choosing a holiday

There are 12 main elements to consider when planning a holiday with your toddler. Get these right, and you are well on your way to the holiday of your dreams! Consider:

- Choosing the right country
- Toddler-friendly resorts and operators
- Weather

- How far you want to go
- How much you want to spend
- How active you want to be
- Town . . . or country?
- Comfort . . . or character?
- Do you want to be alone or in a group?
- Getting your timing right
- Do you want to do it all yourself?
- Beach . . . or no beach?

Choosing the right country

> I always get a warm welcome in Italy and France when I take my children there. We've been there for the past 10 years. My children made friends with the locals really quickly. Everyone seems to be very child friendly in these countries. You always hear children laughing.
>
> Mother of two, Swindon

Aside from the weather and entertainment potential of a country, you really do want to consider the culture. Do they like toddlers? It helps! Later in this book, I've rated each country according to how 'toddler-friendly' it is, and these ratings are based on my research with parents and older toddlers.

For the record, however, the top 10 toddler-friendly countries are, in order:

1. Portugal
2. Spain/Spanish islands
3. Italy/Sardinia
4. France/Corsica
5. Belgium
6. Denmark
7. Turkey
8. Greece
9. Caribbean
10. Australia/New Zealand/Canada

This listing relates to culture rather than facilities offered, and does not take into account climate, budget or the length of time it takes to travel there. But if you want to be sure to be greeted with friendliness by the locals, and catered to rather than relegated to a back room in restaurants, you may want to consider choosing one of these destinations for your holiday.

In Italy Tom and I were mobbed by toddling-loving locals. In England, we are ignored and seem to get in the way of the every day practice of getting from A to B as quickly as possible. Choosing a culture where toddlers feel welcome helps to ensure a successful holiday. It may even limit the need for childcare during meals out, for example, or on the adult-fun part of the itinerary. In my experience, the further east and the further south you go, the more toddler-friendly the place. One exception to this, however, is Scandinavia, where they love toddlers. But take note – smart, Western hotels in any country, even the toddler-friendly ones, tend to be unfriendly. Give them a miss if you can.

The downside of these toddler-friendly countries is that specially arranged entertainment for children seems to be less common than, say, in the UK. Waiters are tolerant of squeaks, shrieks and mess, but you are much less likely to be able to park your children in a childcare centre, unless the resort, restaurant or hotel caters to northern tourists.

It's also interesting to note that travelling with toddlers in less-developed countries can be rewarding. A toddler can open doors that would otherwise remain firmly shut. Though parents mainly worry about their children not being welcome, the reverse can be an issue too. In some countries, notably African and Asian ones, children may be treated as public property. This means they may be touched much more than usual; patted and kissed, or even have their cheeks nipped or pulled. In addition to physical irritation, being a permanent centre of attention can be wearing. And it's a real problem for very blond children, who tend to stand out a mile.

The main solution is to make sure children have plenty of time without this attention (unless they enjoy it), either in your accommodation or in a protected enclave, such as a tourist swimming pool. Many hotels allow outsiders to use their pools for a fee. For little ones

11

a sling or backpack, to keep your child away from other people's hands, may be useful.

Toddler-friendly resorts and operators

As precious as it may sound, it is important to choose a holiday that caters to your toddler's needs. If they don't get what they expect, they tend to be very vocal in protest, which can dampen a holiday in even the most luxurious conditions. But don't forget the fact that if you as parents don't get a real break, it's more likely to be an endurance test than a holiday. A compromise can normally be reached, so aim to include features that will keep you both happy.

When researching destinations, resorts and hotels, don't use just one source of information. Go for a variety. Don't rely too heavily on a brochure when it comes to deciding which is the right holiday for you. If you are simply choosing between resorts, a selection of brochures should offer photographs that give a decent overall picture of what's available. But go beyond the pictures and the fancy words, and ask some questions. What looks good on paper may not be so great in reality.

If you are going for something more adventurous, contact a local tourist office and ask for relevant information. Ask for contact phone, fax or e-mail numbers for the region, in order to be sure that there is plenty to keep all of you occupied. I've listed some of the best operators and hotels (see pages 85 and 117), but if you plan to go to countries outside those mentioned in this book, you'll need to be prepared to put in some research time. And believe me, it's well worth the effort.

Weather

Too hot, too cold or too wet can take all of the pleasure out of a holiday. The ideal temperature for a toddler is tepid, with no rain, no wind and no blistering sun – the sort of weather we expect from the average English summer. Next to budget, this is probably the most important element to consider when picking your destination; get it wrong and you may be miserable. In Spain, Italy and Greece, for example, you can travel during months where the weather is pleasantly warm. But during colder seasons, you may find it extremely uncomfortable, as there is unlikely to be adequate heating. The same goes for seasons where the weather is too hot. You may find air-conditioned accommodation, but chances are you don't want to spend your entire day indoors. Get to know the 'peak' season in terms of weather, well before you travel, and base your holiday plans around this time.

But remember, thanks to global warming, there is no real guarantee that you'll get the weather you expect, no matter how carefully you plan. Holiday brochures can also be misleading. In hotter destinations, brochures indicate temperatures in the shade – not the temperatures reached on the beach, in city centres and certainly not by midday.

In naturally colder climates, weather is quoted at the daily maximum, reached at noon. Winds are not taken into account, and on a sandy beach, a chilling and irritating wind can spoil a day out. Most toddlers will cope with rainy or unseasonably cold weather if you are prepared to brave it yourself. For example, Tom has, on many occasions, wanted to remain on the beach playing in a drizzle, while I shelter under a beach umbrella.

A day or two of poor weather is ideal for sightseeing – although toddlers normally fail to appreciate museums, art galleries and architecture in the same way their parents might. In general, the beach and pool will remain the draw on cloudy, rainy days, just as it will when the weather is fine.

So think in advance about options for bad weather activities and outings. Even in August on the Med you will have a day or two of storms. As well as planning some excursions, look out for toddler-friendly cafes where you can stay for an hour or two, meet other families, exchange ideas for things to do, and allow the toddlers to chase each other around the tables rather than drive you up the wall.

If you think bad weather is a certainty book a hotel room where you feel you could live, as well as just sleep – one with a lounge area, and ideally a TV with a multitude of English channels (BBC Choice, Junior Disney and Junior Nickelodeon have toddler-friendly programmes on most of the day). Look for adequate indoor space and activities (whether in a hotel or self-catering), or nearby alternatives such as play and activity centres. This is a serious consideration, as successfully entertaining your toddler is one of the most basic elements of a good holiday. If you are planning a holiday in the UK, prepare for cold and rain. It will be both!

Weather and the seasons can also add other complications to your choice of destination and when you choose to go. For example, if you have a child who suffers particularly badly from hay fever, check out pollen levels at your chosen resort. You may also note that on a first visit a child may have no problem with a type of pollen never met before. However, by the time of a second visit an allergy may have developed and you'll have full-blown symptoms on your hands.

Pollen alert

• Clarity Line (Tel: 0800 556 610) which operates mid-May to the end of July, and offers details of pollen counts in the UK.

• The European Pollen Information Service (Pollen Research Unit, University of North London, 166–220 Holloway Road, London N7 8DB) advises about pollen seasons across Europe and most of the rest of the world, and can provide information on current pollen concentrations. They also forecast trends in 25 countries. For each enquiry send a cheque for £5, payable to University of North London.

• For the US, check out www.cnn.com/weather

• Useful websites to find out more about international climates is www.worldclimate.com. For a five-day weather forecast just before your next trip try http://weather.yahoo.com. The book, *Weather to Travel*, by Maria Harding (Tomorrow's Guides, £6.99) is also useful.

How far do you want to go?

The distance you are prepared to travel will, ultimately, depend on your toddler. Driving or flying for long periods of time is impractical for both parents and toddlers, unless you have a child who is reasonably good at keeping himself occupied, or sleeping at opportune moments. And remember, the duration of a flight is not necessarily the sum total of your travelling time. You'll need to consider how long you'll be kept waiting at airports or stations, and whether there will be transfers or an extended journey at the other end. Check this out before booking. How far are you prepared to travel with your toddler, and how do you want to travel? Some toddlers are happy to travel in a car for hours, but most are not. Consider this when booking a destination, and when choosing your mode of transport; find out what to expect from airlines, airports, stations, roads and car hire companies well in advance. If you have a choice in the matter, go for one that has special provisions for toddlers.

How much do you want to spend?

Family holidays are expensive, but it's certainly possible to get value for money if you choose carefully and well. The main message here is to forget the holidays you've had alone in the past, and work on the compromise angle. Your toddler is likely to be as thrilled by a week camping in France, for example, as he would be by an all-inclusive with kiddies club in France. And given that a holiday with a toddler or two probably doubles the cost, it's worth considering all of the options, even if they represent the type of holiday you've never considered before.

When Tom was a baby, I was able to travel quite easily, and still continue to do the type of things that I wanted to do. But now that Tom can toddle, asks for things and requires stimulation and entertainment, I've had to rethink my budget plans and focus on the various extra costs involved in keeping us both happy.

So before you start looking for a holiday, it is a good idea to calculate how much you have to spend. Do some research to uncover holidays that might cost slightly less, giving more value for money. Remember to allow a cushion, as you may require extra funds in the event of an emergency, or a treat or two if the going gets tough.

In your calculations, consider:

- The cost of the tour operator or airfare, car rental and hotel if you are DIYing it.
- What you are prepared to pay for childcare or babysitting.
- The cost of meals. Is breakfast included in the deal? Is it worth going half-board or would it be cheaper or more convenient to eat outside the hotel?

- Are there any attractions nearby which your toddlers may find of interest and what do they charge?
- Is there any evening entertainment provided in the hotel or resort – is it free and, if so, is it toddler-friendly?
- If you are not hiring a car, how expensive is local transport and is it practical to take a toddler on board? The locals must have to use it – so presumably so.
- What do you intend to spend on shopping and souvenirs?
- Tips and extras.
- Are there any airport taxes and payment for parking?

The latter is particularly important. When you fly from London airports to JFK New York, for example, you are looking at taxes and parking fees of well over £100. And that's before you've even got there. It's also well worth considering budgeting for regular takeaways or meals out, particularly if you are self-catering. A holiday is no break if you end up slaving in front of a stove the entire time, and you may find that the local fare in supermarkets does not live up to your toddler's expectations.

There are also significant differences in local costs. For example, a short taxi trip in Viareggio might cost £3, but in Rome it would be nearer to £13. While a meal out in Crete might cost around £8 a head, the price in Paris might be nearer to £20. And, last-minute bargains aren't always as cheap as they seem when all the hidden extras are considered. Larger resorts may appear cheaper, but the babysitting and kiddies clubs for toddlers can make a serious dent in the budget.

Is the cost of holidaying prohibitive?

There are alternatives! Why not consider a house swap, which is one of the cheapest and most flexible options, and probably preferable to visiting friends or family unless you know you will get plenty of support. For further details, visit one of the following websites:

---

www.travelgate.co.uk
www.holiswaps.com
www.travel-tree.com
www.budgettravel.com
www.holswap.com
www.phproperty.co.uk
www.holiday-exchange.net
www.tour-britain.com
www.sunswap.com
www.swap-and-go.co.uk
www.homelink.co.uk

Options to fit your budget

One of the most cost-effective options is camping. I personally recommend this option for travelling with toddlers, as it normally provides excellent value for money. Campsites include the ready-erected variety, which may well be successful even for those of you who don't consider yourselves camping material. There are campsites with tents in situ, or mobile homes or even cabins. And the majority of modern campsites on the continent tend to be well organised, family-friendly and fairly luxurious in comparison to the 'roughing it' holiday that they once comprised! For further details on the camping option, see page 158.

Holiday villages have a lot more organised entertainment and a range of accommodation standards, but they can be pricey. For further details, see page 94.

The big tour-operator holidays to sun, sea and sand resorts can be extremely keenly priced. In the past, it was possible to pick up a cheap, last-minute deal, but, unfortunately, operators have become much better at matching demand to the number of holidays on offer. There are a few good last-minute deals on offer, which means that you are pretty much certain to get what you pay for when booking a break. If you find a cheap deal, you are much more likely to get an inferior package. Cheap will usually mean small rooms or self-catering units, often noisy, well away from any centres of interest, and generally in properties of 200 units or more. Food, according to my research, is of inconsistent quality. And you will not only be with your children for the duration of the holiday but also with hundreds of other young families as well . . . all with their toddlers, and all in close proximity. For further details, see page 85.

Self-catering is the main option offered to families. This is obviously a cheaper alternative, as you won't be hit with a bill for dozens of soft drinks and ice cream bars at the end of your break. However, you will either need to do your own cooking or spend a good proportion of your budget on eating out. Note also that food shopping is unlikely to be a bargain in popular resorts. I suggest going for one of the smaller specialist organisations (such as French Life or Balfour France [see page 342]), which offer slightly more expensive self-catering options. The standard of accommodation is normally higher, and it's much more likely to be found in attractive and/or offbeat locations. You'll save money by shopping where the locals do, at local prices, and there is normally the possibility of extra services like cleaning, cooking and babysitting.

Remember, the less known the area, the better value for money the property is likely to offer. Getting there may cost more than to better-known destinations, but you can choose a destination served by a low-cost carrier.

All-inclusive holidays are popular with those wanting to budget carefully. You know in advance exactly what you are spending and there can again be significant savings on toddler's bar and snack bills. However, if the food is inconsistent – which, according to my research, is a real possibility – you are stuck with it. And if you choose a destination that really doesn't suit, you will spend more than you might on a non-inclusive holiday, eating in restaurants outside the complex and hiring a car to get out and about more. Possibly more useful would be a destination that includes a decent breakfast buffet in the price, but leaves you free to eat out later. Beware, however, that breakfast buffets can also be a wonderful source of funny tummy syndrome, to which toddlers are particularly prone (see page 233).

Bed & Breakfasts are an excellent choice for families, although the better ones can be expensive in the UK in particular. This is a good value option in France and increasingly available in countries like Australia, Canada, as well as other European countries. However, those places that don't offer an evening meal can be inconvenient if you have children to put to bed, and you would be well advised to go for somewhere with space outside for running around. There are also some venues that don't welcome children (in much the same way that they would not welcome animals), so ask before you book.

Hotels are getting better at catering for toddlers, but the progress is still patchy and slow. Some of the major chains now provide excellent facilities, and there are pockets of independent, privately owned hotels that are also superb (see page 117). A holiday booked direct means that you have the option of choosing a smaller, more characterful hotel, which offers exactly what you want, where you want. However, it takes some research to find good options. And unless you budget for a large room or suite, the room may be claustrophobic, encouraging you to go out and spend more money during the day.

You may also need specific services such as bottle-warming, a high chair and babysitting services, and you should get confirmation in writing that these will be available. If the kitchen closes at 10pm, you could find that nobody is willing to warm a bottle for you. Provision of high chairs does not mean there will be one available if you need it, particularly if there are only four available in a hotel which caters for hundreds. And if you've had an exhausting day and your toddler isn't up to a trip to the restaurant, you may have to rely on expensive room service, without the option of cooking yourself.

Finally, unless you go for somewhere relatively expensive, you may not get decent sound insulation. For young families this is less about having problems with disturbance from next door and more about worrying about when next door will complain about a child howling at 2am. The bottom line is that hotels are usually expensive, especially in high season.

Getting the best-value holiday

Most families I spoke to had tried a variety of holiday options (from self-catering, camping, skiing, package tours and hotels) and were able to define their most successful experiences and the holiday options they felt had given them best value for money. These, of course were dependent on the tour operator they chose, and the many other considerations that they took into account. And it's important to look around – what may represent good value in one country could be poor in another, while a tour operator might provide excellent accommodation in one area, but sub-standard facilities in another. The parents I surveyed gave me details of which holidays gave them most for their money.

> The overwhelming consensus was that camping, in its many forms, represented the best value for money, especially when the campsite edges on to a beach!

Families got the most value from . . .

1. Camping (caravan/tent – ready erected/bring your own) – usually via tour operator
2. Villa/self-catering – accommodation and flight were booked separately
3. Skiing (through a tour operator)
4. Camping (motorhome or caravan)
5. Holiday village
6. Hotel/resort (a package tour)
7. Cruise
8. Safari (a small selection had taken safari holidays)

Getting more for your money with toddlers

- If you want a mainstream beach resort, you will pay less booking through a tour operator. If you choose a smaller/specialist operator you may pay 10 percent more, but in return receive extras such as private transfers, possibly an office on the spot and greater knowledge of the options when you make your choice.

- If you want something a bit different, away from the better-known destinations, booking direct is cheaper.
- Travelling with toddlers has some benefits over travelling with school-aged children. For one thing, travelling outside the school holidays is usually cheaper. However, if you are beach holidaying in the UK you need to budget for at least some poor weather, when you will spend more visiting local attractions. The cost of these add significantly to the overall cost of the holiday, often making it more expensive than travelling overseas for guaranteed sunshine.
- If you aren't planning to spend much time in your rooms, don't book a room with a sea view or balcony, for which there is normally an extra charge.
- If breakfast is not included in the deal, think about buying something from a local grocery store instead.
- If you are going to be self-catering, take some basics with you from home and enough to tide you over for a couple of days until you have located the best-value places to shop.
- Look for accommodation with easy access to major attractions, such as the beach. Transport, whether public or by hire car, will add to the expense.
- Avoid eating or drinking anything from hotel mini-bars, which are always over-priced.
- When self-catering, check to see if electricity and gas prices are included in the price. If so, you may find that the price is much higher in colder countries, to cover generous use. If it's not included, find out how much you can expect to pay. Remember that in countries such as Italy, you may need considerable heat and electricity in the off-season, and it can all add up.
- Don't make advance bookings for anything you can arrange on the spot. Wait until you are there before you decide what you are likely to enjoy most.
- Check out special local deals, such as family tickets for local attractions.

- Pack light. You will be able to use more public transport to get to your destination instead of hiring cars or taxis, and you won't have to pay for a porter.
- Ask for a discount when contacting hotels, and put a smile in your voice! If you don't ask, you don't get! Almost no-one pays standard rates unless there's a shortage of rooms.
- Ask for special rates. Airlines, car hire and rail companies all operate special deals to encourage business but may not tell you about these unless you ask. Variants include discounts for booking ahead, for travelling midweek/staying a Saturday night, for booking a larger party, plus discounts on upgrades. Last-minute bookings may also qualify for a discount, but this is probably not something you want to gamble on if travelling with children.

Never cut costs on . . .

- Space. Book a room with ensuite, or a separate sleeping area for the toddlers, so you and your partner can have some degree of privacy to read or relax before you go to sleep.
- Extra help. If you have the choice between luxury or extra help with your toddler (such as babysitting or kids clubs), opt for the latter. You will have more of a holiday and feel more relaxed. What good is luxury if you don't have the energy or time to appreciate it?
- Comfort. You'll undoubtedly spend more time indoors with a toddler than you would on your own, and, therefore, accommodation is more than a place to lay your head at night. Make sure your rooms, tents, cabins, etc., are comfortable, safe and clean, with ample space for toddler exploration and play.

How active do you want to be?

Are you looking for total relaxation or lots of exercise or cultural activities? If you simply want to relax, you will need to provide company for your children, or get help with childcare. You may choose to involve your children in your activities, in which case be prepared to put in a little effort, or opt for one of the organised activity holidays for families. Most of these holidays allow you some time away from your toddlers if you so wish.

Remember that an extremely active schedule will likely be exhausting for a toddler, and he probably won't find it as much fun as a relaxing day on the beach. You may need to come to a compromise (weighted more heavily in your toddler's favour) about the level of activity you can expect from your holiday.

Town or . . . country?

City breaks may seem a perverse choice with children, but for families used to urban living, they may well work, although usually for children over five (not toddlers!). Having said that, if you have a robust toddler who likes to be involved, you can find some great city options that involve trips to zoos, galleries and museums with programmes for little ones, fun restaurants, boat or canal trips, parks, a good hotel with plenty of activities going on (and a swimming pool!), and shops that sell treats to keep your toddler keen to carry on.

It goes without saying that the countryside is usually best for toddlers, and the beach is the best of all. Remote areas have the bonus of lots of open space, away from traffic. A number of self-catering specialists can offer options like this. If this prospect seems lonely, or rather bleak, consider an adventure holiday company that caters for children, either in a crèche or by including them in some of the adventure.

Barring foot and mouth disease, countryside holidays can be enormously successful. They tend to be best for children who are still at the stage of wanting to spend most of their time with their parents, or for older children who don't require much entertainment. A property with a pool is a good bet, although you'll want to be sure that it's safely fenced away (and the gate locked) to prevent accidents (see page 112). A working farm break (see page 108) is another fun option, and you and your toddler may be able to watch or even participate in the activities.

Consider the following issues when contemplating a countryside break:

23

- Is the property safe enough for your age of children?
- Is the property on an active agricultural site and, if so, are children welcomed and allowed to visit? If the idea of a farm holiday appeals, see page 108 for more details.
- What standard is the accommodation and what support services are provided?
- How close are the nearest facilities (such as, shops, restaurants, attractions)? If you have to drive, is there suitable parking? If you have to walk, are there pavements/safe roads?
- How long would it take to get to any sights in the area?

Comfort or . . . character?

At the very top end of the market, older, converted, architecturally interesting buildings usually offer a level of luxury unsuitable for toddlers. Character comes at the expense of comfort, and many old houses newly and beautifully converted have long graceful staircases, which parents with toddlers ungracefully try to walk up and down each morning to breakfast. Having stayed in a few of these historic houses with Tom, I ended up opting for room service most evenings.

More interesting accommodation may also have uneven floors, and steep and potentially dangerous stairs. And an older property in the country may well have more insect life than you are used to, as well as countryside noises and smells. If outside the UK, and not British owned, the property may be equipped in an unfamiliar way – without a kettle, for example.

Chain and larger hotels tend to conform to international standards, particularly those properties contracted to the big name tour operators which can impose their own requirements for British customers (see page 107).

Ultimately, however, I suggest you choose comfort over character. It's always possible to take day trips to culturally or architecturally interesting places, and you won't be terrified that your child is going to spill apple juice on an antique, or rip a bit of expensive wallpaper. Choose a place where your toddler can roam free and get on with things, all within easy grasp! If you are nervous about the decor or the other occupants, you'll spend more time restraining your child than relaxing and enjoying your break.

Do you want to be alone or in a group?

This is a very personal choice and one that is crucial to your enjoyment of the holiday. If you do want company and are not taking your own with you, it's a good idea to try to pick somewhere where families are likely to share similar interests and ideologies.

Although a large hotel will provide plenty of potential company, you will also have the option of losing yourselves, if you prefer. This is particularly true if you opt for accommodation- or bed and breakfast- only.

In middle-sized or smaller hotels you may find it easier to get to know people, but you may find yourself trapped if another family makes you their target.

If you are self-catering, and find it easier to cope with your toddler when there are other children around, choose a location where there are other cottages or apartments, and ask for details of other families who have booked for the same period, or local, friendly families nearby.

Getting your timing right

While you can, avoid school holidays, which are more crowded and more expensive. Go off peak, off-season, in the spring and autumn, when the weather is cooler and there are fewer crowds and fewer older children to intimidate your toddler. Consider also when school holidays fall at your destination. There's no point in avoiding the British rush, only to find yourself overwhelmed by local children crowding the beach. August tends to be holiday time for much of Europe, while March, June, July and August see North Americans taking a break. Investigate your destination before you go!

Also avoid festival times. Not all festivals or events will suit those with children but there are a few that might appeal – in Ireland and Belgium, for example.

Do you want to do it all yourself?

Do you want the reassurance of permanent back-up – then a larger tour operator is the best way of finding what you need – or do you seek more independence in your choice of activity? If you want a packaged holiday without feeling packaged, most specialist tour operators can now tailor-make something to meet your requirements.

25

Independent travel is more flexible, but it is important to have a well thought-out framework from which, when appropriate, you can deviate.

It is particularly important to do lots of research about what you will find when you get there, including the nature of any medical support (see page 223). The more remote the destination, the less you can hope for in the way of genuine help from the tourist office. Instead, turn to backpacking guides, which are specifically designed to help those dealing with nitty-gritty issues (see page 424).

Making a detailed itinerary is a good idea. Handling day-to-day issues will take up a reasonable amount of your break, and it is fair to assume that you want time to enjoy wherever it is you are visiting. You may wish to adjust the timetable once you are actually on the spot, but a degree of predictability is likely to make everyone feel more secure. All children thrive on routine, so if you set one in place early on, you'll find that everyone settles in and knows what to expect – and when you can expect to have a break!

Even if you choose to book accommodation as you go along, do consider booking somewhere to stay for your first night, particularly if you are going to be travelling any distance to your destination.

Until you acclimatise to your destination, aim for somewhere relaxed and comfortable. Once you are used to how things work, you will be better able to economise. Take essentials, such as snacks, nappies and drinks, for the first few days so you don't need to rush round to locate shops and work out their opening hours.

Always have an alternative plan of action. If you miss a train or plane, know the alternative routes to your destination, such as travelling to somewhere nearby and then hiring a taxi or car for the last stretch. Pinpointing possible places for an overnight stop would also be useful.

The benefits of independent travel

Despite the extra time needed to research independent travel and prepare for the journey and holiday, there are bonuses. For example,

- A baby or a toddler is a great way of breaking the ice and travelling with one will mean you meet people who would never otherwise have talked to you.
- Any holiday is an opportunity to spend time talking to and listening to your toddler (quality time in the jargon), but this is even more the case if you are travelling independently.
- Independent travel is a great opportunity to do things together rather than simply issuing instructions about how things are going to be done. Map-reading and guidebook interpreting are just two of the ways this can happen. Get your toddler involved in choosing the itinerary. Even little ones will have firm ideas about how they would like to spend their time. Offer choices and have fun fulfilling them.
- Independent travel is a better way of getting to see how a country really works. When operators organise things for you, you tend to see only those aspects of a culture that are known to keep tourists happy. With a toddler at your heels, you will have a great entree to the 'real workings' of a country, and have the opportunity to explore areas that you may never have seen if you'd done it the official way.
- Starting to travel early with your toddler will give you confidence to try more ambitious expeditions as they grow older. Given how fast children grow up, that needn't be too far off.

Beach . . . or no beach?

We've already established that toddlers love beaches more than anything else on their holiday, so being on or near a beach is a good choice.

Seaside hotels are more likely to be geared up to catering for families, with the possibility of babysitting, children's meals, kids clubs and equipment hire (usually via the tour operator). But there are downsides, of course.

Big waves and strong currents are not toddler-friendly. Nor is a beach with little shade. If the beach turns out to be too crowded, expensive or difficult to get to from your accommodation, you may regret your decision. Something less expensive, further inland, and

27

with services such as cleaning, catering, babysitting, and a swimming pool may prove a better option. I would, however, recommend researching your beaches and sticking to the coast if you can.

If you do opt for a seaside holiday check that the beach is sandy (although most toddlers don't mind pebbles), not too crowded or windy (something toddlers may mind), doesn't disappear at every high tide (less of a problem in the Med), or suffer from dangerous currents. Be aware, too, that not all beaches overseas are free and in some countries you pay to use the beach. Watch out for extras, too. Italian umbrella charges, for example, are high, and you may find yourself forking out for more than you had anticipated. Good accessibility is essential: you might have a sea view but do you have to cross a six-lane highway to get to the beach? Do the roads have pavements and safe crossing places? Are there steep steps down to the beach? A 10-minute drive to the beach is OK, but is there parking? Later in the book, I recommend those beaches that have excellent accessibility, are sandy, and safe.

The next step

Once you've established an agenda and a list of what you want and can afford, it's time to consider the nitty-gritty of your break. How will you get there? Let's start by looking at travel by air, which may not always be as straightforward as it seems!

PART TWO

Toddler-friendly Travel

1. Travelling by Air

It wasn't even 6am, and the queue for the ticket counter at London's Heathrow Airport snaked for yards. There were as many families setting out on holiday as there were business people, and everyone was biting a lip or scowling at the counter clerk, or mumbling under their breath about the delay. The entire queue was quietly urging the girl checking in the bags to do it faster. The toddlers were screaming and asking for more sweets and attention. 'We've been here 45 minutes, and the line is hardly moving,' cried one frustrated mother.

The next queue for the outsized luggage was even longer – everyone, it seemed, had brought a buggy. And the queue through security was longer still, as was the one at the gate. There simply wasn't enough room for hand luggage on the packed flight, despite the fact people were frantically trying to bash their bags into compartments that were made to hold something half their size. I had that niggling feeling that, once on the plane, I'd sit with Tom for hours, with no air conditioning, no one telling us what was going on and everyone getting increasingly irritable. After an hour, we took off. But by that time Tom and every other toddler on the flight had used up the store of goodwill that should have lasted the duration, and everyone was scowling in silence. No we hadn't had a nice flight. Have you had an experience like this with your toddler?

'The whole flying experience these days is terrible,' acknowledges

Jeff Zack, a spokesman for the 49,000-member Association of Flight Attendants. 'The problem is more people flying on more planes than ever – to the same number of airports.'

According to the Air Transport Association, each day 1.7 million passengers board 23,000 flights. The crowds are bad, the food is worse, and delays are increasing – especially in the summer when air traffic is always at its busiest. In June last year, there were 50,000 delayed flights – an all-time record. July wasn't much better.

It's frustrating enough to be delayed when you're travelling alone. At least you can spend money in Body Shop or read a book. But with a bored, tired, hungry and slightly nervous toddler on your hands, this type of scenario is a nightmare.

There are, however, ways to make things easier. First of all, you can fine-tune your travel plans to travel at less busy times and from smaller airports. You can also try out some of the tried-and-tested tips below, which help to ease the pain.

Go for the nonstops

They may cost a little more, but by cutting your chances of being delayed twice or missing connections altogether, you have a better chance of making it a painless journey.

• Fly early in the day, too. If your flight is cancelled, it's more likely that you'll be placed on another. You'll also have more time to recover.

• When you can, avoid major airports. The regional airports are quieter, have good facilities, such as baby changing and play areas, and are far less crowded.

• Check the FAA's Web site at www.fly.faa.gov for any general delays at major airports. And, most importantly, call your airline before leaving home. You don't want to be stuck at the airport for longer than necessary.

Know your airports

Check to see if your airport has a play area suitable for toddlers. In the US, there are some excellent play areas, such as those found in Chicago O'Hare, Boston, Pittsburgh and San Jose. Gatwick also has one, but only in one terminal (terminal two), and it's not very large or imaginative. Try out the regionals, which are better all round. Some family travellers come early just to play in them. Check www.expedia.com to take a virtual tour of your airport.

The relative merits of the UK airports are discussed on pages 33 to 35. If you have a choice, go for one that is toddler-friendly. In the event of a delay or other hiccough, it's good to know that you'll be well looked after.

Advance planning
There are a number of ways to make your air journey and airport stay less painful. Consider the following:

Let your toddler help
Toddlers love to carry their own backpack, and if you give him the responsibility of taking care of his own treasured possessions, you'll be exempt from carrying them and possibly him, too! And chances are, he'll be so engrossed, he'll forget that his legs are tired. Go to www.familyonboard.com, or Hamleys (www.hamleys.co.uk), or to www.tesco.co.uk for a great range of backpacks suitable for toddlers.

Take your own food
Don't count on the airlines to feed your junior gourmets. Instead, pack a special lunch in an insulated school lunchbox. You'll save money on the often nasty airport food, too. Let your toddler choose what to bring, and include a few surprises, too (see page 56).

Pack overnight essentials
Just in case your luggage gets lost, or your flight is cancelled late

---

at night, you'll need to have essentials in your onboard bag. You'll also be prepared if your toddler spills drink all over you or, worse (and it's happened to me), your toddler is airsick.

Play games

Come prepared with ideas to keep toddlers and other family members occupied! If you're in for a long airport delay, divide the family into teams and send them off on a scavenger hunt around the airport terminal. There's only one downside: you'll have to spring for a prize for the winners. Bring a few games and puzzles for the flight itself – anything to occupy a busy little body and mind (see page 59).

Take emergency supplies

To keep those bored toddlers busy, stash some surprises in your bag. Toddlers will be satisfied with stickers, a plastic character or a neon marker. And older children are also remarkably easy to please with a few choice, inexpensive gifts – or one big one, such as a CD or an electronic game, which will keep them going for the whole trip. These goodies can be brought out at staged intervals during the flight (see page 57), or during a long airport delay.

Take your own nappies

Don't count on finding any when you need them most. Heathrow Airport has nappy and nappy sacks with wet wipes in automatic dispensers in the ladies toilets in all terminals, and some can be found in chemists. But not all airports are as well equipped, and who's to say what's in stock on the day you need them most? The same goes for baby food and formula, if you use it.

Take a car seat

Your toddler will be safer and you'll be a lot more comfortable if he's securely strapped in a car seat. The FAA (Federal Aviation Authority) in the States recommends using car seats, and you'll have the advantage of not having to fork out for a hired seat at the other end. What's more, a familiar object almost always eases the pain of change, and your toddler will feel much more confident if he's sitting in his usual place, albeit on an airplane instead. It can also be used for a nap in a quiet corner, in the event of a delayed flight.

Know when enough is enough

When the delays are getting worse and your family can't take the airport for one more minute, book a flight for the next morning and head to a nearby hotel. Pick one with an indoor pool. It might be worth checking out possible venues before you travel.

The main trick to flying with toddler is to get clear in your mind what you want, ask for it firmly and keep asking until you get it.

Which airport?

The best airports for toddlers are in Frankfurt, Madrid, Boston and Zurich – and I've been to all of them with my lot. These have the best baby changing and play areas – and when you have toddlers, you need both.

Father of three toddlers who travels with family on business

Airports are number one of the top 10 holiday hates of toddlers, and for good reason. As one toddler from Chelmsford told me, 'They are boring, everyone is cross, it is crowded, in a hurry and there is nothing to do, and no one will play with me'. Quite. In short, airports are not suitable for toddlers.

In the UK, there is, in theory, a babycare policy for all BAA airports, of which the biggest are Heathrow and Gatwick. The relevant area should be unisex, of a minimum of 20 square metres, a temperature of 20°C and well ventilated. Entrances should be wide enough for a buggy and preferably for a double buggy. The areas should provide nappy disposal bins, baby-changing surfaces with guard rail, sink and drainer, paper towels and a bottle warmer. There should be a separate screened area with a chair for breastfeeding, also playpens and an adult-size lavatory.

There is no policy on breastfeeding outside these areas. In practice it is reported it would not be discouraged if discreet (in other words, not upsetting any other traveller).

US domestic airports may provide family lounges, but they are not well advertised and can be hard to find. The best way of locating one is to ring the airport in advance and ask for the custodial department.

Worldwide baby changing areas are not yet the norm, but they are becoming more common, generally installed when airports are refurbished. Feeding areas are less so, except in the best equipped.

However, in the UK, there are airports which, either due to recent expansion (Newcastle); excellent design (Stansted) or because they are quieter and have excess capacity (Edinburgh), have made the waiting process to get on the plane almost pleasurable – even comfortable – if you are travelling with a toddler. Natural light and high ceilings relieve the feeling of claustrophobia that travellers may get in more crowded, poorly designed airports. Choosing a smaller, regional airport is also a better bet than starting your journey from a major hub which should, in theory have more facilities to offer, but in reality, fails to deliver the quantity or quality of product. Of course, if you go on a package holiday, you may have no choice about where you fly from, and who you fly with, but if you do, it is as important to research your airport and airline as it is to research your destination and tour operator. After all, the holiday is supposed to start as you walk out the door – right?

It's not just baby changing facilities that are important. Viewing galleries that are situated close to soft-play areas, which are, in turn, located next to pubs or cafes, are a good idea. Mum and dad can eat or have a drink at the café, watching over their toddler/toddlers in the play area, and together they can watch the planes take off and land from the viewing gallery. Viewing galleries are usually extremely popular with toddlers – they love to watch planes.

The tour operator Airtours has sponsored many soft-play areas in regional airports throughout the UK and they should be highly commended for the initiative. Why don't more allegedly 'family-friendly' companies do this? Each airline and tour operator claims that the holiday starts as soon as you arrive at the airport – so why not make it a more pleasurable experience from the outset?

Those airports that are best for travelling from the UK with toddlers are the newer, better and more thoughtfully designed, regional airports – which have yet to be filled to capacity. If you can choose a regional airport, do so. You will have a far less stressful top and tail to your holiday. And so will your toddler.

The following list of UK airports were mentioned and rated by the young families I interviewed, and given marks out of ten for their facilities, friendliness, accessibility to play areas or viewing areas, and overall design.

Flying from Birmingham 8/10
Birmingham International Airport
Birmingham. B26 3QJ
(Tel: 0121 767 8024, Website: www.bhx.co.uk).
This is the fifth largest in the UK and second largest outside of London. Some 7.6 million passengers travel through two terminals per year, and it was the fastest growing airport in the UK between 1993 and 1998. There are stunning views of the airfield throughout the airport, so toddlers are able to see the planes, as well as over 30 shops – most of which cater for children (although not necessarily toddlers). Over 15 food outlets offer the usual toddler fare of burgers, beans and more nuggets. Check out Madison's Coffee Bar, which has a good play area, and Disney on DVD. Madison's is only in the departure lounge main terminal, while Serendipity – an amusement area with rides for toddlers – is located on both sides of the security gate. Bottle-warming facilities and baby food are available in many of the catering outlets, as are high chairs. There is a dedicated children's play area in main terminal departures and three dedicated baby rooms. Most toilets have baby-changing facilities. There is also a widescreen TV and DVD player in Madisons, showing Disney, Bob the Builder and Thomas the Tank Engine.

Fifty airlines serve the airport, with scheduled flights to over

55 destinations and 15 capital cities; 64 percent of travel is scheduled and 36 percent is chartered. Voted best UK business airport four times in six years in the Business Travel Awards, Birmingham Airport is not bad with toddlers either. It also has one of the best punctuality records among UK airports – according to CAA figures – which is a bonus if you have toddlers with you. Charter flights include Air 2000, Air Malta, Airtours, Britannia, British European, Canada 3000, Excel, Eurodirect, JMC Airlines, Monarch, and Pegasus Airlines. Scheduled airlines include Aer Lingus, Air Malta, American, BA, British Midland, Brymon, Continental Airlines, Corssair, Cyprus, Emirates, Czech Airlines, KLM, Lufthansa, Maersk, Manx, Ryanair, Sabena and SAS.

Flying from Cardiff 9/10
Cardiff International Airport
The Vale of Glamorgan
(Tel: 01446 711 111, Website: www.cial.co.uk)
There is an excellent, well-equipped children's play area located in the departures lounge, and it's open throughout the year. The facility is unsupervised and is free of charge to all passengers. There are child-changing facilities in the ladies toilets located on the first floor and in the departures lounge. On landside there is a large restaurant area featuring Buddy's (burger, hot dogs, kiddies' meals, chips and soft drinks) and Cegin Cymru (sandwiches, baguettes, hot food, pastries and snacks, plus special deal kiddies' meals). High chairs are available here. A World News shop is located on the first floor, selling books, magazines, confectionery, gifts and toys. A World News shop is also located in the departures lounge, plus a tax and duty-free shop selling an extensive range of confectionery, gifts and toys. The Deli offers a range of sandwiches and pastries, plus hot and cold drinks.

Airlines that fly from Cardiff include British Regional Airlines (part of the BA group), KLM, Manx Airlines, Ryanair and Air Wales. Charter airlines from Cardiff include Britannia, Airtours, Air 2000, JMC, Spanair, Futura, Eurocypria, Monarch, Jersey European, Air Europa, Air Transat, Via Est Vita, and Tyrolean Airways. These airlines fly to the major holiday destinations in Spain, Greece, Turkey, Portugal, Cyprus, Tunisia, Bulgaria, plus Toronto and Florida.

Flying from the East Midlands 8/10
East Midlands Airport, Castle Donington
(Tel: 01332 852 852, Fax: 01332 850 393,
Website: www.eastmidlandsairport.com).
Breastfeeding parents' rooms can be found on the first floor adjacent to the Trent Café, in the international departure lounge and in the international arrivals hall. Baby-changing facilities are available in the departures hall, on the first floor adjacent to the catering area, in the international departures lounge and in the arrivals hall. The information desk carries supplies of baby food and nappies for use in emergency or delay situations.

Select Service Partner operates all of the catering outlets at East Midlands Airport. The Trent Café on the first floor of the terminal building has four high chairs available and offers a bottle-warming service. Crayons and colouring pads are provided free of charge and the café offers a range of children's meals and kiddies party packs. The Burger King outlet offers children's extra value meals as well as promotional toys. There are also a number of snacks available, such as cheese triangles, diddy cones and apple fritters. High chairs are available in the Local Hero Pub, as are soft drinks and snacks. This non-smoking pub has a 'child friendly' area with a TV. The Meden Café in the International Departure Lounge offers high chairs, bottle-warming facilities and kiddies lunch packs. The Bar des Voyageurs has high chairs available and a range of soft drinks and snacks. A children's play area, sponsored by Airtours, is available for all children in the terminal building. A children's play area can also be found in the international departures lounge. Boots the Chemist offers a range of products, such as nappies, baby food, and children's swimwear. Dominoes Toys sells a large selection of games, toys and crafts suitable for children of all ages. East Midlands Airport offers children up to the age of 12 free membership to the Rascal Rabbit Kids Club. Members of the club receive a birthday card and a quarterly newsletter. For a membership application form, call 01332 852 814.

The main airlines that fly from East Midlands Airport are: JMC, British Midland, Air 2000, Spanair, Airtours International, Britannia, British Regional, EAF, Eurocypria, Hemus Air, Eastern Airways, Onur Air, Air Malta, Virgin Sun and Iberworld.

Flying from Humberside 8/10

Humberside International Airport,
Kirmington, North Lincs, DN39 6YH
(Tel: 01652 688 456, Fax: 01652 680 524,
Website: www.flyfromhumberside.co.uk)

An Airtours-sponsored play area is located in the main terminal. A variety of toys and play equipment is available. This area is not supervised, and parents must take adequate care and be responsible for their children at all times. There is also a small amusements facility – Slots of Fun – located within the international departures lounge. Baby-changing facilities can be found in the main terminal concourse, the international departures lounge and arrivals hall. Nappy dispensers are available in all areas. There is a restaurant in the main terminal offering a selection of hot and cold food and drinks. Children's meals and high chairs are available; and food/milk warming is also provided if needed. Snacks and beverages are also available in the departure lounge. In the main terminal, BooksPlus sell a variety of newspapers, magazines (including children's), books, sweets and other travel goods. In the international departures lounge, Travel Value sell a variety of tax- and duty-free goods. Vending machines are also situated in the terminal building.

Airlines that fly from Humberside include Air Europa, Airtours International, Britannia, Eastern Airways, Futura, Helios, Iberworld, JMC, KLM UK, Onur Air, Spanair, Sunbird and VLM.

Flying from Leeds or Bradford 7/10

Leeds Bradford Airport, Leeds LS19 7TU
(Tel: 0113 250 9696, Fax: 0113 250 5426,
Website: www.lbia.co.uk)

Nine miles north of Leeds, this airport is ideal if you live close to Leeds or Bradford. It hosts a large unsupervised play area, sponsored by Airtours (in the international departures lounge). There are four restaurants and cafes, all of which have non-smoking areas. The White Rose café has excellent views of aircraft taking off and landing, and the Woolpack Pub has a large family room. There are bottlewarming and nappy changing facilities, and the staff are extremely helpful in the event of any other requirements. Breastfeeding parents' rooms are situated next to the information desk and in international departures.

Airlines that fly from here include British Airways, British Midland, KLM, Sabena and Ryanair.

Flying from Manchester 5/10

Manchester Airport, (Tel: 0161 489 3000, Fax: 0161 489 3812,
Email: Info@manchesterairport.co.uk,
Website: www.manairport.co.uk)
Manchester Airport is one of the UK's principal airports, handling over 18 million passengers a year. In addition to its new £172 million second runway, Manchester has invested more than £100 million on improving its three Terminals. A growing number of major airlines now offer services to over 85 scheduled and 108 chartered destinations all over the world.

In terminal one, there is a babycare facility landside in both domestic and international arrivals, as well as at the baggage reclaim. Before passport control there are baby changing rooms in the women's lavatory, in the shopping area, and also in the food concourse. Lancaster Brasseries, New Covent Garden Soup Co., and Pizza Hut are your best for families with hungry toddlers, and Harry Ramsden (fish and chips) offers good value. After passport control there are two toilets, both of which have baby changing facilities, and a soft play area.

In terminal two, there is a babychanging room beside the bureau de change in the arrival area, and facilities for both parents in the departure lounge. Café Europa is the eatery of choice for toddlers, with a free, supervised play area (maximum use half an hour) opposite the café.

There is a baby changing room beside bureau de change. Terminal three is linked directly to terminal one and shares the facilities.

British Airways, Lufthansa, Delta, British Midland, Aer Lingus, Air Canada and Air France, among others, fly from here.

Flying from Newcastle 7/10

Newcastle Airport, Woolsington,
Newcastle-Upon-Tyne, NE13 8BZ.
(Tel: 0191 286 0966, Fax: 0191 271 6080,
Website: www.newcastleairport.com)
Newcastle airport has recently been extended, and the new development is well designed. It has a 5 million passenger capacity, although

only 3 million fly from the airport at present. The soft-play area is close to the viewing gallery, and the pub and café. There are also four baby-changing rooms, one unsupervised play area, and six restaurants, all of which are toddler-friendly.

Air France, Sabena, KLM, Britannia Airways and Air 2000 are among those airlines flying from this airport.

Flying from Southhampton 6/10

Southampton Airport, Southampton,
Hampshire SO18 2NL (Tel: 0239 262 0021,
Website: www.baa.co.uk)

Southampton became one of the most modern regional airports in December 1994 with a £27 million development, opened by HRH the Duke of York. Over 767,000 passengers fly through this airport annually to over 200 destinations worldwide, via Amsterdam, Brussels, Dublin, Frankfurt, Manchester and Paris. It has excellent road access via the M27 and M3 and the closest plane to train connection of any airport in Europe, with three trains an hour to London Waterloo (a journey taking approximately one hour). It's small, so it has few retail outlets and even fewer eateries. But waiting time while we were there was short. But bring your own entertainment and pray for no delays. There is a baby care room located in the main concourse, with a private feeding cubicle and bottle warmer. Contact the information desk if you need any additional equipment or help.

Airlines that fly from Southampton include British Airways, Manx, Air France, Scotairways, British European, Aurigny.

Flying from the London Area

London Heathrow 5/10

Heathrow Point West, 234 Bath Road,
Harlington, Middlesex UB3 5AP.
(Tel: 08700 000 123, Fax: 020 8745 4290,
Website: www.baa.co.uk)

The largest airport in the UK and busiest in the world, Heathrow has over 63 million passengers a year travelling with over 90 airlines to around 160 destinations worldwide. About 60 percent of travellers are passing through on holiday rather than business. Readers of Business Traveller magazine have consistently voted Heathrow one of the top five airports in the world. But how do they do with toddlers? Sometimes size matters and in this case it does. Although the airport has increased its retail space – especially in terminal three – play areas for toddlers do not seem to be one of the areas on which they have focused.

Depending on which terminal you are flying out of, you will be able to entertain your toddler for a few minutes to hours. For example, if you are on terminal one, go through to the departure lounge as soon as possible. There is more to entertain both you and your toddler there. Eateries such as Burger King, Café Nero, Est Est Est and Pret A Manger seem to cater well for toddlers, and they are less busy than on the landside. There is also a Disney Store to keep toddlers occupied for a few minutes more.

Terminal two, landside, has a larger choice of eateries as there is a Food Village featuring outlets including Village Grill and Health Shelf as well as Burger King. All of these have high chairs. But I would head straight for the departure lounge, as there is a Hamley's toy shop on the other side.

Terminal three has outlets and eateries on both sides, but the departure side will be less crowded. In terminal four, definitely head for the departure side. There are lots more shops, including Hamleys and The Disney Store, and many more eateries, such as Caffe Uno, McDonalds and Garfunkels, which cater for toddler appetites.

There are babychanging facilities in all departure lounges, and in most landside lavatories. Sometimes cramped, and certainly not custom built.

All major airlines fly from London Heathrow.

London Gatwick 3/10

West Sussex RH6 0NP
(Tel: 08700 002 468, Website: www.baa.co.uk)
Handling over 30 million passengers a year, with 102 airlines serving over 280 destinations, there are many developments planned for both north and south terminals to expand the catering, seating and

shopping areas – which is needed. The travel through this airport is predominantly for leisure, but Tom didn't seem very amused. However, it's been voted Top UK Airport by travel trade publication Travel Trade Gazette four times in six years. The south terminal has more to offer at the moment.

Stay landside, which has a wider range of toddler-friendly eateries and Warner Bros shops. The north terminal is poorly served both on landside and airside, with slightly more in the way of food and drink in the departure lounge. But Tom got very restless in an area which seemed to have little to entertain toddlers – or children of any age. There is a recently opened World of Fun toyshop (owned by The Nuance Group) in the airside lounge at Gatwick's south terminal. To attract the children and their parents, the shop design is colourful, fun and entertaining, and most products are at the perfect height for children to touch and see for themselves. There is a video wall screen that plays cartoons and Disney films throughout the day and a wide selection of pick and mix sweets to take away and munch on the plane. The shop contains an exciting array of toys and souvenirs.

In terms of practicality, Gatwick is getting the message. There are baby changing facilities at both ends and the centre of the check-in area, with a booth in 'zone A' in the south terminal. All facilities are signposted (look for bottle or cot symbols). There are showers available at the arrivals end of the mezzanine area, where there is another baby-change facility. Children's play areas are tucked away in the Gatwick Village (south terminal).

Most major airlines fly from London Gatwick.

London Stansted   10/10
Essex CM24 1QW.
(Tel: 0870 000 0303,
Website: www.baa.co.uk)
BAA is investing £200 million in the expansion of this airport, to double its capacity from 8 million to about 15 million. The UK's fourth busiest airport and the fastest growing in Europe, it serves over 90 scheduled destinations, mostly European and Mediterranean plus Tel Aviv and North America, and is used by 24 scheduled airlines.

Compared to Gatwick and Heathrow, it is a haven of civility, excellent design and helpful staff. There are over 68,500 square feet (just under 30 square metres) of retail space with a limited range of shops, none of which particularly interested Tom, but travelling was made easy and pleasurable due to the excellent design. The small things matter. For example, you can pay for your parking ticket if you have parked in the long stay car park while you are waiting for your luggage. There are all the usual baby-change facilities, but what sets this airport apart is the design, which makes travelling with and entertaining a toddler a breeze – large wide gangways and doors, thoughtful construction, easy access to viewing areas. It's all here.

Airlines which fly from Stansted include Buzz, Go, Ryanair, KLM, Lufthansa, SAS, British European, BA, British Midlands and Air Malta.

Flying from Scotland

Prestwick (Glasgow)   7/10
Aviation House, Prestwick, Ayrshire, KA9 2PL
(Tel: 01292 511 000, Website: www.gpia.co.uk)
This airport handled a million passengers annually by end April 2001, and is increasing at a rate of 40 percent per annum. The airport has a children's play area in the departure lounge. High chairs are available. For all holiday charters there is a children's entertainer who provides balloons, a short magic show and general children's entertainment centred around the play area. Also, to assist families, the airport provides free porters for every holiday flight. Changing facilities are available for babies and toddlers. Prestwick has one of the finest aircraft viewing areas of any Scottish Airport, which looks out over the passenger apron and in the spectators terrace there is a separate coffee bar. Prestwick is relatively compact, and there are no long distances to walk. It is, therefore, easy to be landside at the cafeteria, or in the spectators' gallery, and then to go through security to the play area. All of the facilities are on the flat, except the cafeteria which is one floor up, as is the spectators' gallery. There is, however, a lift in which to take toddlers and toddler paraphernalia.

The airport has its own rail station connected by covered walkway to the check-in area. Trains run every 30 minutes to Glasgow Central (journey time 44 minutes). On production of their ticket or Ryanair internet official confirmation, all airline passengers are entitled to half-price rail travel to or from any Scotrail station in Scotland. If passengers are travelling on Ryanair, check-in closes 30 minutes before departure, hence the time at the airport is relatively short. On charters with longer check-in times, the airport does not force customers into the departures area and they have a choice as to where they want to wait.

Prestwick Airport handles 15 Ryanair scheduled flights a day to London Stansted, Paris Beauvais, Frankfurt Hahn, Brussels Charleroi, and Dublin. The airport also has holiday charter flights with Airtours, Club Travel 2000, Seguro Holidays, Direct Holidays and Airways to a range of European and Florida destinations.

Flying from Aberdeen 7/10
Aberdeen Airport Ltd, Dyce, Aberdeenshire
(Tel: 01224 722 331, Fax: 01224 725 724,
Website: www.baa.co.uk)
Seven miles north west of Aberdeen, and the smallest of the BAA Airports in Scotland, Aberdeen carries only 2.6 million passengers a year, 18 percent of which fly in and out via helicopter. This airport has a very decent area to keep toddlers entertained for a few hours, but no more than that. A baby-care unit is next to the airport information desk, within the disabled toilet facility in the international departures area, and within the ladies' toilet facility in the domestic departures area. A children's Lego table is available in the waiting area, and there are a few eateries including Delifrance and Brophy's self-service buffet; high chairs are available. Two restaurants are particularly suitable for toddlers: the Gallery Café, with a play area and children's menu, and Cloud 9, which has an entertainment centre for young children. To help keep toddlers entertained, colouring books and crayons are usually available, free of charge, from the airport information desk, where there is a Duplo play table and a fun table. Further fun tables are located in the domestic and international departures lounges and on the main concourse.

Atlantic Airways, Eastern Airways, Gill Air, SAS, Coastair, Braathens, Easyjet and British Airways all fly from this airport. Parents requiring a taxi with a toddler seat fitted should pre-book the facility by tele-phoning the Airport Taxi Rank on 01224 725 728. There is a first aid room located next to the airport information desk, where all staff are trained first-aiders.

Glasgow Airport 8/10
Glasgow Airport Ltd, Paisley,
Renfrewshire PA3 2ST
(Tel: 0141 887 1111, Fax: 0141 848 4586,
Website: www.seeglasgow.com)
Nearly 7 million passengers fly in and out of Glasgow Airport each year. Nine miles west of Glasgow, this is the busiest major airport in Scotland, ranking fifth in the UK with an extensive range of inter-national destinations for both business and leisure activities. There are four babycare rooms in the terminal building. Any of the catering outlets will be happy to heat babies' bottles and food. Restaurants and bars before passport control include McDonalds (which always has an enormous queue and never sufficient seats), Weavers Café (Pizza Hut, Harry Ramsdens and Upper Crust – which is always just as full), and Garfunkels. At Glasgow they have two children's soft play areas – one in the international departure lounge and one located on the first floor of terminal one. Both are fairly large facilities.

Air 2000, Atlantic Airways, American Airlines, BA, British Midland, Continental Airways, Easyjet, KLM, Icelandair, Jersey European, Manx, Aer Lingus, Air Canada, Air France and Air Malta all fly from this airport. Greater Glasgow & Clyde Valley Tourist Board operate a Tourist Information Desk located in the international arrivals concourse, providing information on accommodation, events and places of interest. Public transport information is available from Strathclyde Passenger Transport Travel Centre on the ground floor at UK arrivals. Contact 0141 848 4330.

Flying from Edinburgh 7/10
Edinburgh Airport Ltd, Edinburgh EH12 9DN
(Tel: 0131 333 1000, Fax: 0131 335 3181,
Website: www.baa.co.uk)
Seven miles west of Edinburgh, this airport caters for 4.5 million

passengers a year, mostly flying to the London airport network, Amsterdam, Paris, Brussels and Dublin. So you don't see many children about. Baby-care rooms are sited next to toilet facilities in the UK arrivals hall, on the first floor departures concourse and in the departures lounge. There's a Burger King on the first floor within a Granada food village, which also hosts a Village Grill, Franklins of Boston and Brioche Dorrée. Village Grill, and Wetherspoons, Baby bottles are available on request. Two baby-care facilities are located in the terminal, plus there's a private lockable nursing room and a unisex toilet. The food court has a play table, colouring sheets and crayons for toddlers. There are three Lego play points in the departure lounge. Early learning and story books can be purchased in Books Etc.

Air 2000, Air France, BA, British Midland, Crossair, Go, KLM, Sabena, Scotairways, Tyrolean, Easyjet, KLM, Icelandair, Jersey European, Braathens, Aer Lingus and Lufthansa all fly from this airport.

Useful contacts

Belfast City Airport (Tel: 02890 457 745)
Belfast International Airport (Tel: 028 9448 4848)
Blackpool Airport (Tel: 01253 343 434,
    Website: www.blackpoolairport.com)
Bournemouth International Airport Ltd (Tel: 01202 364 000)
Bristol International Airport (Tel: 0870 121 2747)
Exeter and Devon Airport (Tel: 01392 367 433,
    Website: www.exeter-airport.co.uk)
Gatwick Airport (Tel: 08700 002 468)
Guernsey Airport (Tel: 014812 377 66)
Humberside International Airport (Tel: 01625 688 456,
    Website: www.humberside-airport.co.uk)
Leeds Bradford International Airport (Tel: 0113 250 9696,
    Website: www.lbia.co.uk)
Liverpool Airport plc (Tel: 0151 288 4000,
    Website: www.livairport.com)
London Luton Airport (Tel: 01582 405 100,
    Website: www.london-luton.com)

Londonderry (Tel: 0800 010 100, Website:
    www.derrynet.airport.index)
Norwich Airport Ltd (Tel: 01603 420 620,
    Website: www.norwichairport.com)
Plymouth City Airport Ltd (Tel: 01752 204 090)
Regional Airports Ltd (Tel: 01256 862 059)
Scottish Airports Ltd (Tel: 0141 887 1111)
Teeside International Airport (Tel: 01325 332 811,
    Website: www.teesside.com)

Which airline?

Your choice of destination will, obviously, limit your choices, as will the airport you wish to fly from. It's a good idea to scout around between airlines if possible, as there can be a big difference in the way they cope with toddlers, and the experience they provide. In fact, a good experience is very much dependent upon the airline's child policy, the crew and, of course, the route.

What you should research in advance are the facilities the airlines offer. Even something as simple as the seat pitch (the distance between one seat and the next) makes a difference to comfort. Ideally, you'll want some space where your child can comfortably kick the seat in front, and possibly make a fort or a makeshift bed on the floor between rows. It's always a good idea to double-check what amenities – if any – you can expect on your flight, since airline policies are always subject to change.

Increasingly, airlines are providing kiddies packs and child menus, the best of which is provided by Virgin Atlantic, who pioneered the concept of targeting children. Virgin's website (www.flyvirgin.com) has pages dedicated to showing customers what they can expect when flying Virgin, and obviously understand the truth in the saying 'toddlers are the customers of tomorrow'. You can expect kiddies meals, a backpack full of goodies, a trip to see the cockpit, and more. British Airways and Cathay Pacific had the best toddler packs, according to the toddlers I spoke to.

Stopovers

These are a good idea only if you are travelling on a long-haul flight. Try to avoid stopovers on journeys that can be made in under five hours. For longer journeys, they can be a bonus, particularly if you are allowed into the transitional airport for a 'stretch'. Stopovers make flights to countries like Australia, for example, much more bearable. You may even be able to find shower facilities to use if you have an hour or more to spare. They usually cost a few pounds – easier if you have some local currency – and make you feel human again.

Better still, though, is an overnight stopover, or even two. If just one night think about sleeping at an airport hotel so you don't have to worry about transfers. The lost time will probably be gained on arrival because you will feel in better shape to start moving.

But stopovers can have their drawbacks. You'll have double the potential trouble with ear problems on take-off and landing, and you may face the same lengthy delays in queues before boarding.

How much will it cost?

• All of the airlines offer special discounts when booking a seat for children under two years old, while lap babies fly free. I encourage you to buy that extra seat – for peace of mind in unexpected turbulence and for a more comfortable, less stressful flight. Over the age of two, most airlines offer a seat at a set percentage of the adult fare. Normally, this discount applies up to the age of eleven or twelve, after which full adult fare applies. All children who pay for a seat are allocated the full baggage allowance. It's worth shopping around, however, to find the best deal. There is a wide variation between prices for toddlers and young children.

• If your baby or toddler does not take up a seat, you normally pay around 10 percent of the adult fare, but only one child is allowed per adult in this arrangement. Additional children pay half the adult fare, or a set discounted rate. Babes in arms are not entitled to child meals or even a baggage allowance.

> • Business class costs at least double the price of economy, some-
> times considerably more, and despite the extra space, it may not
> be a better option. It is not unknown for parents of a noisy baby
> to be moved back into the economy to keep the peace with other,
> irritable passengers. And in case you are wondering, first class is
> likely to cost at least two-thirds more again!

According to those parents who had flown with their toddlers to both long- and short-haul destinations worldwide, the top 10 airlines are listed below. They all scored highest on entertainment value – with goodie bags, individual TV screens with cartoons and games (in the case of Virgin, Cathay Pacific, Qantas and Singapore Airlines) – and allowed sufficient time to board the plane before other passengers. These airlines also had the friendliest and most efficient cabin crew, according to the survey.

1. Virgin Atlantic (Tel: 01293 747 747, Website: www.flyvirgin.com)
2. Air New Zealand (Website: www.airnz.co.nz)
3. British Airways (Tel: 0845 773 3377,
   Website: www.britishairways.com)
4. Singapore Airlines (Tel: 0870 608 8886,
   Website: www.singaporeair.co.uk)
5. Quantas Airways (Tel: 0845 774 7767,
   Website: www.quantas.com)
6. Cathay Pacific (Tel: 020 7747 8888,
   Website: www.cathaypacific.com)
7. Emirates (Tel: 020 7808 0033, Website: www.ekgroup.com)
8. Ryanair (Tel: 0870 333 1231, Website: www.ryanair.co.uk)
9. Austrian Airlines (Tel: 020 7434 7350)
10. Swissair (Tel: 0845 758 1333, Website: www.swissair.com)

The best time to fly

To a degree your choice of destination will dictate what time you fly, particularly if you are taking a charter. However, there a few things that you can do to help ease the pain of the journey:

- If possible, choose a departure time that will allow relatively normal sleep patterns to be maintained. Travel early in the day from the UK, if you can, which gives you time to get organised at the other end. On short-haul flights this shouldn't be too much of a problem.
- On longer flights, a night flight might be the best option, but only if your toddler is likely to sleep. If both you and your toddler are unable to get any rest, you're likely to have chaos at the other end, and probably an unpleasant flight trying to keep a wakeful child from disrupting other passengers, and, of course, occupied. Some night flights leave lights on until the early hours, which can make sleep difficult for anyone, particularly an excited toddler. If you don't think sleep is likely, go for a day-time flight instead.
- Day flights will almost certainly be a better option if your child/children are not easy sleepers, though you may have to devote more time to entertaining them and to planning entertainment beforehand.
- Aim for flights that are unlikely to be busy. Very early morning and after 7pm on shorter-haul routes are reportedly good bets. Early morning is best for toddlers, but may not be best for you. Quieter days are reported to be Tuesdays and Wednesdays. It is probably also a fair bet that cheaper flight times are the less crowded ones.
- Your airline may not allow it, but you can try to reserve split seats – one on the aisle and the other by the window, for example, and ask reservations to indicate that you have a child with you in order to discourage other passengers from taking the middle seat. Airlines sometimes leave free seats next to families in the central section, filling these only as the plane is occupied. This seems more common practice in North America than in Europe.

The best time to fly with babies and under-twos

- If you are travelling with a baby, pre-booking a bassinet or 'sky cot' can be useful. These generally take infants of up to 22lbs (10kg), though this varies from airline to airline, as does the design. Ideally look for one with a net over the top so you do not have to take the baby out if the seat belt sign goes on (Qantas offers this, for example). Sky cots are not common on charter flights.

- If your child is under two years old (40lbs/18kg in weight, in the US) you are permitted to travel with them on your lap. However, think hard about this if the flight is more than an hour. If the plane is not full, you will be able to use a spare seat beside you, but you can't count on there being one.

Before the Flight
Checking in

Allow plenty of time for this, particularly as arriving early gives you a better chance of getting your preferred seats. If travelling as a sole carer and/or with small children it is worth going straight to the business or even first-class desk to avoid an economy class queue. You are unlikely to be turned away, though it is a possibility.

Apart from giving you a better choice of seats, arriving early for check-in should eliminate the chances of being bumped from your flight.

Where to sit

- Try to pre-book seats with your airline before travelling. This is more complicated than it might seem, largely because different aircrafts have different layouts.
- Most airlines are now non-smoking, but a few remain that allow passengers to smoke at the back of the plane. Ask if there is smoking on board and, if so, make sure you are as far away as possible. Remember that there may be a smoking row in business class, too, so you may not want to be seated right at the front of economy class. The answer is, really, to choose a non-smoking airline.
- A seat at the side of the aircraft is probably the most useful for parents with toddlers. The fallout of any accidents – spills, sick, messy meals, for example – will not affect strangers, who will similarly be protected from kicks and other physical expressions of boredom and frustration. A toddler will want to exercise at least a little and a gentle walk down the aisle can be useful entertainment when the crew do not want to use the gangway. A seat at the side however will minimise how much the child can get out and

possibly trouble other people. However, the lights running down the side of the cabin are pretty bright and generally the last to be switched off, which is not useful if you are trying to get a child to sleep.

- Those with babies and young children may be placed near emergency exits for safety reasons, but not in the exit row itself because of the statutory obligation to keep the route to the exit free.
- If you have booked a bassinet (sky cot) you will almost certainly be given a bulkhead seat as the cot is generally fitted against the bulkhead wall. It is partly because there are a limited number of bulkhead seats that cots are not guaranteed, though frequent fliers seem to get priority.
- There are disadvantages to bulkhead seats. They are generally right under the film screen, which may disturb a baby. There are often no pockets in front for storing books and small toys. What's more, the seat arms rarely lift, so getting in and out when the cot is in place often means climbing up on to your set and then out, possibly over someone else. The fixed arms also make it impossible to spread yourself comfortably over a vacant seat should there be one. Families with little ones are often placed in these seats, so it can be noisy.
- Having said that, the bulkhead seats often provide a little more floor space, without the inconvenience of a seat in front being leant back. It can be the perfect place for a makeshift bed, a fort, or a play area for a bored or sleepy toddler.
- If you want to sleep, avoid anywhere with noise, near the galley for example.
- Ventilation is generally better at the front of the plane than the back so you might prefer to go nearer the front.

Overbooking and bumping

A recent report by American Express indicated that one in 10 passengers have been bumped from their flights in the previous 12 months because of overbooking by airlines. Most airlines overbook on the assumption that there will be cancellations; however, this is not always the case, and more often than not, they find themselves with too few seats for passengers.

You are slightly less likely to be bumped if you have a pre-assigned seat and have both booked direct and reconfirmed with the airline. You are more likely to be bumped if you have a restricted, economy ticket.

EC regulations stipulate that airlines should make a particular effort to ensure that handicapped passengers and unaccompanied children can fly as planned, there is no mention of anything similar for families.

If you are bumped, your airline must give you the choice of a full refund on your ticket (half the return fare), another flight as soon as possible, or another flight at a later date of your choice.

Airlines must also pay you compensation in cash (unless you would prefer vouchers). The amount depends on the length of the missed flight and how late you are getting to your final destination. Compensation for flights of up to 3,500km with a delay of up to two hours would entitle you to a payment of ECU75 (around £50). If the flight is further than 3,500km and the delay more than four hours the payment is ECU300 (around £200).

However, regulations do not specify any details on payment for children and infants and while some airlines will make payment for a full fare, others point to the fact that regulations refer to the compensation not exceeding the price of the ticket, and so pay less.

In addition, airlines should get a message through to your point of arrival, provide meals and refreshments, plus accommodation if the delay is overnight. For further information, see the AUC website www.auc.org.uk, or ring them on 020 7240 6061.

Luggage

Given the effort that it may require to get items out of an overhead locker, you might like to pack a small bag as well, which can be removed and placed under the seat for instant access to toys, snacks, wet wipes, nappies and drinks.

A toddler without a seat is not entitled to a baggage allowance. If you travel heavy, this will be a problem. A baby bag will almost certainly be allowed as extra hand luggage, but the size and weight allowed varies widely between airlines. Find out in advance what is permissible, as you may find yourself hastily unpacking before boarding the flight. British Airways, for example, says that the maximum extra permitted weight is 6kg (about 15 lbs). Charter flights will undoubtedly have a lower allowance.

Most airlines will permit you to take buggies, pushchairs and prams right up to the boarding gate, where they will take them to load into the hold. The area in which airlines differ is how soon the buggy is returned on arrival. Some will provide this at the gate, others will only return them with the rest of the luggage in the baggage hall, which can mean a fairly long walk with toddler and belongings being carried. Ask in advance how you can expect to retrieve your buggy, and remind the flight attendants that you will need it as soon as you land. If you anticipate problems, you may want to use a sling or backpack instead, as these can be stored in an overhead locker and used immediately upon landing. You'll also have the advantage of having two free hands, for carrying onboard bags and/or other toddlers.

Officially, carry cots are not permitted on board, but you may be able to swing it if your flight is not crowded. Check in advance to see if there is a possibility that you will be allowed to use a cot, but be prepared to have it sent down to the hold at the last minute.

Forwarding luggage

If you are taking a lot of luggage you can send it, unaccompanied, to your destination, to await your arrival. This may be possible with the more sophisticated scheduled airlines or you can use a tailored service.

Before you board

Assuming that you have arrived in good time for check-in, you will have some time to kill at the airport. As these become more and more like shopping malls, there are a growing number of ways to spend your money and time.

If you prefer not to spend your holiday budget doing some advance shopping, you might like to park yourselves somewhere near a window, probably near the embarkation gate, to watch planes land and take off. Some airports offer children's play areas, but these are still pretty much a novelty (see page 34), particularly during off-peak travel seasons.

During peak periods, many airports will lay on children's entertainers – great for short distractions, and always free.

Your best bet is to plan a little entertainment in advance, with some colouring, snacks, a little shopping, a puzzle or even just a few good books to keep your toddler occupied during a long wait.

Extra precautions
It is wise to take any toilet-trained toddler to the loo before boarding as they will not be allowed to use the in-flight loo until after takeoff. Similarly take them before landing.

Boarding

Airlines generally allow passengers with children to board first but, in practice, this depends on the airport crew and the airline's policy. If you would like to pre-board, chances are you will be permitted – if you ask in advance. Although it may mean a longer time on board before take-off, it gives you a chance to stow your on-board luggage and get yourself organised for the flight before the aisles fill with other passengers.

The alternative is to board among the last passengers. This allows your children to burn off any last-minute steam with a quick runabout, and means a shorter time sitting strapped in before take-off. Remember, however, that you may end up with your on-board bags in inconvenient places.

Use the time before take-off to chat to the cabin crew about any special treatment you may require, such as bottle-warming or chilling, sky cots, extra blankets or pillows, or inflight entertainment. If they are given advance warning, they can normally help to make your journey more comfortable.

On the plane

Most long-haul airlines now provide some sort of goody bag for children. This is a fun idea, but the contents of these bags may not be appropriate for a toddler, or your toddler's interests. Best to go prepared with your own distractions (see page 59).

If the airline operates seat-back screens, there is normally a children's cartoon channel that should keep them amused for hours.

Beware, however, that some toddlers explore the options and have horrified parents who find them watching highly unsuitable films. You'll need to take charge of the controls, and keep a close eye on what your child is watching. Many toddlers find the earphones difficult to manage, so you may need to rely on another form of entertainment.

Aircrafts with seat-back screens also tend to have a shallower seat pitch, offering children less space to move, and a greater likelihood of banging into the seat in front, necessitating apologies.

Meals are an obvious diversion, but they can be so unpalatable that you may prefer to take your own food along. Children's meals normally have to be ordered well in advance of the flight, and it's probably better than taking chances with adult fare. Check in advance what your child's meal is likely to include, and supplement it with other goodies if you anticipate little interest from your toddler.

Try to get your toddler served before you, so that you can help him with his meal without the two-tray juggling act. Either that, or ask for yours early, and bolt it down quickly. You may also consider asking for a low salt or vegetarian meal, as the special diet meals are generally better than the standard ones. Other alternatives are cold meals (brown bag meals in the US), a simple fruit platter, or some sandwiches.

Remember that once the service begins, you are unlikely to be able to get your child to the toilet for some time. Ask in advance about when you can expect to be served, and fit in a pit stop before that time.

Food and drink

• Feeling good after a flight has a lot to do with your digestion and this is particularly true for toddlers. At altitude, the digestive process can take a third longer than usual, so it is best to stick to lighter foods, such as pasta and white meat (so no burgers) or fish. Lower-fat foods are recommended, as they are more easily digested, so avoid fish fingers, chips and other fatty fare.

• Offer plenty of fruit, which encourages the action of the liver.

• It's a good idea to eat little and often, so bringing your own snacks, rather than relying on in-flight meals may be preferable.

Bear in mind, too, that the body is better able to digest food earlier in the day. And in the case of travelling across time barriers, this refers to the time at your point of departure.

• Drink and offer your toddler plenty of fluid, preferably plain water, which keeps the digestive system working, and helps to counteract the dryness of the air.

• Experts recommend that you include potassium in your diet (a mineral that can help to prevent cramping). A good natural source is bananas.

Pre-planned distractions

If you are flying during the day, be prepared to spend the majority of your trip entertaining your toddler, until, that is, he's old enough to enjoy the in-flight entertainment, or draw or read.

When providing your own entertainment, try to prepare something new for every hour on board. Obviously infants will need much less stimulation, as will children who are old enough to be handed the latest Harry Potter.

Bring along a selection of gift-wrapped goodies, such as treats, crayons, a new pad of paper, some plastic cartoon characters, a magnetic puzzle or two, some new books, a story tape to fit into a walkman or small tape player, a colouring book, a small game and even a selection of coloured plasticine. You can pack these in your own bag, and offer them as required throughout the flight, or put them in your child's backpack and let him explore at agreed-upon times.

Make sure you bring along a favourite toy or comfort object, such as a stuffed animal or a blanket. Something familiar will undoubtedly make your toddler feel more confident in his new surroundings.

For those old enough to read a map you can point them in the direction of those in the in-flight magazines showing the route, or you can provide your own rather more detailed map for the purpose.

Get up and walk around. You may even be able to organise a trip to see the pilot.

Sleeping on board

If they aren't already on your seats, ask for a blanket and pillow as early as you can to ensure you are not left without. If you are counting on your toddler sleeping on the flight, bear in mind the fact that the lights may not go out until some hours after takeoff. Distractions will need to be provided until that time. And be prepared that he may not sleep at all!

Tips for encouraging sleep:

- Fly on red-eyes for long trips. Your child should sleep, particularly if you keep him busy throughout the day before. Take him on board in his pyjamas, and bring along his favourite sleeping companion.
- Use your normal car seat on board (see page 63). Safety aside, children are used to sitting still/sleeping in them, so they are more comfortable with the confinement.
- Board the plane at the last possible moment. You may choose to pre-board one person with the gear, but put the child on the plane at the last possible moment.
- Offer a snack and a drink. Have babies nurse/drink a bottle for takeoff and landing. Feed dry foods during the flight so your child will be thirsty upon landing. Once in the air, ask the flight attendants to avoid disturbing you unless absolutely necessary. You can opt out of meals and duty-free shopping if you let them know early on.
- Once the plane is in the air, you may be able to unbuckle your child's seatbelt and prepare a little bed for him on an empty seat, or even on the floor in front of you. Most airline crew are happy for you to do this, but remember that you may have to waken him to buckle up if the seatbelt sign goes on.
- Offer some soothing, warm herbal tea (see page 61) or milk, take a trip to the loo, read a story and settle him down just as you would at home. It may not work, but a familiar pre-sleep routine may set things in motion.

Entertainment en route

If your toddler needs fairly consistent distraction, aim to supply one (very small and light) toy for every hour en route. The top 10 distractions are as follows:

1. Books. Choose interactive ones, with flaps, mirrors, smells and folding bits. Bring a selection of favourite books for comfort value, and some new ones to stimulate. There is normally a good book-shop at the airport (if you are flying), or choose a book together at a bookshop closer to home.

2. Stocking fillers are ideal for travel. Wrap up little inexpensive gifts and offer them every hour or so.

3. Personal stereos. Sing along to Thomas the Tank, Bob the Builder, Teletubbies and nursery rhymes. Or get your child's favourite books on tape (you can make these yourself by taping as you read) so that he can look at the pictures as he listens.

4. In-flight cartoons. Not all airlines offer these (see page 49), but many do. If you have a long-haul flight ahead of you, it's worth choosing an airline with an in-house entertainment programme set up.

5. Games. Scissors, paper, stone is a good one, and never fails to entertain (possibly because they have a good chance of beating their parents).

6. Colouring-in, join-the-dot and sticker books. Choose age-appropriate ones so that they won't need constant supervision or help (see page 431).

7. Playing finger puppets (see page 78).

8. Magnetic puzzles and games, which avoids pieces being eaten or dropped down the side.

9. A visit to the pilot (this can also cause problems as they don't want to leave the cockpit). Ask if this service is available before you promise a trip.

10. Beanie babies (preferably two, so one can talk to the other).

Toys to avoid:

• Anything with small parts that will get lost in the sand, down the side of the seat, etc.

- Anything noisy (for your sake, and to keep the peace with other passengers).
- Toys that are large and heavy to carry.
- Toys that require banging (hammer and 'nail' sets, stamping sets, etc.) will irritate other passengers, and, possibly, you.
- Felt-tips, unless they are washable.
- Crayons, if the weather is hot.

Extra comfort

Though not all airlines may be happy about this option, you may want to lay your baby on a sheepskin or blanket on the floor, in order to provide a comfortable place in which to sleep. Furthermore, a blanket draped over the seat-back table can make a peaceful tent when the overhead lights are still on.

Changing nappies

- New aircraft are generally supplied with changing tables in the lavatories. If you are unlucky enough to find yourself on board one without this kind of facility, you may have to change a child on the seat or seatback table, potentially incurring some displeasure from neighbours. Or try to find a surface in the lavatory itself, which may be unhygienic. A folding changing mat would be useful.
- One tip is to use an extra-absorbent night-time nappy to avoid unnecessary in-flight changes.
- Note that hygiene restrictions may mean that cabin staff (who handle food) cannot take a dirty nappy for you. Come prepared with nappy sacks to dispose of them easily.

Read up on the subject!
Stress-Free Flying, by Robert Bor, Jeannette Josee and Stephen Palmer (Quay Books, £10.99 ISBN 1-85842-167-8) is a title written by three psychologists to help those who experience difficulty flying. It includes a chapter on flying with children, noting the stress that a strange environment can cause for the child, as well as examining children's potential fears about flying and suggesting practical and emotional preparation. The authors suggest trying to spend a calm day before travelling, and setting out for the airport in good time.

Happy Flying
Aromatherapist Daniele Ryman (www.danieleryman.com) offers the following advice:
• Give them as much outdoor exercise as possible before the flight to help them to deal with the non-activity on board, as well as the lack of space.
• Give them a good meal before they fly, with freshly squeezed citrus juice for the vitamin C and minerals.
• Add honey to their drinks for its natural vitamin B and vitamin A content.
• Offer lots of apples, which act as a sedative to the nervous system. Take some for the flight, along with some fresh carrots. The latter is particularly useful if they have sore gums. In fact, most raw vegetable will help to soothe teething problems, and the chewing action will help to prevent earaches caused by pressure on board.
• Bring a flask of lukewarm herbal teas, mixed with honey. The best herbs to choose include orange flowers, vervain, orange leaves and chamomile. If you like, mix them with a little warm milk.
• Blend 1 to 2 drops of essential oils of lavender and chamomile in a little almond or sunflower oil. Rub it gently under your toddler's nose, and massage the tops of their hands and the nape of their neck. They will sleep for the entire flight . . .

Knocking them out

Although it can be tempting to encourage sleep and a painfree flight by using drugs to sedate your toddler, it's not really a good idea. First and foremost, your child will probably suffer from a hangover effect upon landing, and/or suffer a reaction from the drugs. And it's worth noting that many of the drugs suggested for sedating children onboard may well have the opposite effect!

Antihistamines, which are most commonly used, can actually encourage hyperactivity in some children. You may not want to take the risk! By giving large doses of antihistamines you may knock your toddler out but, as *Times* newspaper doctor, Dr Thomas Stuttaford, suggests, 'Your child does indeed sleep, but when it wakes the next day its irritability may be unimaginable.'

This kind of drug does not encourage the REM sleep which is crucial for real rest. And unless you are prepared to use large doses, you may find your child more manic, talkative and over-excited. He'll have lost his inhibitions and worries, but he may become more grizzly and too over-tired to sleep.

Safety restraints for toddlers

The issue of keeping a child safe on an aircraft is a minefield, according to Roger Hardy of the Cranfield Impact Centre, largely because there are few air crashes so little material for research. As a result, children are not offered the same protection as adults on board.

There is some dispute about what the safest option actually is, so there are different rules for carriers registered in different countries.

It is recognised that a single adult belt is dangerous for a small child because, in the event of an impact, it will focus the pressure on a small soft tissue area (not the pelvis as in adults), which is likely to suffer severe damage. Because of this, rules in the US and other countries do not allow the use of belts or lap belts for under fours.

However belts do have to be used by children on carriers registered in the UK and certain other European countries. According to Roger Hardy the belts are not ideal but do offer a degree of protection. They also prevent the child from becoming an potential free-flying missile.

UK Legislation

The Civil Aviation Authority's regulations for UK airlines are based on research at Cranfield and state that:

- Children under the age of six months must sit on an adult lap with a loop/belly belt; in other words, a belt that is attached to the adult's belt by a loop.
- Children between six months and two years must be restrained as above or in any car seat meeting British safety standards. They may also be seated in a 'care chair', which is a seat specially designed for use on an aircraft.
- Children between the ages of two and three must use a car seat as above or an adult belt on the aircraft seat. Children over three years must use an adult seat belt.

Using a child car seat

A child seat, though only suggested by the UK authority, is recommended by the American Federal Aviation Association, which states that all US domestic carriers must accept child car safety seats as long as these carry a label stating that they conform to federal safety standards. This ruling applies to children up to around two and a half stone (30lbs, 12kg, or about four years of age).

The Cranfield Centre has recommended an upper age limit of four, as in the US, but the CAA has selected three years as being the upper age limit, possibly because size is the real criteria and this avoids such a seat being used by children too large for safety.

While UK carriers are not permitted to use rear-facing seats, because it is felt that airline belts are not a safe enough anchor, the FAA recommends the use of rear-facing seats for babies, as in cars. They recommend their use until your baby is about 22lbs (10kg, or about nine months old).

An alternative is to take your own car seat. In addition to the safety on board, taking your own car seat means you can probably use it in any car at the other end of the flight. However, there is no guarantee of this as not all car seats fit all cars.

Even where accepted in principle, there is no guarantee that an airline will accept your child's car seat for use on board. In addition you will need to check that the seat fits the airline seat. Seventeen inches is the standard economy width.

The disadvantages of taking a car seat are the hassle of carrying it and the way it restricts the amount of space in which your toddler has to fidget. They can, however, be useful as a point of familiarity for your toddler, and can help in cases of turbulence.

If you are not sure that your seat will be accepted you can take it to the gate with tape and black bin liners. Wrap it and hand it to cabin crew to be placed in the hold if it is rejected.

Given the quality of most baggage handling, this is not ideal, particularly if it is a hard plastic-framed seat which could sustain invisible damage. Better would be one of the polystyrene models.

Some airlines, including BA, are introducing bulkhead seats specifically for children on some flights. However, there have been no further announcements about this.

Health issues

Flying is not a particularly healthy activity so you might like to think about some of the relevant issues. First of all, every parent should be aware that airlines will not carry children with infectious diseases, severe cases of middle ear infection, or sinusitis. Here's what to do for the main problems that might crop up on board:

Ear problems

Around a quarter of travellers suffer from ear pain or discomfort when flying. Pain is caused by inequal pressure on either side of the eardrum, the result of changes in air pressure and often a blocked Eustachian tube, which runs from the throat to the middle ear on each side. Normally air moves to equalise pressure in the ear, but when it becomes trapped, anything from a mild discomfort and 'deaf' feeling, to extreme pain can be experienced.

Toddlers are often more at risk of this kind of pain, first and foremost because they have smaller Eustachian tubes, which are more susceptible to blocking, and also because they often have colds, snuffles and excess mucus, which compounds the problem.

What to do

- If possible, avoid travelling when your toddler has a heavy cold, severe hay fever, or any form of ear infection or sinusitis.
- Swallowing can help to reduce the pressure. Babies should be offered a bottle, or your breast when breastfeeding, to encourage sucking during take-off. Beware of starting too soon. Your plane could end up stuck in a queue on the runway. Offer older children a drink, or chewing gum. Yawning also helps. Encourage long, jaw-splitting yawns, which will help to prevent a build-up of pressure.
- A word of caution! While you are encouraged to give liquid during landing to promote swallowing and prevent pain in the ears, you may not reach a loo on the ground until quite some time after disembarkation. This can be a particular problem at larger airports like Gatwick and Heathrow.
- If your child's ears do get blocked, or he is suffering pain, encourage him to inflate his cheeks with air, pinch his nostrils and blow hard with his mouth closed. This has the effect of pushing air up through the back of the nose to the middle air, which helps to equalise pressure. A fun alternative is to bring along a balloon, which can be blown up by older children.
- Painkillers and/or nasal decongestants can help if the pain is severe, and many airlines carry these on board.
- There are now earplugs available, which are designed to help equalise the pressure in the ear. Cirrus Health Care offers a product called Earplane, silicone ear plugs which provide a seal within the ear canal and pressure regulation. These plugs come in adult and child sizes.
- Bring along the homeopathic remedy Chamomilla. If you can't find it, go for teething granules, which contain it. It will help ease the extreme pain of ear blockage on board.
- As awful as it may sound, crying will help to open up blockages, so it's a good idea to allow it.
- If all else fails, fill two paper cups with paper napkins soaked in hot water to put over your toddler's ears. The idea is that the warmth reduces the pressure. It may also help to massage the area on the neck, just below the ears.

- Whatever you do, keep calm and try to bear in mind that the pain can be excruciating. Patience is the order of the day!

Dehydration

Under normal circumstances, water vapour forms some 70 to 80 percent of the atmosphere. Levels between 30 and 60 percent are considered to be comfortable. However, on most flights, water vapour forms only 10 to 20 percent of the air, and this figure is often lower.

The result is dehydration, which is often made worse by the fact that airlines may cut ventilation rates in order to make savings on their fuel bills. Furthermore, in order to encourage sleep, the temperature on most long-haul flights is increased after the meal has been served. This can be helpful, but when levels rise above room temperature, dehydration is further encouraged. Add to that the fact that many toddlers (and adults) simply do not drink enough on board, and you have a potential problem on your hands.

What to do
- Ensure that all of you drink plenty of liquids both before the flight and while on board. Avoid anything containing caffeine, such as cola and chocolate, which acts as a diuretic.
- Offer plenty of juicy fruit, such as fresh grapes, citrus fruits and crunchy apples, which will keep your child hydrated. Fresh vegetable sticks and fruit purees will also be useful.
- Avoid offering crisps or anything salty, which can encourage the problem.
- If you have a reluctant drinker on your hands, consider buying him his own water bottle. Fill it with water or diluted fruit juice and allow him to 'be in charge' of his own intake. If it's got a favourite TV character on the outside, it's sure to be a hit.
- Although a toddler's skin is usually supple enough to cope, you might like to take along an emollient moisturising cream to make them more comfortable, particularly if they suffer from a skin problem such as eczema. Lip balm might also be a good idea, as well as a water spray – if they can be trusted not to run riot with it.

- If you are breastfeeding, it's doubly important that you drink enough.

Air sickness

Always a possibility, particularly on a turbulent flight! Go prepared with extra sick bags, just in case.

What to do
- Encourage your child to eat small, regular meals before the flight. Blood sugar swings can make the problem worse. Avoid fatty, sugary foods before flying, choosing fresh fruits and vegetables, toast and rice cakes instead.
- Invest in some Sea Bands, small stretchy bracelets that circle the wrist and press on acupressure points that help to prevent motion sickness.
- Offer small sips of drinks rather than whole bottles. A full tummy can make the problem worse.
- Bring along a small bottle of ginger ale or chilled lemon and ginger tea, sweetened with a little honey. Ginger helps to settle an upset tummy.
- Ensure that your toddler gets a good night's sleep before flying, and that he has a chance to get some fresh air before the flight. If he's well rested, he'll be much less likely to suffer.
- If he does begin to vomit, keep calm and try not to show anxiety, which can make the problem worse. Place a cool cloth on his head and encourage him to look out the window, or to shut his eyes and listen to a favourite story.

Plaster casts
Because the body tends to swell in the highly pressured air of the airplane cabin, it's not a good idea to travel with a limb in plaster. Swelling in tightly confined space can stop the blood flow. If your child is in plaster, see your doctor before flying.

Airplane air

The dry air of the cabin is uncomfortable, but there are other problems.

• Many viruses seem to survive better in low humidity, and because the air is recycled, you and your family are much more likely to be in contact with infectious agents. This is particularly problematic on planes with poor ventilation, and on long-haul flights.

• In addition, the carbon dioxide produced by all those bodies breathing can build up, which causes stuffiness and even headaches.

• There may be pollutants in the air, such as kerosene, particularly if the aircraft has been standing on the tarmac for any length of time. And while the airplane is refuelling, at a stopover, for example, you may be in contact with a wide number of noxious chemicals.

Flying babies

Babies should not fly in their first 48 hours of life because their heart and lungs cannot cope with the reduced levels of oxygen.

In 1998 there was a report that flying, particularly long-haul, might be connected with cot death. The theory was that even in a pressurised aircraft cabin, the lower levels of oxygen might be a contributory cause. Researchers found that when they provided an equivalently low level of oxygen to babies of around three months, the level of oxygen in the blood of some children fell. Subsequent research has, however, thrown this theory into doubt. Experts now claim that flying is safe for babies.

On the other side

If you've had a long flight, it might be a good idea to arrange care for your toddler when you arrive, so that you can get some much-needed rest. You'll also need to be prepared for time differences and, potentially, jetlag (see below).

Pack a little bag of emergency items to have on hand when you arrive, as well as a foreign language phrasebook, if appropriate, and some local currency. It's a good idea to have prebooked a cab or a hire car before leaving the UK, to avoid disappointment or long waits. Keep all confirmation documents in a safe place that can be easily accessed upon your arrival. Have some snacks, nappies, drinks, pyjamas, toothbrush, a story book and your child's comfort toy to hand for when you arrive at your destination. You may find that you have little time to unpack these necessaries.

Preventing jetlag

A degree of dislocation is likely with time differences of any more than a couple of hours. If your flight crosses more than three time zones (there are three in the US, for example), you might experience jetlag, an argument in favour of travelling north or south rather than too far east or west.

It is believed that the direction of travel affects the severity of jetlag. Travelling east seems to be more disruptive, as it involves shortening a day, while travelling west lengthens it. But individual experiences differ, depending on your departure and arrival times, and whether or not you were able to sleep on board the flight.

Symptoms include tiredness during the day and insomnia at night. You may also experience loss of appetite, irritability, stomach and bowel problems, plus increased sensitivity to light and sound. As a rough guide, in adults symptoms tend to last for up to two days per time zone crossed.

Jetlag seems to be less of a problem for toddlers than adults, and seems to be of a shorter duration. But it can play havoc with sleep routines, so be prepared!

What to do
• Plan a couple of easy days on arrival at either end of your journey.
• Start adapting to local time at your arrival point by setting your clocks and trying to eat and sleep at the appropriate times.

- It is particularly helpful to aim to arrive in the late afternoon or early evening. After a short walk and meal you can all go to bed at the usual time to recover. If travelling overnight in an eastwards direction, it is considered better to depart later so that arrival time is closer to your normal wake-up time.
- Get into the sunlight as soon as possible on arrival and then go to bed when it is dark. The body clock takes its timing from natural light.
- Drink plenty of water, avoiding caffeine (including in colas and chocolate), which can play havoc with sleep patterns.
- Lavender oil is widely used essential oil that is safe for even the smallest children. It soothes, relaxes and encourages sleep, when required, but as it is adaptogenic, it will invigorate and restore as well. Put a couple of drops on the pillow or a couple in a bath. Even if the effect is merely Pavlovian it may be helpful to put some on your children's bedclothes for two or three days before depart-ure, so the smell is associated with sleep. If you would like to know more about what essential oils to use for toddlers and when, see *The Fragrant Pharmacy: A complete guide to aromatherapy and essential oils*, by Valerie Ann Worwood (Bantam, £7.99).
- Isocones, from the manufacturers of Sea Bands, are designed to help you get a better night's sleep after flying, using the prin-ciples of acupressure. They cost £6.99 from chemists.
- There are a number of jetlag supplements now available, and because they are mainly based around vitamins and minerals, they are safe for children. Follow the instructions on the label. Good products include Jet Ease.

Best travel website for families (not just toddlers)

The Family Travel website at www.family-travel.co.uk offers exten-sive information for parents on all aspects of holidays and travel with children – from tips on flying to holidays for single parents, and everything in between.

2. Travelling by Rail, Road and Foot

On the train

My research shows that taking the train is one of the most popular, enjoyable, time- and cost-effective, safest and most practical ways to travel with toddlers. That's according to the parents I questioned. This was an absolute consensus. And it appears that toddlers agree. Here's how they most like to travel:

TYPE OF TRANSPORT	RATING
Train/tram (steam or otherwise)	10/10
Boat (cruise ship*)	7/10
Plane (depending on duration and airport chosen)	6/10
Car (length of journey and traffic congestion has most impact on toddler temperament)	3/10
Miscellaneous (tuk tuk, horse-drawn carriage, buggy, on foot; for short distances only!)	10/10

*Toddlers who have travelled with their parents on ferries and/or cruise ships (see page 126) are more concerned the ship may sink than they are about falling over board. However, in general, they like the idea of travelling on a boat if it is not for prolonged periods, and when there are lots of things to do.

So whether we are aware of it or not, toddlers perceive their parents to be most relaxed when travelling by train (commuter rush hours excepted). It appears the toddlers sense that their parents are more relaxed during train journeys than travelling on a cruise, plane or in a car. Parents appear more distracted and stressed when travelling by car, or plane. This may be perceived or actual stress. However, the effect is that a toddler becomes stressed as well.

Most toddlers love travelling by train – Thomas the Tank Engine being a fairly key influence. If you are able, travelling by train in this country and overseas is an ideal option. There is space, the potential to move about on board, and lots of people inside and things outside the window to entertain. Given the cost of petrol and motorway tolls, not to mention the probability of having to make an overnight stop, travel by train can work out a cheaper option than travel by car. It is also generally far more relaxing than either driving or flying, and everyone can play and picnic together much more easily. Furthermore, the chances of travel sickness are considerably reduced.

Most tour operators will arrange travel by rail (see page 85), and the tourist boards of the countries to which you are travelling will also be able to provide schedules, prices, and details of onboard facilities (see Part three, page 261).

Making the most of rail travel

- It is particularly helpful to reserve seats so you don't have to worry about being able to sit together. Near the buffet is good for little outings, though prices for these seats can be higher, and there will undoubtedly be a fair bit of through traffic. Remember, too, that the buffet may be out of stock, or closed. Trips for meals and snacks will be difficult if the train is crowded, but carriages further from the buffet will probably be less crowded, making them more attractive if you have children.
- While a seat near the door is useful with a pre-crawling child, it can be an accident waiting to happen when you have mobile children. A central carriage seat, though less convenient, is a better bet.
- On old-fashioned train carriages, aim to find seats in the centre, rather than over the wheels, to prevent the possibility of travel sickness.
- If you are not embarking at the main terminus, it is useful to ask where your carriage is likely to stop. If you have toddlers you can request help from the nearest person in rail uniform to ensure you all get on safely.

- When it comes to disembarking, remember that there may only be a short stop at your station. It's worth being well prepared, standing at the door with all luggage and toddlers so you can get off swiftly.
- Consider taking a map, so you can follow your route as you travel. If you are feeling really enthusiastic, a guidebook telling you something about the towns you pass might also be fun.
- To make life easier, book accommodation at the other end, and arrange to be met at the station upon arrival.
- Consider all of the on-board entertainment and snack ideas outlined in Travelling by Air (see page 29).

On the road

Babies love travelling by car, as every parent who has circled the neighbourhood at midnight to get a wakeful baby to sleep will know. Toddlers, however, are utterly bored by the experience and are usually very vocal about their frustration. They are tied into one position for a duration and most hate the confinement. They need loads to entertain and divert them from whinging about where they are going, when they are going to get there and how soon they can get to the toilet.

Making it work

To make any sort of journey by road – in your own car, a hire car, or by coach or taxis, the following tips will help to ease the pain:

- Taxis are extremely helpful when travelling with toddlers as they deliver straight to your destination, saving your toddler's energy for the attraction itself. But drivers can and do take advantage of tourists and may be particularly likely to do so if they see hassled parents. To avoid problems, always insist the meter is used. Agree a price for the journey before anyone gets in. Ask locals, including hotel reception staff, what the going rate should be.
- Note that seat belts in rear are not common outside the UK and in the event of an accident this could have serious consequences.

73

> • Consider using Taxihop, a professional, pre-booked taxi service in the UK (www.taxihop.com)

- Although drivers in less developed countries will be happy to pack in large numbers of passengers, where there are regulations about such things, families of five or more might have to take two separate cabs. Allow for regular stops on route to allow toddlers to get around and move around. If you don't feel you are up against the clock and will miss your deadline, you'll be less tense about potty or picnic stops.
- Drive during your toddler's normal sleeping times. Tom, for example, sleeps between 12.30 and doesn't wake until about 3pm.
- Start early in the morning, pack the car before loading your toddler, and set off before they are fully awake. Drive until mid-morning for a late breakfast and potty stop.
- Encourage your toddler to use the potty or toilet every time you stop. This will hopefully curb the cries of 'I want to go' when you are rushing down the motorway at 70mph plus.
- Toddlers are less likely to suffer from motion sickness on motorways as there are fewer stops and starts. But there is also a lot less for them to see out of the window. Service stops on motorways, increasingly in the UK, but especially in the States, Canada and France, have an excellent range of facilities (such as games machines, play areas and outdoor playgrounds) to entertain toddlers en route. This presents a slight problem as it is often difficult to get them back in the car. Telling them there is a more interesting one further on the way doesn't work. I tried it with Tom.
- If you have toddlers stop off at picnic areas, where there are toilets, and benches and tables for an al fresco meal. The French autoroute has some excellent picnic sites, and it gives your toddler a chance to burn off a little energy with a ball or a Frisbee, as well as having an inexpensive, pre-packed lunch.
- Take a potty in the car, even if your toddler is potty trained. Invest in a travel potty, if you can. It's worth the expenditure and can

reduce accidents substantially, particularly when stuck in traffic jams or on a motorway with few facilities.

- Provide shade from the sun's rays when travelling. Muslin draped over the back windows is fine, but you can also buy purpose-built shades for cars.
- Try to purchase a laptop table before you travel. Many car seats come with these tables, or you can purchase some that attach to the seat in front. A hard surface is essential for snacks, minimeals, colouring sessions and play. Be prepared to do lots of picking up from the floor!
- Make the destination seem inviting. A treat of some kind, such as a swim in the resort or hotel pool as soon as you arrive may be a good idea.
- Make the day before you travel one of activity for the toddler – they will be more tired during the journey.
- Rural cottages, villas in the Med, French gîtes and North American cabins are never within walking distance of local amenities. It is highly probable you will need a car and, unless you can take your own, you will have to hire. If you are going to a city with good public transport like London (hmm), New York or Paris, or a resort that is either compact or with good public transport links, a car is an unnecessary expense.
- If driving in a warm climate, invest in air conditioning. Do not accept a car without it.
- According to a survey commissioned by Hertz, the typical car-hire crash occurs immediately after leaving the airport. A long, tiring flight impacts on concentration, and you may need to drive on the opposite side of the road, from the opposite side of the car, which can be daunting. Arrange a transfer from the airport and collect or arrange for the car to be dropped off to your hotel the next day.
- Don't drive like a tourist. When you book your car, make sure it has local number plates and doesn't carry a car hire sticker. If you are in doubt about security, keep the door locked while you are in the car. Don't leave maps or guidebooks on the front seat. Areas that are poor or crime-ridden seek out tourists who may be easy prey.
- Always talk about the trip with your toddler in advance of departure. You'll be surprised at how much toddlers understand,

particularly when put in familiar terms. For example, you might tell a toddler that a two-hour drive is like watching two Bob the Builder programmes. For a longer trip, liken it to being at nursery school for an entire day, in their seats!

- Comfort is a priority. I take pillows, sometimes blankets, so that Tom is able to cushion himself for sleep. Plus, he likes to see out of the car window without difficulty.

- Dress intelligently. Snug clothes should be saved for arrival. Your toddler will inevitably get dirty on the journey, so don't count on looking fresh and clean at your destination. Better to find a bathroom a few miles from the end of your journey in which to change. Bring sweatshirts if you plan on turning the air-conditioning on high.

- Humour goes a long way in changing the mood when cooped up in a car. Turn a complaint into a joke. Acknowledge that being in a car is unpleasant by poking fun at it. I've found Tom giggles through the tears when doing this.

- Juice-in-a-box, I am convinced, is designed for travelling families. Just be careful not to squeeze the box when inserting the straw! Freeze several the night before taking off; these will keep other items cool for most of your trip, and provide refreshing drinks all day long. Try to avoid sugary drinks, though. The last thing you need is a hyperactive toddler on your hands.

- Make a plan to be at a set destination by 5pm. This pre-dinner period, in addition to being the time when toddlers are at their most irritable, is when the barrage of questions from the backseat seem never-ending. More importantly, it's also when hotels fill up. Having a destination in mind will help you give the kids both a sense of security and something to focus on.

- Log expenses, distances covered, sights visited, etc., and create a journal of your trip. Lots of parents like to do this because it involves interaction and creates memories.

- Never stay in an unpleasant situation you can avoid. Traffic is a prime example. If you can't get off the motorway completely, pull over and jump rope, throw a ball around, or have an impromptu picnic. Nothing is worse than being stuck in a car that's not going anywhere.

- Organise your belongings in a manner that works for your family, both inside the car and in the boot. I put Tom's stuff on top, since he always needs something 'now'.
- Pack a day bag in the front of the boot and, depending on the season, include swimsuits, towels, rain macs, hats, gloves and a change of clothes for everyone. That way you'll be prepared for all emergencies. A toothbrush and a pair of Pjs are also a good bet for emergencies.
- Quiet time helps everyone. Don't attempt to entertain your toddler every minute. Toddlers who learn to amuse themselves develop valuable self-sufficiency skills which will serve them well in later life. Napping is fine, too; kids are generally not as enraptured with the scenery as adults are.
- Underplan. Don't include too many must-dos or must-sees. Go with the flow.
- Vary the types of roads you take, including some motorways and some backcountry roads. Change seats from time to time if your toddler gets really irritable.
- Wake any sleepers about 10 minutes before you plan to stop so that they can re-enter the world with a minimum of grogginess (and get their shoes on).
- Lock the doors while travelling and when you leave the car. But make sure you have the keys first!
- Expect the unexpected. Something unforeseen is sure to crop up – a too-good-to-pass-up street fair, a flat tyre, a detour. Here's another occasion when a sense of humour and common sense can be tapped to advantage.
- Young toddlers with excessive energy are the hardest to satisfy. Early communication, involvement and lots and lots of stops where they can release energy will work wonders.

Top travel games

• I Spy. (Choose things with phonic sounds for younger children, or colours.)

• 20 Questions. (Someone thinks of a person or object and the rest of those present try to work out what or who this is in just 20 questions; questions have to have a 'yes' or 'no' answer.)

• Granny Went to Market and She Bought . . . (A game in which each player adds another object to those purchased by the fictional granny and repeats those listed by all players before him.)

• The Minister's Cat (Players take turns to describe the cat with adjectives beginning with the letter a, b, c, etc, losing a life if they have to move on to a new letter. You can guess how many lives each player has . . .)

• Motorway Snap (One player picks a colour and model of car. The next person to see one the same shouts snap and scores one point)

With equipment . . .

• Nought and crosses, hangman and battleships (if someone is willing to draw up the grid).

• Hand or finger puppets. Can be invaluable from around three and a half up.

• Toys with plenty of moving parts (but not noises or bits that come off).

• Toys with suction cups so that they will not slide on tables (on planes or trains, for example).

• Felt picture toys because can be re-used endlessly and the pieces are less likely to disappear.

• Drawing Material (Toddlers can doodle, to reassure themselves with drawings of their favourite objects, or to draw what they see around them, both on the trip and for example 'copying' works in art galleries.

• A clipboard for drawing or paper pad with card back. Old-fashioned pencils are best and Berol produces a range which do not need sharpening.

Hamley's top ten travel toys

Website: www.hamleys.co.uk

• Tomy Megasketcher/Pocket sketcher.

• Marvin's Magic board. A drawing board with no paints or crayons.

• Tweenie fuzzy felt collection.

• Winnie the Pooh activity tree. (Tiger Electronic)

• Read along Bob the Builder. A cuddly Bob and book set.

• Alfie my Alphabet Friend. An interactive bear which has a number of games and letter games. (V-Tech)

• Talking Treasure Adventure. An electronic book shaped and themed on a pirate ship.

• Electronic Looney Tunes piano.

• Activity toy Octopus. A soft toy with multiple sounds, textures etc. Suitable for six months plus.

• Little Smart Nursery Rhyme book. An electronic book.

Car seats

• Only use child seats that are appropriate to your toddler's age and size. Hire or borrow if you don't have a suitable seat.

• Regulations in each country differ about child protection in cars. I have referred to individual requirements in the respective country chapters (see pages 266 to 420).

• Car seats through car hire firms can pose a problem. Car seats are not included in the hire charge, and tend to be levied when you collect your car. None offers guarantees that child seats will be provided, although you can normally book a car seat in advance from reputable companies.

• In the US, car-hire companies are aware that the law requires children up to the age of five to travel in a child seat. By law, therefore, companies must provide seats for toddlers.

• If you choose to hire a car seat from a car hire company, ask for a British/US-style model.

• If you choose to take your own car seat, don't take a hard plastic model. The baggage carriers may drop and damage it. A polystyrene model is more durable, but they are less adaptable to different seat fixings.

- If you have three or more toddlers requiring child seats, you have a particular problem. Most seats require shoulder straps for fixing. Few cars offer this for all three seats in the back, although some operators seem to be unaware of this. If this is pointed out, operators suggest putting one child in the front and need to be reminded that this is not safe if there is an airbag. If you have three toddlers, you may need to go for a people carrier, which has its own advantages and drawbacks.
- Make sure all child safety seats are properly secured in the car. Experts claim that approximately 80 percent of all safety seats are not properly secured in the car. So read the safety seat manual as well as the car manual. Some cars, for example, are equipped with Automatic Restraint Systems and child seats can not be safely used. Continuous loop lap and shoulder belts need a locking clip to keep the seat firmly in place.
- Make sure that your child's head is protected by the back of the car seat or head rest. Don't use a booster seat if the middle of your child's ear is above the top of the seat of the car.
- Check your car manual to see if seat belts need a locking clip, and use it to stop seat belts from coming loose.
- Purchase a new car seat for each child.

Caution
Never use a seat that is more than 10 years old.

- Any seat that has been involved in an accident should be discarded promptly.
- Take advantage of any safety programmes in your area that check the installation of car seats.
- Make sure that all toddlers are properly secured in their seats. Infant shoulder harnesses should be tight and you should only be able to put two fingers between your child's chest and the harness.

- Toddlers should always be placed in rear seats. Never place rear-facing infant seats in the front seat.
- No child under 12 should ever be seated in the front seat in a car with an air bag.
- Never place infant car seat carriers on tables. If you have to, don't stray more than an arm's length away, and never turn your back on your baby.
- Never place infant car seat carriers on soft furniture or beds. There is a risk that the seat could turn over and your baby could suffocate.

Which car hire?

No car hire company will guarantee a child seat, so it's worth considering bringing your own. Problems start, however, when you find that your seat model doesn't fit your car model. Ask in advance about specifications, and go for a car that will work with your seat. Alternatively, get a written guarantee that a car seat will be available and fitted in your car upon arrival.

While the larger companies have more to lose if they fail to deliver a seat, standards of safety, quality and staff service vary dramatically. There are differences between countries, and even regions within those countries. Whatever the local policy, you'll find that it's the car hire operators themselves who decide whether or not a seat is safe for use. To be on the safe side, ask for confirmation of when the seat was purchased, whether or not it has been involved in an accident, and what, if any, special instructions need to be taken on board. You are fully within your rights to reject a seat if you don't feel it is safe.

There is no guarantee that the seat you end up with will conform to the high safety standards of the UK but here are the major companies who adhere to safety standards – at least in the UK.

• Alamo, Tel: 08705 994 000 (operates in the US with 135 locations)

• Avis, Tel: 0870 606 0100 (operates in 160 countries and more than 4200 locations worldwide)

• Budget, Tel: 0800 181 181 (operates in 3200 outlets in 120 countries, with 130 outlets in the UK)
• Hertz, Tel: 08705 906 090 (operates 6100 outlets in 140 countries. In the UK, there are 133 outlets)
• Holiday Autos, Tel: 0990 300 400 (operates in 4000 outlets world-wide). The Holiday Autos Freedom Behind the Wheel guide gives advice on how to avoid family hassles – before travelling and once on the road – by offering tips such as how to keep the kids amused, what items to have at hand and how to avoid stress. This free guide is available on-line at www.holidayautos.co.uk.

Note that you will need a first aid kit in the car in Switzerland, Germany and Belgium.
See page 225.

On the coach

This is not the transport medium of choice if you are travelling with children. It takes a lot longer, doesn't offer as much space as the train, is not as flexible as travelling by car, and the motion may induce travel sickness. The argument in its favour is, of course, price, and occasionally convenience, though with family discounts, the train might work out as cheaply, particularly on the Continent.

Coping on the coach

If you do need to travel by coach, however, the following tips will help you to cope:

• Ask if they supply car seats and, if they do, what type. If they aren't included, make sure your own seat is compatible.
• If you have to do more than a transfer by coach from airport to resort, think about doing so at night, when the children may sleep.

- Rest stops are pretty curtailed and unlikely to suit children who may have a real need to stretch their legs. Make the most of them when you get them.
- If motion sickness is a problem, arrive early to get seats in the middle of the vehicle rather than over the wheels. It has to be said, however, that seats at the front offer a better view of the road and more leg room.
- Luggage is almost invariably stored under the vehicle, making it inaccessible during the journey. Therefore, you'll need to pack on-board luggage in much the same way as on board a plane (see page 53).
- Go for a luxury option, with video and on-board lavatories.
- If travel sickness is a potential problem, see page 239.

Legging it

The journey to your destination is not the only journey you'll be making during your holiday, unless you have chosen an all-inclusive resort where everything is within walking distance. Only you will know best how far your toddlers can be expected to walk. If they are small, the answer will be not very far, so you will need some way of trans-porting them while you are on holiday. Ultimately, how you carry your toddler will depend on you and the destination.

Tom was far too heavy to carry at just two years old. He is now three and walks fast when I want him to slow down, slows down when I want him to speed up, and walks in circles rather than in a straight line. Most toddlers are the same. Journeys on foot, therefore, take much longer.

Toddling with a toddler
- Suggesting a treat at the end of the walk, such as a visit to a park or swimming pool, is a good idea, to keep your toddler motivated.
- Consider introducing different sorts of walks, like a kangaroo, for example, or a tiger.
- Teach road sense from an early age, and make sure toddlers know how dangerous cars can be. Even stationary cars pose a risk, as

they can set off very quickly. Teach your toddler to stay by your side at all times.

- Pedestrian crossings, one way signs and red traffic lights are often ignored in southern Europe, so it is even more important to be on guard.
- Reins are an alternative to keeping a toddler on a leash, if you don't feel he is fully aware of the dangers. These work with some toddlers and not others. Tom doesn't like them and on several occasions I have dragged him along the floor on his bottom, which he seemed to enjoy but I didn't.
- Only walk on the marked trails in the countryside and ask locals for advice. There are no public rights of way in some parts of the world and private property may be defended with guard dogs, which should never be approached, particularly by toddlers.
- In busy city centres, such as London, carry your toddler or use a pushchair. Children are too easily lost in the crowd, and shoppers and businessmen have little respect for mothers with two year olds, especially in the UK.
- In cities, buggies are difficult to use in crowded places and as unwelcome on trains and buses as they are on planes. However, if carrying or walking with your toddler is too painful, check out how easy it will be to use a buggy at your destination, and ask where it can be stored en route. Lighter, umbrella-style models are ideal for travel, and can be slung over an arm if you are forced to abandon pushchairs in favour of carrying your toddler.
- If your toddler is small enough, a front carrier is much more practical than a buggy. You will have your hands free and less luggage en route.
- For toddlers capable of sitting on a hip, a sling such as the 'Huggababy' can be useful for shorter distances, such as the trip from plane to luggage carousel, or when popping into shops. They are, however, less comfortable for longer walks. If you will only need one for short periods and want something light, the Active Birth Centre in London sells a string version. For details of where to find these products, see page 428.

3. Toddler-friendly Tour Operators

Every tour operator claims to offer holiday options that are 'fun for all the family'. Take this with a pinch of salt. As I've discovered, this statement is a contradiction in terms. There are, however, some tour operators that have, at the very least, developed a product that works for families with one to four year olds, and each offers a little bit more than the rest. The operators below have excellent, tried-and-tested kiddies clubs that cater for this age group – albeit not exclusively. And the toddlers I asked all enjoyed themselves and talked about the 'club' as being one of the highlights of their holiday. That, the beach, and the friends they made. None could name where they had been, or the country to which they had travelled, but they had fun and that's what counts.

Each of the companies listed below has a good website, but none gives exact details about the toddler age group, so ask a travel agent about toddler-friendly products as well as checking it out on the internet. Be persistent!

Crystal Holidays, for example, recently launched their new family website www.crystalfamilies.com, which currently provides information on skiing with children, but will be developed to cover all Crystal products.

From my research, it's better to start off with a destination you personally like, and identify whether any of the following operators offer packages to these countries. Direct contact with their agents, using travel agents and the internet, will tell you much more than any guide book can or will. All of the tour operators below offer good-to-excellent nanny, crèche or toddler club facilities, and each has devised their childcare programme in response to direct feedback from their customers. Reason enough to keep telling them what you want and how you want it.

The best

Crystal France
Tel: 0870 888 0023, Website: www.crystalfrance.com
Crystal France actively targets families with toddlers by providing nanny and childcare services and accommodation specially equipped for families with small children. For summer holidays to France, Crystal offers a unique 'Flying Nanny Service' and will provide a qualified nanny to travel with the family (or fly out separately) to care for up to four children (over two years old) or three children if under the age of two, for the duration of the stay. This is available for children between the ages of six months and 12 years, and includes six days of nanny service and an evening babysitting.

At two family holiday villa complexes, the Domaine de Beaumont and the Domaine de St Apolis, Crystal France offer villas that cater specifically for families with small children. Each Domaine is equipped with bottle sterilisers, toilet steps and seats, potties, non-slip bath mats and baby packs (which should be requested at the time of booking). Also available are cots, high chairs, baby listeners, buggies and back carriers. Family-plus services are free of charge but need to be pre-booked.

Crystal France operates Pepi Penguin childcare clubs, but these are only applicable to children between the ages of four and 10. Crystal France offers travel to France by rail, air and self-drive through the tunnel, by ferry or Hoverspeed.

Caribtours
Tel: 020 7751 0660, Website: www.caribtours.co.uk
Caribtours offers toddler-friendly accommodation in many Caribbean destinations including Barbados, Jamaica, St Lucia, Antigua, Anguilla, Nevis and Turks and Caicos. Children's clubs are available and vary according to the resort and the ages of the child.
They have supervised club-style activities with some resorts accepting children of all ages, including babies, although some take children from four. Stick to those destinations that have direct flights to the island (see page 386).

British Airways Holidays
Tel: 0870 242 4243 (Florida and City breaks),
0870 242 4245 (rest of world), Website: www.baholidays.co.uk
Destinations include Africa, the Caribbean, Florida and the Far East with the hotel, villa, apartment, all-inclusive and fly-drive holidays. They offer 'child stay free' places and reduced fares for children, with children under two travelling to Florida for free. Toddler-friendly hotels are clearly identified in the BA Holiday brochures, though really only a few are suited to toddlers. Most have kids clubs that cater for children between the ages of four and 12. Check that your choice caters for toddlers.

Neilson Active Holidays
Tel: 0870 909 9099, Website: www.neilson.com
Neilson Active holidays feature flotilla sailing, surfing, cycling and also ski holidays to destinations in Greece, Turkey, Spain, the Caribbean and the Alps. Children's clubs are available from the age of four months, at destinations in Greece, Turkey and Spain. The Starfish Club is for babies from four months to two years. Sea Urchins is for toddlers from two to five years. Each Sea Urchin and Starfish receives a personalised Sea Urchin sack containing suncream, sunhat and a mobile listening device on loan till the end of the holiday.

Powder Byrne
Tel: 020 8246 5300, Website: www.powderbyrne.com
Destinations cover both summer and skiing holidays (see page 151). Summer destinations include Sardinia, Crete, Elba, Mallorca, Provence and the Algarve. Clubs for children from six months are available. There are crèche facilities for babies from six months to three years, run by NNEB or equivalent nursery nurses, and they feature Hamley's toys.

Sunsail
Tel: 023 9222 2222, Website: www.sunsail.com
Sunsail offer 11 Watersports Beach Clubs, including nine around Greece and Turkey, as well as centres in the Caribbean, and world-wide sailing holidays. Kids clubs are available for babies from four

months. Care for children over the age of two is free, but there is a charge for children younger than this. The Mini Club is geared for children between the age of four months to two years, and supervised by qualified nannies. The Penguin Club is for the two to four age group, and supervised by qualified nannies. Check out the Galini Club on the Greek Island of Lefkas.

First Choice
Tel: 0870 750 0001, Website: www.firstchoice.co.uk
First Choice has teamed up with Looney Tunes to provide a programme of activities. Toon Tots are crèches for children aged 15 to 35 months. The crèches are managed by fully trained nannies – one to a maximum of three children – and equipped with a range of Little Tikes toys, bottle warmers and sterilisers from Avent. Sessions last one and a half hours, run six days a week and can be booked before your departure. You can book more sessions when you arrive, subject to availability. For three to six year olds, the Tunes Squad provide games and activities eight times a week.

Familyplus holidays are available in a wide variety of destinations, including the Balearic Islands, the Algarve, the Costa's, Greece, Tenerife and Tunisia. First Choice Holidays has baby packs for hire to guests staying in villas and apartments in Majorca, Menorca, Fuerteventura and the Algarve. Packs include cots, high chairs and pushchairs, plus bottles and sterilisers.

Airtours
Tel: 0870 241 2572 (family first hotline), Website: www.airtours.co.uk
This operator asked its customers what they wanted from their holiday – in particular, what they expected from their tour operator – and delivered. In response to customer demand, they offer short-haul flights (less than 5 hours); the ability to sit on the plane together and order meals before boarding; daytime flights; less than 90 minutes' journey time to and from airport and resort; no lengthy check-in procedure at resorts; low-rise apartments, family helplines; 24-hour medical attention on call; indoor soft play areas; spacious rooms; toddlers' splash pool; and rooms decorated for children.

A crèche with qualified NNEB nannies is open six days a week, for six hours. Babysitting is available in the evening, as are early meal sittings for families, and there is an excellent soft play area and adventure playground for babies and toddlers respectively. There is a kiddies club for three to ten year olds, open six days a week. Airtours has Family First resorts in Majorca, Minorca, Gran Canaria, Tenerife, Fuerteventura, Cyprus and Corfu, which have crèches catering for babies to three year olds, plus baby equipment for hire, including toys, paddling pools, cots, high chairs, pushchairs, nappies and sterilisers. This operator has also sponsored many play areas in airports around the UK – so parents of toddlers owe them a debt of gratitude, as many airports would be even more bleak if this facility was not available.

JMC Holidays
Tel: 0870 758 0194, Website: www.jmc.com
JMC Holidays offers pre-bookable items, including buggies, playpens, and babypacks with a changing mat, cutlery and a cup. From check-in, children are given plenty to occupy them with a fold-out puzzle showing scenes of the airport and beach, designed to keep them guessing prior to take-off. Once air-borne, a new kids pack is given out, specially designed following research carried out in schools, and with the help of leading educational publisher Usborne. The result is an activity pack that is both fun and educational, with a 3D puzzle that older kids can build into a cube and younger children can enjoy as a jigsaw puzzle, a joke book, luggage tag and a lolly. It's certain to keep them busy throughout the flight.

Last year, JMC invested in a new range of kids clubs at resorts, available at the family focused FamilyWORLD properties. The club is targeted at a specific age range; all run by JMC Representatives carefully selected for their personalities, experience and qualifications. Their sole job is to plan treasure hunts, organise games and competitions and generally make sure that children have the time of their lives.

Beach Babes Crèche (for children between the ages of six months and two years) and Paddlers (for kids between the ages of three and four) are available at all FamilyWORLD properties, in destinations ranging from Majorca to Turkey.

JMC's FamilyWORLD properties offer supervised early suppers for children, available several nights a week in all half-board, full-board and all-inclusive accommodation. In most properties a separate child buffet counter is available, offering specially selected dishes, designed to cater for children's tastes.

Babysitting is offered during the evening at all of JMC's FamilyWORLD properties for its 'Beach Babes' club members. The service for 'Beach Babes' takes place in the children's club crèche from 7pm to midnight and is chargeable by the hour. Qualified NNEB, or equivalent nannies staff all the 'Beach Babes' crèches babysitting services.

Recreational play is provided at most FamilyWORLD properties through indoor soft play areas for two to five year olds, developed in conjunction with Miracle Recreation – the world's largest manufacturer of commercial play equipment, all of which complies with EU and British safety standards.

JMC is also easing the travelling burden for parents, with pre-bookable Cosatto buggies and play pens, Tough 'n' Tumble baby and toddler Packs, Tomy soft bed rails and Jackel Pod UV protection shelters – all of which are waiting in FamilyWORLD accommodation, on arrival at the resort. All FamilyWORLD properties are equipped with well-known brands, such as Boots, Stabilo, the Early Learning Centre, Cosatto and Red Fox publishing. Many families prefer the privacy gained by staying in a villa and with JMC's Beach Villas programme, a baby pack is provided completely free of charge in the following resorts: Majorca, Menorca, Costa Blanca, the Algarve, Cyprus and Corfu. This baby pack is for families with children under three years of age at the time of travelling and includes a high chair, luxury travel cot and a buggy with sun canopy. Requests for a baby pack must be made at time of booking.

Popular family destinations include Majorca, Menorca, the Canary Islands, Cyprus, the Greek Islands and Turkey. JMC Airlines has a dedicated fleet of 28 aircraft, carrying over 2.8 million customers a year to 584 resorts in 44 different countries.

Thomson
Tel: 0870 514 3499, Website: www.thomson.co.uk
Thomson Superfamily resorts provide crèches and baby packs for an additional fee, including branded baby food, plus a babycare pack including toiletries, and a toy pack with beach products.

Research commissioned last year by Thomson Holidays showed that the majority of people see children's clubs as a central attraction for a family holiday. Parents view children's clubs as beneficial for their children because it allows them to meet other children, and helps to avoid boredom, thus maximising enjoyment for all. Parents enjoy seeing their children happy and learning new skills, and they also enjoy the free time it gives them. Thomson Superfamily was launched in the last year (2000 was the first year in resort, but the brochure came out 1999) specifically to cater for families with children who are of pre-school and primary school age. It also suits customers who are willing to pay a little more to make sure their family holiday is perfect.

Baby and toddler equipment is supplied by Mothercare. These facilities can be pre-booked, which means you don't have to worry about packing everything before you go. For toddlers you can book play sets for children up to three years of age, and they include a castle bucket and spade set, sand moulds and ball.

Activ is the only children's club open all day, and geared towards kids aged three to five. Pagers are now available for parents who holiday in the Balearic or Canary Islands or Mainland Spain, so Activ reps can contact them immediately if necessary. The Breakfast club is available at selected Superfamily hotels three days a week. The ACTIV reps collect the children at 8am and entertain them until 10am.

Virgin Holidays
Tel: 01293 456789, Website: www.virginholidays.co.uk
Virgin destinations include the Balearic islands, Canary Islands, Greece, Mainland Spain, Portugal, Turkey, USA and Caribbean. Accommodation options include hotel, apartment, villa, self-catering and all-inclusive. Children's clubs are available at most resorts, with crèche facilities at selected Club Virgin hotels. Virgin Sun kids clubs are free of charge and each club is supervised by trained representatives for two to four hours per day, six days a week. Pickles is for three to six years. One of the best resorts for toddlers is the Club Virgin Hotel in Menorca.

Simply Travel

Tel: 020 8541 2222, Website: www.simply-travel.com

This company does not charge per night, only per week. Infants under two travel for a small sum per week, while children between the ages of two and 12 get a discount, depending on destination. Simply Travel hires fully qualified nannies (NNEB, RGN or equivalent). Any children over the age of two that go to their 'Shrimps Crèche' (for children between the ages of six months and five years), or 'Sea Urchins' children's club (for five to 10 year olds) are given their own 'Shrimps' or 'Sea Urchins' rucksacks and T-shirts. These facilities are available within the company's Turkey, Corsica, Crete, Ionian and Ski programmes. They also provide a private 'flying nanny service' in the Algarve. The company confirms that they do target families with toddlers. Simply Travel are the preferred travel partner of Leapfrog nurseries (a network of day care centres for pre-school children in the UK).

Cosmos

Tel: 01233 211 303 (brochures),

Website: www.cosmos-holidays.co.uk

Children who are younger than two years of age, with a cot in their accommodation, and seated on an adult's lap during flights, travel free of charge. Children over the age of two pay the applicable child price. This varies greatly, depending on the destination and property. For children under three, they offer the Baby Bugs crèche, which is bookable on a first-come, first-served basis. These specially designed and fully equipped crèches, organise activities such as arts and crafts, story times and free play. They can be found in six properties for Summer 2002. Children in the crèche are cared for by qualified nursery nurses, and have a staff child ratio of one to three, for toddlers under two, and one to four, for toddlers between the ages of two and three.

For three to six year olds, Cosmos offers the Starbugs kids club. Staff are all NVQ qualified, and the club has no more than 15 children at one time.

Cosmos also now offer pre-bookable toddler packs, created in conjunction with Sainsburys. Introduced into specially created Family Focus properties and selected Planet Kids properties, each pre-booked pack will be waiting for you on arrival in resort. The Xenos Beach in

Zante is perfect for toddlers because of its safe surroundings and brilliant facilities for families.

As well as the Baby Bugs and Starbugs, Cosmos also offer pre-bookable flight seats, a book and toy library, late check-out facilities, and a welcome pack in each apartment on arrival. Babysitting service is also available for toddlers over the age of two. There is an indoor play equipment room for toddlers aged between six months and four years, and a special children's snack menu, designed to be child-friendly.

Buggies are available for hire, and they can be pre-booked. Pagers are given to parents when children are in the kids club, so that parents are safe in the knowledge that they can be contacted at any time. Cosmos flies to the following short haul destinations: Majorca, Menorca, Ibiza, Tenerife, Gran Canaria, Lanzarote, Fuerteventura, Costa Brava, Costa Dorada, Costa Blanca, Costa del Sol, Algarve, Malta, Cyprus, Italy, Zante, Kefalonia, Corfu, Kos, Rhodes, Crete, Turkey and Lapland (Christmas programmes only). The most suitable destinations for toddlers are those with a shorter flying time and lots of facilities aimed at young families. These include Majorca, Menorca, Ibiza, Costa Dorada, Costa Blanca and the Algarve.

Sun Esprit
Tel: 01252 618 300, Website: www.sun-esprit.co.uk
Sun Esprit offers Alpine holidays designed for families. This company developed their nurseries and crèche facilities using direct feedback from their customers. They noted that parents want some space to do their own thing, while also spending time with their children. Nurseries are held three days of the week by qualified NNEB or equivalent nannies, with stringent nanny-child ratios. There are specific activity groups for the three to four-year-old age group (Mini-Alpies).

4. Holiday Villages

This is a totally hassle-free holiday. We arrive, we stay, I may or may not cook – the option is mine. The kids are looked after and we have a break. Just make sure the holiday park you choose has clubs that cater for the under-fours. So many start at four and over.

Mother of two in Lewisham

The holiday village option may appeal to you if you feel most comfortable staying in one place. It also works if your toddler enjoys kids clubs and the company of other children. At the more sophisticated all-inclusives, where self-catering is not an option (such as Club Med, Superclubs and Mark Warner) you will be able to find all you need on site, at a relatively high standard. In addition, many sites are car-free except for arrival and departure days, making them very safe for little ones. Accommodation and facilities at the holiday villages are, in general, becoming more refined, but unless they are rated with four or five stars, they can be cramped and very basic. Mark Warner and Club Med have always targeted the more affluent sector of the family market, so they are normally a safe bet if you want to ensure quality.

While this type of holiday is ideal for some families, it may not be for you. Some parents commented that they felt as though they were trapped 'in a compound' that they weren't able to leave, while others enjoyed the 'everything rolled in' part of the experience. Of course, in some parks everything is genuinely included and you don't pay anything. At other villages, you do need cash. Alas, only a handful provide good childcare facilities for toddlers under the age of four. Infuriatingly, most have kiddies clubs that start at four or five years of age.

With the exception of swimming areas, most activities must be paid for as extras. While villages almost always see plenty of families, on the Continent these may not be English-speaking, but at least your toddler may be able to learn a new language in the process. Never go in high season as most holiday villages become very crowded and the facilities that are free are spread very thinly. If there are restrictions on cars, single parents in particular may wish to ask for a property near the car park to make loading and unloading easier.

The best bets

Domestic holiday villages
Butlins Family Entertainment Resorts
Tel: 0870 242 1999, Website: www.butlins.co.uk
A recent £139 million refurbishment with a modernised version of traditional entertainment has made this a fun-packed and viable option for families with toddlers. Singles parties of four or more under 30 are banned and almost all changes directly benefit families – although not necessarily all with toddlers. Based in Minehead, Bognor Regis and Skegness, apartments house up to four without a kitchen and self-catering facilities for up to eight. Among other toddler-friendly channels, TVs feature the in-house Red TV. Toyland-themed accommodation includes a second bedroom with matching wallpaper, beds and duvets, a Noddy play table and Toyland video cassette and player. Young guests also receive activity packs and are invited to a Noddy welcome party. Facilities include a weather-proof Skyline Pavilion with street cafés and live entertainment. Food outlets include Burger King and Harry Ramsden. A Toyland mini-town with Noddy, Mr Plod and Noddy's car offering rides, Tessie Bear's Teacups, a Kids 'Rumble in the Jungle' outdoor adventure play area includes three themed sections. Toddlers have a soft play area and a shallow pool play area. For entertainment there is a Cirque de Masquerade with acrobatics, juggling, music and dance, plus uni-cycling and other street performers, a conjurer, and a storyteller in the Skyline Pavilion at intervals. There are also live appearances mid-week from Fox Kids characters. Shows for children include one of three musicals with

95

effects. On Monday evenings children's TV personalities present a show of their own.

Equipment is supplied by Mothercare, including cots and high chairs, and nappies and baby toiletries are on sale. Day-time nursery services are available for toddlers between three months and five years. Babysitting is charged per the hour and a Night Owl service (which runs between 8 and 11.45pm) is available in the nursery for babies between three and nine months. Parents using this second service will usually be given a bleeper, to be contacted quickly if necessary. Parents must provide the name, address and phone number of a GP who knows the child's medical history.

Centre Parcs
Tel: 08705 200 300, Website: www.centreparcs.com
Founded in the 1960s in the Netherlands and imported to the UK in the 1980s, the company now reports the centres always at least 90 percent full. In 400 acres of ground, the 700 villas and apartments are arranged to allow some degree of privacy. Based at Longleat, Elveden and Sherwood, accommodation consists of variable standards from two- to four-bedroom villas to executive villas of up to three bedrooms. All have live fires fuelled by smokeless logs. Executive villas come with a maid service. Facilities include a subtropical swimming paradise – at rainforest temperatures, with pools plus cafés, shops and restaurants (although the feedback about the food has been poor). Indoor sports include squash, tennis and short tennis; at Elveden Forest a 10-pin bowling alley is also available.

All three villages have a mini-health spa with treatments including thalassotherapy, aromatherapy and reflexology. Fitness and beauty weekends combine fitness classes with complementary therapies. Although no entertainment aimed at toddlers is provided, there is a kindergarten for children three years and over, with face-painting, badge-making, and dressing-up, among other things. A crèche is available at Elveden and babysitting is also available at a cost. There are children's play areas in the restaurants; a wooden adventure playground with safety net; kiddie trailers to attach to the back of bikes; and, baby dolphin classes that introduce toddlers to swimming. The baby dolphin pool is for under threes only. Restaurants are geared for families, with child menus, Lego tables (although not all restaurants have this facility) and play areas.

Centre Parcs are better suited to families with school age children as most clubs start at four plus, although they do provide babysitting and crèche facilities.

Water safety

The parents I interviewed had many recommendations on how to stay safe on the beach, by the pool or by any type of water, such as lakes and streams. Here are the most fundamental and some of the less obvious:

• Never leave children of any age unsupervised.

• Toddlers are able to drown in a few inches of water in a few minutes. Teach them to stay out of the water when no adult is supervising them.

• Toddlers should learn how to swim at the earliest possible age, taking lessons that include safety instruction.

• Teach toddlers never to dive into the water (they mimic the older children).

• Teach toddlers to stay away from frozen lakes, rivers and ponds.

• Make sure your toddler understands your family's basic safety rule, such as no running, pushing, or hurting other children, respect for other children and people using the beach or pool, and never, ever push anyone under the water.

• Check the beach or pool area for safety including any chemicals that may be around pool area.

• Always leave a pool or lake if a storm is approaching.

• Lifejackets are a great idea for toddlers; inflatable toys are not safety devices and play must be closely supervised.

• Long hair should be tied up and loose clothing should not be worn in the pool.

• Toddlers should not go into spas or hot tubs.

• Always wear life jackets in boats.

• Warn toddlers to stay away from drains, filters and drain covers in pools and hot tubs, which can be very dangerous.

Poolside safety

For hotels, resorts and self-catering villas/apartments that have pools, consider the following:

• Swimming pools in warm, undeveloped countries can be a real problem and if in doubt about permitting your toddler to swim, insist they do not put their head or mouth under the surface, which will reduce the risk of eye, ear or internal infections. For more information contact The Royal Life Saving Society (UK) on Tel: 01789 773 994.

• Check if the pool has lifeguards on hand to watch over your toddler, alongside you.

• The best toddlers' pools have a soft spongy surface, are heated, slope very gradually and are never very deep. They are also usually well away from the main pool so that adults and older children do not intimidate the toddlers with their splashing and diving (which toddlers may wish to mimic).

• You can catch diarrhoea and hepatitis A or typhoid from contaminated swimming pools, so you should feel confident that the water is cleaned (filtered and disinfected) to a level appropriate to the number of people using it. Sometimes the system used is not sufficient for numbers over peak periods. Check that the pool is filtered and ask how often the filter is checked. If a pool is shared you could also check how many people in total use it, as peak use can put a strain on filter units.

Overseas Holiday Villages

Calister Travel

Tel: 0208 650 1414, Website: www.calister.co.uk

This operator books VVF Vacances holidays at 24 sites in France, including Normandy, Brittany, the Atlantic coast, Aquitaine, Languedoc Roussillon, Provence and Rhone Alps. The resorts are normally three-star, with between 50 and 200 units. Three of their resorts offer a half-board option, and some have accommodation spread through real villages. Facilities include a restaurant and usually a delicatessen, TV room, launderette and small shop, as well as a sports ground and pool.

Cots, high chairs, baby baths, iron and ironing board, board games and books are available from reception. Babysitting or nanny services are available on request and payable locally. A baby club for children between the age of three months and two years is sometimes available for an extra charge. For two to six year olds, activities include craft workshops, shows and competitions, and outings. In half-board accommodation parents can share meals with children or leave them in the children's restaurants.

Centre Parcs
Tel: 01623 872 997, Website: www.centreparcs.com
Centre Parcs caters for three million customers a year, more than three-quarters of whom are on a short break. And 65 percent of those customers return. There is one in the Netherlands, three in the UK (see above), two in Belgium, two in France and one in Germany. No more than 10 percent of each site is reported to be developed, but each village averages 650 villas, with between one and four double bedrooms, equipped kitchens, central heating and a furnished patio. Children's cottages have a children's bedroom with toys and doll's house. VIP cottages include breakfast and freshly made beds each day.

All sites have a subtropical swimming paradise – a transparent dome housing water activities including paddling pool. The temperature is kept a constant 84°F and the setting is landscaped with polished rocks, tropical trees, plants and flowers. At one Dutch and one Belgium site are the Discovery Domes – indoor play areas featuring a deserted bay with shipwrecked galleons, mist-cloaked lakes and underground passages. Covered plazas house the sports, shopping and eating areas. Outdoor streams, lakes and waterways have been created and wood-land houses wild animals. Health and beauty spa offer treatments including thalassotherapy and aromatherapy. Eateries include fast food, Dutch pancakes, plus a restaurant classed as gourmet. There is also a village supermarket and themed shops.

Pierre & Vacances Holiday Villages
Tel: 01892 677 777, Website: www.pierre-et-vacances.com
These holiday villages comprise nine sites dispersed between the Atlantic and Mediterranean coasts of France, in Cote d'Opale, Brittany, Vendee,

Aquitaine, Languedoc, Cote d'Azur and Provence. They have traffic-free streets and squares, and are self-contained holiday complexes. Accommodation is available in apartments (ground floor ones are normally given to families with young children), larger houses, and in the hotel (children under 12, sharing with an adult, are free). Children under three can also eat free. The facilities include paddling pools, animal farms and playgrounds for young children, all available free of charge. They also offer crèche facility and toddlers clubs (Club Poolpy), involving puppet-making, mini-golf, nature walks and team games.

A different type of holiday which might be of interest are the Austrian farmhouses. Dispersed throughout villages in the Tyrol region, many of them are branded 'children friendly', which means that they are adapted specifically with young children in mind. There are, therefore, enclosed gardens, playgrounds, playrooms, small animals and pets, babysitting by appointment, organised children programmes, and healthy food, not to mention all the farm activities they offer, such as hay-jumping, pony-riding, fruit-picking, animal-feeding and more.

The price of the stay usually includes everything available on the farm (apart from some specific services) and parents can choose between accommodation in self-catering apartments or in rooms on a B&B basis (children under four are free).

Crystal Holidays
Tel: 0870 888 0023, Website: www.crystalfrance.com,
Email: franceres@crystalholidays.co.uk
Located in France, and operated independently or by companies such as Pierre & Vacances, Maeva and VVF Vacances, the accommodation comprise apartments and villas from studios to apartments sleeping up to seven. There are optional sea views, and most have dishwashers and TV hire. Pierre & Vacances is the most toddler-friendly holiday park of the group, with playgrounds, and children's clubs available in either the morning or the afternoon. All are suitable for toddlers. Crystal Holidays will advise on prices and age ranges when you book, and will prebook the P & V clubs at most featured residences. Some include theatre performances, circus schools, beach activities and games. Those aimed at younger children have crafts, activities, games and excursions.

Cots and equipment hire are available, and there is plenty for adults to do, including golf, tennis, rock climbing, boules, archery, cycling and canoeing, if you have the energy or inclination. Note that not all facilities are available at every site. There are pedestrianised buggy-friendly walkways, launderettes, bars, restaurants and games rooms, as well as evening entertainment.

EuroVillages
Tel: 01606 787 776, Website: www.eurovillages.co.uk
Operated by Pierre & Vacances, Maeva/.Latitudes, VVF Vacances, Independent, Gran Dorado and Roompto, in France, Spain, Italy, the Netherlands and Germany, accommodation comprises apartments that are mainly designed for families with toddlers. Pierre & Vacances villages are three to four star, and include playgrounds, a crèche for babies between three and 36 months (running from 9am to 7pm at all Pierre & Vacances villages except Cap Coudalere). For three to five year olds, the Poolpy Club offers painting, handicrafts, walks, sports and games and has some English-speaking staff. Pre-booking is advised.

Superclubs
Tel: 0208 339 4150, Website: www.superclubs.co.uk
SuperClubs is a family-owned company that pioneered and specialise in all-inclusive holidays in three categories. Superclubs' Super-Inclusive holidays include accommodation, meals, use of all land- and water-sport facilities, with equipment rental and instruction; entertainment; recreational activities; complimentary weddings; hotel taxes; and airport transfers – with absolutely no tipping allowed. Breezes resorts feature Children's Camps, which offer a nursery, designed for infants up to the age of two, and operating from 9am till 10pm with qualified babysitters on hand to keep little ones content. Three youth programmes are also available, The Kids Club (for children between three and seven) is available from 9am till 5pm and 6pm till 9pm, featuring a wide range of age-appropriate activities such as circus school, kid's Olympics, nature walks, trampoline and juggling classes, a variety of sports, video games, the internet and more. After hours, babysitters are also available at a nominal additional fee.

Superclubs run 12 properties and are currently open or under development in Jamaica, The Bahamas, St Kitts, St Lucia and Brazil. These include Superclubs Breezes Resorts, Breezes Golf and Beach Resort; Breezes Montego Bay and Breezes Negril in Jamaica, plus Breezes Bahamas; Breezes St Lucia and Breezes Costa do Sauipe in Brazil. The operator says that they introduced the Children's Camp concept in the Breezes resorts as they noticed a growing trend towards luxury family travel.

Note that the Hedonism and Lido resorts, which Superclubs also operates, are not suitable for families with toddlers. At time of going to press Superclubs are planning to expand the Children's Camp concept to additional Breezes resorts planned for the future. Superclubs have plans to significantly expand the resort group over the next five years with four more hotels in Brazil, three more hotels in Cuba and its first hotel in St Kitts-Nevis.

Beaches Negril
Tel: 08701 626030, Website: www.beaches.com
Beaches Negril is situated on a sandy seven-mile long beach on the western tip of Jamaica. The resort follows the Beaches philosophy of welcoming everyone from families and singles to couples and groups. At all Sandals and Beaches Resorts, all meals, drinks, room accommodation, entertainment, airport transfers, taxes, gratuities, sports activities and instruction are included in the package price. The Beaches Kids' Kamp is also included in the cost. Beaches Kids' Kamp is available for children aged over the age of six months (and separate programmes are available for both younger and older children).

The Kamp is available all year round, with an average of four or five fully licensed and insured nannies. The nursery is open until 10.30pm, but nannies are available after this time at no extra cost so you can benefit from a night spent in one of the resorts' nearby bars or a romantic meal in one of the five gourmet restaurants on offer. At the Kids' Kamp, toddlers enjoy a range of entertainment. They have their own separate pool, a playroom filled with toys, including trikes and plastic cars, as well as a painting room for those developing an artistic flair. Beaches Negril is open all year round but if you are travelling with children be aware that August and September can be prone to hurricanes while June and July can get very hot. Children under two years stay free.

Motours
Tel: 01892 677 777, Website: www.motours.com
Motours books Pierre & Vacances and VVF in France, Sunparks in Belgium, as well as independent holiday villages in Holland, Germany and Denmark. Pierre & Vacances have nine holiday villages dispersed between the Atlantic and Mediterranean coasts of France. These villages have traffic-free streets and squares and are self-contained holiday complexes. Accommodation is available in apartments (ground floor ones are normally given to families with young children), in larger houses if you need more space, and in the hotel (children under 12 are free). Children under three can also eat free.

The facilities include paddling pools, animal farms and playgrounds for young children, all available free of charge. They also offer crèche facilities and toddlers clubs (Club Poolpy, which is pre-bookable) involving puppet-making, mini-golf, nature walks and team games.

Mark Warner
Tel: 08708 480 480, Website: www.markwarner.com
Mark Warner holidays are on a seven-night basis so cannot be reduced to a nightly charge. For infants between the ages of four and twelve months, there is one trained nanny for every two babies. For babies between 13 months and two years, there is one nanny for every three kids. For toddlers between three and five, there is one member of staff for every six children, supplemented by waterfront staff, Baywatch staff and instructors.

In the Toddler Club (13 months to two years) children are provided with an indoor and outdoor play area with plenty of stimulating games. The Mini Club (three to five) is based in in-house crèches which are well equipped with toys and crafts. They also enjoy nature walks, swimming, paddling, games on the beach as well as excursions out on the water and even ice cream trips. Safety is paramount at all times.

The children's clubs run six days per week, from 9am to 5.30pm, with a break from 1pm till 3pm when all the children rejoin their parents for lunch. No childcare is provided on the Club hotel changeover days. The children's clubs are in great demand and places are limited. All the children's clubs have been inspected and approved by a British safety specialist.

There are nine club hotels in France, Italy, Corsica, Sardinia and Greece. However, Ziglione in Corsica, Punta Licosa in Italy and Palm Beach in Turkey do not accept children under six at any time of the year. All the other Club hotels are child friendly and encourage families with kids of all ages.

Flights operate from Gatwick and Manchester (with a supplement from Manchester). Airlines used are Monarch Airlines. All flights fly into the nearest airport to each of the resorts.

Can you drink the water?

In most developed European countries tap water is perfectly safe and the same is true in the vast majority of North America and Australasia, although you have to be more careful in desert and wilderness areas. However, given that children may be affected by even relatively harmless local bugs and different chemical treatments, you might prefer to take precautions.

Bottled water is generally safe, although higher levels of bacteria have been found in bottled water than are permitted in tap water in the UK. Furthermore, true mineral waters have a high mineral content, in particular, sodium, which can be hard on young kidneys. Look for waters with less than 20mg of sodium per litre. Choose bottles with the seal intact, and keep it cold once opened, to prevent a build-up of bacteria. If you use refillable, individual water bottles, wash these daily with hot water and soap to prevent bacteria.

Purifying water

Boiling is the best purifying method. Simply bringing tap water to the boil, and then allowing it to cool in a sterilised container will make it pure enough for most uses, but babies should only be offered water that has been boiled for a full five minutes. For the

---

record, longer boiling is needed at higher altitudes, as water boils at lower temperatures.

Note that hotel kitchens may well not boil the water for any length of time and may even simply heat rather than boil it. Ask to oversee the process. In self-catering accommodation, it can be relatively simple to boil water yourself, and some hotels will provide a kettle in your room if you explain your position in advance. Boiled water must be left to cool before using, should be covered to prevent contamination, and placed out of reach of children.

You can also purchase water purifying tablets, which can be used abroad in an emergency. They tend to be rather full of chemicals, but certainly superior to local tap water.

Safety notes

• Remember that bathwater and even water used to brush teeth can carry bacteria and disease. Use bottled water for everything you can, and discourage your child from drinking the bathwater. Mouths should be kept tightly shut in the shower.

• Foods washed in local water should be avoided. This includes salads and many fruits and vegetables. If you can, choose foods that can be peeled, but wash them in boiled water first (or with an antibacterial hand wipe), to prevent transmitting disease with your own hands.

• You can buy fruit 'wipes', which remove surface chemicals, bacteria and other germs. These are probably a good idea if you have a fruit-loving toddler.

• Avoid ice cubes, unless you make them yourself with boiled water.

• Make your own squash, or dilute fruit juice yourself, using boiled water.

• Use antibacterial soap when washing your hands.

Club Med
Tel: 0700 2582 633; Website: www.clubmed.com
Club Med operates 81 children's villages on five continents (56 villages with child supervision, 25 without). This operator pioneered the all-inclusive, geared to providing an up-market family option. Since the 1970s, children seem to have reigned supreme at Club Med villages. In fact, they represent one of the club's outstanding features. Depending on age group and village facilities, Club Med offers creative activities (such as drawing and painting) and sports (such as, inline skating, windsurfing, flying trapeze, judo, mountain biking, kayak, football and water sports).

Children are supervised by 2000 qualified GOs. The range of children's Club Meds is broken down into four age groups – two of which are suitable for babies and toddlers. Baby Club Meds are open to children from four to 23 months old, Petit Club Meds are reserved for two and three-year-olds. Each group is organized into subdivisions according to age and has its own areas and facilities (there are often 'subgroups' of different languages or tastes as well). Some activities vary throughout the week, while others are offered on a permanent basis.

Feeding areas are provided in all villages with a Baby Club Med. Pleasantly decorated and well laid-out, these areas are specially designed to give parents and their babies a warm welcome (offering, for example, nutritional advice). You'll find everything you need from utensils to prepare meals as well as some basic provisions. In all of the villages welcoming children with or without supervision, you will find cots, highchairs in the restaurant, bottle-warmers and microwaves. In villages with Baby Club Med and Petit Club Med, buggies are also available. There are seven Baby Club Meds for the summer 2002 season, catering for children from four months to two years old and open six days a week from 9am to 5:30pm, and 30 Club Med villages that cater for two and three-year-old children, six days a week from 9am to 9pm (with a shower and dinner break from 5:30 to 7:30 each evening). All are supervised.

5. Toddler-friendly Hotels

We've visited this particular hotel in Scotland for the past three years because we know the staff are patient and genuinely like toddlers, the rooms are very large and the facilities are great. It gives us a bit of flexibility and a bit of luxury at a good price, making it a value-for-money option. We've found, with the all-inclusive resorts we've tried, that we don't see the children for most of the time as for that amount of money you feel obliged to take advantage of the kids clubs. Fine if you want a break from your toddlers – but then why take them with you in the first place? Choosing the right hotel, with lots for them to do and see nearby, we get to have more quality time as a family. I don't do the cooking so it's a holiday for me, too, but I know the food will be good, which it isn't always in these all-inclusives. We've also tried other hotels that claim to be 'family-friendly' but they weren't. Well not with our family.

Mother of two toddlers from Newcastle, talking about
the Polmaily House Hotel, Scotland

In most of the countries listed in this book, I recommend that families with toddlers choose self-catering accommodation, farmhouses or camping as the ideal way to holiday with a toddler. These are usually excellent options, offering value for money and allowing a degree of flexibility in a relaxed atmosphere. But self-catering is only appropriate for those parents (or mothers!) who are happy to continue with the same home regimes – cooking, looking after family, and cleaning. This may not represent much of a holiday for many of you.

True, there are an increasing number of self-catering accommodations – from apartments and gîtes, to villas and paradors, which include daily maid service within the package, and some even provide chefs or are close to many reasonable restaurants, so you don't need to slave away at a hot microwave. In general, however, self-catering is pretty much a DIY affair.

Self-catering and all-inclusives both have their downsides. Farmhouses, usually surrounded by lots of countryside in which children can safely play, are intimate and cosy, and the food is generally excellent and fresh. Toddlers will adore helping to feed and stroke the farm animals. But staying in a farmhouse or on a farm may not appeal to you as much as it does to your toddler.

All-inclusive resorts do everything for you, including taking your toddler at nine in the morning till the early (or even late) hours of the evening. So although you don't see much of your children, at least you have a break. But many of these resorts are similar to compounds, where you feel obliged to use the facilities because everything is included. For some families, this narrows down the options and personal freedom to an unacceptable level.

An alternative is, therefore, staying in a hotel, where you are looked after but are also able to share the experience (and the room) with your toddlers. This is an option that would simply not have been viable 10 years ago. Many hotels are now geared to handle toddlers, and the prices have come right down.

These days, certain hotel groups and independent hotels are progressive in their attitude toward families with toddlers – albeit affluent families. They appear to have researched the market well, and identified the needs of families with young children. Their staff are genuinely child friendly, and they combine that with a relaxed atmosphere that makes parents and toddlers feel both at home and on holiday.

In resort hotels, the property needs to have around 200 rooms before making it worth providing special facilities for families. If you are going to be keeping company with your toddler, a place where they regard toddlers as fully paid-up members of the human race may be all you need. There are some up-market hotels falling into this category and, in general, the smarter the hotel, the better the service – for toddlers as well as grown-ups. Some of the UK's very best hotels fall into this category.

Smaller, family-run hotels may also set out to attract the young family market, with a host of activities, special meals, babysitting services and entertainment as part of the package. You may need to look a little harder to uncover these gems, but once found, you may find that you return again and again.

What to ask

Whatever the hotel you are considering choosing, it's important to ask a series of questions before committing to a booking. For example:

- Do they have family rooms or suites?
- Is there family pricing or discounts for children between the ages of one and four (for some inexplicable reason, some hotels begin to charge for children older than three)
- Are there children's menus available and are the meal times set in stone?
- If there are child menus, are they limited to burgers and beans? In other words, is there a healthy option?
- Are toddlers allowed in the restaurant/ restaurants. At all times or restricted times? Is room service available for toddlers and are high teas provided? How fresh is the food? Forget buffet foods, which may not be fresh and may harbour food-borne illnesses. Diarrhoea is the most common health complaint among toddlers on holiday. It's main cause is eating the wrong sort of food.
- Is your toddler a fussy eater? Will he eat only at certain times. Choose room service or pre-order for your toddler before arriving at the hotel restaurant. It will save hassle on arrival. Can the hotel cater for special (meat-free, wheat-free, dairy-free, nut-free) diets?
- Is your hotel close to the garden/beach/pool and do you need to cross a busy road in order to get to it? Are the roads paved in the resort/around the hotel?
- Are there baby-listening devices or babysitting services? If so, what is the cost (per hour) and are the sitters qualified and certified?
- Can they tell you who will be providing the care and something about their experience and any qualifications? You will, at least, want to know their age. In the US, for example, babysitters tend to

109

be very young and not ideal for looking after babies or toddlers. Note, too, that provision of a baby listening facility does not necessarily mean that there will always be someone in reception listening to it.

- If babysitting is booked, can you leave the premises? This is not always allowed. It might be wise to check out the standard of in-house catering if you are not going to be able to eat elsewhere.
- Is there supervised childcare available during the day and are the carers qualified?
- Are any books, games or toys made available for toddlers during the day?
- Are there cots and high chairs in the restaurant?
- Are children allowed in the restaurant in the evening? If so, until what time?
- Do they have an area designated for toddlers? Is it fenced in? Paved or grass? Are there any specific facilities for toddlers? Kiddies clubs? Places with childcare almost invariably come at a price. You will get what you pay for. And a hotel that offers a kids club is not necessarily child-friendly; indeed, the club may not be any good. What age are they allowed into the club? Is there a toddlers' pool? Does it have a lifeguard on hand watching over the bathers? Are toddlers allowed in the adult pool? If so, when and how are they supervised? And what are the charges per hour for any special facilities for toddlers? Are they charged on an hourly basis or by the day?
- Are there many steps or steep slopes to negotiate? Usually a hotel that offers facilities for disabled people is also very toddler and buggy friendly.
- To avoid the heat of the midday sun, are arranged excursions possible in the early morning and late afternoon?
- Are there any no-go areas for toddlers – with steep drops, rivers or lakes without barriers, or pools without lifeguards near to your hotel room?
- If you are near the beach, how steeply shelved is the beach? Is it sand or shingle, and how far is it to the water? How calm is the water and are there strong currents? Is it warm water? What

facilities and equipment are offered on the beach (such as umbrellas, showers, pedalos)? Is the beach usually crowded at particular times of the day? Which part becomes most crowded? Where does the sun rise and set?
- Where is the nearest supermarket to buy nappies, wipes, drinks and snacks?

And there are safety issues to consider as well (see page 112). You want to be sure that the facilities are toddler-proof and safe for inquisitive little hands and fingers.

Does your family fit the bill?

Many hotels have all kinds of rules and regulations surrounding evening meals. Children may only be allowed 'high tea' at 6pm, and then banned from the restaurant after 7pm. While this may have advantages if you'd like a quiet meal with your partner, with your toddler tucked up in bed with a caring sitter, it does put pressure on your family to be incredibly organised. You may be expected to feed your children and get them into bed at an early hour, which may not be practical if you've had a busy day out, or you are running late.

Some hotels only 'welcome' children for part of the year, notably in the Caribbean. Treat these with caution! They are probably not well set up and the other guests are often the kind hoping for a chic holiday on the cheap. And avoid places that state in advance that they only accept well-behaved children. Your normally placid toddler will misbehave as soon as he arrives.

One reason why hotels are reluctant to provide facilities for toddlers is that it pushes up the staffing costs. Toddlers require so much more attention than young children, and hotels can often not afford to cater for their needs.

How safe?

Parents and toddlers have variable needs and expectations when it comes to safety. If you have a toddler or toddlers beware of stairs, slippery marble floors, balconies with low walls, busy roads near by, cots, babysitters without suitable qualifications, stairways with banisters and so on. Nowhere is 100 percent safe.

Hotels, self-catering apartments, villas and gîtes are unlikely to be as safe as your home, which has been adapted over time to deter your toddler from their preferred methods of getting into trouble. There are some obvious things any parent would do to prevent problems, but there are some tips you may not have thought of.

Before you arrive

Ask the following questions:

• Are the floors hard and/or highly polished (marble or lacquered wood) or carpeted?

• Are there stairs and do these have balustrades or gaps between the steps into which small children could wedge heads or limbs?

• Is a pool fenced or at least within eyeshot of the sitting area (to check that no-one is getting in unsupervised)?

• What are the plug sockets like and can socket covers be provided? Many countries use the round two-pin system so you will not be able to provide your own from home. Electricity overseas, even in Europe, may be less safe than in the UK. Mains electricity poles and cables in the street should be treated with extreme caution. South African sockets have three round holes, large enough for a toddler's finger.

• Is there a fence or gate to prevent children from leaving the property alone?

• How close and busy is the nearest road?

• Are there any full length glass windows? Is glass toughened?

• Are there windows that can be opened by toddlers? Casement windows above the ground floor can be a particular concern.

• Are there balconies with balustrades or barriers that toddlers could climb over or squeeze through?

- Are there any open fires and, if so, do these have firmly fixed fireguards?
- Are there any breakable items such as ornaments or glass coffee tables which would be best removed?
- Are there any steep drops on or at the edge of the property?

When you arrive

- If you feel that for some reason your property is not safe (there may be balconies without rails, doors opening easily on to an unguarded pool, or other hazards), ask to change rooms immediately. In a multi-unit self-catering property it should also be possible to swap. In a villa this is considerably less likely, making it even more important that you book through an operator that can offer reliable advice on the options.
- Check the safety of child equipment provided. It is wise to give cots a good shake and to ensure that they have been properly assembled. A baby can be seriously injured by a collapsing cot. For your own peace of mind check also the width of any bars. If they are wide enough to get a head through, a towel wound in and out between them may prevent your toddler getting stuck.
- To prevent accidents with sockets, take a roll of gaffer tape to cover any potential problem points (while the toddler isn't looking, so that you don't arouse curiosity!) Tuck away any trailing flexes, including to the phone.
- If there are plate glass windows make big crosses of tape to prevent anyone walking through one. Or mark with toothpaste or children's washable paints.
- Check which tap is hot and which is cold to avoid anyone scalding themselves. In Italy, for example, C stands for caldo, which means hot, and caliente is Spanish for hot.
- Remove the in-room tea making facilities, ashtrays and all other magnets for toddlers.
- If there is a gas cylinder in the kitchen, turn this off, making it impossible for toddlers to leave on the gas on the cooker.

- If there is an easily opened mini bar, your toddler will open it. Ask housekeeping to remove it or its contents.
- Roll or .fold up mats over which toddlers will trip. If floors underneath are tiled or polished wood, discourage toddlers from running round in socks.
- Take rubber bands or masking tape to keep shut doors to items like the microwave, plus any cupboards with items that need to be kept safe.
- Wedge open heavy doors that could crush little fingers if swung shut.
- Check in cupboards, in the bathroom and kitchen for dangerous products, such as insect and mouse poisons.
- Remove plastic bags from waste bins.
- Check that the lift is safe for toddlers to use, particularly if yours are old enough to venture round the hotel on his own. Even when accompanying toddlers, be wary of old-fashioned cagestyle lifts through which small people could stick fingers/hands/feet.
- Warn about hands and feet getting stuck in lift doors or any revolving doors.

Getting the room you want

To avoid a shock when you arrive in your hotel room, it's sensible to find out in advance exactly what you are getting for your money. Don't be afraid to ask questions, to ask to see photographs of the room and its layout, and to ask for something different if what you see doesn't seem right for you and your family. Base your questions on the following issues:

- Ask the dimensions of the hotel room, and its layout.
- If you have more than two toddlers, extra beds and the rates that apply are usually only for a third or fourth bed. But check this out.
- Do you need privacy? Do you want your toddlers to sleep with

you or in a separate room? Do you have the option of an en suite facility, connecting room, annex or area where the bed/cot can be placed away from the main bedroom?

- How sound-proof are the walls of the hotel? Can you hear your neighbours flushing the toilet? If you can, it is 100 percent guaranteed that they can hear your toddler crying.
- Ask what kind of bed is provided? Are they all with sprung mattresses or will some people be sleeping on sofa cushions, zed beds or other?
- If you are self-catering, ask about kitchen equipment. Is there a dishwasher or microwave?
- Is your hotel room above a busy road, noisy bar, or nightclub? If so, you don't want to be there.
- Do you need a balcony to dry clothes (such as swimming costumes or cloth nappies)? If you need a drying space, ask for one.
- Can you easily navigate the hotel, lifts, and corridors with a buggy? In some resorts there are few pavements and you will need to walk on the road. Ask for a ground floor room in hotels that don't have lifts.
- Where exactly will your room be? Baby monitors may not be able to work if the hotel has thick walls, steel girders or generators to interfere with transmission.
- Is the cot provided with bedding and a mosquito net in hot climates? If so, what type of cot will it be? Countries overseas use different designs, sometimes with lower sides and wider gaps than in the UK. They may be incorrectly erected. The safest option is a travel cot. Although taking your own adds to luggage, a cot with sides will ensure that your toddler is less likely to decide from an early hour that you are there in the same room to be played with.
- Your toddler may be unhappy in a shower, so ask for the option of a bath.
- Can they guarantee high chairs for your toddlers each day at meal times (or are they available on a first-come, first-served basis)?
- Is there a fridge for storing boiled water and toddler's food? If you have a mini-bar in your room, is it childproof or can it be emptied of alcoholic drinks that toddlers may be able to open and drink?

Other factors to consider

- If you are going to be using a kids club, you need to check on the carer-child ratios, the space available, hours, charges and age groups, so that your child is not overwhelmed by older children or bored by younger ones.
- If your toddler is old enough, make sure that they know the name of your hotel and the hotel room number.
- If your hotel has a lift, review safety concerns with your toddler. Suggest they always keep their fingers from the lift doors, which close very quickly without warning. Tell them never to play with the emergency button as it will break the lift. Encourage them never to leave the lift with a stranger, or to go to anyone else's room without a parent. Show your child how to get straight to the ground floor, and reception, in the event that they find themselves alone in a lift.
- Review hotel fire escape procedures and locate exits. Check your room for safety including, but not limiting, electrical outlets, furniture with sharp corners, loose equipment. Get down on all fours and take a look from a toddler's perspective.
- Move all furniture away from any windows.
- Put all soaps, shampoos and toiletries out of reach.
- Remove dry cleaning bags or place them out of reach.
- Ensure that glasses are out of reach of your toddler.
- Make sure your toddler can not reach coffee maker or hairdryers while in the bathtub.
- Put any matches that may be in the room immediately out of reach of your toddler.
- Make sure you check the hot water for the bath to ensure that the water is not too hot. Cool down the tap before your toddler goes into the tub and instruct them not to play with the taps.
- If your toddler is afraid of the dark or used to a small night-light, take it with you and use it in the room.
- If you are drinking alcohol in your room, make sure it is out of reach of your toddler including empty glasses.
- If you are supplied with a cot in your room, double-check that it

is properly and securely set up. Check that the mattress is firmly supported and that it has a tight fit.

- If the cot is a mesh cot, make sure sides are securely locked up. Children can suffocate in mesh cots if the sides are down.
- Some hotels have started putting bunk beds in rooms for children, and while these can be fun and convenient, it's important to bear a few facts in mind. First of all, never place children under 6 in the upper bunk. Make sure that the top bunk has guardrails on all four sides, and that the mattress fits tightly into the frame. Check the frame for sturdiness, and ensure that it is all fastened together safely. Discourage bouncing on bunk beds.

Top-rated hotels

Which hotels around the world received the most praise from families with toddlers? They are listed below. Beware, however, that many are in the higher price bracket.

The Best
Jumeriah Beach Hotel, Dubai
PO Box 11416, Dubai, United Arab Emirates
Tel: 00971 4 3480000, Fax: 00971 4 3482273
Website: www.jumeirah-beach.com
Absolutely fabulous for parents and toddlers. There are 551 deluxe rooms and 49 suites in this sumptuous and multi-award-winning hotel. In fact, according to several travel magazines, it is one of the best hotels in the world. There are kids clubs, swimming pools, toddler-friendly restaurants, babysitting services and much, much more, all in complete luxury. Emirates and British Airways, both of which fly to Dubai, are recommended in the top 10 airlines for toddlers. Which doubles the reason to go.

Small and personal
Ballimaloe House, Shanagarry, Co. Cork, Ireland
Tel: 00353 21 4652531
With 33 bedrooms en suite, lovely countryside, an excellent cookery school, toddler-friendly staff, some of the best golf in Europe just 10 minutes' drive away, and a five hole course in the front garden, this hotel is a perfect break for families.

Close to home
Fowey Hall, Fowey, Cornwall
Tel: 01726 833 866
This hotel has 23 en suite bedrooms, Nintendo rooms and landscaped grounds of 12 acres. It's the perfect hotel for parents of toddlers who don't want to slide down market just because they've upsized. There are crèches and play areas for the toddlers, while adults can enjoy the many, varied facilities.

Luxury for kids
Four Seasons Hotels
Website: www.fourseasons.com
The Four Seasons has a department known as 'Kids for all Seasons', which provides child entertainers, babysitters, nanny services, and all-day crèches. Two of the best in the group are in Palm Beach and Nevis (see below).

Fairmont hotels
Website: www.fairmont.com
The Fairmont Group of hotels (see page 398) are based all over Canada and the US (with a collection of 38 distinctive city centre and resort hotels) and have excellent kiddies programmes – some of which cater for toddlers. For luxury combined with security and entertainment for the toddlers, try Quebec at Le Chateau Frontenac (001 418 692 3861) and Le Manoir Richelieu (001 418 665 3703) in Canada. Perfect for a Christmas stopover – there is guaranteed snow and even reindeer.

Putting on the . . .
The Ritz Carlton Group
Tel: 0800 234 000, Website: www.ritzcarlton.com
The Ritz Carlton Group of resorts is one of the best in the world for toddlers. There are toddler's menus in all restaurants, as well as activities and special events.

Best-kept secret
Babington House, Bath
Tel: 01373 812 266
One of the most toddler-friendly bastions of style and civility in England, Babington is a wonderful retreat for families. The 'little house' crèche will take your toddlers from 9am to 6pm weekdays, and from 7am to 6pm on weekends. Fully qualified nannies entertain toddlers, while adults can pamper themselves in the health spa, sauna, steam room or in one of the two pools. The stable rooms, which have a lounge area and two bedrooms, allow enough space for even the most hyper of toddler.

Check out the web
The best websites providing information on toddler-friendly hotels are www.johansens.com and www.slh.com, which offer advice on luxury hotels and resorts with excellent toddler facilities or special programmes for children. Another good site to try is www.hotel guide.com.

Toddler-friendly hotel groups

You may have faith in a certain hotel chain or group providing a pleasing level of service. When you have a family, it is always a delightful surprise to discover hotels that cater for young families alongside couples, business people and singles. In fact, certain hotel groups have woken up to the fact there are a growing number of holiday makers who enjoy staying in hotels because they trust their brand, and would like to continue to do so with their families. Here are the best of the bunch.

Choice hotels
Tel: 0800 444 444, Website: www.choicehotels.co.uk
Choice is a very large chain, with over 5000 properties worldwide. With so many hotels, it's very difficult to be precise about facilities for toddlers; the hotels generally cater for children across the age ranges, rather than target in on specific groups. Also, the chain largely comprises franchised hotels, which tend to differ between countries. The best hotels within the group that cater for toddlers are in Ireland and Scandinavia – both countries that cater well for children in general. In Ireland, the Quality Hotel & Leisure Centre Clonakilty, Clogheen, Clonakilty, Co. Cork, and the Quality Hotel & Leisure Centre Galway, Oranmore, Galway are particularly toddler-friendly.

Le Meridien
Tel: 0800 028 2840, Website: www.lemeridien-hotel.com
Le Meridien hotels feature excellent 'Penguin Clubs' at most of their resorts worldwide, catering for all ages, including toddlers. The crèche facility includes a fully equipped nursery with cots for naps. The shaded, enclosed play area where the staff accompany and play with the more active young ones, is generously supplied with a variety of safe toys. Water wings are available for those old enough for a little dip in the pool and protective head wear, sun lotions and creams are always at hand.

Rosewood hotels and resorts
Tel: 020 7313 2000, Website: www.rosewood.com
Although not all the hotels in this group are toddler-friendly, it boasts a few that are. The hotels that make up the Rosewood hotels and resorts, include Las Ventanas in Mexico, The Lanesborough in London, Badrutts Palace in St Motritz and Caneel Bay in the US Virgin Islands among others. Both Badrutt's Palace, Little Dix Bay in the British Virgin Islands and Caneel Bay cater extremely well for toddlers.

Starwood hotels
Website: www.starwood.com
This group acts as an umbrella for the following hotel chains: Sheraton, Westin, W Hotels, Luxury Collection, Four Points and Regis. The company has a global presence, with a wide number of facilities on offer for toddlers. The best in the group are as follows:

The Westin La Paloma Resort & Spa, Tucson, Arizona
Tel: 001 520 7426000, Website: www.westin.com/lapaloma
Unlike many resorts that offer children's activities, La Paloma also focuses specifically on toddlers. The hotel participates in Westin Kids Clubs, and all children are given an age-appropriate gift on arrival. La Paloma's 'Children's Lounge' offers supervised childcare for children between the ages of six months and 12 years. The lounge features an array of games, activities, and story time, as well as a secure outdoor play area. Children under 12 eat free in the resort's Desert Garden Bistro, 365 days a year.

Sheraton Nusa Indah Resort – Bali
Tel: 0062 361 771906; Website: www.sheraton.com/nusaindah
This resort features the Little Stars Club, which is suitable for kids two and over. The facility includes a classroom, sleeping room, computer room, a shop and outdoor play area with structured activities. Children under three require a guardian or parent present. There is also a small zoo and aviary, home to animals and birds saved by Indonesia's Quarantine Department from illegal export (which in all probability saved their lives).

Sheraton Algarve Hotel & Resort, Albufeira, Portugal
Tel: 00351 289 500100, Website: www.luxurycollection.com/algarve
Porto Pirata – the children's village – is a well-conceived play area, with two huge pirate ships right at its heart. Toddlers from six months are supervised by qualified nannies. A swimming pool, bouncy castle, a car and skaters track, a basketball field and 18-hole mini-golf course (this is the Algarve after all) are among the other attractions. The team of carers has created a daily activity programme, which includes treasure hunts, team games and handicrafts. Lunch is optional.

Shangri-la hotels

Tel: 020 8747 8484, Website: www.shangri-la.com

The Far East probably offers the best value for money world wide, when considering the standard of food, overall service and accommodation you get for your money. The Shangri-La group, which is the largest Asian-based luxury hotel company in the region, currently manages 37 hotels in 10 countries, including China, Hong Kong SAR, Taiwan, Singapore, Philippines, Malaysia, Thailand, Indonesia, Myanmar and Fiji Islands. Spring or autumn tend to be the best times of year to visit the area, if you want to catch some good weather. The best resorts for toddlers are:

Shangri-la's Mactan Island Resort

Punta Engano Road, PO Box 86,
Lapu-Lapu City 6015, Cebu, Philippines
Tel: 0063 32 2310288, Fax: 0063 32 2311688,
Email: mac@shangri-la.com

The playroom is called 'The Galleon' and has organised activities for children three years old and older. These include fish-feeding, paper-doll making, jogging, basketball, leaf-painting, face-painting, body-painting, making snowflakes and collages, walking along the beach, garden tours, hydrobics, soccer and baseball. The resort has an exclusive kiddie club called the 'Mactan Gang'. Members get newsletters regularly, or emails sent by the resident mascot. They also receive cards and treats to mark special occasions, such as birthdays.

Shangri-la's Fijian Resort, Yanuca

Private Mail Bag (NAP 0353), Nadi International Airport, Fiji Islands
Tel: 00679 520155, Fax: 00679 500402, Email: fij@shangri-la.com

The resort has a 'Little Chief's Club' for children aged two to 12 years. The Little Chief's 'Club Bure' is located at the back of the Lagoon Block, right next to the children's park. Membership is free and there are fun activities, such as building sand castles, 'mocktail' parties, face-painting, visits to Fijian villages, boat rides, mini-golf and crab-hunting, all organised throughout the day. Children receive the Little Chief's Club daily activities schedule when they first check into the resort.

Shangri-la's Rasa Sentosa Resort
101 Siloso Road, Sentosa, Singapore 098970
Tel: 0065 2750100, Fax: 0065 2750355, Email: sen@shangri-la.com
The resort provides a specially equipped nursery and playhouse for children between the ages of two and 10. A pool with waterslides and children's bicycles are also available. Babysitting services are available.

Shangri-la's Tanjung Aru Resort, Kota Kinabalu
Locked Bag 174, 88995 Kota Kinabalu, Sabah, Malaysia
Tel: 0060 88 225800, Fax: 0060 88 217155, Email: tah@shangri-la.com
The resort provides babies and toddlers below the age of four with babysitters upon request. These sitters are available around the clock, if required, and the service is chargeable by the hour. A baby pool, a safe playground and tricycles (for children aged three and above) are available for children looking for outdoor fun. The resort staff are trained to cater to the needs of parents and will offer help whenever necessary.

Hyatt hotels and resorts
Website: www.hyatt.com
Hyatt have just under 200 hotels worldwide. The Camp Hyatt programme is designed to cater for families, and is now offered at over 15 hotels across the US and the Caribbean, as well as at selected resorts worldwide. Camp Hyatt offers a supervised area where children over three enjoy a daily programme of activities. Some resorts offer supervision for babies from the age of six weeks to three years. Charges made for the use of the Children's Clubs and activities vary according to the resort visited. The best resorts for toddlers are The Hyatt Regency Grand Cypress Resort in Florida, Hyatt Regency St Lucia and Hyatt Regency Beaver Creek Resort in Avon, Colorado in the US. For further details check out the website www.hyatt.com. Some camps are only operational in the summer months.

A good night's sleep

Hotels are for . . . sleep, right? Maybe not. This subject is top of my list because problems with sleep can ruin even the best-planned holiday. And, unfortunately, toddlers are all too prone to sleep problems, and believe me, they need their sleep. Not only can sleep problems mar your enjoyment of your holiday, but you may feel far less equipped to deal with them without the support of family or friends back home. This is particularly relevant if you are staying somewhere with no childcare facilities.

Points to consider

• Toddlers, like most adults, can be fussy about changing the place they sleep. Taking some of your child's own bedding and his pillow can help.

• If your toddler has his own travel cot, take it along if you can. Anything familiar will help to ease potential problems.

• Place it in the holiday room facing the door, or in the same direction as they usually sleep in their own room at home (in other words, towards the window/natural light).

• Take their favourite cuddly toy (especially if it is small and they can carry it themselves. I suggest buying three of their 'favourite toys', just in case they lose one en route. Beanie Babies make excellent portable toys.

• If you are going to stay with friends who have insufficient beds, it might be worth taking your own light air bed. Again, if your toddler is already familiar with the bed, it might be better than an unfamiliar bed.

• All toddlers build up their own routines, but a change of place and timetable can upset this. Try to stick to your normal home routine as closely as possible, particularly the presleep sequence of events.

• If your toddler takes a nap at home, try to make time for something similar in the day. Consider introducing a family siesta, enabling everyone to rest together. Eat together in the cool of the evening, and put your child to bed after a family meal. It might be a slightly later bedtime, but they will probably sleep later in the morning.

• Think about trying to arrange things so that small children can't see you the minute they wake up. They may also give you an extra 15 minutes of rest if they have a toy or two to distract them.

• If your toddler won't settle down at night, consider a warm bath with a drop or two of chamomile essential oil, and a light massage with a few drops of the same oil, or lavender, blended into a little warm olive oil. Another drop on a hankie tied to the cot is also useful.

• Many toddlers are incensed at the idea of being put to bed before everyone else. If you are desperate, the whole family can pretend to settle down for the night, and then slip out of bed when the going is good.

• Bring along a favourite book or lullaby tape, and make this part of your sleep routine.

6. Get Cruising

My first thought when someone suggested that I take Tom on a cruise ship was that he would be sure to jump off at any given moment, and that I would be in a perpetual state of stress. So, perhaps, you, like me, feel that the idea of taking a toddler on a cruise ship sounds daft. But there are an increasing number of families who are cruising with their toddlers – and certain cruise line companies are admirably catering for this market. In some cases, they are doing so brilliantly.

A new style of cruising

The days when cruise ships were the sole preserve of the wealthy and elderly are long gone (although you will still find a lot more 50-something than those in their thirties). Only recently, a joint venture between First Choice and Royal Caribbean launched a new cruise company, Island Cruises, specifically targeting young families with children.

Cruising in the new millennium really is a holiday for the family – and that includes toddlers. And some of the latest generation of cruise ships have children's facilities that would put many land-based resorts to shame. Cruising has certain advantages over land based resorts – even all-inclusives.

- Unlike stay put holidays in land based resorts, cruise holidays take travellers to a host of different destinations, keeping toddlers stimulated with the new sights and sounds. The challenge with most all-inclusive resorts is you may feel confined to your 'compound' and see very little of the country around you. When cruising, the destinations come to you.
- It's also worth noting that the big three tour operators (First Choice, Airtours and Thomson) fly you direct from almost

anywhere in the UK, and they usually send the coach to meet the plane on the tarmac in Europe, thereby missing out the hassle of customs and the airport.

- Another benefit is that you can effectively travel light. Once you arrive, there is no need to move from one gîte, hotel or apartment to another. You have a variety of destinations without the hassle of actually moving to each one.
- Some of today's ships allow parents free time, thanks to supervised children's programmes aimed at keeping toddlers entertained in a safe environment.
- On the latest generation of giant cruise ships, toddlers get their own dedicated play areas and even their own exclusive pools, as well as age-related activities ranging from face-painting and quizzes to treasure hunts and talent shows.
- On some ships, there are even night nurseries and slumber parties, so you can enjoy a romantic evening, secure in the knowledge your toddler is safe and supervised.

Which cruise?

Cruising is a vast and varied business, and there are as many different types of ship as there are cruise passengers. When seeking a family cruise, the first question to ask yourself is whether you'd enjoy a large, floating, resort-style cruise ship or an older, more traditional vessel.

Ships, such as those offered by Thomson, Airtours, First Choice, P&O and MSC have a cosier feel than the state-of-the-art mega-ships run by companies like Carnival Cruise Lines, Royal Caribbean International and Princess Cruises. Their prices are also lower – a key consideration for a family on a budget. But toddler facilities are more limited on the smaller ships and be aware that many of the clubs for children are only relevant to children above the age of three or four. So, basically, they are no good for parents with young toddlers.

Thomson's Emerald and Topaz ships, for example, have fairly small playrooms, though they have fully supervised children's clubs and use areas of the decks and even some of the ship's lounges for meetings, games and activities. At the other end of the price scale, babies and toddlers can sample life in a traditional nursery – staffed by fully trained Norland nannies – aboard Cunard Line's classic Southampton New York liner, the QE2.

But for the biggest, best and glossiest children's facilities, the latest generation of megacruise ships are hard to beat. Most cruise ships winter in the Caribbean and spend summer and spring in the Mediterranean.

Carnival Cruise Line (which also owns Cunard, Costa, Holland America and Seabourn) gives toddlers their own pools, deck chairs and playrooms, as well as a Camp Carnival activity programme. A prime example of the Carnival style is the 2040-passenger Elation, which entered service in 1998. Facilities include a 2500-square-foot 'Children's World', comprising three areas – a computer lab, an arts and crafts centre and a climbing/adventure/activity area. There is also an outdoor play centre in the shape of a schooner, and an arcade featuring state-of-the-art virtual reality games.

Norwegian Cruise Lines, Princess Cruises, Royal Caribbean International and Celebrity also offer extensive and fully supervised children's programmes, mainly during school holiday periods.

These companies run ultra modern, beautifully designed ships with imaginative facilities for youngsters. Celebrity, for example, has American-style slumber parties, as well as a wide range of age-related activities like treasure-hunting, designing T-shirts, and quizzes and contests.

Holland America Line gives youngsters the chance to enjoy a real adventure on its Alaska cruises, with a dedicated shore excursion programme aimed specifically at children. It's not particularly suitable for toddlers, as activities include mountain hikes and sea kayaking, but fun nonetheless. On Princess Cays, the company's private hideaway in the Bahamas, toddlers can enjoy themselves at Pelican's Perch, a fully supervised play area specially constructed on the theme of a pirate ship.

And Norwegian Cruise Line gives toddlers the chance to explore their own talents as entertainers with a Circus at Sea, in which they can learn juggling, clowning and other circus skills to (near) performance standard. The circus is part of NCL's Kid's Crew programme, which, like most of the big ship children's programmes, is divided into four age groups.

All of these companies offer not only activities and play areas, but also special menus designed to appeal to young appetites, and even kid's newsletters detailing the day's activities.

Latest to join the ranks of family-orientated cruise lines is entertainment giant Disney's new cruise arm, Disney Cruise Line. Disney's first ship, the 2400-passenger Disney Magic started operating three- and four-day cruises to the Bahamas in July 1998, combined with stays at Florida's 46-square-mile Walt Disney World resort. Though it attracts singles and couples as well as families, Disney has gone big on children's facilities; the newest Disney films are shown in the new ship's cinema, and youngsters get almost an entire deck to themselves. Disney now has two twin ships, Disney Wonder and Disney Magic.

Disney characters are on hand to play with the littlest passengers, and there is also an extensive, fully supervised activity programme split into five age groups. Toddlers are pre-registered for this facility before their cruise, and then get a personal greeting and schedule on arrival. And parents are guaranteed peace of mind, with pagers to help them keep tabs on their toddlers.

Families who prefer a British atmosphere over a 'have a nice day' American-style cruise will also find excellent children's facilities on board P&O Cruises's newer ship, Oriana. The play centre, Peter Pan's, has different sections for each age group. Each ship features extensive age-specific facilities that are fully staffed and equipped with everything from toys to video game machines.

On both ships, children up to the age of five can be left in the supervised night nursery (from 6pm to 2am), and on Oriana there is an in-cabin baby-listening facility.

Points to consider
Before choosing to go on a cruise with your toddler, consider the following

- Not all cruise ships are child-friendly, and not all of those who say they cater for 'children' cater well for toddlers. Others have extensive kid's facilities during the school holidays, but offer little at other times of the year. The best way to find the ship that's perfect for your needs is to consult your travel agent. Be assertive and specific about your needs. Ideally, you will need babysitting, a kiddies club that provides supervised care, child-friendly meals, and cabin listening. You'll also want to be certain that there will be fully qualified medical staff on board.

- Do remember that agents who belong to PSARA (Passenger Shipping Association Retail Agents) scheme are likely to be the most knowledgeable about cruising. Look for a PSARA sticker in the window.

- Some cruise lines are quite strict about pregnant women, so if you've got a toddler and are pregnant with Number Two (or more), check the final date up to which you can travel safely.

- Most shore excursions are not geared to toddlers. It's often better to arrange car hire through the purser or do your own thing in port. Island (08707 500 414), a new British cruise line that will be sailing the Mediterranean this year, is introducing an innovative range for children. For example, in Rome, passengers will be able to visit the famous Olympic stadium where Rome's football giants, Roma and Lazio, play. For children (and toddlers), there will be the option of seeing where gladiators fought, or a trip to the beach. Island is a joint venture between tour operator First Choice, and cruise company Royal Caribbean.

- Do contact the Passenger Shipping Association (0207 236 2449 or visit the website www.cruiseinformationservice.co.uk) for information on any aspect of cruise holidays. It is an excellent source of information.

- Don't regard children's programme as a licence to forget about the kids for a week or so – many ships won't accept children under four in children's clubs unless a parent comes, too. You may need to be there.

- Don't book full-day shore excursions on your own if you have very young children; most companies insist that at least one parent stays on board during a full day in port, in case a child becomes distressed.

Sense in the Sun

I'm seeing increasing numbers of skin cancer patients because toddlers aren't protected from the sun on their travels and sunscreening is essential – not least because toddlers discard hats, shirts and everything else at the soonest opportunity . . .

Dr Jane Wilson-Howarth, Your Child's Health Abroad

Not only is a sunburned toddler a real trial to have around, but we now know that sunburn in babies and children is related to the development of skin cancer in later life. By one estimate, six serious bouts of sunburn in childhood doubles the chances of skin cancer. The younger they are when burnt, the more likely it is that problems will arise.

Children have less mature skin, and have a long life ahead of them during which skin cells can develop damage, so they are in particular need of protection. Furthermore, according to the Imperial Cancer Research Fund, children's skin reacts in a slightly different way to the sun, indicating, once again, a greater need for care.

While UVB rays cause the burn, UVA rays – which are almost as strong in winter as in summer – cause skin ageing. The combination of rays can lead to cancer. Remember that UV rays can penetrate clouds, so ensure that your child is sunscreened no matter what the weather or climate.

What to do
- Take a barrier lip moisturiser, as standard creams may not be suitable for use on the lips. If your toddler is like Tom, he will want to eat it!
- Anything placed on a child or baby's skin is likely to be absorbed to some degree. Therefore, choose brands with lots of natural ingredients, and fewer chemicals. Don't, however, be tempted to forego sunscreen. The damage caused by sun will be a lot worse than any effect of chemicals being absorbed into the skin.
- Expose toddlers to the sun gradually, remembering to include time spent in the car, under clouds, and walking around, as well as on

the beach. All toddlers have sensitive skin, some more than others.

- Toddlers should wear a hat with back flap (covering the neck) at all times, to prevent sunburn and other effects of sunlight and UV rays.

- It takes three days before an adult's body starts to produce the melanin that creates a tan, and The National Radiological Protection Board reports that a tan offers no more protection than a sunscreen of SPF 2 to 4.

- Avoid exposure between 11am and 3pm (when your shadow is shortest). This is particularly important, the closer you get to the equator.

- Be aware of the possibility of thermal burns to sensitive skin when you get into a hot car. Try to park in the shade. If this is not possible, provide some shade inside by putting a towel over the seats and any metal buckles. Use sun shades in the windows, to reduce the impact of the sun on the car.

- Take particular care when there is light cloud or a breeze. You may not feel the sun's power until it is too late. It is possible to burn in as little as 15 minutes on cloudy days, as up to 80 percent of ultraviolet rays pass through light cloud, haze and fog.

- You will also burn in shallow water, so your chosen sun protection must be waterproof and water resistant.

- Encourage your toddler to swim in a T-shirt. The reflection of the sun on the water increases the impact of its rays, and toddlers are also more likely to spend longer periods outside when they have some cool water to dip into.

- If relying on a standard buggy sunshade, consider lining it as the fabric is unlikely to offer much serious sun protection.

- Look for sunglasses with UVA and UVB filters, as only these provide proper protection against the sun. Like most toddlers, Tom loves to wear sunglasses, but they are easily misplaced. A clip, much like a dummy clip, can be attached to a Tshirt and one arm of the glasses to prevent loss. Don't be tempted to choose fashion or 'cute' glasses. Go for the ones with real UV protection. For more information see the Shades of Summer leaflet from the NRPB (National Radiological Protection Board). For the best protection look on the label for the British Standard BS2724: 1987.

- Remember that all family members need to practise sun safety. As parents, we have a responsibility to teach our toddlers how to be safe in the sun, by example as well as by education.
- The homeopathic remedy Sol (at 30c dilution) can help to reduce the impact of sun. Take once or twice throughout the day.

Know your sunscreen

• The sun protection factor (SPF) rating indicates protection from UV rays. Grading is not universal, but for young children a minimum SPF of 15 is recommended. The star rating indicates a ratio of UVA to UVB protection. For young children three stars is recommended. If an unprotected child would burn in 10 minutes, a cream with a SPF of 15 would allow him or her to spend 15 times longer (two and half-hours) in the sun. But an SPF15 cream may not be good enough. Look for a high sun protection sun factor (SPF) broad-spectrum sunscreen. For toddlers, choose those with a SPF of 30 or higher (although recent reports state that anything above 25 has the same impact as an SPF25 cream). Thicker creams usually cover and stick better than thinner lotions and oils.

• Sweat, as well as swimming, washes off the cream and while water-resistant options last for longer, they too are rubbed off by towels and clothing.

• If your child reacts to a particular product you will need to check the ingredients and try another. According to one dermatologist, the most likely culprit is titanium dioxide, though complementary practitioners often also recommend avoiding zinc.

• Given the possibility of an allergic reaction, it is best to opt for a perfume-free brand, and one without mosquito repellent. Further chemicals add more variables to the cocktail and although the basic chemicals have all been tested individually, the combinations very rarely have. However, risks are still very low.

• Whatever you use you should ensure that the product is applied to all exposed areas including ears, neck, hands and feet. According to the Health Education Authority's Sun Know How campaign, most

---

people apply cream too thinly, so they provide less protection than the SPF on the bottle suggests. It can be helpful to put a higher SPF on highly exposed areas such as noses and even collar and cheekbones, to avoid burning. Common sites for skin cancers are tops of ears, face, back or hand. You may want to try one of the coloured sunscreens, so that you can see that you have applied it all over the body.

• All pharmacies stock sun barrier creams but, given how important the issue is, it is worth looking for one which will provide the extra protection children need, in the best way possible.

• MASTA (Medical Advisory Services for Travellers Abroad) suggests E45 cream which 'uses only non irritant, mineral-based sun screens which form a protective shield on the skin to reflect away sunlight'. It is reported ideal for sun protection of infants and children. Containing paraffin, lanolin and monostearin, it is also excellent for many dry skin conditions.

• Nomad offers both a basic No Ad (no advertising) product or Uvistat, which is 'considered to be one of the best sun protection creams' and one of the most pure. It is water resistant, hypoallergenic and lanolin free, and offers a range of SPFs, from 6 to 30; all are rated with four stars. The company also sells a Babysun range with lotions and creams, while Uvistat Sunsplash is waterproof for up to five hours, useful for children in and out of the water. Uvistat also produces three lip screens Factor 15, Factor 25 with Tea Tree oil to help heal and protect, or Factor 30 with Vitamin E to minimise skin damage.

• An alternative is the Forever Living sun tan lotion, recommended by complementary practitioners as safe for children. Although it has no official SPF rating, and may only offer protection of around SPF10, it is reported to be extremely effective when combined with Forever Living's Aloe Gelly. This product encourages collagen production and adds moisture. Unlike most Aloe vera products, this one is produced by one of the few companies who have managed to stabilise Aloe vera.

• For children who hate the feel of sticky, thick creams, go for a spray brand (Coppertone has a great one for kids), which allows full coverage with the minimum of fuss. Or choose one of the 'wet wipe' brands, which are, effectively, simply towels soaked in a liquid sunscreen. They are quick and easy to use, and come in many high SPFs.

• Always choose waterproof and water-resistant brands. If you are heading for the beach, get a sunscreen that will not be rubbed away by sand. Many brands for children offer this feature.

• The higher the SPF, the longer it takes for the skin to burn. However, this does not give you licence to spend whole days in the sun. Even sunscreens cannot completely prevent sunburn, if you spend too long in the sun's rays. It simply protects the skin for longer.

• Suntan lotion is not sunscreen.

• Take sun protection products with you – they may not be easily available, especially where permanent residents have darker skin.

• Apply lotion according to directions

• Shake well, rub it in well to make sure you get even coverage on all exposed parts of the body.

• Apply suntan lotion on toddlers before they get dressed so you don't miss any edges around clothes. Repeat the application throughout the day, particularly after bathing.

• Avoid contact with eyes and mouth. If lotion gets in the eyes, flush thoroughly with water. If more than a lick is ingested, contact your local doctor's office to ensure that there is no real problem. If a rash occurs, discontinue use of that brand immediately and consult your doctor.

• Suntan lotion's active ingredients do expire. If your bottle is two or more years old, throw it out. Expiry dates are usually on the bottom of the bottle – if not, make a note of the date you bought it.

Sunburn

Despite your best efforts, your toddler may become burnt in the sun. For details of treating sunburn quickly and effectively, see page 144.

Sun safety gear

There is a growing range of items on the market designed to protect children from the sun. Here are a few suggestions:

1. Toddler togs

Standard clothing offers some protection against UV rays, the degree depending largely on the closeness of the weave, though darker colours are reported to offer more protection than lighter ones.

While densely woven Tshirts may fall into the maximum protection category, thinner fabrics may offer no more than SPF4. It may, therefore, be sensible to invest in safer sun protection clothing.

Sun protection wear with an SPF of 40 should provide a total block, but some companies offer a range of SPF clothing with an SPF factor of up to 100. You can buy these in sports shops (Speedo sell a range), chemists (such as Boots) and also from kids catalogues (Great Little Trading Company and Outdoor Kids, for example).

Swimsuits, covering shoulders, upper arms and thighs, and 'French Foreign Legion'-style caps with neck flaps, are especially good designs.

2. Sunglasses

Eyes need to be protected from the sun with glasses with a UV filter to international standards. Neoprene bands may help keep sunglasses in place or at least prevent loss.

3. UV protection cabanas

A growing number of suppliers are offering pop-up cabañas (shades). These are helpful if you want to take little ones to the beach, for example, especially if they want to sleep. Note, however, that these will still get hot so you should not leave a baby in one for any great length of time.

For further information contact The National Radiological Protection Board (NRPB), on Tel: 01235 831 600. They produce a leaflet entitled 'Ultraviolet Radiation', and offer reports, features and other documents about the issue of sun.

Top-rated liners

These cruise liners offer the best facilities for toddlers although, in some cases, the facilities are only appropriate to children older than two or even three. So ask before you book. Each defines toddlers in a slightly different way. Other cruise lines are more suited to older children, but those listed below are the ones that have received most positive comments from my research and first-hand experience.

Carnival Cruises
Tel: 0207 940 4466
Carnival has designed their modern Superliners to be ideal for families. Their excellent activity programme for children offers a similar atmosphere to the extremely popular American 'summer camps', with a huge range of optional daytime activities and excellent children's amenities, in this case for toddlers aged two and upwards.

Camp Carnival hosts supervised daytime activities for children aged two to 16, in three age groups. Children between the ages of two and four would take part in the 'toddlers' group, and younger children can attend activities if accompanied by a parent or guardian. Times and locations of these activities are printed in the daily Carnival Capers shipboard newspaper. A team of qualified youth staff are in charge of these activities, which could include face-painting, puppet-making, ice cream parties and 'Learn your ABC'. And Tom loved them all.

Dedicated Superliner facilities for toddlers include an indoor play-room, partitioned-off deck area (with pirate ship or other permanent play feature) and wading (paddling) pool. High chairs (in the restaurants) and cots (in cabins) are available on request. Special children's menus include hamburgers, fried chicken and chips, ice cream and the usual fare that they like and we don't like to give them.

Babysitting is available at a nominal fee and this takes place in the playroom in a 'pyjama party' atmosphere, after the last evening activity has ended. Babysitting is also available on some afternoons in port. Passengers must sign up for babysitting before 5pm each day and a day ahead for time in port.

Costa Cruises
Tel: 020 7940 4499

This cruise line offers excellent facilities for children, particularly in the Med but also on board its Florida-based ships, the Costa Victoria and Costa Romantica. During the school holidays, the ships run supervised clubs for children, offering a range of activities and entertainment. But the activities provided for toddlers are limited – and out of school holidays many of the activities stop all together.

There is a 'mini-club' for three to six year olds, with organised entertainment. A babysitting service is available for kids under three. The Fun@Sea programme is distributed to children under 12 years of age. There is one for the 'mini-club', listing all activities offered during the cruise; these include treasure hunts, chocolate parties, visits to the bridge and face-painting. Mini clubs are run between 9am and 12pm, 3pm and 6pm, and 9pm and 11.20pm. A communal babysitting service for children from three years is available free of charge upon booking the previous day with the Children's Entertainment Director. This service is available from 11.30pm until 1.30am.

Two theme suppers are offered on weekly cruises, with a menu designed for children.

P & O Cruises
Tel: 020 7800 2222

With up to eight sailings a month from Britain, and cruises ranging from four days to over three weeks, P & O offers a vast array of itineraries encompassing the Mediterranean, Baltic's Atlantic Island, Canary islands and Norwegian Fjords. With P&O's Family Savers and Family Savers Plus deals, children can benefit from huge discounts (see page 139).

P&O Cruises prides itself on its supervised facilities for toddlers. Each ship has playrooms for children aged two to nine. On Aurora, 'Toybox' caters for the two to fives. On Oriana, 'Peter Pan's' is for the two to nines, and on Victoria, there is a junior club available on cruises departing between 14 July and 22 December each year. Each is open from 9 am until 10.30pm (Victoria closed during lunch), with an extensive programme of play, sport and entertainment. On Aurora and Oriana, the younger age range have a paddling pool as well as their own reserved pool.

Children under five are catered for at night on both Oriana and Aurora. The night nursery, which is complimentary, operates on a first-come, first-served basis daily. Additionally, there is an in-cabin baby-listening facility. Book early – this is popular, as you can imagine.

Normally toddlers sit with their parents at breakfast and lunch, but a special children's tea is hosted on Aurora and Oriana. This means that parents are able to enjoy an adult dinner if they wish. It's worth noting that one parent must be onboard the ship at all times if their child is in the children's centre or involved in any activity.

P&O Cruises offers very substantial fare reductions for toddlers. On some cruises they travel free of charge, on others there are discounts of up to 90 percent of the adult fare.

Princess Cruises
Tel: 020 7800 2468
To make cruising as a family easier than ever, children can now travel aboard all Princess ships in the Caribbean and Alaska from the age of six months, with youngsters over 12 months old being welcomed on cruises in Europe and those over 18 months accepted on voyages to more exotic destinations. All nine Princess ships can cater for junior cruisers, while the three newest 'Grand Class' Superliners offer fully equipped children's facilities.

Eight Princess Cruises ships (Grand, Golden, Ocean, Dawn, Sea, Sun, Regal and Crown Princess) feature a children's centre. Youth activity co-ordinators will supervise children over the age of two and under the age of18, in groups according to age, with a variety of activities to keep them entertained. Supervised activities include arts and crafts, afternoon ice cream, birthday parties and Nickelodeon TV.

Princess Pelicans, the children's programme for two to 12 year olds, has a wide range of supervised activities, including:

- arts and crafts
- pool games
- scavenger hunts
- deck parties
- afternoon ice cream
- videos and cartoons

- birthday parties
- special Nickelodeon TV programmes
- A play area, complete with pirate ship playground and sandbox, on Princess Cruises' private island, Princess Cays.
- An 'adventure ashore' programme
- A pizza party during one night of a cruise, where children dine with friends and without parents

Royal Princess and Pacific Princess operate a programme of activities when 15 or more children are booked in any one cruise. Neither ship has a specific child centre. Childcare times and babysitting rates for Royal Princess are the same as for the rest of the fleet. Pacific Princess closes the childcare facilities at 10pm and there is no group baby-sitting offered. Only a limited number of children can be accommodated on individual cruises.

It's worth noting that the youth activity co-ordinators in the children's centre will not change nappies (very frustrating), organise bottle feeding or administer medication to the children (understandable), nor can a meal service be provided (again very annoying).

Supervised pool times are as advertised in the daily programme; adult supervision is required at other times. Private babysitting is not available on any Princess ship. A toddler (defined as being between the ages of two and four) pays 50 percent of the lowest grade cabin price. About 10 percent of the customers on Princess are families with toddlers.

Thomson Cruises
Tel: 08705 502 5628
Thomson Cruise has three ships – the Emerald, Topaz and Stella Solaris – featured in the cruise brochure. Stella Solaris does not have a children's club. Topaz is the only fully inclusive ship operated by a tour operator.

Thomson runs a children's club, 'Little T Club', for children aged between three and seven years (so just within the toddler bracket). Two to three hours of activities and games are arranged, six days a week. Children are welcome at the T Club as long as there is a parent or guardian onboard the ship. Some babysitting services are available, so it's worth checking when booking. A children's menu is available, with 'home from home' dishes and smaller portions. It's the pretty standard fare of chips, nuggets and beans.

Thomson is an excellent company, but comments from parents who have travelled with their toddlers on cruises have led me to believe that this company is geared more to older children than toddlers.

Royal Caribbean International
Tel: 0800 018 2020
RCI operates four kids clubs on boards its fleet, under the umbrella 'Adventure Ocean'. Each club is specially designed to meet the needs of each different age group, with activities arranged accordingly. For all toddlers three years and above, the Adventure Ocean programme is an excellent idea. Beware, however, that toddlers must be toilet-trained. But the programme is free of charge. Toddlers enter the 'Aquanauts' group (three to five years), while kids between the ages of six and nine are 'Explorers'. The nine to 11 age group become 'Voyagers', and 12 to 14 year olds are 'Navigators'.

All children's activities are supervised by male and female youth staff who are graduates in education, recreation or have college degrees in related fields, including, I am told, 'qualified experience in working with children ages three to 17'. A worryingly large age group, as many anecdotes will testify!

Activities in the Aquanauts group include finger-painting, dressing up, building blocks, playdough sculptures, music activities, dot dancing, animal, colour and shape bingo, pillowcase colouring and a talent show – which makes them all very competitive, I am told. Island activities include building sandcastles and collecting seashells.

Group babysitting is available, supervised by the youth staff, from 10pm to 1am. Children must be three years of age and toilet trained. In your cabin, babysitting is available through the purser's desk, and must be booked at least 24 hours in advance. It's subject to availability, so book early. In-cabin babysitting is supervised by the ship's staff members.

There are excellent and inventive children's menus (not just the usual burger, beans and bun wrapped up as a 'salty sea captain's' nibble), and an excellent selection of movies for toddlers shown on cabin televisions. At mealtime, young cruisers can dine from their own eight-page menu, featuring word and picture games, plus pictures to colour (crayons come with the menu, although Tom decided to eat his). In addition, the Adventure Ocean dinner programme allows children to eat dinner with their favourite youth staff and friends in either the Windjammer Café, the Solarium or Johnny Rockets (depending on which ship they are on). This programme, which is scheduled three times on a seven-night cruise, and once or twice on shorter cruises, offers a complete children's menu between 6pm and 7pm and gives parents the opportunity to enjoy a romantic meal without the toddler. Sort of.

Check out the web

For up to date cruising information visit www.cruiseandferry news.com, www.seaview.co.uk or www.cruise2.com. Also check out *Cruise Traveller*, a glossy but independent consumer magazine, published quarterly and covering everything from summer Mediterranean cruises to round-the-world voyages. There are also destination features, interviews and comprehensive listings of which cruise lines operate where. The magazine also covers family cruising and in 2002 will conduct a major survey on cruise products available for the family market. *Cruise Traveller* is available on subscription. Visit www.cruisetraveller.co.uk, or www.gpca.co.uk, or call 020 7751 2080 for subscription details.

Health issues

Cruising can be great fun for families with toddlers, but there are always health problems that can crop up and it's sensible to know what to do, particularly if medical care is not available round the clock. Many problems can be prevented with a little common sense.

Sunstroke and overheating

Toddlers and particularly babies are prone to overheating quickly. Heat exhaustion occurs in extreme temperatures, and is exacerbated by excessive sweating and inadequate liquid replacement. In the case of babies, overheating may occur because their bodies are not sufficiently developed to sweat efficiently, if at all. High humidity is also an aggravating factor, as are high levels of activity (a common feature of toddlerhood).

What to look for

Severe and inexplicable tiredness, headache, nausea, cold and clammy skin are common symptoms. A young baby may cry inconsolably, and feel warm. Heatstroke (also known as sunstroke) can follow heat exhaustion. If your child's temperature is above 40°C, you should consult a doctor. Toddlers generally acclimatise in a day or two – much faster than adults.

What to do

- In hot climates, encourage toddlers to eat more salty foods than usual, which helps the body to retain water. Local foods may well be more highly seasoned anyhow. Don't, however, be tempted to offer salt tablets, which are not appropriate for children.
- Avoid drinks with caffeine, including colas, as caffeine is a diuretic.
- In the wet tropics, humidity usually rises through the day, usually falling with an afternoon rainstorm. Try not to stay outside during these hours. A break in the pool or an air-conditioned cabin might be just what your toddler needs to cool down.
- Avoid car travel, without air conditioning, in high temperatures.
- Keep a supply of cool drinks available all the time and, if possible, access to a swimming pool for cooling off.
- Invest in hats with flaps, which protect the nape of the neck. The nape of the neck is reported as being a part of the body that is most directly connected to the brain's system of temperature regulation.
- Water, ideally containing an oral rehydration sachet, is recommended as a counter measure in extremely hot temperatures.
- Blowing on or fanning the skin, or sponging all over with cool water, cools the body. Don't use ice, as this causes shivering and actually increases temperature in the short term. A cool

compress on the forehead or nape of the neck may help.
- Remember that it is possible to get heatstroke in the shade, so when it is very hot it is best to avoid being outdoors between noon and 4pm.
- Choose accommodation with air conditioning, if available, not merely ceiling fans. If the accommodation is too hot (either due to inadequate or non existent air conditioning), think about taking excursions on an air-conditioned coach or aim for places like caves and other underground sites (remembering that they may be chilly so be prepared with extra layers).

Motion sickness
See page 239.

Sunburn
Although every attempt should and can be made to avoid sunburn, there are times (such as during long periods in the pool, or on a hazy day when you've been caught unawares) when your child's skin may become burned by the sun. And it's easily done – toddlers and babies have extremely sensitive skin, and it doesn't take much sun to cause a burn.

First and foremost, follow the precautions noted on page 131. If your child does become burned, it will be fairly obvious, with reddened, painful skin, and possibly even blisters.

What to do
- Run cool (not cold) water over the affected area, or run a tepid bath where your child can play. This will help to take the heat out of the burn, reduce damage to the skin, and possibly relieve some of the pain. Cool compresses also help. Don't use ice as it can put an ice burn on top of the sunburn.
- Pain-relief tablets or syrup may help reduce the discomfort of sunburn. Check with your doctor or pharmacist if your child is under two. Paracetamol should be useful, as it has anti-inflammatory action as well as being a painkiller. Never give aspirin to children.

- A local pain-relieving spray may help to ease the pain, but check that it is suitable for children.
- Consult a physician or hospital emergency if the sunburn is serious or if your child is under one year old.
- Never pull peeled skin, nor prick blisters.
- If there are no blisters, lotions, such as calamine, aloe vera or after sun, may help to soothe.
- If there are blisters, keep area clean and only apply healing lotions when the blisters have dried.
- Essential oil of lavender was first discovered for its ability to heal burns. Blend one or two drops into a little cool olive oil and gently massage into the affected area (although only if there are no blisters). It will help to encourage healing, prevent infection, and ease the pain.

Other problems on board ship may include 'funny tummy', and nausea. These are covered in detail on pages 233 and 235.

7. On the Slopes

Its worth packing an extra one piece (if they have it) for three to four year olds. They can get soaking wet playing in the snow. Older children don't seem bothered about wearing damp kit, but youngsters don't like it. Choose a company with a tumble dryer in the chalet – you will need it.

Mother of two, from Tottenham

In my experience, tour operators who specialise in or offer skiing holidays are better equipped for toddlers than their summer counterparts. Those parents I interviewed seemed to agree. After camping, and self-catering, skiing appears to be a popular holiday for both toddlers and grown-ups (see page 20). Perhaps because this type of holiday tends to be more expensive per capita, the childcare and facilities are great, and the overall attitude to toddlers is encouraging. In fact, this is one segment of the travel industry where taking toddlers on holiday is not a 'grey area'. This is a refreshing change.

You may want to consider preparing your child for a ski holiday by arranging some dry slope lessons in the UK before departure. These can be a huge advantage, although many of the parents I spoke to felt that waiting for the real thing worked just as well. If you plan to leave your child on the slopes for at least some of the time (in a club or ski school), you may want to try a little practice in advance, just so he feels confident enough to be on his own once you reach your destination.

What's on offer?

There are a surprising number of tour operators offering excellent crèche and nanny facilities during your stay. All of the nannies are English-speaking and fully qualified, and most of the toddlers clubs run for at least five days a week, usually for the entire day. The tour operators will also be able to advise you about suitable kit for your toddler during the holiday, and in most cases supply a suitable outfit. The maxim with most companies is that 'you can never start them too young' on the slopes, but this will very much depend on the child. Usually there is no attempt to start them on the slopes until the age of three and then only on the most gentle of nursery slopes.

Some of the operators offer hotel accommodation, others house you in chalets. The latter allows greater flexibility and privacy, and as each chalet is usually supplied with its own nanny or crèche, there is usually a smaller ratio of children to carers. In a hotel, the childcare and other facilities tend to be much more regimented and fixed, but no less effective.

Points to consider
Some ski resorts are also more suited to families than others. You may want to think about the following before booking:

- What is the proximity of the resort from the airport? Some resorts are literally hundreds of miles from the nearest airport, and you will probably want to avoid a long car journey.
- How close is the accommodation to the slopes?
- Is the resort car-free and predominantly pedestrianised?
- Are there plenty of après-ski activities, and programmes for non-skiers?
- Are there doctors on site?
- Are there plenty of nursery slopes for adventurous toddlers to try out their skills?
- What's the weather like at the time you hope to book? If the snow is unreliable, you may end up stuck inside all day.
- Are there local attractions or activities for non-skiing days?

- How many children take part in activities, and do you need to be present?
- Are ski school and crèche facilities included in the price? If not, what can you expect to pay?
- Do they offer hire equipment for little ones, or will you have to arrange to bring your own?

Toddler-friendly resorts

The most family-orientated resorts, with good nursery slopes and family facilities, include:

- Soldeu in Andorra, Kitzbuhel, Obergurgl and Mayrhofen in Austria (in Mayrhofen under fives can learn to ski for free).
- Geilo in Norway is also excellent.
- Les Arcs, Avoriaz, La Plagne and Flaine – all of which are good for families. Les Arcs and Avoriaz are car free. Note, however, that Les Arcs and La Plagne have a long transfer time (time it takes to get from airport to resort).
- Switzerland has many family-friendly resorts – Grindelwald, Murren, Wengen, Villars and Zermatt all have excellent nursery slopes and childcare facilities.
- Killington and Stratton (in New England, on the East Coast of the US) are also worth considering if you are prepared to journey for over seven hours.
- The Canadian Rockies have lots of great resorts for kids. Outstanding ones include Silver Star and Big White in British Columbia.

Check out the web

Websites worth checking out are www.skiclub.co.uk – the website for the Ski Club of Great Britain – and www.kidznsnow.com, which has further reports and reviews of ski resorts and their toddler/child friendliness. The Ski Club of Great Britain also produced an excellent 'skiing with the family' video, in conjunction with Neilson Holidays. For further details, contact the club on 020 8410 2000.

What you'll need

One drawback of skiing is that you do need a fair bit of equipment that you will have to borrow or purchase. Check out nearly-new sales, twins' club sales, and local papers for used equipment and clothing. Many ski shops also sell nearly new gear. Given how quickly toddlers grow, it's probably better to go down this route than invest in entirely new kit that will only see the light of day on one skiing break. If you are planning a skiing holiday, you'll need pretty much all of the following:

- A warm snow/ski suit that is both wind and shower-proof
- Warm undergarments – vests and all-in-one 'long-john' type garments are best
- Sunblock and lip block
- Warm mittens – avoid wool if you can, which becomes saturated very quickly. Tie them to a piece of elastic and run it through the sleeves to avoid losing them. For the record, mittens keep hands warmer than gloves
- Warm ski socks (several pairs, both for layering and to allow drying)
- Sunglasses or goggles
- A warm hat, again not wool, and preferably one that fits over the chin and neck as well
- A ski helmet (which can be hired from most ski hire shops in resort)
- Waterproof, warm boots suitable for wearing in snow
- Clothes suitable for layering under snowsuits

- A small purse with some money for drinks/snacks during the day
- A piece of paper with your child's name and the telephone number of your accommodation for him/her to keep in a pocket

Top-rated operators

The following tour operators all offer excellent and creative crèche facilities and personal nannies either in a chalet or hotel scenario. Most offer clubs with ski schools designed for coaching toddlers from the age of three on the slopes. These companies all provide great facilities for one to four year olds in the resorts mentioned above.

Hillwood Holidays
Tel: 01923 290 700. Website: www.hillwood-holidays.co.uk
This operator offers nannies and crèche facilities in resorts in Soll, Austria; Les Gets, France; Argentiere, France; and Whistler, Canada.

Fantiski
Tel: 01622 844 302, Website: www.fantiski.co.uk
Offers nannies and crèche facilities in resorts in Les Gets and Val d'Isere in France, and Aspen in the US.

Skibeat
Tel: 01243 780 405, Website: www.skibeat.co.uk
Offers nannies and crèche facilities in resorts La Plagne, La Tania and Val d'Isere in France.

Simplyski
Tel: 020 8541 2209, Website: www.simplyski.co.uk
Offers nannies and crèche facilities in resorts Courchevel, La Plagne and Verbier in France.

Ski Blanc
Tel: 01306 743 996, Website: www.skiblanc.co.uk
Offers nannies and crèche facilities in resorts near Meribel, France.

Meriski
Tel: 01451 843 100, Website: www.meriski.co.uk
Offers nannies and crèche facilities in Meribel, France.

Ski Esprit
Tel: 01252 618 300, Website: www.ski-esprit.co.uk
Offers nannies and crèche facilities in Chamonix, Courchevel, La
Plagne, La Rosiere and Verbier.

Ski Total
Tel: 020 8948 3535, Reservations 0800 980 9595,
Website: www.skitotal.com
Offers nannies and crèche facilities in Les Gets, Les Contamines, Lech,
St Anton and Val d'Isere.

Family Ski
Tel: 01684 564 488, Website: www.familyski.co.uk
Offers nannies and crèche facilities in La Plagne, Val Thorens and Portes
du Soleil (Ardent).

Mark Warner
Tel: 08708 480 482, Website: www.markwarner.co.uk
Offers nannies and crèche facilities available in some resorts and specific
chalets only. Available in La Plagne, Val d'Isere (not chatelhotel Morris),
Courchevel (not chatelhotel Bellevue) and St Anton (not chatelhotel
Rosanna).

Ski Famille
Tel: 01223 507 808, Website: www.skifamille.co.uk
Offers nannies and crèche facilities in Les Gets in France.

Powder Byrne
Tel: 020 8246 5300, Website: www.powderbyrne.com
Offers nannies and crèche facilities in the Villars Courchevel 1850,
Flims, Grindelwald, Zermatt, Arosa, Klosters and Saas Fee Zurs.

Crystal Ski Holidays
Tel: 08708 880 252, Website: www.crystalholidays.co.uk
Offers nannies and crèche facilities at hotels and chalets in Alpe D'Huez, Chamonix, Courchevel, Flaine, La Plagne, La Rosiere, Les Deux Alpes, Morzine in France, and Bardonecchia, Courmayeur, Claviere and Val di Fassa in Italy. Nannies are provided in specific hotels in Mayrhofen, Zell am See, Bad Hofgasten Neustift and Rauris in Austria, and Meribel and Val d'Isere in France.

First Choice
Tel: 0870 754 3477, Website: www.fcski.co.uk
Offers crèche facilities and nannies in Les Deux Alpes, Alp d'Huez and Les Menuires in France.

Thomson
Tel: 0870 606 1470, Website: www.thomson-ski.com
Offers many nanny and crèche facilities in Andorra.

Erna Low
Tel: 020 7584 2841, Website: www.ernalow.co.uk
Can pre-book crèche, kindergarten and ski school for clients in their three main resorts: La Plagne, Les Arcs and Flaine.

Toddlers and snow

In general, toddlers love the snow more than they do sunshine, which can make them hot, and sticky and uncomfortable. On the other hand, snow is so much more fun. You can build things in it, toboggan down slopes, make snow angels and snowballs, build forts and dig trenches. It's unusual (to a toddler) texture is like nothing else, and falling in it hurts a lot less than tumbling anywhere else. Usually. If you wrap up your toddler well – like a thermal Michelin man – he'll be able to play for hours.

However, the snow in the back garden or local park is quite different to that found on skiing holidays, where there are numerous other hazards to negotiate. The following safety checklist was supplied by the Ski Club of Great Britain:

- Check the weather report and heed precautions and advisories. If weather warnings suggest a severe wind chill or extremely low temperatures, consider avoiding outdoor activities until the weather improves.
- Be aware of avalanche warnings.
- Be aware of symptoms of and treatment for hypothermia and frostbite.
- Dress in layers. It is very important to keep warm and dry while enjoying outdoor activities in the winter. When not wearing a helmet, wear a hat and a neck guard. Keep ears covered, too. Noses can be covered with a neck guard.
- Make sure clothing is comfortable. Tight clothing restricts circulation and can increase chances of frostbite. Ask your toddler if their clothes are too tight. They will tell you.
- Dress toddlers in brightly coloured clothing, so they are more easily seen.
- Take extra care when dusk or evening approaches, as reduced visibility can lead to accidents.
- Goggles with sun safety features can also protect eyes from cold, wind and snow.
- Remove all drawstrings from toddler's snow suits and avoid using scarves to reduce the risk of strangulation.
- Don't overdo activities.
- Try to maintain healthy eating and sleeping habits.

For parents:
- Try to avoid alcohol, tobacco, drugs and consider reducing caffeine consumption. You need your wits about you with toddlers in the snow.
- Teach toddlers never to touch metal during cold temperatures.
- Toddlers should be taught never to throw snow at other people. Snowballs can contain ice chunks or stones that can cause harm, including damage to eyes.
- Never bury anyone in snow as there is a risk of suffocation. Teach toddlers never to make tunnels in the snow.

> • Toddlers should never play on snow piles near parking lots or on the road side. Make sure your toddler never goes near snow-ploughs or areas being ploughed.

Health issues

It's worth being prepared for health problems that can crop up on ski-ing holidays. Toddlers tend to be more susceptible than adults, mainly because of their size, so keep an eye out for symptoms, and act quickly if you suspect illness.

Hypothermia

Hypothermia results from exposure to low temperatures, wind and moisture over a period of time. It can occur on the ski hill, in a car, by falling in water that is cold or anywhere else where extreme cold causes the body temperature to fall below normal. As a parent you need to be aware of the causes and symptoms of hypothermia in chil-dren as well as other adults, and know what to do when you suspect hypothermia. Seek medical attention immediately if you suspect or observe any symptoms, which can include:

- Complaints about being cold and irritability
- Uncontrollable shivering
- Impaired or slurred speech or vision
- Clumsy movements
- Blurred vision
- Severe symptoms can include stiff muscles, dark and puffy skin, irregular heart and breathing rates and unconsciousness

What to do

If any of these symptoms is present, move the toddler to a warm, dry place as soon as possible. Remove any wet clothing and seek urgent medical attention. Never rub the skin. Bundling in a warm blanket will help to keep the heat in. Keep your child next to your body, so that he can share your body heat. This will also help to keep him calm.

Frostbite

Frostbite results from exposure to low temperatures, wind and moisture over a period of time. As a parent you need to be aware of the causes and symptoms of frostbite in toddlers, as well as other adults and know what to do.

There are two degrees of frostbite:

- Superficial frostbite looks like grey or yellowish patches on the skin, especially the fingers, toes, face and ears. It can, however, occur on any exposed skin. The first symptoms are usually numbness, itching and prickly pain. The skin remains soft but becomes red and flaky after it thaws.
- Deep or severe frostbite looks like waxy, pale skin, which feels cold, hard and solid to the touch. The areas turn blue or purple when thawing and large blisters may appear when the area warms up.

What to do

- As soon as you suspect frostbite, get out of the cold and to a warm place.
- Seek medical attention immediately.
- Remove any tight clothing to increase circulation.
- If affected area is partially thawed, place in warm (not hot) water (102–106°F). If the water is too cool, thawing will take too long. It takes about 20 to 40 minutes for tissues to soften.
- Encourage your toddler to drink warm (not hot) fluids to help increase circulation and warm the body. Avoid caffeine and alcohol completely.
- Never rub or massage the affected area and never put snow or ice on the frostbite. The area can be protected with a fluffy clean bandage and aloe vera cream can be applied.

Altitude sickness

Altitude sickness occurs when the body does not adjust well to having less oxygen to breathe at higher altitudes. Anyone can be affected by it, but toddlers are more prone to it. Reduce the risks and identify the symptoms by:

- Considering resorts that are at lower altitudes, or ascend to high altitudes in gradual steps to allow the body to adjust.
- If any member of the family has a predisposition to altitude sickness, check with your doctor before you go on holiday. Medicines are available to help prevent this illness.

It's important to keep an eye out for symptoms, which can mimic other health problems. You may spend your time treating a tummy bug when there is clearly something else at the root.

Watch out for
- Headaches, dizziness, nausea, vomiting and fatigue.
- Poor appetite, trouble sleeping, and pale, cool skin are also features of this condition.
- Changes in behaviour in toddlers. Toddlers exhibit symptoms more quickly and become much sicker than adults.
- An unusual and uncommon form of altitude sickness causes fluid to collect in the lungs. If a family member exhibits a cough that becomes wetter, with more difficult and faster breathing and a faster heartbeat, seek urgent medical attention.

What to do
- If you suspect altitude sickness, seek medical attention as soon as possible. You may need to descend to a lower altitude to relieve symptoms, and mild symptoms may be relieved by rest and eating lightly.

Toboggan troubles

Toddlers will also love their first toboggan trip, but it can be an experience that is riddled with potential problems. Some toddlers, like Tom, are naturally adventurous, and may love the roller-coaster ride down a hill. Others will be more nervy, so start slowly and stop if you have a reluctant surfer on your hands.

If you do choose to slide down the slopes on a sled, consider the following safety advice:

- Don't toboggan at night or dusk as visibility is reduced.
- Maintain control and look for a clear path before you go.
- If a slope is beyond your ability or conditions become unsafe, don't go down the hill.
- Never toboggan near or onto a lake, river or other ice.
- Teach toddlers to sit forward, not backwards, head first or lying down, to get out of the way at the bottom of the hill, and to roll off the toboggan if heading for danger.
- Avoid scarves and loose clothing, and tie up long hair that can get caught.
- Under no circumstances should toddlers go down the hill alone – get a toboggan that is large enough for an adult to share the ride.

8. Camping

Choose a campsite that is on, not close to a beach. 'Close to' in brochure-speak could mean a 10-minute drive. If you have to do that every day with three toddlers, the appeal quickly weakens. Choose a site close to the airport and on a beach. And one that has the option of a toddlers club. But that's not the most important thing. The beach is the most important thing. Your children will remind you every day you are there.

Mother of three from Barnet

Most toddlers love camping and caravan holidays, largely because there is a sense of adventure, excitement and freedom that other holiday options can't quite deliver. They are in an environment where they can make mess, and it just doesn't matter. And according to those parents I interviewed, adults like it too. In fact, camping offers the best-value getaway for both short breaks and longer stays with a toddler. You'll be away from busy main roads, have your own space, and the opportunity to make friends as and when you wish. And if parents are relaxed, your toddlers will be too. It's no wonder that the toddlers I interviewed listed camping as their number-one holiday choice.

Chances are, too, that you can catch some good weather. Try camping overseas in the late spring and early autumn to avoid school holidays. The South of France, Spain and Italy are all good destinations, and you'll be pretty much guaranteed weather that is not unbearably hot, and you'll miss the crowds.

There are many ways to camp, according to your budget, how much luxury you require, and, of course, the age of your toddler. You can take your own tent or caravan, hire a motor home or camper van to tour a vast area of wilderness, stopping off at parks en route. Or you can choose to stay in one of the ready-prepared, permanent camps, where the cabins, tents or caravans are already in place. Whichever you choose, camping is pretty much an outdoor experience, with guaranteed fresh air, if not sunshine.

Holiday parks

Holiday parks should not be confused with 'holiday villages', which are discussed on pages 94 to 106. Holiday parks – where you rent a caravan holiday home, or take your own touring caravan or tent – can be a toddler's paradise. There's freedom to toddle in a green and friendly environment, other youngsters to meet and play with, plus play-grounds and other distractions, all within toddling distance.

Parks are a pretty good bet for parents, too. Many have a wide variety of activities available for family members of all ages, and you can, if you like, spend your entire holiday on site. Some even have restaurants. A caravan holiday home is much like a miniature house, with separate eating, sleeping and living rooms, allowing you to put your toddler to bed and relax in peace and quiet in another room.

Holiday parks have traditionally catered for the family market, and most are fully geared-up for younger guests. Cots can be booked in advance, cafes and restaurants serve child-friendly and child-sized meals, facilities such as swimming pools have provisions for toddlers, and many parks even lay on entertainment for different age groups, from nature trails to sandcastle-building competitions.

Holiday parks can take you right to the heart of the countryside, and many parents view them as an opportunity for toddlers to spend some time closer to nature and the natural world. The 300-plus UK holiday parks that were awarded accolades this year are not just those that are tucked away in quiet corners of the countryside. Among the winners are much larger centres, in popular holiday areas, which offer a wide range of attractions for guests, such as heated swimming pools, indoor and outdoor play areas, supervised children's entertainment and light-hearted competitions.

Some parks are out-and-out family affairs, and it's here you'll find features such as swimming pools, play areas, and clubs for toddlers.

But you may choose a different type of holiday experience. There are also many parks designed specifically for couples, and families who enjoy quieter away-from-it-all surroundings. The main attraction of these types of parks is a beautiful setting in the peace of the countryside, or on the coast and away from the main holiday resorts. You may want to fill your break with outdoor activity and adventure, and there are holiday parks for you, too. There are, in fact, a long list of parks that pitch you right into the heart of the action on water or on land, with equipment hire and professional instruction included, if you wish.

The wide choice available helps to explain why British parks, in particular, have become one of the most popular ways to take a toddler on holiday in the UK, and many of the parents who offered advice and tips agree.

Babies and bugs

In Europe, bugs, such as mosquitoes, are more of a nuisance than a danger, but bites can, if scratched, become infected, which can pose problems. What's more, itchy bites can cause toddlers and babies great distress, disrupt sleep and literally spoil a holiday.

More seriously, however, mosquito bites can, in some parts of the world, carry disease such as malaria, dengue fever, sleeping sickness and much more.

The key to solving this particular problem is prevention, and taking steps to keep your toddler away from bugs, and protected from them, is essential.

Preventing bites

Location

• Go somewhere where mosquitoes are not a problem. This option rules out most warm places with fresh water, and anywhere tropical. Seaside areas are usually OK, but avoid those with low-lying land, marshes and/or lagoons (such as the Camargue or the west coast of Scotland in summer). Arctic and Scandinavian summers mean lots of mosquitoes and 'no-see-'ums'.

• Malaria-carrying mosquitoes don't survive at higher altitudes, for example above 1500m, even in tropical areas, so this might be an option if you are feeling deprived of adventure.

• If you are simply worried about avoiding malaria you do not have to restrict your choices quite so thoroughly. The southern Mediterranean would be fine, for example, or try Queensland in Australia, though there is a slight worry there about dengue fever.

• Don't think that it's safe just because local toddlers are running around uncovered. They get bitten, too.

Clothing

• Light-coloured clothes are recommended in the evening (dusk is a major biting time), with arms, legs and necks covered. That means providing long-sleeved shirts or Tshirts, and long socks to go under trousers so there isn't a biting gap. Mosquitoes can bite through lightweight fabrics, so a certain density is preferable. Coverage is more important than colour.

• Long, loose cotton trousers tucked into socks or boots can also protect legs and ankles from bites when out and about during the day.

• A sun hat with a brim and a neck flap offers a degree of protection against bites on the face and neck. Corks hung from the brim, Australian-style, can discourage flies and mosquitoes.

Washing and skin products

• Mosquitoes are attracted by the smell of sweat, so it's wise to wash or shower at the end of the day. Avoid highly scented perfumes, soaps or sprays. Some after-sun products are best avoided for this reason.

• Choose skin products with tea tree oil, which helps to deter insects.

Nets and screens

• Use nets and screens that are close fitting and free of holes. Keep all doors/windows/screens shut, particularly at night when mosquitoes are most active and when they may be attracted by lights. Close door and screen before switching on a light or lighting candles or lamps. Just for the record, most bites are reported to take place during the hours of sleep.

• Bed and cot nets are especially effective if treated with Permethrin insecticide against night-biters. Most travel clinics and outdoor shops offers nets impregnated with Permethrin. You can also get a kit and do it yourself. The treatment lasts six months or until you wash the net – whichever is sooner. Make sure that the net doesn't touch your child's skin or mouth, though, as permethrin is a powerful neurotoxin. This type of preventative measure is really only necessary if you are going to countries where insect-borne diseases are a problem. In the end, the potential effects of permethrin are far outweighed by these types of diseases.

• The World Health Organisation recommendations allow for a slightly larger hole size in the net if it is impregnated, allowing better air circulation and more comfort. Ideally look for one with a generous skirt to tuck under the mattress.

Repellents

• The most effective chemical repellent is DEET (dimethyltolu-amide) but, again, many experts now claim that it is not really suitable for long-term use on children. If insects are a nuisance rather than a real danger (carrying diseases, such as malaria), then go natural (see page 163). However, if there is a risk of insect-borne disease, products containing DEET are probably your best bet. Make sure your child does not apply the product himself, and keep away from eyes, mouth and nose.

• Beware of manufacturers' claims of repellent time. Complete cover will probably be for only about 30 percent of this time. For effective protection you will need to reapply.

• Avoid aerosol sprays, which may lead to your toddler inhaling the product. Opt for a lotion or a pump spray.

• The aroma that attracts mosquitoes is believed to come from certain points on the human body, so the best prevention is to use repellent on these key points. First put the product on your child's ankles, then on the back of his or her hands (to avoid sucking it off fingers) and then use the backs of the hands to rub a little on either side of the neck. Don't allow your toddler to rub in the product himself, unless he washes his hands thoroughly (or you do it for him) afterwards. It will almost certainly end up being consumed, probably along with anything eaten with fingers at dinner.

Natural alternatives

There are a variety of alternatives to DEET, but none is quite as good at repelling insects:

• There are a growing number of natural products on the market, largely relying on citronella essential oil, although eucalyptus and pyrethrum flowers may also feature, and cedar and lavender are considered good general insect repellents. Neal's Yard Remedies warns that the skin of children under 18 months reacts to essential oils differently from older children and adults. Using oil on the skin before this age, even when diluted, can make your child's skin more sensitive (particularly to sun). Use on clothing may therefore be preferable. Where they work these options do so usually for between 30 and 60 minutes (though the manufacturers may claim differently). Try Alfresco – a moisturiser that acts as a mosquito repellent, and is made from botanical ingredients including Melissa, geranium and lavender, plants traditionally known to deter biting insects. The School of Hygiene and Tropical Medicine in London have recommended it as being safe for use on toddlers.

• Mosi-guard Natural is made from a blend of lemon and eucalyptus oil, has been clinically tested, and is recommended by the London School of Hygiene and Tropical Medicine. The product is suitable for toddlers, and is said to be effective for up to six hours and so probably fully protects for two to three.

• Mozzi Patch, a fabric patch containing citronella, can either be attached to something like a belt, headboard or pram, or used in a small plastic holder round the wrist or ankles. The benefit of this method is that there is no direct contact with the body.

• Natrapel, the top-selling DEET-free repellent in North America, contains 10 percent citronella in a water-based solution, and is available in either a pump spray or lotion. I've had several reports that it is extremely effective.

• Soak a cotton ball in geranium oil, and leave by the bedside (out of arm's reach) to repel insects while sleeping.

Other options

• Autan, originally with DEET, now uses Bayrepel from the manufacturers Bayer, reported to be as effective as 10 or 20 percent DEET repellents. A family formula lotion is reportedly safe for children from the age of two years. Autan is available from Boots and other good chemists.

• Try using a repellent only on clothes or nets, not on the skin. The advantage is that the substance is not absorbed through the skin. Skin repellents can be used on clothes, or there are special repellents for fabrics. They are designed not to stain fabric.

• Repel Clothing Treatment from Healthway Medical or Safariquip can be used on cuffs, collars, trouser bottoms and hats, and is reported to last seven days. Plus, Bug Proof from Nomad, is reported to last for two weeks.

• Consider using an electric insecticide device – which normally comprises a plug-in burner that burns a vaporising tablet. These are available from MASTA, Nomad and Travelextras (with dual voltage function and either liquid or standard tablets) as well as high street outlets, including some supermarkets during the summer months. Note that different countries have different voltages and sockets orientated vertically or horizontally, sometimes depending on the installing electrician! Open models for use in one type of socket will not hold the tablet when placed in the other. A model with flex, which would work with either type of socket, is available from Safariquip. Check the room volume, as a single device is insufficient for a large, high ceiling room.

• Insecticide coils. These are lit at the tail end for a slow burn to create smoke, so are not ideal with children, particularly as the recommended place to locate them is on the floor, so that smoke can deter insects from biting ankles, before rising into the room. However, Homeway and Safariquip offer metal covers for them, which offers some protection. Remember that coils cut bite rate by only 50 percent. Coils are especially worth considering when camping or staying in accommodation without electricity.

• Note that ultrasound buzzers are actually completely ineffectual.

Bug bites
If your child does get bitten, follow the advice on page 201.

Choosing a park in the UK

If you decide on a park holiday, how do you choose where to stay? An excellent starting point are the Freedom Guides, available free from BH&HPA (British Holiday and Home Parks Association). The guides cover six different regions of the UK (Southern England, Western England, Central and Eastern England, Northern England, Scotland and Wales), and contain descriptions of the holiday area, the main attractions and a profile of the holiday parks with their most recent quality grading.

For copies of these publications, write to BH&HPA, 6 Pullman Court, Great Western Road, Gloucester GL1 3ND. Please state which brochures you are requesting.

Alternatively, Internet users can pay a visit to www.ukparks.com where more than 2,500 BH&HPA-member parks are featured. Planning your holiday on the site is easy: just choose the location on the map, and tick the preference boxes. You'll be given a list of sites that most perfectly match your requirements.

Top-rated holiday parks

Domestic holiday parks

Axevale Caravan Park
70–395 Colyford Road, Seaton, Devon EX12 2DF
Tel: 0800 068 8816, Website: www.axevale.co.uk
A quiet family park with superb views. Town, beach, footpaths, bird
watching, attractions and pubs all within walking distance. Caravans
have all amenities including satellite television. Shop and playground
on park.

Bay View Caravan & Camping Park
Old Martello Road, Pevensey Bay, East Sussex BN24 6DX
Tel. 01323 768 688, Fax. 01323 769 637, Website: www.bay-view.co.uk
Situated next to the beach between Pevensey Bay and Eastbourne –
an ideal family park with play area, all facilities and small shop.

Beulah Hall Caravan Park
Beulah Hall, Dairy Lane, Mutford, Beccles,
Lowestoft, Suffolk NR34 7QJ
Tel: 01502 476 609, Fax: 01502 476 453
Sheltered, grassy, family-run site, situated midway between Beccles and
Lowestoft, and close to award winning beaches and amenities. There
is a free swimming pool.

Beverley Park
Goodrington Road, Paignton, Devon TQ4 7JE
Tel: 01803 843 887, Website details: www.ukparks.com
There is lots in this park for toddlers, including outdoor and indoor
pools, play zones and a choice of nearby resorts.

Bridgnorth Park Grange Holidays
Morville, Bridgnorth, Shropshire WV16 4RN
Tel: 01746 714 285, Fax: 01746 714 145,
Website: www.parkgrangeholidays.co.uk

Small, family-friendly park with goats, poultry and a pony. Small wildlife and fishing ponds.

Brighouse Bay Holiday Park
Brighouse Bay, Kirkudbright, Dumfries & Galloway,
Scotland DG6 4TS
Tel: 01557 870 267, Website: www.ukparks.com
This award-winning family park on the beach has an indoor pool, bistro and lots for little ones to explore.

Corpach
Fort William, Highlands PH33 7NL
Tel: 01397 772 376, Fax: 01397 772 007,
Website: www.linnhe-lochside-holidays.co.uk
One of the best and most beautiful lochside parks in Scotland. Magnificent views over Loch Eil and to the mountains beyond. Private beach and free fishing. Park for children, and pets welcome.

Darwin Forest Country Park
Darley Moor, Two Dales, Matlock, Derbyshire DE4 5LN
Tel: 01629 732 428, Fax: 01629 735 015,
Website: www.darwinforest.co.uk
A tranquil woodland area in the heart of the beautiful Derbyshire Peak District offering many on-site facilities including indoor swimming pool, tennis courts, mini golf and a toddler-friendly restaurant and play area.

Fallbarrow Park
Windermere, Cumbria LA23 3DL
Tel: 01539 444 422, Website: www.ukparks.com
This is a quiet park on the shores of Lake Windermere, with first-class family facilities, including play areas.

Fisherground Camping
Fisherground Farm, Eskdale,
Lake District, Cumbria CA19 1TF
Tel: 01946 723 319, Website: www.fishergroundcamping.co.uk

Adventure playground, station on Ravenglass and Eskdale miniature railway. Quiet family site on a traditional lakeland fell farm.

Holgates Caravan Park
Silverdale, Carnforth, Lancashire LA5 OSH
Tel: 01524 701 508, Website: www.holgates.co.uk
Winner of many awards, this quiet park has a lovely pool, as well as safe play areas and woods to explore.

Holiday Resort Unity
Coast Road, Brean Sands, Somerset TA8 2RB
Tel: 01278 751 235, Fax: 01278 751539, Website: www.hru.co.uk
Indoor and outdoor pools, fun park, children's club and many special offers.

Honeypot Caravan & Camping Park
Wortham, Eye, Suffolk IP22 1PW
Tel: 01379 783 312, Fax: 01379 783 312
Six and-a-half acres of parkland surrounding two lakes. It's family run and quiet, with fishing and play areas for the kids.

Kenmore Caravan & Camping Park
Kenmore, Aberfeldy, Perthshire, Scotland PH15 2HN
Tel: 01887 830 226, Fax. 01887 830 211,
Website: www.taymouth.co.uk
Set in the heart of Highland Perthshire by river and Loch Tay, this lovely park has modern facilities and the Byre Bistro restaurant, which is extremely toddler-friendly. Kenmore golf course is adjacent, and there is walking, fishing, golfing and watersports on offer.

Lady's Mile Holiday Park
Exeter Road, (A379), Dawlish, South Devon EX7 0LX
Tel: 01626 863 411, Fax: 01626 888 689,
Website: www.ladysmile.co.uk
Just 20 minutes' walk (and a much shorter drive) to the beach. Indoor and outdoor water flumes. Bar and entertainment, kids clubs and mini golf.

Looe Bay Holiday Park
East Looe, Looe, Cornwall PL13 1NX
Tel: 01392 447 447, Fax: 01392 445 202,
Website: www.weststarholidays.co.uk
Situated on the southeast coast of Cornwall, a short distance from the fishing villages of Looe and Polperro, there are brilliant all-weather facilities, including a free indoor heated pool, children's clubs and live entertainment.

Lydstep Beach Holiday Park
Lydstep Haven, Nr Tenby, Wales SA70 7SB
Tel: 01834 871 871, Website: www.ukparks.com
This is a quiet family holiday park on a secluded bay. There are play areas, an outdoor pool and boat trips nearby.

The Monk's Muir
(Environmental Camping and Caravan Park)
Haddington, East Lothian, EH41 3SB
Tel: 01620 860 340, Fax: 01620 861 770,
Website: www.monksmuir.co.uk
Set in a little-known but unusually lovely and interesting area very close to Edinburgh which is renowned for its 60 kilometres of glorious beaches, picturesque villages, and beautiful hills, the Monk's Muir is an environmental haven, small, civilised, tranquil, and informal.

Mullion Holiday Park
Mullion, Nr Helston, Cornwall TR12 7LJ
Tel: 01326 240 428, Website: www.weststarholidays.co.uk
This site offers indoor and outdoor pools, and it's close to lovely sandy beach and coves. There's free entertainment and a restaurant on site.

Nunnington Farm Camping Site
Rookwood Road, West Wittering, Chichester, West Sussex PO20 8LZ
Tel. 01243 514 013
Family site one mile (1.4km) from safe sandy beach. Picturesque coastal walks, and small animal park on site.

Par Sands Holiday Park
Par Beach, Par, St Austell, Cornwall PL24 2AS
Tel: 01726 812 868, Fax: 01726 817 899,
Website: www.parsands.co.uk
Alongside large sandy beach, indoor heated pool, tennis courts,
bowling green, crazy golf. Modern facilities.

The Plassey Leisure Park
The Plassey, Eyton, Wrexham, North Wales LL13 0SP
Tel: 01978 780 277, Fax: 01978 780 019
The multi-award winning The Plassey Leisure Park is set within 247
acres of quiet farm and woodland in the beautiful Dee Valley. The
Parks amenities include a heated indoor swimming pool (open May
to September inclusive), badminton, table tennis, golf, clubhouse,
toddler-friendly restaurant, coffee shop, craft centre and children's play
area.

Priory Hill Holiday Park
Wing Road, Leysdown-on-Sea, Isle of Sheppey,
Kent ME12 4QT
Tel: 01795 510 267, Fax: 01795 510 267
Hosts a swimming pool, clubhouse, excellent entertainment for
children and adults, shops, a coastal park, mini-golf and a beach.

Roundhay Park Caravan & Camping Site
Elmete Lane Leeds, Yorkshire, LS28 2LG
Tel: 0113 265 2354, Fax: 0113 237 0077

Sandford Holiday Park
Holton Heath, Poole, Dorset BH16 6JZ
Tel: 01392 447 447, Fax: 01392 445 202,
Website: www.weststarholidays.co.uk
Close to the Purbeck Hills and many of Dorset's finest blue flag beaches.
All-weather facilities including free indoor and outdoor pools and chil-
dren's clubs.

Sandy Balls Holiday Centre
Godshill, Fordingbridge, Hampshire SP6 2JZ
Tel: 01425 653 042, Website: www.ukparks.com
A pretty location with a superb pool complex. There is toddler-friendly
pony trekking and walks in the New Forest.

Searles Of Hunstanton
South Beach, Hunstanton, Norfolk PE36 5BB
Tel: 01485 534 211, Website: www.ukparks.com
This site offers lots to occupy toddlers and parents, including pools,
entertainment, beaches and places to play, all in the beautiful Norfolk
countryside.

Strathclyde Country Park Caravan Site
366 Hamilton Road, Motherwell, North Lanarkshire ML1 3ED
Tel: 01698 266 155, Fax: 01698 252 925
A highly recommended camp and caravan site, with many facilities.
There are watersports and fun boats, guided walks, a land train, sandy
beaches and play area. A few minutes walk from site are the Inn keepers
Fayre and M&D's theme park.

Thurston Manor Holiday Home Park
Innerwick, Dunbar, East Lothian EH42 1SA
Tel: 01368 840 643, Fax. 01368 840 261,
Website: www.thurstonmanor.co.uk
This is a luxury holiday park that caters for parents as well as chil-
dren. It's close to Scotland's cleanest and safest beaches, so perhaps a
good one to try.

Trevornick Holiday Park
Holywell Bay, Newquay, Cornwall TR8 5PW
Tel: 01637 830 531, Fax: 01637 831 000,
Website: www.trevornick.co.uk
Family Park specialising in touring and camping with a full enter-
tainment programme and children's club. Pool, golf course, fishing and
Holywell Bay fun park next door. Safe swimming and surfing beach
only 10 minutes' walk away.

Ty Newydd Leisure Park
Llanbedrgoch, near Benllech, Isle of Anglesey LL76 8TZ
Tel: 01248 450 677, Fax: 01248 450 711
Small family run park with toddler-friendly restaurant, swimming pool, health club, kid's playground and more.

Waxholme Road, Withernsea, near Hull,
East Yorkshire HU19 2BT
Tel: 01964 613 319, Fax: 01964 612 915
A quiet park in a rural setting, close to the sea and town centre. Full amenities including pub, shop, laundrette and play area.

Westermill Farm
Exford, Minehead, Exmoor TA24 7NJ
Tel. 01643 831 238, Fax. 01643 831 660,
Website: www.exmoorcamping.co.uk
Beautiful secluded valley fields by shallow river, and in the heart of Exmoor National Park. Waymarked walks over 500-acre working farm, and Scandinavian style cottages with woodburners.

The Willows Caravan Park
Bromholme Lane, Brampton, Huntingdon, Cambridgeshire PE18 8NE
Tel: 01480 437 566
Near to the river Ouse, with fishing, a play area, toddler-friendly restaurant, walks and local to beautiful scenery.

Overseas Holiday Parks
All of these companies come highly recommended from parents of toddlers, who found the facilities and general service to be excellent. Eurocamps and Keycamp were considered to offer the best all-round service. The tour operators are rated, on a scale of 10, for the quality of the facility and its accessibility from airport/road.

Carisma (8/10)
Tel: 01923 284 235, Website: www.carisma.co.uk
Carisma is a family company that specialises in family holidays in luxury mobile homes on campsites that are directly on the beaches of

France's west coast. Under fours are free at all their sites. On all four campsites, Carisma provide a babysitting service, with trained staff. Note, however, that their kiddies club does not accept children under the age of four. This operator offers self-drive holidays with the channel crossing included in the price. Resorts particularly good for toddlers include La Foret, in Southern Brittany, La Tranche, in the Southern Vendee, and Biscarrosse, on the south-west coast. These sites are exclusive to Carisma and cannot be found in other companies' brochures.

Keycamp holidays (9/10)
Tel: 08707 000 123, Website: www.keycamp.com
Children under four travel free at all Keycamp holiday parks. All children are provided with a children's pack. The pack for one to three year olds contains a bib, car sunshade, scribble pad and jumbo crayons. Keycamp has identified 15 campsites that are particularly suitable for toddlers. On these sites, the company runs a 'Harry's Garden' play area for the exclusive use of Keycamp toddlers in May, June and early July. The playground is well equipped with a range of sturdy outdoor play equipment in a safe, fenced-off area outside a mobile home where parents can make tea and coffee. On each of these sites, Keycamp also offers free all-terrain buggy hire, and free cots and high chairs. Accommodation is designed to be child-friendly and includes stairgates and night-lights. In addition, most sites provide baby baths, nappy-changing facilities, and washing machines and dryers. Most campsites also have paddling pools and play areas.

Keycamp produces a mini-brochure aimed specifically at families with babies and toddlers. Included within the brochure is information on the Harry's Garden play areas, with anecdotes submitted by families with young children who have taken Keycamp holidays. There is also a 'questions and answers' panel highlighting some of the common queries raised by parents of small children. Keycamp offers luxury tents (with four bedrooms) and mobile home accommodation at 120 campsites in eight European countries: France, Spain, Italy, Germany, Holland, Austria, Switzerland and Luxembourg. Of these 120, 15 campsites – in Normandy, Brittany, the Loire and on France's west coast – are designated as being particularly suitable for families with toddlers.

All holidays are self-drive (with any ferry crossing), although families may book a flydrive package if they prefer.

Canvas holidays Ltd (9/10)
Tel: 08709 022 022, Website: www.canvasholidays.com
This operator has recently launched 'The Canvas Toddler Group', specifically targeting the toddler market. The Toddlers' Group meets two to three times a week in May, June and September, in a specially designated mobile home at 11 campsites. The Toddlers' Group is designed to let parents meet for coffee and a chat while their toddlers play in a specially designated and equipped play area. The service is free. Facilities at these sites are well suited to families with young children. They are often smaller sites, typically quiet at night, and within a day's drive of the channel ports.

The operator provides an infant pack, which comprises a high chair, baby bath and travel cot (which can also be used as a playpen). There is a charge for this pack. They also provide lightweight buggies on site (reserved at time of booking). All mobile homes are fitted with a child restraint rail that converts one of the single beds into a child's bed. There is also a de-mountable rail that can be fitted across the double doors to the mobile. Families can, therefore, have the double doors open to enjoy the fresh air, safe in the knowledge that their young child cannot wander out of the mobile or indeed fall down the steps. Mobile home cookers also have pan rails fitted for added safety.

The Canvas tent has a unique layout, with a separate kitchen area. A child safety gate is fitted as standard between the kitchen area and the bedroom/living area of the tent. Young children can therefore play safely in the main tent area, while a parent is preparing and cooking food on the 4-burner gas cooker in the kitchen. No other camping tour operator provides this safety feature. Many children have difficulty sleeping in the dark, so all Canvas tents and mobile homes are fitted with a small electric nightlight or dimmer switch, which provides a low light all night if needed. The sites in Normandy, Brittany and the Vendee are the most suitable for toddlers.

Canvas holidays cannot book flights for customers. The majority of their customers cross the channel by ferry or Eurotunnel and drive to their resort.

Haven Europe (9/10)
Tel: 0870 242 7777, Website: www.haveneurope.com
Holiday prices for Haven Europe are based on two adults sharing, while children under 18 are free. Families can stay at one park, tour a number of parks or simply enjoy a short break. The PAWS club is an organised free activity club where parents and children can enjoy a variety of specially designed play sessions together. It is ideally suited for parents with children from between 12 months and four years of age. Activities include arts and crafts, with shapes, paint and crayons, toys, dressing-up costumes, music with instruments, and dance and movement sessions. There are trained lifeguards at the toddlers' pools and a babysitting service is available. There are also special Junior Tents designed for the younger members of the family, and these can be booked when adults stay in a Royale Tent. There are free board games to borrow. Action packs, which include boules, bats, racquets and balls, are also available.

The best parks for toddlers are the eight Haven-owned parks in France: Domaine de Kerlann, Le Bois Dormant, Le Bois Masson, La Pignade, Les Charmettes, La Reserve, La Carabasse and Le Lac des Reves. Haven Europe offers flexible travel arrangements – most people travel by car, using one of the ferry options available. If you choose to fly, Haven Europe are unable to book with one of the main low-cost airlines, as these deal directly with the public, but the cost of the holiday will be reduced if you choose to take the fly-drive option. All childcare facilities are included in the holiday cost, except for children under two.

Eurocamp (10/10)
Tel: 01606 787 878, Website: www.eurocamp.co.uk
Twice winner of the Tommy Award for the most parent-friendly tour operator, in 1999 and 2000, Eurocamp is an obvious first choice when considering toddlers and children of all ages. Some 52 holiday parks across Europe have been singled out as being specifically toddler-friendly, as they tend to be quieter, with safe play areas, grass and shade.

For low-season holidays, between 9 June and 7 July, Eurocamp's Toddler Service really comes into its own. During this period,

Children's Courier supervises free playgroups at 30 parks for five hours a day, six days a week. And families can pre-book a free toddler package, to be waiting for them at their chosen accommodation, including cot-cum-playpen, high chair, baby bath, changing mats and bed safety rails. Mountain buggies are also available for hire on many of the toddler-friendly holiday parks.

Friendly holiday parks

Spain
Canet-Plage Brasilia
Camping Le Brasilia, Hôtel de Plein Air BP 204, 66141
Canet-en-Roussillon, France. Tel: 0033 468 802382
This site is seven miles from Perpignan airport, with direct access to the beach and a toddler service.

Noja
Camping Playa Joyel, Playa de Ris, 39180 Noja, Spain.
Tel: 0034 942 630081
This site is 57 miles from Bilbao airport, and has direct access to the beach and a toddler service.

Torroellade Montgri
Camping Caravaning El Delfin Verde, Afveras S/N, 17257 Torroella de Montgri, Spain. Tel: 0034 972 758454
This site is 35 miles from Gerona, has direct access to the beach, but no toddler service.

France
The Vendée
Ile de Re Interlude
Camping Interlude, 17580 Le-Bois-Plage-en-Re, France.
Tel: 0033 546 091822
The beach is 50 metres from the site, which offers a toddler service.

St Hillaire Ecureuils
Camping Les Ecureuils, 100 Av de la Pége, 85270 St Hilaire de Riez,

France. Tel: 0033 251 543371

The beach is 550 metres from the site, which offers a toddler service.

Jard-sur-mer

Camping Les Ecureuils, 85520 Jard sur Mer, France.

Tel: 0033 251 334274

The beach is 800 metres from the site. There is a toddler service available.

La Tranche-du Jard

Camping du Jard, 123 Route de la Faute, 85360 La Tranche sur Mer, France. Tel: 0033 251 274379

This site has a beach 800 metres from accommodation, and a toddler service.

Portiragnes Plage

Camping Les Sablons, Portiragnes-Plage, 34420 Villeneuve les Beziers, France. Tel: 0033 467 909055

This site has direct access to the beach, and is located 45 miles from Montpelier airport. No toddler service is available.

Brittany

Beg-Meil Atlantique

Camping de l'Atlantique, Route de Mousterlin, 29170 Fouesnant, France. Tel: 0033 298 561444

The beach is 550 metres from the site, which offers a toddler service.

Raguenès-Plage

Camping Raguenès-Plage, 19 Rue des Iles, 29920 Nevez, France.

Tel: 0033 298 067682

The beach is 250 metres from the site, which offers a toddler service.

La Trinite-de la Baie

Camping de la Baie, 56470 La-Trinite-sur-Mer, France.

Tel: 0033 297 557342

The site has direct access to the beach and a toddler service.

Trinite-de la Plage
Camping de la Plage, 56470 La-Trinite-sur-Mer, France.
Tel: 0033 297 557328
There is a beach 200 metres from the site, and a toddler service.

The Loire Valley
Saumur
Camping L'Etang de la Brèche, 49730 Varennes-sur-Loire, France.
Tel: 0033 241 512292
This site is 35 miles from Tours airport, and offers a toddler service.

Mesland
Camping Le Parc du Val de Loire, Mesland, 41150 Onzain, France.
Tel: 0033 254 702718
The site is 25 miles from Tours airport, and offers a toddler service.

Picardy
St Valery
Domaine du Château de Drancourt, BP22, 80230 St Valery-sur-Somme, France. Tel: 0033 322 269345
The beach is 50 metres from the site, which offers a toddler service.

Holland
Kootwijk
Camping Kerkendel, Kerkendelweg 49, 3775 KM Kootwijk, Holland.
Tel: 0031 557 456224
This site is 50 miles from Amsterdam airport. No toddler service is available.

Italy
Lake Garda
Gardameer-Fornella.
Camping Fornella, 25010 San Felice del Beuaco, Italy.
Tel: 0039 036 562294
Just 36 miles from Verona airport, this site has access to a lake beach, and offers a toddler service.

The Adriatic Coast
Caorle
Camping Pra delle Torri, 30020 Porto S Margherita, Italy.
Tel: 0039 421 299063
Approximately 44 miles from Venice airport, this site has direct access to a lake beach, as well as a toddler service.

Lido de Pomposa
Camping Vigna sul Mar, 44020, Lido di Pomposa, Italy.
Tel: 0039 533 380216
Just 50 miles from Rimini Airport, this site offers direct access to a beach, as well as a toddler service.

Luxembourg
La Rochette
Camping Birkelt, Larochette, L-7601 Luxembourg, Luxembourg.
Tel: 00352 879040
This site is 15 miles from Luxembourg airport, and a toddler service is offered.

How safe is your playground?

Toddlers love playgrounds and most of the hotels, attractions, resorts, cities and regions I have recommended in this book offer playground facilities. Those playgrounds that are well maintained, imaginative, suitable for rainy as well as sunshine days, and well thought-out will amuse toddlers for weeks and days, not just hours. The perfect toddler-friendly playground should have a soft surface of sand, pea gravel or wood chips, at least 6 inches (15cm) deep or soft rubber mats to protect children when they fall. Grass, asphalt, concrete and dirt can cause serious injury in a fall. The most important thing you can remember, however, is: Never leave your toddler unsupervised.

Here is a checklist of things you should consider:
• Cloud or no cloud, make sure your toddler is well protected from the sun – ideally with hat, sunscreen and glasses.
• Always check to see if the equipment is age appropriate for your

---

children. Many playgrounds have equipment suitable for older children only, which can be very frustrating if you have chosen a hotel or resort principally for this facility. Brochures regularly fail to mention this minor detail, so you should speak to your travel agent, or the hotel or resort direct, and ask before you decide.

• Before letting your toddler loose, show them how to use the equipment properly and make sure they know that there is to be no running, pushing or hurting other toddlers. They should also learn to have respect for other children and people using the equipment.

• Tell them that they must hold handrails at all times

• Always keep toddlers within arms' reach.

• Ideally they should stay within 5 feet (2 metres) of the ground.

• Remind toddlers every hour or so not go in front of swings.

• Check the equipment for safety and inquire if the resort/hotel conducts weekly safety inspections.

• Check that your toddler's clothing cannot get caught on the equipment, and remove any strings, scarves and dangling bits.

• Check that metal slides, steps and platforms are not too hot to touch

• Toddlers should wear shoes at all times on playgrounds – sharp objects and glass are always a concern

• Tell children to slide down equipment feet first, one at a time.

• Most stationary equipment should have at least a 6-foot (3-metre) use zone in all directions.

• Any openings that can trap children (in guardrails or between ladder rungs) should be less than 3.5 inches (8cm) apart or more than 9 inches (22cm).

• Guard rails should surround all elevated platforms and should be at least 29 inches (72cm) high for preschool-age children and 38 inches (95cm) high for school-age children.

• Look for exposed concrete footings, tree roots or rocks that could trip children.

• Check for sharp edges and dangerous hardware, like open 'S' hooks or protruding bolts.

• Playgrounds should be maintained regularly. Report any problems.

Motorhomes

> We were touring Canada – the Rockies and Banff. I don't think we could have seen as much as we did if we'd stayed in a hotel or guesthouse. The campsites were great, the views were spectacular and the driving was a doddle on those roads. One thing, though, we did need to take lots of pit stops to stretch legs, which may make the journey take longer than you planned.
>
> Father of two, London

If you don't mind driving, this type of holiday may appeal. If, however, you don't enjoy spending a good proportion of your holiday behind the wheel, don't bother reading on. You will hate it.

Recreational Vehicles (RVs) provide a comfortable and familiar place to sleep each night on touring holidays. Packing and unpacking is simpler and, as a motorhome is usually higher than a car, your toddler will have a better view of the surroundings. An on-board kitchen offers convenience and potential savings, if you do the cooking and choose not to eat out. Campgrounds, which are particularly well maintained in France, North America and Britain, offer lots of facilities, and are great places for toddlers to meet other toddlers.

Motorhomes provide a unique way to explore the dramatic wilderness in countries around the world, including North America, New Zealand, Australia and South Africa. They are perfect for anywhere with a vast landscape that needs to be driven through to be appreciated, or when there are long distances between urban sprawls.

Popular motorhome destinations

In North America, the most popular areas are the South West (California, Arizona, New Mexico, Nevada, Utah and Colorado); North West and the Rockies (Washington State, Oregon, Idaho, Montana and Wyoming); New England and the North East. Also popular are New York state, the Capitol region (Washington DC, Maryland, Pennsylvania, Delaware and the Virginias, using the

---

Capitol KOA campground and one of their guided tours of Washington itself); Florida; and Alaska. Other beautiful destinations include Salt Lake City for a trip to the Grand Tretons and Yellowstone, Denver for a Wild West tour, the Pacific Coast route between Los Angeles and Seattle, or a Great Lakes tour starting in either Chicago or Toronto. Calgary and the Canadian Rockies are extremely popular, in Canada, or try a trans-Canada journey from Vancouver to Nova Scotia or Newfoundland.

In South Africa, the Garden Route is popular, with its beaches and scenic walks. Up through the Eastern Cape is the Shamwari Game Reserve, Addo Elephant Park, and traditional villages. KwaZulu-Natal offers Durban for beach front, Drakensberg mountains for drama, Hluhluwe-Umfelozi Game Reserve for wildlife, and more traditional villages. The Western Cape around Cape Town offers the wine regions. Motor homes are also popular in Kruger Park.

The more popular areas in Britain are Scotland (vast wilderness again), Devon and Cornwall, with smaller numbers visiting the Lake District, Wales and Yorkshire. Ireland is a popular destination to travel through in a motorhome – head up to the Giant's Causeway and Donegal and then down the west coast. Or head through Northern Ireland to Bangor, a popular seaside resort.

France is also easily travelled in a motorhome, and there are many campsites and parks to visit en route. More experienced and adventurous travellers may like to drive through France and down to Italy and Spain, or north to Scandinavia through Germany and the Netherlands.

Motorhome basics

Expect the vehicle to be just over 2 metres wide, close to 3 metres high, and between five and seven metres long. Vehicle options include motorhomes, camper homes (basically pick-up trucks with a caravan moulded on the back), van conversions, High Tops and A Class, all of which have variable living space. Hiring a motorhome shouldn't cost much more than a top-of-the-line car, but they can cost considerably more to run. Remember, however, that the cost of a motorhome covers your transportation (excluding petrol and other costs) as well as your accommodation, which can save you money. Be prepared to pay to park at campsites and holiday parks.

Before hiring a motorhome

- Don't choose this type of holiday if you don't like camping or outdoor life. You will be living in a fairly confined space for a period of time, and unless you are confident driving and love touring, forget the idea. As long as they are given sufficient pit stops, toddlers will love it.
- As with hire cars, you must pre-book a car seat for your toddler (see page 81) as well as a harness, if required. Be aware, however, that you may be let down by your operator if seats are in short supply. If you can, bring your own, checking in advance that it is compatible with the vehicle.
- The issue of seatbelts can also be a problem. Most car seats can only be fitted on forward-facing seats, with shoulder belts. If there are only four of these, you may find yourself without an appropriate seat – and belt – for all of your passengers in a five or six-berth motorhome. Unlike cars, motorhomes are not required by law to include rear seat belts. Contact the Motor Home Information Service (Tel: 01444 453 399) for further information.
- If you do decide to hire a motorhome, consider hiring for three weeks or more. There are frequently discounts if you hire for longer periods.
- Don't be tempted to take too much with you. Most vehicles are equipped with everything you will need, apart from bedding and towels. Gas cylinders, toilet chemicals, cutlery, crockery and glassware are usually included, though check when you book. A few will also include a guide to campsites. You will, however, need to bring your own toddler gear, such as bottle warmers (if required), changing mat and highchair. Some operators offer extras, so ask before you book.

- Watch out for the extra costs. If travelling to Ireland or the Continent you must notify your rental company so that they can arrange breakdown and other insurance for the vehicle. Note that you will need a bail bond if you are travelling to Spain. These extras will cost anything from £80 to £150 per week, dependent on which operator you choose. Ferry tickets usually need to be arranged independently and should be booked well in advance.
- Consider if you would like a walk-through model, which allows access from the driver's cab to the living area.
- Look for vehicles that have passenger seats close to the driver and front passenger. Your toddler will want to be able to communicate with you, and it saves having to stop every time you want to pass back a drink, snack or book.
- Always book well in advance to avoid disappointment. The months between April and October are always busy, with the peak time running in July and August. There are minimum rental periods, normally two weeks in high season or when travelling to foreign countries. You can normally book for a week in the off- or mid-season.
- If you are flying to a destination to pick up your motorhome (in the US, for example), it's a good idea to book an overnight stopover. You'll be able to start driving when you are rested and it gives you a little time to organise your belongings and to purchase any necessities before you hit the road. It's worth noting, too, that many operators will not allow you to begin driving on the day of arrival.
- Book a place at a campground for your first night. After that, try to book a few nights ahead of proposed stays. Campsites and parks can become very busy, and you may find yourself with nowhere to park. Depending on season and the advice of the operator always book a few nights ahead of yourself to ensure you have a space. It's sensible to plan a route (which can be fairly flexible) in advance, making reservations and bookings for your proposed stopovers.
- Get a good guidebook, either from your tour operator, or in bookshops, and research your journey before you plan to go. Most motoring organisations can provide you with a triptych, which is a

series of maps plotting your journey. These are extremely useful, as they normally provide up-to-date information on problem areas, such as roadworks.

Canada in a caravan

Matthew Collins has just written a book charting his experience crossing Canada with his two sons (seven and nine). It's worth reading to get a flavour of life with family in confined spaces – regardless of the weather. It's entitled *Across Canada with the Boys and Three Grannies*, published by HarperCollins, and available from all good bookshops.

Motorhome operators

In the UK you will probably have to go to one of the smaller operators – normally vehicle dealers who also rent. For details, contact the Motorhome Information Service on 01444 453 399 or on their website www.motorhomeinfo.co.uk. This is the best central information source with lists of UK companies.

Overseas operators

Motorhome Holidays

Tel: 01424 814 100

This company works with Cruise America and Cruise Canada, plus Maui, but you would have to book flights and other accommodation separately. This company operates in North America, Australia and New Zealand, and offers motorhomes that sleep anything from three adults to a maximum of four adults and three children. They operate in North America, Australia and New Zealand.

North America Highways

Tel: 01902 851 138, Website: www.northamericanhighways.co.uk

This company operates in Alaska, with rentals from Anchorage, tours generally up or down the Alaska Highway from Dawson Creek British Columbia to Fairbanks or into the Yukon. They offer special deals with prebooked campsites, and even one-way Alaskan cruises, with deals for toddlers.

Frontier Canada
Tel: 0208 776 8709, Website: www.frontiercanada.co.uk
An operator specialising in adventure and activity holidays to Canada, and also an agent for Canadream Campers, reported to have the best fleet in Canada. They do offer rentals for one-way journeys (in other words, you don't have to return to your point of departure). This company operates only in Canada.

Cruise America
Tel: 08705 143 607, Email: cruiseam@compuserve.com
This North American operator operates a fleet of 4000 vehicles, and books your first night hotel. Worth a visit.

Hemmingways
Tel: 01737 842 735, Website: www.hemmingways.co.uk
A specialist experienced in motorhome travel to many different destinations, this operator can also arrange flights, rail and ferry. Offers standard family VWs, pick-up campers, van conversions, fifth-wheel caravans and pick-up trucks, as well as mini- and full-size motor homes. They operate in North America, Australia, New Zealand, South Africa and parts of mainland Europe (principally France, Germany and Holland).

Combining holidays?
If you would prefer to combine a motorhome holiday with other types of accommodation or activities, motorhomes can be booked through the following.

Australasia
The Destination Group, Tel: 020 7400 7037
Travelmood, Tel: 020 7258 0280

Gold Medal, Tel: 08706 063 001
Airline Network, Tel: 0870 241 0003

North America
Airline Network, Tel: 0870 241 0003
American Connections, Tel: 01494 473 173
Bridge the World, Tel: 020 7916 0990
Flightbookers, Tel: 020 7757 2000
Just America, Tel: 01730 266 588
Jetset, Tel: 0870 700 4000
Premier Holidays, Tel: 01223 516 688
Quest Worldwide, Tel: 020 8547 3322
Trailfinders, Tel: 020 7937 5400

South Africa
Travelbag, Tel: 0142 088 724
Bluebird Holidays, Tel: 08705 320 000

Useful contacts
The Caravan Club
Tel: 01342 326 944
Membership benefits include ferry discounts and pre-booking at sites. Members should own a caravan or motorhome, or be hiring with view to buying.

Camping Cheque
Tel: 01892 559 855, Website: www.campingcheque.co.uk
This is a voucher system operated by the Caravan Club for members to prepay access onto a wide number of sites in France.

The Camping and Caravanning Club
Tel: 0247 669 4995
Membership provides foreign travel service to 18 countries, a technical advice service, a monthly magazine with tips, discounted insurance, maps, guides, and related items such as language videos for children.

The club operates 93 UK sites (all of which are toddler-friendly), and 1500 farm sites exclusive to members. They also hold pitches at 155 sites on the Continent, and produce a guide to UK sites with over 4000 entries, and a symbol indicating family friendliness. An affiliated French club produces a similar guide to over 8500 sites in France. The club provides a similar system to indicate child-friendly sites.

What you'll need

The prospect of camping with a toddler can be daunting, particularly when considering the extra clothes, toys and other items that might be required for what is effectively a self-catering holiday.

But don't get carried away. Most holiday parks and camps have washing facilities, and tumble dryers or lines, so you can pack pretty much the bare minimum and rinse or wash clothing as required. Furthermore, you'll find mini-marts on site at most camps, and hyper-markets or grocery stores in nearby towns (often better value), so take only a few food items and other necessaries to get you through the first day or so – until you find your feet and work out what's required. As a basic guideline, stick with the checklist on page 257, and add the following:

- Bug sprays and zappers (see page 162), a must for any outdoor holiday
- Sunscreens
- An extra towel or two (there's nothing worse than a wet towel, and they take some time to dry)
- Trial sizes of kitchen items, such as washing-up liquid, bleach, olive oil, pepper, and ketchup. Aim to fill a medium-sized cosmetic or zip-lock bag, and no more
- A waterproof sheet, which can be used on the ground, if in a tent, under a blanket on the beach or on a damp lawn, or as an impromptu tent in the event of a downpour
- Baby formula (if you are using it) or a long-life version of your child's normal milk
- Some small cereal boxes (for that first morning)
- An extra fleece or jumper for everyone
- A cagoule for everyone

- A fleecy blanket, which can double (triple) as a picnic blanket, a throw on chilly evenings, and an extra blanket on the bed

Health issues

Camping can be an exciting and relaxing holiday for parents and toddlers alike, but any holiday that takes place in the outdoors can increase the risk of health problems. The main issues will be oversun (see page 131), insect bites (see page 160), funny tummies (see page 233) and possibly problems with the water (see page 104). It's a good idea to be prepared for all of these possibilities, and you'll find details of a good first aid kit on page 225.

9. On Safari

I wish my parents had taken me on safari when I was a toddler.
All I thought about was lions and elephants, and its never quite
the same in a zoo. I now take my young children on safari in South
Africa, and just seeing the look on their faces is pure magic.

Mother of three from Devon

Most toddlers love animals – preferably those that they can touch and
hold. That's one reason why holidaying on farms, or visiting zoos and
theme parks with pet corners are such excellent toddler-friendly
holiday ideas. Wild animals are that much more exciting and exotic,
but obviously untouchable. In fact, the experience of seeing 'big', wild
animals can be unforgettable for toddlers.

The prospect of safariing with a toddler might fill parents with
horror, as it can be impractical, potentially dangerous and expensive.
In some African countries, such as Malawi and most parts of Kenya,
there is a good chance of catching malaria, and children are more
prone to this disease than adults. Yellow fever is also a risk in some
African countries. Furthermore, most toddlers do not fully undersand
the concept of danger, and may be tempted to pet, chase or stroke
real-life versions of their fluffy pets from home.

But safariing with a toddler is not only possible, but great fun,
when it's done safely, and under the supervision of a reputable operator that caters for children. In fact, the tour operators, African tourist
boards and parents who have undertaken successful safaris with
toddlers, all claim that it is the holiday of a lifetime. If you carefully
choose your game reserve, and a tour operator which offers a tailor-
made service for families with toddlers, its perfectly possible to have
a great, safe break. It is, however, all available at a cost! Safaris are

an expensive holiday, but if you've got the budget and the courage, give them a try!

Points to consider

- There are safaris and safaris. Canoeing and walking safaris are not good ideas with a toddler, partly because you and your child will be more exposed, but also because there is a risk of becoming separated. Choose a safari that is undertaken from a land rover or coach. Perhaps not as dramatic, but certainly safer for parents with young children.
- Africa is a big country, and not all of it is safe. In fact, the only two places I would recommend as safe safari destinations are South Africa and certain parts of Kenya. Kenya holds the danger of malaria (see page 199), which means that you may want to avoid it altogether, although inland sites hold much less risk. Try the ranches around Mount Kenya (such as Lewa and Borana) and the Rift Valley. South Africa has a lot to offer in terms of safaris that are toddler-friendly.
- Toddlers have a limited concentration span and, quite frankly, it is not worth taking very young children on game-viewing safaris, whatever the lodge or operator says. Children soon get bored and parents end up having a miserable time. You can expect to spend long hours without much to see, and big distances to travel. Unless you are prepared to entertain your child throughout the period, and possibly give up the possibility of seeing animals yourself, it's better to give it a miss.
- Be prepared to have an operator organise a private safari, as most operators will not allow children under the age of 12, unless they are travelling in a big party of people who know them and are willing to take responsibility for them. There are a few operators who will organise private deals, but parents must be aware of the malaria risk at all times.
- Toddlers will not be able to participate in the regular game drives. Babysitters and nannies are provided by specific tour operators, but you must book these at the time of check-in. Activities such as

191

videos, books and colouring are normally laid on. Shorter game drives (free of charge) can be arranged, subject to availability of land rovers and rangers. These services cannot be pre-booked.
- If you do plan to go on safari, contact MASTA (01276 685 040) or Nomad Pharmacy (020 7833 4114), who will advise you on medical issues, such as malaria and yellow fever.

Best information sources
- The African Travel and Tourism Association is extremely helpful and can provide advice and guidance about safariing with toddlers. Contact them on 01983 872 216, or on their website, www.atta.co.uk.
- Another useful site is www.safarilink.com.

Top-rated operators

The tour operators listed below have been recommended by parents who have tried and enjoyed the safari experience.

Ngala Private Game Reserve (9/10)
Kruger National Park, South Africa
Tel: 0027 11 809 4447, Website: www.ccafrica.com
Toddlers are welcome at Ngala Private Game Reserve, which prides itself on being child and family-friendly, offering specially structured children's programmes. On arrival at Ngala, all children are presented with a special eco-guide for planet-managers, containing a quiz, a learning guide and tips for spoor and animal identification. Rangers will help the kids complete their eco-guides, help them collect pods, feathers, bugs and leaves and teach them to identify different animal species. When all of the activities in the guide have been completed, the ranger will sign a certificate at the back stating that the child has graduated as a planet-manager!

Children are given aprons with specially designed pockets for collecting leaves and dung, as well as bug-boxes for bug-collection. Rangers take children on special 'Pooh Walks', during which they are

taught to identify dropping and spoor. There are also fishing and frog-
ging safaris, bark-rubbing expeditions, visits to the garage to oversee
land rover repairs, and lessons in making recycled paper, which can
be taken home.

If they aren't exhausted by all of this, the chef welcomes children's
assistance in the kitchen, baking cookies for afternoon tea. If there are
a group of children keen to eat in the boma (an open-roofed enclosure,
which keeps the wind and cold out), they'll have a special table set
for them, and they'll be given their own fire and marshmallows to grill
over the coals – always under a ranger's watchful eye. Parents can rest
assured their children will always be safe and well-cared for both on
and off game drives.

Other lodges within this group that cater for families include, Phinda
Mountain Lodge, Tau and Bongani.

Jack's Or San Camp (7/10)
Tel: 0026 34 860 064, Website: www.classicafrica.co.zw
Kids love the young guides at Jack's, as well as the quad bikes. They
have on occasion been known to strap baby car seats onto the handle-
bars with no complaints emanating from the babe involved. They don't
charge for babies under one year old. However, the minute that they
are mobile, they do charge full price because 'they are actually more
high maintenance than adults'. They will serve high teas, and serve
different meals for toddlers at different times, if required.

Ol Donya Wuas Lodge (8/10)
Tel: 0025 42 882 521/884475/882240, Fax: 0025 42 882 728,
Website: www.richardbonhamsafaris.com
At this safari lodge, there are seven individual cottages, built with local
material, and all with spectacular views of Mount Kilimanjaro. Each
cottage has an en-suite bathroom, and the electricity and hot water is
generated by a solar system. Two cottages have an additional bedroom
for young children. These family cottages are all on ground level with
good security for young toddlers. Both the family cottages are near the
dinning room, and arrangements can be made for one of their staff
members to stay with the young in the evening while their parents
are at dinner.

The open plains, rolling Chyulu Hills and snow-capped peaks of Mount Kilimanjaro evoke images of Africa as it was in the earlier part of the century; abundant game and Maasai herdsmen living as nature intended, show an unspoilt corner of Kenya.

The managers and the friendly crew of Kenyans organise the daily activities, to ensure that everything runs smoothly and to provide high standards of cuisine and personal service. Guests can go horseriding. walking or view game from open 4 x 4 vehicles. There are bush break-fasts, sundowners on kopjes and wonderful candlelit three-course dinners with a sky full of stars.

The owners – Richard Bonham and his sister Trish Luke – both have children. Richard actually lives in the Chyulu Hills with his family, which includes three and five year olds. and the managers also have a toddler (aged two) who is at the Lodge the whole time.

Mutumaiyu Lodge (8/10)
Tel: 0027 11 809 4447, 0025 42 882 521/884475,
Website: www.richardbonhamsafaris.com
Mutumaiyu comfortably accommodates up to six guests in three African-style cottages, traditionally thatched using 'makuti' (palm leaves) over a vaulted wooden frame. This is a family home, so books, art and music collections are yours to enjoy while you stay. The cottages are built of local stone and furnished with king-sized or twin beds. The rooms are large and can very easily accommodate an extra bed or cot for a toddler. The rooms are secure and the area around the lodge is walled in, so toddlers are very safe.

The managers will happily design a programme for the guests, which includes birdwatching, riding or walking with local Samburu tribesman and their camels. Donkey treks to the floor of the Rift Valley, a guided visit to the sacred Galla graves or a hosted visit to the primary school on Mugie ranch can be arranged.

Mutumiayu has a heated swimming pool with an unbelievable view across the plains. Lunch and drinks are served here. Other entertain-ment options include day and night game drives, guided bush walks, day trips to the local marketplace and farm tours. They can also arrange bush breakfasts or picnic hampers to take out on game drives.

During dinner, toddlers can, if the parents wish, stay with a staff member in their room. The managers have two young children, and a very capable nanny who would gladly look after any other toddlers visiting the lodge.

Both Ol Donya Wuas and Mutumaiyu are in radio contact with hospitals in Nairobi, and both lodges have airstrips.

Safari tour operators

Abercrombie & Kent (9/10)
Tel: 020 7881 9890, Website: www.abercrombiekent.co.uk
This company has just launched its first family-friendly brochure, which is excellent for those in search of ideas for travelling with toddlers. They recommend Ant's Nest and Horizon Horseback Safaris, as do the parents I interviewed. Ant's Nest can be contacted direct (Tel: 0027 14 755 4296, Website: www.waterberg.net).

Africa Exclusive (7/10)
Tel: 01604 628 979, Email:africa@africaexclusive.co.uk.
This operator offers tailor-made itineraries to Kenya and South Africa, among other places. All Kenyan camps recommended are fenced, making them safer. Flights in light aircraft can be arranged.

Africa Explorer (8/10)
Tel: 020 8987 8742, Brochure line: 020 8987 8742
Specialists in self-drive Land Rover safari holidays, either independently or with a guide. They focus on South Africa, among other destinations, and have a centre in Cape Town. Safari camping is reported to be very popular with toddlers and camps are fenced to protect them from the animals.

Africa Travel Centre (7/10)
Tel: 020 7387 1211, Email: africatravel@easynet.co.uk
This company has offices in Kenya. They recommend 'The South African Family Tour' of 15 days, travelling to the White River in the Eastern Transvaal, to the Movenpick Kruger Gate Lodge in a family room, on to Swaziland, Kwazulu Natal, and two nights at Shakaland, Durban and the garden route, and Cape Town.

Art of Travel (8/10)
Tel: 01285 650 011
Art of Travel offer a safari designed specifically for families, taking them to South Africa's malaria-free game lodges. Based in the Madikwe Game Reserve, the 16-day itinerary features:

- Bakubung Lodge (half-board), a comfortable base with all mod-cons, a vast hippo pool and regular game drives, swimming pool, tennis, and children's adventure playground.
- Madikwe River Lodge (8/10; full board), with 16 luxury chalets, swimming pool, bar, lounge, daily game drives and bird-viewing deck.
- Jaci's Safari Lodge (9/10, full board), which opened last year and comprises just eight thatched canvas-and-rock cabins overlooking a waterhole and the edge of the Marico River. The main complex, complete with local shop, curves around a huge anthill! The camp caters for children as young as two.
- Tau Game Lodge (8/10, full board), with 30 luxury chalets (each with en-suite bathroom, outdoor shower and private deck), overlooks the rolling Inselbergs hills. There is a bar, dining room and boma for bush dinners.
- Safari costs per person include flights, accommodation, most meals, transfers, guided game drives, activities, and park entrance fees.

Carrier (8/10)
Tel: 01625 582 006, Website: www.carrier.co.uk
Up-market tour operator Carrier features Jaci's Safari Lodge (see above) and Makwetti, a luxury lodge in Welgevoden Game Reserve, which caters for only 10 guests at a time. The reserve offers spectacular scenery, and chance to view the 'big five' and the endangered Brown Hyena.

Classic Retreats (8/10)
Tel: 0027 21 671 3102, Website: www.classicretreats.co.za
Not really wildlife safaris but giving a taste of it. The following Classic Retreat members welcome toddlers.

- Hout Bay Manor – Cape Town, Western Cape (This has babysitting facilities and a children's room. They also arrange packages for toddlers)
- Constantia Uitsig – Cape Town, Western Cape (Offers babysitting facilities and family suites, as well as children's menus)
- Roggeland Country House – Northern Paarl, Western Cape (Has family rooms and babysitting facilities)
- Le Quartier Francais – Franschhoek, Western Cape (With family suites, children's games and childrens' menus, and babysitting facilities)
- River Bend Country Lodge – Eastern Cape (Has children's room, children's menus, and babysitting facilities)

Classic Africa Safaris (9/10)
Tel: 0026 34 860 064, Website: www.classicafrica.co.zw
This company operates safaris to Jack's Or San Camp (see page 193), which welcomes toddlers.

Conservation Corporation of Africa (10/10)
Tel: 0027 21 425 0222, Website: www.ccafrica.com
CCAfrica is a multi-award winning, environmentally-friendly, world-class ecotourism enterprise with 27 lodges and camps in six Southern and East African countries: South Africa, Namibia, Botswana, Zimbabwe, Tanzania and Kenya. The company won environmentally friendly awards from both Conde Nast Traveller and Tatler in 2000 and 2001 respectively. Ngala, Tau and Bongani lodges (see page 192) are also award winners.

CCAfrica is Afro Ventures' preferred safari lodge operator for children. The company takes pride in their range of specially constructed children's safari programmes which bring the magic of Africa alive to youngsters through fascinating and entertaining activities. Children are presented with a special 'Eco-guide for Planet-Managers' (see page 192).

Richard Bonham Safaris (8/10)
Tel: 0025 42 882 521, Website: www.richardbonhamsafaris.com
This company operates safaris to the excellent Mutumaiyu, described

by a recent visitor as 'Heaven on a Hill'. It is a magnificent family-owned house in Northern Kenya, named after the ancient, twisted olive trees growing around it. Blending into the rock-strewn hillside, Mutumaiyu house is part of Mugie Ranch, a 49,000-acre working farm that rolls out across the plains of the Laikipia plateau, on the edge of the Great Rift Valley. They run their stock side by side with the wildlife (see page 194).

An alternative is Ol Donya Wuas, which is Maasai for 'Spotted Hills'. Ol Donya Wuas lies in the foothills of the Chyulu range, halfway between Tsavo and Amboseli. It is set on a concession of 300,000 acres of communal Maasai owned land, which is also part of the Amboseli eco-system (see page 193).

What you'll need

If you are thinking seriously about safariing, you'll need to discuss your plans in advance with a reputable tour operator or safari lodge. Depending on the local weather and types of insects, you'll require different clothing and sprays to combat insects and/or heat. This is one case where it's a good idea to go with the heavy-duty bug sprays, even if they are not something you would normally consider for a young child (see page 162). The risk of insect-borne disease is high in most safari regions, and it simply doesn't pay to take any chances. Go through the checklist for the basic beach holiday on page 257, and consider the following:

- Long trousers with socks and long-sleeved shirts for the early evening and morning, when mosquitoes swarm to feed
- A good supply of high DEET (appropriate for children brands only) concentration repellents
- Any prescription or OTC drugs you require regularly, as the selection is normally limited and expensive
- A camera with lots of film (and a zoom lens) and extra batteries
- Hats with shade brims
- Sunscreens
- Lip sunblocks
- Casual clothing that will layer. Choose lightweight materials, such as cotton

- Bring jumpers and jackets (light) for higher altitude destinations
- A comfortable pair of closed-toe shoes for everyone
- Short sleeves are necessary during the day, but long sleeves are essential in the evenings and early mornings
- Traditional safari colours (khaki and olive) are the best because they blend in and will not alarm the animals, but they are not essential
- A bathing suit and cover-up (most lodges and tented camps have pools)
- Nappies (if required) and formula, which may be difficult to get
- Boxed drinks and snacks
- First aid kit

Health issues

Travelling to any country in Africa can pose health risks, and it's sensible to prepare for the worst possible scenario. On page 231, you'll find details of vaccinations required before travel, as well as treatment for common health problems, such as diarrhoea. Here, however, we'll look at some of the main health issues that will affect travellers on a safari holiday.

Malaria

Think seriously before considering travelling to a country with malaria. Some experts report that malaria, which until 10 years ago was relatively easy both to prevent and cure, has now become resistant to virtually all drugs. If you need to go somewhere where there might be malaria, go to the experts for advice. It is a very serious disease, which kills millions of children every year, especially in Africa, south of the Sahara. Babies and toddlers are more vulnerable than adults.

Malaria is a parasitic disease, spread by mosquitoes. The disease produces severe fever and, in some cases, complications affecting the kidneys, liver, brain and blood, which can be fatal.

The period between being bitten by the mosquito and the appearance of symptoms is usually a week or two, but it can be as long as a year in someone who has been taking antimalarial drugs (which may suppress rather than prevent malaria). Symptoms include shaking, chills and fever, the latter being the classic determinant of the disease.

The fever normally has three stages – a cold stage of uncontrollable shivering, a hot stage in which the temperature may reach 40.5°C, and finally a sweating stage, which drenches the bedclothes and brings down the temperature. There will also be a severe headache, general malaise and vomiting.

Even people who take antimalarial drugs and precautions may contract malaria. Anyone in whom a fever and headache develops after returning from the tropics should see a doctor as soon as possible.

What to do

GPs rely on advisory organisations and experts when advising patients about preventing malaria, which is technically called 'prophylaxis'. Every six months the British National Formulary is published jointly by the British Medical Association and Royal Pharmaceutical Society of Great Britain, and covers all aspect of drug treatments, including malaria. As the insects evolve tolerance to drugs, the goalposts shift constantly and you and your GP need to consider the latest information when deciding how to protect your children. Not all drugs suitable for adults are suitable for children, and certainly not toddlers.

Different malaria regimes may be suggested by advisors in different Western countries, causing concern and confusion when parents compare notes in the field. And for the record, eating Marmite, or taking zinc and Vitamin A supplements, do not provide immunity against malaria as some reports suggest.

All malaria medications taste pretty horrible. Chloroquine is available in syrup form but this form is still bitter to taste, and must be taken after food. Take my word for it – your toddler will not willingly take it. One suggestion is to crush the tablets and mix with a little jam on a spoon, but even so you will need co-operation. Bear in mind that you will have to keep doing this for four weeks after you return.

Another alternative is to go for tablets. Mefloquine and Larium can be given to children above 3 months or 5kg in weight, and can be used where malaria parasites are resistant to chloroquine or proguinal/Paludrine.

Malaria information

For more detailed information about malaria, contact:

• The Malaria Reference Laboratory (Tel: 020 7636 3924)

• Malaria Healthline (Tel: 09065 508 908; £1 per minute at all times)

• The Malaria Foundation International was set up to 'facilitate the development and implementation of solutions to the health, economic and social problems caused by malaria' and produces up-to-date press releases and academic articles as well as a calendar of malaria oriented conferences and events (Website: www.malaria.org).

Insect bites

In Africa, insects can be a lot more dangerous than they can in Europe or even North America, largely because they are carriers of disease. On page 160, there is a good section on preventing insect bites. If your child does get bitten, however, the following will help ease the pain or discomfort.

What to do

• Dab the area with essential oil of lavender, which will help to encourage healing, soothe and reduce itching. It can also prevent scratched bites from becoming infected. Tea tree oil will do much the same thing.

• Calamine lotion can help itching. Dab it on and let it dry.

• If your child has a number of bites over his body, an oatmeal bath (a handful of oatmeal added to tepid water) can help to ease the itching.

• If your child does scratch the bites, cover them with small plasters to prevent infection.

• If the itching is unbearable, a mild antihistamine may be appropriate. But check with a local doctor before administering any medication, particularly if your child is taking antimalarial drugs.

Sunburn
See page 144.

Sunstroke and heat exhaustion
See page 142.

Vomiting and diarrhoea
See page 233.

10. Toddlercare

> I booked this resort hotel because it advertised a toddlers club and the activities for the toddlers sounded great. It also had great facilities for adults. I asked if the club would accept my two children – aged two and three – and the travel agent contacted the hotel who told her that they would. But when I arrived, I was told that the club was only suitable for children three years and over, despite the fact my two-year-old toddled very nicely. It was very inconvenient. We were there for two weeks and the younger child felt left out and frustrated. We were left to entertain him, which was fine, but it turned into a completely different holiday than planned and not as relaxing. Both my children are now over three, but I won't go there again out of principle.
>
> Mother from Suffolk, about resort hotel in the Caribbean.

Has this happened to you? The definition of a toddler varies from hotel to hotel, and from resort to resort. Most kids clubs offered by resorts and hotels start at three or four year olds, despite the fact that they claim to cater for toddlers. If you have a two-year-old who needs more stimulation that a babysitter can offer, you are likely to be out of luck.

The fact is that many parents are keen to involve their toddlers in at least some activity during the day, both to give them a chance to meet other children, and to allow some free time for parental rest and relaxation. The most successful family holidays appear to be those that cater for both parents and children, so that each gets a break and some fun time on their own.

According to the letters I received, it's not uncommon for parents to find that the kids club they booked well in advance is simply not suitable for their child, or the facility itself refuses to accept children so young. Make sure that you get all offers of places in writing, and ask them to stipulate the ages at which children are accepted. A great many clubs start from age four, so beware.

A potentially useful website is www.hotelguide.com, which lists the facilities available in most hotel resorts world-wide – identifying those with kiddies clubs, although not necessarily whether they are suitable for toddlers. The Ski Club of Great Britain also lists resorts that have kiddies clubs suitable for the under fives (contact them via the web, on www.skiclub.co.uk).

Preparation is the key to making a holiday with a toddler work for both you and them. Find out well in advance what is on offer, and make sure you ask the right questions. It's one thing to have problems that affect adult activities, but if your toddler is bored or unhappy, the entire holiday can be spoiled. Remember that childcare – in the form of babysitters, kids clubs, crèches, or just occasional organised activities – will only work if your toddler is happy with the situation. Only you know your toddler's interests and needs. Ask lots of questions and make sure that you are satisfied with the results.

Before making childcare decisions . . .
Consider the following:

- From around eight months onwards, children can suffer separation anxiety. Some parents feel that they just have to get over this. Others find that they feel unable to use the expensive childcare because they don't have the heart to leave a wailing infant. You may feel you have to spend time at the crèche while your toddler acclimatises, again wasting the money that was supposed to buy you time off.
- There are cultural differences in childcare. For example, in Asia, parents are happy to have their children in a much more competitive environment, where only the older children win. French childcare can be much harsher than most British toddlers are used to, for example on the subject of potty training. By contrast, Italian childcare will probably be much less proactive than the average British toddler is used to. Check out the facilities

yourself, and watch and listen before committing. If you think your child will be unduly daunted, give it a miss.

- You need to consider the issue of the carers' main language. Some parents considered this to be a problem at Club Med resorts in Europe. Toddlers who are able to talk can be extremely reluctant to stay with carers with whom they cannot communicate. Pre-verbal children, on the other hand, may settle well with almost anyone in a pro-child country because they sense the goodwill. And it's worth noting that toddlers left to their own devices with just a few foreign children, seem happy to find a way to play, despite having scarcely a word in common. This easy-going approach to play seems to fall off after the age of about eight.

- The quality of care is not what you were expecting: children are simply parked in front of a TV, carers spend more time talking to each other than with the children, there is a poor child to adult ratio, or all age groups are simply lumped together. What happens then? While there is little you can do in advance about unenthusiastic staff, you can check into the other issues. If there is anything in writing, for example in a brochure, you will be in a better position to complain if it isn't provided. Ask specific questions in advance, and request replies in writing.

- What if there aren't any toddlers of the same age as your own? Unless you go to a real specialist, this sort of thing can be difficult to check in advance. However, you can up the odds by travelling outside of school holidays with pre-schoolers, and throughout school breaks if you have school aged children who need companionship. If you are simply going with another family, try to ensure there will be reasonably matching ages. It can be horrible being three years younger than all the others.

- It is worth thinking through what your choices are before paying for something that might not work out, and simply won't be used.

- For younger toddlers (those in nappies) you need a crèche or other facility where you can feel safe leaving them. The physical area needs to be well set up, with lots of space out of the sun in hot climates, for example, sleeping areas and safe, supervised play things.

- Check what kind of activities are offered, what meals and equipment are provided, and the ratio of time spent in and out of doors.
- The best guarantee of quality is to use a reputable British operator. All those listed in this book follow the UK guidelines for carer-child ratios. Furthermore, if a company has invested in setting up this kind of childcare system, they'll be likely to ensure that the service is reasonable.
- With slightly older toddlers, you not only need to feel that the child is safe with the carers but also feel happy that the child feels he or she can communicate well and is comfortable with the other children there. This can be a particular issue in crèches run in non-British/English speaking resorts or hotels as well as resort crèches, for example in ski centres. Ask in advance how many English children are usually present.
- You should check how far you can roam when your child is in care. Some crèches only cater to children whose parents remain on the premises.
- If there is only a crèche rather than a kids club an older child may well be bored by the entertainment or the lack of playmates. This can be a problem outside of school holidays. It might be useful to book holidays when other countries have their breaks. Even if the children don't speak the same language, there will be someone there to kick around a ball, or to play in the pool.
- Don't forget to check out the age groups. Toddlers at the upper end of a division may well find themselves bored if most of the others in the group are much younger. With a specialist operator you should be able to check the ages of those already booked. You may find that your mature three-year-old would fare better in the four to six age group, rather than the two to three bunch. Note also that if divisions are too rigid siblings who would prefer to stay together may find themselves split up.
- If no provision for younger toddlers is mentioned, you can safely assume that they are not catered for until out of nappies. Even then, the emphasis is usually on slightly older children, and unlikely to suit under fours.
- If your children are gregarious enough to get on with any single

carer provided, and you have the budget, villas with single nannies might be the option to go for. Some selfcatering operators are also able to arrange childcare. Depending on what you and your toddler needs, this might be more suitable than having to fit in with kids club hours and activities. However, though this can be helpful, you need to consider what to do if the nanny and children don't hit it off.

How safe is the beach?

Pollution is on the increase, thanks to improved standards of living. The tourism industry is aware that dirty beaches and raw sewage in the sea damage earnings and there are constant initiatives to try to clean them up. Increased awareness about caring for the environment has resulted in more intensive monitoring of certain measurable markers, in particular the quality of the water. This is vital when travelling with toddlers, who are more vulnerable to infection than adults.

If you are travelling to a sand, sea and sun destination its important to know that the beach is safe for your toddler. Bathing water standards in continental Europe are generally higher than in the UK; more mainland European beaches have 'Blue Flag' awards.

On page 269, I have listed some of the safest beaches in the UK. For European destinations, check out http://europa.eu.int/water/water-bathing/index_en.html. This website, edited by the EU, covers all beaches in the EU and indicates where standards have been met. Some of the final detail links seem to be missing but this does include a tourist atlas of tourist beaches which provides some useful information.

Top tips for beach safety

Here are some other tips for ensuring a safe beach-side holiday with your toddler:
• Make sure toddlers don't wander off unsupervised when you are on a beach and always keep them in your direct vision.
• Beware the possibility of diseases, mainly gastro-intestinal, skin,

---

ear and eye infections, transmitted by water. Freshwater carries a different range of diseases to seas. For example, bilharzia or schistosomiasis is found only in freshwater.

• Ask locals about safety. British waters are dangerous due to high tidal ranges (among the world's highest), rip currents in some places, currents, low water temperatures and changeable weather.

• Look for steep shelving which means that children could get out of their depth without realising it.

• Check tide times. This is less of a problem in the Mediterranean but potentially significant elsewhere, especially around the UK, Ireland and the Bay of Fundy in Canada. UK Coastguard statistics indicate that around a quarter of incidents involving marine rescue services involved people being cut off by the tide or stranded.

• Check wind direction. In some places there is a daily offshore wind, for example in the afternoon, which can make inflatable items like lilos particularly dangerous. Rubber dinghies, air beds and surfboards were responsible for a further quarter of problems handled by UK coastguards.

• Most resort beaches should be served by lifeguards in season. However, you should check that they are operational.

• If you see anyone in trouble on the UK coast you should dial 999 and ask for the coastguard.

• Overseas, ask in advance what to do if anyone does get into trouble. There may be lifesaver services but it would also be useful to know about any first aid post or telephone.

• Take it in turns to be responsible for watching out for your toddler, or being with them in the water.

• In even shallow water toddlers can be knocked over by waves or by the wash from passing boats. If they can't swim or they panic, they can drown. Even in the Mediterranean in July you can find waves strong enough to knock over a teenager.

• In the UK, a red and yellow flag means a lifeguard is on patrol. A red flag means do not go into the water, a quartered black and white flag means it is an area for surfers and body boards, but not safe for swimmers and bathers.

- Overseas, different flag codes are used. Broadly, a red flag means danger and advice not to swim. A yellow flag means you are allowed in but it may be hazardous. A green flag indicates an all-clear and a chequered flag may indicate that the lifeguard is not currently in attendance. At Agadir in Morocco, black means danger, red is a warning and yellow means safe. Swim only between the marker that indicates an area is patrolled by lifeguards. If there are no flags don't assume it is safe.
- For more information on Sea Safety in the UK, see www.sea safety.org.uk. This is the Royal National Lifeboat Institute website and has an hyperlink to Sea Smart, PO Box 6, Hampton, Middlesex TW12 2HH, the national safety campaign run by the Maritime and Coastguard Agency.

Kids Clubs

No two kiddies clubs are alike. Confident and outgoing toddlers will enjoy meeting new friends, even if only some of them speak the same language; less gregarious toddlers, however, might have nightmares about returning to the place each day. Gear your choice of kids clubs to your individual toddler, and make sure that the arrangements are flexible. You may find that he enjoys it so much that he wants to spend whole days at the club, or you may find that your pre-booked, full-time club is simply not appropriate for more than a few hours a day. Choose clubs that can gear arrangements to individual toddler's needs.

Furthermore, some clubs will be better managed than others, with qualified staff who have a limited number of toddlers under their care. Check the staff-child ratio before you book. Some clubs cater for very young children, while others only take children from the age of three or four. Don't, however, be put off by stiff regulations. If you have an extrovert two-year-old, who is more than able to hold his own in the three-plus club, ask them to make an exception. Some tour operators have realised that flexibility is a much better policy, and have adapted their product accordingly.

Checking out the kids clubs

When I first started to travel with Tom I actively looked for hotels and resorts with kiddies clubs. To my disappointment I found lots of family-friendly hotels and restaurants, but they were only appropriate if you had a baby or a child of school age. It became increasingly obvious that toddlers are non-people.

Here are some tips to find out if the kids clubs you have chosen are designed with you and your toddler in mind:

• Review safety concerns with your child and staff
• Check for age appropriateness and safety before leaving your child
• Review pick-up procedures with staff
• If your toddler has any special needs, allergies or fears, make sure that the staff are aware of them. Call ahead to inquire about allergy precautions
• Advise staff of your whereabouts while your toddler is in the club, and make sure they know how to contact you, or a friend or relative in case of emergency
• Resorts/hotels with this kind of facility should include this information on the child information sheet. This should be updated each time a child is left in the club if necessary
• While not always available, it is preferable that the club/kids room have exclusive use of lavatory facilities designed for children
• Before children are taken to a club, they should be sunscreened, even if the majority of the activities take place inside
• Check staff ratios to children so that you feel comfortable with supervision of the children. Suggested ratios are: for infants under 18 months, three staff members for every 10 infants; for toddlers aged between 18 and 30 months, there should be one staff member for every five children; preschool children (30 months to five years) should be cared for with one staff member for every eight children; five to six year olds need one staff member for every 12 children, while children over the age of six should have one staff member for every 15 children. If activities take place by water, all of these ratios should be improved

> • Overseas hotels and resorts have no obligation to adhere to these standards, though British operators offering this kind of service generally report that they do

Are kids clubs for you?

- As childcare is expensive, you may find that a good proportion of your holiday budget is wasted if you don't use it. Consider your needs well in advance of travelling, and if you really don't want or need childcare, avoid resorts that offer it in the price. It's a hidden extra that you will be subsidising whether you use it or not.
- Todder's behaviour can rapidly descend to the standards of the lowest common denominator. In broad terms, this means that the more children there are around, the worse behaved they may all be. For parents who require good behaviour from their offspring, running around at meal-times, shouting, throwing food and more, can all become extremely wearing and probably not worth the bonus of the extra childcare offered.
- Good places with childcare can be very heavily booked and tend to exploit this so, for example, all meals have to be booked well ahead, especially at key times like Sunday lunch. This can make what is supposed to be a relaxing experience feel far too regimented.
- You simply may not be comfortable leaving your child on his own all day. If you have reservations, you may want to consider some of the other, more flexible options, or give it a go on your own.

What if there is no kids club?

Choosing a destination that is more family orientated and welcomes toddlers is one way to ensure that you are surrounded by many other families with the same needs and tolerance levels. This can work well in resorts or destinations where kids clubs are simply not available.

211

However, problems can arise when children of different ages are thrown in together. Toddlers will and do become intimidated by older children, and this is particularly apparent in mixed pools. For this reason, I recommend choosing resorts that either have specifically targeted kids clubs for toddlers, or special parts of the resort or pool area for little ones only. Toddlers need extra special care.

If all you need is the occasional night's babysitting, a good operator should be able to organise this for you.

Beach entertainment

Toddlers understand the beach, and you'll find that they can pretty much create their own entertainment with a little sand and surf to hand. Buy a couple of inexpensive toys (balls, spades and buckets), as well as a set of water wings (arm bands) for safety, and you'll be set.

Holiday childcare options

If you don't want to pay for childcare, sharing a holiday with another family can be a good bet. Consider holidaying with people with whom you can share childcare. One option is to self-cater with another family, or even willing grandparents. Meet up beforehand to ensure you are working to similar budgets, and go for an equal financial division of everything, from the deposit onwards. Financial equality is important to keep everyone happy. Make sure there is advance discussion of any expected exchange of childcare/babysitting stints, particularly with older relatives who may be looking forward to spending time with you.

Arrange in advance what toys you are going to be taking in order to get a wide selection that can be shared. But avoid prized items which are likely to be fought over and those (like felt pens) which, in the wrong hands, could cause expensive damage. Beware of couples whose relationships appear to be in trouble. A second family may be invited simply to shore it up. And don't do it at all if you think that the stress of holidaying together could harm the friendship. Even the best friendships can hit rocky ground when you are spending 24 hours a day together. Choose wisely, and preferably someone with whom you already spend a great deal of time.

Remember, too, that although the parents get on, it doesn't necessarily mean that the children will, too, even if they are of appropriate ages. Children quickly develop a pecking order and this can create tensions in parents.

Take adjoining self-catering properties rather than one large one. Then, socialising can be restricted to whatever is comfortable, particularly in bad weather when toddlers can be difficult. It also means a crying or disruptive toddler won't wake others. If two properties are out of the question, at least consider separate bathrooms. Bathroom habits can be a particular cause of trouble. Lastly, try to take your own cars so you can go off as separate parties when you feel like it.

What do you need?

Whatever style of care you opt for, you should consider in advance the number of hours you will need. Pay-as-you-go can work out to be better value than advance block-booking, particularly when you don't know what you will need. You may find, for example, that both you and your toddler are happier on your own, with plenty to do and see. Conversely, at peak periods you could find that the crèche is full if you haven't booked ahead.

In general, the major childcare providers are completely booked up over the summer holidays, but you might be able to book on the spot at other times. Childcare arranged through self-catering operators is much more flexible.

Though full daycare leaves parents free to spend whole days exploring (or relaxing) on their own, for those who want simply to give the children some time with playmates, and then spend family time together, it can be cheaper and just as successful to go for somewhere offering shorter hours. A combination of three hours a day, alternating between mornings and afternoons, can be particularly useful as it allows for different types of outings together.

Check if you can arrange care once you have started your holiday. Sometimes you don't know what will suit until you get there, and some children who are fine with carers at home hate being left by parents with strangers in a strange place.

It may sound obvious, but it is a very good idea to tell your babysitter as much as you can about your toddler and his likes, dislikes and habits. Children are raised very differently in countries around the world, and your toddler may be thrown by a completely strange approach. What's more, your sitter may have little idea about such things as administering medicine that may have been prescribed to your child. Provide as many details as possible, and don't forget to let them know where you will be!

Taking childcare with you
Some families prefer to take their own nanny, au pair or babysitter with them. This usually means less privacy and it can be complicated setting boundaries between work and relaxation in a holiday environment. Even those who can afford it often find that it did not provide the degree of relaxation they had hoped for. If you are considering this, here are the factors to consider:

- Define working hours and time off, as well as details of pay, well before you set off on holiday. You should also clarify whether or which meals will be eaten together and whether she or he will be joining the family on outings/evenings out.
- Looking after toddlers in an unfamiliar environment can be harder work than at home, with none of the usual fall-backs. There may also be homesickness to contend with. Some extra consideration, time off or perks would therefore be a good idea.

Other arrangements
You may be able to arrange childcare once you arrive at your destination, and it's a good idea to keep an open mind about the options. As long as you have a clear idea of what you expect from care, you should be able to negotiate a successful arrangement. Consider the following:

- If you are at a small hotel and can see how well one of the staff gets on with your toddler, that may be good enough for your purposes.

214

- If you are using a more formal set-up, for example an agency recommended by your hotel, qualifications are a useful marker of the quality of what is being offered. You might also like to check out the carer in person, though this may only be possible too late in the day to be of much practical use. In more developed countries you could look at least for the qualification required to work in the local summer camps.
- In the US the minimum requirement for those employed in crèches is child first aid and two years' experience with children. If the childcare is on dedicated premises, carers should be licensed, bonded and insured. Note also that privately employed babysitters in the US tend to be very young (around 16) and not really capable of looking after a baby, whatever the local custom.
- In smaller centres in countries like Greece, Turkey, North African countries and further afield, carers tend to be found more informally. In many larger resort hotels you may well find people who are missing their own children and are only too happy to play with yours. A potential disadvantage is that the children may well get spoilt in these kind of environments, being fed all kinds of sweets and treats you might prefer that they avoid.
- However you arrange babysitting, always check whether the price you are quoted is per child or for all of the children.
- Once they reach an age when they can be relied on not to stray or do anything dangerous, children may not need designated carers. Self-catering properties with a single shared pool (common in Corsica and found also in Tuscany, northern Portugal and mainland France) can be a good way for children to mingle with peers without all the club issues.

Before you book

If you are arranging childcare, whether through a tour operator, your accommodation, a local agency or a personal contact, you should check:

- What amount of notice is required.
- What the rates are.

- Whether the sitter has any experience of dealing with children of the age and nationality of yours.
- Whether the sitter speaks English.

Food for thought

When Tom was a baby, he would feed regularly and often. Now that he is toddler he is fussier about when and what he will eat and the whole process of meal times can become very fraught. Ironically, it is much easier when we are travelling as the boredom factor fails to set in.

Local food is often a much better option than choosing western-ised food which your toddler may recognised but may not be cooked as well or under the same conditions as at home. Local food is also fresh, appropriately seasoned for the climate (for example in hotter, more humid climates where toddlers could get dehydrated and lose salt, local foods are usually more highly seasoned) and easily avail-able. Tom tries all sorts of foods at home (Italian, French, Indian, Thai, etc.) so he's more adventurous when travelling overseas. For that reason, it's a good idea to try out a little 'local' cuisine before you go. Annabel Karmel's series of books for toddler food have some brilliant, tried-and-tested menus and recipes. Worth a visit before you travel!

It's a good idea, however, to stick to bland, familiar foods when you first arrive at your destination. The digestive system of toddlers can be easily upset, and it's best to introduce new foods more slowly – including interesting tropical fruits and vegetables – to avoid a bout of upset tummy or diarrhoea.

Most restaurants are flexible about producing food that your toddler will know. Rice, pasta, noodles and potatoes are always good and safe standbys. Bread is found in virtually every country round the world, and is usually a safe bet.

If your toddler has an allergy, go prepared. For example, Tom is allergic to dairy produce, and we use a goat's milk formula instead. This can be easily prepared for cereals in the morning, or anything else that requires milk, and is transportable without fuss. It's particularly useful in countries, such as the Far East, where dairy produce is hard to come by.

Don't forget snacks! Always bring along a supply of familiar, easily transported snacks, such as muesli bars, biscuits, rice cakes, raisins and dried fruit bars, which can be relied upon in an emergency. This is ideal when your toddler refuses to eat anything else and is particularly useful when travelling off the beaten track.

Encourage your toddler to try food from your plate. There is something tantalising about other people's food, and it works for toddlers, too!

Finally, when purchasing food in other countries, stick to organic whenever possible. There are international guidelines for the production, manufacture and even transportation of these goods, and you can be sure that you are getting something that is untainted and healthy. This is particularly important if your toddler is very young. Good brands, such as Baby Organix, are invaluable on holiday. Bring along a few jars for emergencies.

Dining out

- When eating out, visit the restaurant before you make a decision to go. This will allow you to see if your toddler will be welcome and if they have the general facilities to cope with your bundle of fun. Avoid restaurants, cafes and brasseries that only welcome 'well-behaved children'. There is no such thing as a well-behaved toddler – ultimately, your toddler will behave how he feels on the day.
- Avoid places that pride themselves on being bastions of quiet civility and sophistication. You may love it, they will loathe it and neither of you will enjoy the experience. A tugged tablecloth, for example, can result in the entire contents of the table ending up on the floor/over your toddler.
- Take all temptations such as nibbles and breadbaskets from the table to avoid your toddler consuming the basket and not touching the food about to be served.
- Go to places with a child's menu (most offer nuggets, chips,

burger, chips, and more chips). Although you may not want to choose the offered fare, the fact that they have a menu means that they have at least acknowledged the existence of toddlers. More restaurants now offer adult meals in child-sized portions. If it's not obvious, ask.

- Choose restaurants with patios or outdoor conservatories. Noise is much less of a problem and there is often running-around space where children can let off steam while waiting for the food to arrive and adults to finish. As long as the weather is good, your toddler will be able to draw and play games without being scowled at.

- I always try to choose restaurants with high chairs. These come in a variety of different styles – from the designer versions at the Conran restaurants to the more basic versions at Burger King. Many high chairs consist of no more than a chair with an attached table. This can be difficult if you have a child who grabs everything within arm's reach. If the chair comes with a table take a wet wipe to clean before use.

- Now Tom is older I take a booster seat. Clip on seat or one of the fabric restraints can be equally as useful but the safety of any of these is variously reliant on how tightly you can secure them to the chair or table and whether the chair or table is stable enough to hold the weight/wriggling of the child concerned. Check this before getting settled.

- If you are new to eating out as a family, do so at lunchtime when your toddler will not be quite as tired, and when even serious restaurants are more relaxed and less busy.

- If I am eating with Tom in the evening, I make sure that he has an afternoon nap. Think about offering a light snack before going out, to avoid spiralling hunger (and inversely proportionate behaviour) while you wait!

- 'Ethnic' restaurants (Indian, Chinese, Thai, Indonesian, Turkish, Lebanese and African) are the best option with toddlers, unless they are very smart and fashionable.

- Always make a reservation and use this opportunity to check attitudes to toddlers. If you use a buggy you might like to check in advance whether this is allowed in the restaurant at the table. This is less likely in the more cramped but characterful spots.

- Be assertive and ask for your toddler to be served as soon as you are seated. This might mean ordering on the telephone in advance, or while waiting in a queue, but it's well worth the effort.
- Introduce the concept of toddler-friendly restaurants as early as possible (Café Rouge, Brewsters or Pizza Express in the UK are good bets), so that the idea of sitting, waiting and eating at a table is not alien!
- Aim to eat before peak times so that the kitchen can process your order faster, the staff is likely to be more attentive and your children are less likely to irritate co-diners.
- Take along something to entertain children while they are waiting, such as pencils, a colouring-in book or a small portable game, which isn't likely to end up too riotous. Books are great, though a bit anti-social, if your toddler is able to read himself or you aren't going to be embarrassed by reading aloud. Best of all teach your children to play card games; a pack of cards is easy to take anywhere and even 4-year-olds can manage snap.
- Restaurants with aquariums are a good choice for toddlers.
- Avoid restaurants where they cook at the table. This is exciting but dangerous with toddlers.

Lots to drink

It's important to remember that toddlers will become easily dehydrated in hot countries, and they will need plenty of fresh water throughout the day. A good bet is to supply a leakproof water bottle, which they can carry on a strap around their neck, or in a backpack. Wash it carefully every night, and freeze freshly boiled, cooled water (or mineral water, see page 104) so that the drink remains cool the following day. Remember that juices and artificially sweetened drinks can actually increase thirst rather than quenching it.

If milk still forms a significant element of your children's diet you need to think about the quality of what you might find on the spot or what might work as a substitute. If you have doubts

---

about the purity of the local milk you could buy or take your own UHT milk cartons. These are heavy and take up space but will leave plenty of space for packing souvenirs on the way back. Many toddlers really dislike the flavour, so get them to try it before filling your suitcases with gallons of the stuff.

Yoghurt is normally widely available even where milk is not (in India, for example) and it normally contains healthy bacteria that wards off more inhospitable germs. A good choice in a hot country. If your child is still drinking formula milk, take enough to cover the whole trip, plus more. If you run out you may be unable to find the same brand.

In an emergency, take an empty tin to the local pharmacy and ask for the nearest replacement. Don't buy powdered milk not designed for babies, which does not have the same nutritional value as formula.

10 Tips for Healthy Eating on Holiday

1. Chopped fresh fruit is a nutritious food that a child can hold and eat alone on a long journey. If you are giving your toddler non-organic fruit, wash and peel it first (in bottled water if necessary). Don't offer any fruit with a broken skin.

2. Avoid citrus fruits until your child is at least a year old. When introducing, do so gradually and monitor your child for any allergic reactions. Once your toddler is past the critical stage, citrus fruits are a great snack and contain lots of vitamin C.

3. When on long journeys, choose foods and drinks that are nutritious and non-perishable. Items like rice cakes, breadsticks, fruit, cereal bars, dried fruit and even frozen 'tubes' of fromage frais, are a good choice for toddlers. Avoid anything slippery, such as chocolate, bread and jam and soft fruits, like bananas. Cut up anything that could present a choking hazard, such as grapes. Freeze boxed drinks and water bottles the night before, to ensure a supply of cool liquid.

4. Ensure foods are well cooked and served hot, right after

cooking. Never eat leftovers or food that has been displayed for a long time. Avoid raw seafood wherever possible.

5. Make sure dairy products (milk, cheese, yoghurt) are pasteurised. Milk may harbour disease-producing organisms. If you aren't sure, boil the milk before serving.

6. Avoid ice cream in all developing countries.

7. Rice, grains and pulses are nutritious and safe if cooked properly. Always eat rice when it is hot and never reheat once it has become cold.

8. Spicy food can be very popular with toddlers, but be careful not to overdo it. Always taste the food first when you are abroad, as it can be considerably spicier than we are used to in the UK.

9. Use bottled water in parts of the world where chlorinated tap water is not available (see page 104). Try to avoid tap water and ice in these areas, which could be contaminated. Bottled water is generally declared safer while travelling, and a good tip is to ask for the bottle with the lid still on, when eating in a restaurant. That way you will know that the water is as on the label. If in doubt, ask for carbonated and make sure it fizzes!

10. If you would prefer fruit juice, and you can't take your own, this is safer if it is pressed in front of you.

11. In Sickness and in Health

Toddlers are more prone to illness and accidents than any other group of children, and according to the thousands of letters I received from parents while researching this book, it can be a real problem when travelling.

In reality, however, toddlers are just as likely to suffer from illness and accidents if you stay at home, so there is little argument in favour of doing so. The best advice is to be prepared for all eventualities, and to know what to do if your toddler does become ill. A little knowledge goes a long way.

While most parents set out to be vigilant about what their toddlers eat, where they walk, and what they touch, it's virtually impossible to keep tabs on them 100 percent of the time. And it's in those few moments, of course, that most accidents happen.

But there are ways to prevent accidents from happening, and with a little foresight, you can help to ensure a healthy, happy holiday. The same goes for health problems. Inevitably your child will resist anti-malaria medicine, for example, or develop an unhealthy fascination with a rabid dog, so be prepared to deal with problems that might arise. Most healthcare involves using common sense, staying calm, and administering treatment with the minimum of fuss. Whatever happens, don't panic. Your toddler will sense your concern, and things can only become worse.

Bring along a first aid kit on all travels, and talk to your GP or practice nurse before you go, to ensure that you have treatment for all possibilities covered. They will also be able to advise you on which vaccinations (if any) are required. Another good source of information is the British Airways Travel Clinic Hotline (Tel: 01276 685 040).

Be prepared

Don't burden yourself with unnecessary tablets and bandages if you are travelling to a holiday village in Northern Europe, for example, or any other place with a fully equipped medical centre on site. A basic travel first aid kit will do the job. On the other hand, if you will be travelling extensively, and in countries where the medical care may not be readily available or even up to scratch, it's worth bringing a fully equipped kit, to prepare you for all eventualities.

You'll also need to take steps to ensure that your toddler stays healthy, by making sure they get enough sleep, eat well and healthily, are dressed appropriately for the climate, are protected from the sun and from insects, and are immunised against any potentially dangerous diseases. A little preventative action can help to keep your toddler healthy and happy throughout the holiday.

Planning your medical care

- Once you have decided on a destination contact your GP, practice nurse or the British Airways Health Clinic Hotline (Tel: 01276 685 040) to update yourself on necessary vaccinations. Give details of your travel plans, including region within the country, season and type of accommodation and activities.
- Purchase a relevant advice book (*Your Child's Health Abroad*, by Jane Wilson-Howarth and Matthew Ellis, is a good starting point).
- If you are travelling to a part of the world where extra immunisations (see page 231) are recommended, you need to consider which vaccines your toddler requires at least eight weeks before travel. Some vaccines, such as oral polio, MMR, and yellow fever jabs, should not be given within three weeks of each other. You will need to be sure that your toddler has worked through any reactions before travelling. Yellow fever vaccination should only be given to babies under nine months if there is no alternative. Ideally, babies should not travel to yellow fever areas. General guidelines are widely available but advice should be taken for an individual itinerary, as there are often different recommendations for different parts of countries.

- Pick up an E111 form (at the back of the 'Health Advice for Travellers' booklet) from a UK Post Office, or by phoning 0800 555 777, from Monday to Friday, between the hours of 8am and 6pm. This form, once completed and stamped, will entitle you to various levels of reciprocal medical care in other countries, principally in the EU. But note that the care offered is seldom of the level provided at home, and almost always costs more.
- In many countries, including those that are less developed, pharmacists are highly trained, often speak English, and may be able to supply the help you need on the spot. But don't rely on this facility. I suggest going to the nearest international chain hotel and ask for the house doctor, who is certain to speak English.
- If you are particularly concerned about a specific health issue and have booked through a tour operator, demand to be provided with appropriate details in advance. The operator should be able to give you the name and contact number of a suitable doctor or clinic. One company – Options Travel Insurance – details approved clinics to travellers to Spain taking out a travel policy with the company. Note that not all medical care is equal and even going private fails to guarantee the highest standards.
- Wherever you go, remember that many less developed parts of the world are still enthusiastic about medical drugs in a way that people in the UK are not. Injections are often given when tablets, syrup or suppositories could be given instead. If you are offered a prescription, ask for details of potential side effects. Check the expiry date of all medication you are offered.
- Always take out health insurance, either through your tour operator, or privately.

Health on the web

Check out www.doh.gov.uk (health advice for travellers from the British Government including details of Form E111); www.medi search.co.uk (medical site with details of what immunisations you need for where); www.fco.gov.uk/travel (travel advice from the Foreign & Commonwealth Office); and www.worldclimate.com (for climate records and information). There are also literally hundreds of website devoted to health problems, so it might be worth reading up on the treatment of common ailments before you travel. A good one to try is www.netdoctor.co.uk.

First aid kits

First aid kits are a requirement in some countries, and an absolute necessity in countries where the medical attention is patchy or poor. While a ready-prepared kit can be extremely useful, it's worth considering an individual kit, made of the types of things that you are most likely to require. Remember things like extra contact lens lotion for yourself; in some countries, it's difficult to find what you need. Your first aid kit should, ultimately, be your own personal pharmacy. But don't go overboard. Most countries will have what you need. Find out in advance what's available, and create your kit to fill the holes, and to have the obvious treatments for common ailments to hand. Plasters will, of course, be number one on your list.

Ready prepared kits
If you don't have the time to prepare your own first aid kit, buy one from one of the specialists in this field. You will need to check that the contents are suitable for babies and toddlers.

Car first aid kits are compulsory in some European countries, such as Switzerland. They are also recommended in Germany and Belgium.

DIY kits
The following list offers a variety of different items that might be useful for various health problems and accidents. By no means do you need to take them all. Check the ones that are most appropriate for your family (if you have a toddler who is susceptible to tummy bugs, for example, you'll almost certainly want to include treatment for these), and put together a kit designed for your individual needs. While some of these items may be available in other countries, your toddler may

feel more comfortable with a label he recognises, and you will also feel happier that you know what you are offering. Drugs with labels in foreign languages, dispensed by non-English-speaking physicians or pharmacists, can be difficult to comprehend, and you may not be at all certain what you are taking.

- Rehydration sachets (Dioralyte, Rehidrat, Electrolade taste the best of the bunch, and come in a variety of different flavours). This is essential for all ages and should form part of every travel health kit.
- You can also make your own oral rehydration solution, using 2 teaspoons of sugar and 2 pinches of salt in a glass of fresh water or juice.
- Paracetamol, Calpol, Disprol or other infant analgesic (not aspirin for under 12s), with measuring cup, spoon, dropper or oral syringe. Note that paracetamol is called acetaminophen in the US.
- Antihistamine tablets for bites, allergies and itchy skin conditions (such as poison ivy or poison oak).
- Calamine lotion for insect bites and itchy skin problems.
- Treatment for sunburn, such as Aloe vera lotion, lavender essential oil, or cooling sprays.
- Plasters.
- Bandages. High-tech dressings are now available, and may be appropriate. Consider the ActivHeal range, which is designed to help the natural healing processes and reduce scarring. It is available from independent pharmacies.
- Antiseptic wipes.
- Antiseptic solutions, such as TCP, Dettol, tea tree oil, iodine or Savlon dry spray.
- The homeopathic remedy Arnica, in tablet and ointment form for bumps and bruises, or any injury.
- Calendula ointment for cleaning minor cuts and grazes.
- Sterile (ideally waterproof) dressings. Melonin non-stick dressings may be useful.
- Micropore or zinc oxide tape, to fix dressings.
- Steristrips and butterfly closures are useful for more serious cuts that do not need professional stitching.

- Pointed tweezers for splinters and spines. Finger and thumb or a drop of alcohol is enough for tick or leech removal. Also useful can be a needle and a little olive oil. When removing a bee sting, ensure that you grasp the barb from the side, parallel with the skin, and do not squeeze the venom sac.
- Safety pins and nappy pins.
- A thermometer. Mercury thermometers are banned on airplanes. Chemical strip thermometers are less accurate but more portable.
- If your toddler is prone to infections that are normally treated with an antibiotic, I recommend you ask for a prescription so you can take some with you on holiday.
- Adequate supplies of any drug that may be regularly required. Know its generic name, not just the UK trade name, which may be different overseas. You can check with the relevant embassy or high commission if you have any doubt about whether the medicine can be taken to the country you intend to visit. Carry a doctor's letter stating the drug name, dosage and reason for use, which is very useful when communicating with Customs officers, doctors or pharmacists overseas.
- Activated charcoal is used in some cases of poisoning; by binding the poison in the stomach, it reduces absorption. It can be given safely to any conscious casualty, ideally within 2 hours of taking the poison, or longer for slow release drugs. It is particularly useful for preventing the absorption of drugs such as antidepressants which are toxic in small amounts. UK products include Carbomix by Penn, Liqui-Char by Oxford and Medicoal by Concord.
- Any allergy medications, including those appropriate for wasp or bee sting allergies. If you or your child has an allergy, you are advised to bring along an epipen, which allows self-injection of adrenaline in an emergency.
- Hyoscine tablets (UK trade names include Joy-rides, Kwells and Scopoderm; beware! in the US, Kwell is a headlice treatment) for motion sickness for children over 2 years of age. You might be better off with something natural, such as Seabands (see page 428), or homeopathic remedies.
- Cough medicine and/or throat lozenges.

- Cotton balls and swabs.
- Gauze for cleaning wounds, as cotton wool fibres are often left behind.
- Teething medicine.
- Large plastic bags or airsick bags.
- Medication for upset stomach.
- Nasal Aspirator (if your toddler will not blow his nose).
- Tissues.
- A clean handkerchief.

For prevention
- Sun cream with a high SPF (Sun Protection Factor, see page 133).
- Insect repellent. DEET is the most effective chemical ingredient, although more natural products are also available (see page 162).
- Blister relief, such as moleskin or Opsite waterproof film (Smith & Nephew).
- A reusable ice pack.
- Opsite waterproof pads to cushion cuts and grazes while swimming.
- Chamomile to make tea is recommended for upset stomachs, heat rash (used topically) and sleep problems.
- The homeopathic remedy Chamomilla, for teething and intense crying and irritability. Also useful for the pain of earaches.
- The homeopathic remedy Belladonna, for fevers.
- The homeopathic remedy Aconite, for health conditions, such as colds and earaches, that come on suddenly.
- Vinegar plus dry powder such as talc for marine stings (alternatively, St John Ambulance recommends a meat tenderiser used for barbecues containing papain, an ingredient reported to inactivate venom).
- Aloe Vera for skin problems, and for healing cuts, grazes, burns and blisters.
- Lavender essential oil for sleep problems, cuts, burns and hysteria.
- Tea tree oil, for its antibacterial and antiviral properties. It also helps to keep insects away.

228

First aid courses

If you can find or make the time, consider taking a course in first aid before you travel. Knowing what to do in an emergency can make a big difference. It's also worth knowing that adults and children are treated differently (for example, in cases of choking or drowning), so it's important that you learn how to treat your toddler in case of injury.

- The British Red Cross Society (9 Grosvenor Crescent, London SW1X 7EJ, Tel: 020 7235 5454) organises courses specifically for carers of toddlers and babies. A certificated childcare course covers resuscitation, bleeding, asthma and other baby ailments. Cost depends on location but is kept as low as possible. You will find branches under British Red Cross in your local phone book or details are on the website.
- St John's Ambulance (National Headquarter, 1 Grosvenor Crescent, London SW1X 7EF, Tel: 0870 2355 231) runs courses in most parts of the UK, and will gear your lesson to toddlers if you ask in advance.
- In Scotland, first aid training is also provided by St Andrew's Ambulance Association, St Andrew's House, Milton Street, Glasgow, G4 0HR.

Homeopathic remedies

Homeopathy is a lovely, gentle way to treat children, and there is no risk of side-effects. Treatment can be difficult because there are literally hundreds of remedies available, but there are some that work effectively for common health problems. I've listed some in the DIY first aid kit checklist (see page 225), but other good ones to consider include:

Aconite – for fear, anxiety, restlessness, sudden illness (including a cold, raging fever, violent diarrhoea or vomiting, that comes on suddenly), intense pain.

Arnica – for cuts, grazes, broken skin, bruising, burns, scalds, nose-bleeds, stings, sprains, dislocated joints, fractures, muscular aches and pains, eye injuries and shock.

Apis – for stings, hives, water retention, cystitis, allergies affecting the throat, mouth and eyes, bites and puncture wounds.

Arsenicum – tummy bugs, diarrhoea, burning discharge (from nose, etc.)

Belladonna – for fever, earache, hallucinations, sensitivity to light, noise, touch, motion or pressure during illness, complaints that come on suddenly and with great violence, intense burning, swelling, congestion with throbbing, hot head and cold extremities.

Bryonia – for fractures, sprains, strains, swollen joints, heat exhaustion, colds, flu, bursting headache with nausea, illnesses accompanied by a 'bear with a sore head' feeling, painful chest, dry mucous membranes, great thirst.

Calendula (cream or tincture) – for burns, cuts and grazes.

Cantharis – for blisters, burns, scalds, burning diarrhoea, any stinging or burning sensation.

Chamomilla – for teething, insomnia, severe earache, illness with bad temper, babies who are distressed when put down (during illness), anxiety dreams, severe pain, great irritability and sensitivity to pain.

Hypericum – for cuts, grazes, bruising, lacerations, puncture wounds, cut lip, shooting pains, diarrhoea and indigestion.

Ledum – for cuts, bruises, insect stings, black eye, sore eye, bites, sprains and strains, particularly when they feel numb.

Nux vomica – for travel sickness, digestive problems, nausea with headache, overindulgence (after a party, for example).

Pulsatilla – for thick, yellow-green and bland catarrh, tearfulness, digestive complaints (particularly those that are worse after eating), one-sided fevers, headaches, etc.

Rhus tox – for red, swollen, itchy blisters, nappy rash, torn muscles, swollen joints, dislocated joints, cramp, muscle stiffness, arthritic or rheumatic pain which is helped by moving.

Silicea – for splinters, recurrent colds and infection, migraine, spots.

• Homeopathic remedies should not be taken with food or drink, just placed on the tongue. Most toddlers love them! They are also available in granule form, for tipping into little mouths.

• Try not to put your remedies through an Xray machine, which can render them less effective.

• Store them well away from strong-smelling substances, such as essential oils, mint (including toothpaste) and perfumes.

• Bring along a good book to help you make choices about the right remedy for your child. I suggest *Homeopathy for Mother and Baby*, by Miranda Castro (Pan, £9.99), or *Commonsense Healthcare for Children*, by Karen Sullivan (Piatkus, £12.99), which also outlines practical solutions, including natural remedies, herbs, foods, essential oils and flower essences for hundreds of health complaints, many of which will crop up on your break.

Vaccinations

No vaccination offers 100 percent immunity. If you are seriously worried about your toddler catching a disease, it is best to avoid a destination where this could happen. If you are simply looking for a standard level of protection and travelling to Europe, North America or Australasia, they may be fine as they are, as toddlers are usually more up to date with their immunisations than adults.

The Hospital for Tropical Diseases has estimated that travellers have about a one in 50,000 chance of catching a disease against which they have been vaccinated. It's also important to ensure that your toddler has had his normal jabs. Measles, for example, is much more common in other countries, particularly those without an immunisation programme in place. Your unimmunised child could become very ill and possibly suffer complications if he is not protected.

If extra shots are required, it's worth nothing that travel vaccines tend not to be quite as effective in toddlers. They are advised, because they offer some protection, but extra care will need to be taken.

If you do not want to immunise or choose not to follow the

recommended schedule for babies and children, even non-conformist practitioners recommend at least polio and tetanus if a child is travelling outside Western Europe, North America or Australasia. Note, too, that some countries will not accept a decision not to immunise. You may have no choice in the matter.

If you are travelling in areas where yellow fever is present (many parts of Africa, for example), immunisation is recommended and may be compulsory. However, the vaccination is seldom given to young children under nine months, so avoid these destinations with young children and babies. A certificate is given with yellow fever vaccination. Immunity begins 10 days after the jab, and officially lasts for 10 years. Yellow Fever jabs can only be given at certain vaccination centres, and should not be given alongside polio or MMR vaccines. Remember that the insects that spread yellow fever live in countries other than Africa, such as South America, and you may need to show proof of vaccination before travelling in these countries.

Caution

Infants under the age of nine months should only be vaccinated against yellow fever if there is an unavoidable risk. The vaccine should not be given to anyone, of any age, with an impaired immune system.

Before you travel, take steps to ensure that your toddler's immune system is in tiptop shape, so that his body can deal effectively with any diseases to which he comes into contact. A healthy diet, good sleep patterns and exercise are all important for good immunity, but you may wish to enhance the process by adding in some natural remedies. If you already see a complementary practitioner, contact him or her at least two months before travelling, to allow the programme to take effect. Remember, too, that most diseases are either carried by insects or caused by poor hygiene. Take special care to protect against these possibilities.

Vaccination alternatives

If you want to know more about alternatives you can contact:

• The Informed Parent, PO Box 870, Harrow, Middlesex HA3 7UW, Tel: 020 8861 1022. Send an SAE for travel information and pointers on alternatives.

• Some experts believe that homeopathic nosodes (infinitesimal quantities of a disease taken in tablet form) work as effectively as vaccinations, and there is a fairly strong body of research in favour of this view. Other experts, however, have expressed concern about this approach. If you wish to find out more, contact the British Homeopathic Association, Tel: 0207 566 7800.

Common health complaints

Diarrhoea and vomiting

Diarrhoea is normally caused by a change in diet, medications such as antibiotics, or an infection. You can reduce the risk by paying careful attention to hygiene, washing your hands before eating and after going to the toilet. Drink bottled or treated water and avoid ice in drinks. Take steps to ensure that your child's diet is appropriate, healthy and safe (see page 220).

Most cases of diarrhoea resolve by themselves, but it can be very serious in babies and toddlers if they lose too much fluid and become dehydrated. This is more likely in a hot climate or when accompanied by vomiting.

The signs of dehydration are drowsiness, lethargy, irritability, lack of response, sunken eyes, dry mouth and skin, increased thirst, scant urine (fewer wet nappies than usual), perhaps accompanied by an increased temperature. Skin becomes less elastic – if you pinch a fold of belly skin, it should spring back to normal immediately. If it doesn't, this is a danger sign and you should consult a doctor urgently. A dehydrated baby's fontanel will become sunken, and this is a very serious sign. If you think your baby or toddler is becoming dehydrated (particularly if only taking small amounts of fluid) seek emergency medical attention.

What to do
- It is very dangerous to stop giving solid food or bottled feeds, although children will probably eat less than usual. Stick to plain, bland foods, such as toast, rice and stewed apples, and avoid anything spicy or fatty. Bananas are gentle constipants and, when ripe, build up the natural flora (healthy bacteria) in the bowels. They should be eaten regularly. Very ripe bananas are best.
- It is vital to encourage a dehydrated child to drink clear fluids. Fresh, cool, previously boiled water is your best bet.
- Oral rehydration solution (properly made up) can not do harm, so give it sooner rather than later, to prevent dehydration becoming more serious. You can not give too much oral rehydration solution.
- The homeopathic remedy Arsenicum is worth trying, as it is indicated in many cases of diarrhoea, vomiting and food poisoning.
- If you are breastfeeding, try to increase the number of breast feeds. Offer oral rehydration solution after each loose bowel movement. It is important that you make the solution up according to the instructions on the packet. Do not add juice or squash, which could make it less effective. It is vital to check that the solution does not taste more salty than tears before giving it to your child.
- If you are bottlefeeding, offer oral rehydration solution and cooled boiled water alongside the feeds. Once the diarrhoea is settling then it is safe to reduce oral rehydration solution.
- Avoid dairy foods until the diarrhoea has been resolved. Live yoghurt, however, is good when the problem has settled down, as it will help to restore the healthy bacteria in the gut, which will have been affected by illness.
- Avoid giving any antidiarrhoeal medication to babies and toddlers, unless advised by a doctor or pharmacist you trust. Diarrhoea is, in fact, a flushing process, and it can rid the body of infection.

Vomiting

There are a number of reasons why toddlers may vomit, including overeating, chest infections, coughing, food poisoning, infections and even travel sickness. Babies and toddlers can become dehydrated if they are unable to keep fluids down, particularly in hot climates. If the vomiting persists, or if it is accompanied by a high temperature or signs of dehydration, see a doctor.

What to do
- Follow the advice for diarrhoea, offering food only when your child feels hungry. It's essential, however, that he continues to drink.
- If your toddler finds it difficult to keep down drinks, offer ice lollies or even ice cubes (made with cooled, previously boiled water) to suck.
- A mild, cool ginger tea solution can help to ease nausea. Offer with a little honey to sweeten.
- If you suspect food poisoning, see your doctor immediately. And if vomiting continues for more than 48 hours, you must get some medical attention.

Altitude sickness

See page 155.

Constipation

Constipation can be uncomfortable for toddlers, and may affect appetite and even sleep patterns. Chronic constipation may be a sign that your child is not getting adequate liquid in his diet, which can be worrying if you are travelling in hotter than usual climates.

What to do
- Offer plenty of fresh fruits and vegetables.
- Offer freshly squeezed fruit juices, which can move things along in no time at all. Beware, however, that these can be very powerful and cause the opposite effect if used too frequently.
- Choose foods that are high in fibre, such as rices, wholegrains, wholemeal pastas and cereals. Don't be tempted to add bran to

your child's diet, which is too hard on the digestive tract for toddlers.
- Ensure that your toddler drinks plenty of water throughout the day, at frequent intervals. Aim for at least 500ml per day.
- If available, natural live yoghurt can help to balance the intestinal flora, making the bowel more efficient.
- If available, natural live yoghurt can be helpful.

Cuts and grazes

Treatment will be much the same as you are used to at home, but remember that extra care will need to be taken in hot climates, particularly those with high humidity.

What to do
- Use plenty of warm soapy water to clean cuts and grazes thoroughly. Antiseptic wipes are ideal for when you are out and about, but not necessary for mild grazes and cuts.
- Clean the area with Calendula, which can help to encourage healing.
- Do not use plasters or bandages unless the cut is deep enough to become infected. It's better to let the air encourage the healing process.
- Anything serious should be seen by a doctor. Ask for steristrips or butterfly closures rather than stitches, if you are given the option, and carry some in your first aid kit for emergency DIY treatment.
- A deep cut on the head may be cleaned thoroughly and then closed by tying together strands of hair.

Earaches

An earache is often triggered by swimming, particularly in polluted water, or changes in pressure caused by flying or crossing high passes by road or rail. Colds or congestive conditions may also cause earaches, as the Eustachian tubes can easily become blocked in toddlers and young children. Some toddlers are prone to earaches, a problem which they usually outgrow.

What to do
- If the earache is caused by swimming, keep the ear dry for a week or two, or use earplugs when swimming.
- A complementary approach for prevention and treatment is to put a drop of garlic oil (warmed olive oil in which you have steeped garlic cloves) in the ears before and after each swim. Pop in a cotton ball to ensure that the oil stays in situ.
- Antibiotics may be offered for an ear infection, although these are not widely used on the Continent. A wait-and-see approach has proved to be just as effective as antibiotics in clinical tests.
- If the ear is very painful, offer the homeopathic remedy Chamomilla, as required. A drop of lavender oil, in some warmed olive oil, can be dropped into the ear canal, and rubbed into the area around the ear and neck.
- Painkillers, such as paracetamol can help, especially to aid sleeping.
- If the ear is blocked, flying or crossing a high pass can be painful. Consult your doctor who might prescribe a decongestant as a preventive measure.

Skin infections
Skin infections (particularly fungal infections) may spread quickly in warm, moist enviornments so you should take extra care when drying after swims.

What to do
- Complementary practitioners recommend tea tree oil, which is anti-fungal as well as anti-bacterial. It is available in light creams, or can be added to olive oil and massaged into the skin.
- Another idea is to pack a medical anti-fungal powder or cream.
- Grazed knees and mosquito bites go septic quickly in hot, humid climates, so you may wish to use antibacterial or antiseptic agents more often than you might at home. Many essential oils are natural antiseptics. Try lavender or chamomile in the first instance, as both are suitable for toddlers with sensitive skin.

Hypothermia
See page 154.

Infectious diseases

If your toddler is suffering from chickenpox or another infectious disease, most airlines will not allow you to travel, and you may be put onshore if the condition crops up on a cruise. In this instance, it's worth taking out health insurance cover, in the event that you are forced to stay at your destination for longer than planned.

What to do
- If your child does become ill on holiday, don't hesitate to see a doctor. Most childhood illnesses do not require treatment, as they soon pass, but you can get some help to deal with the symptoms, which may be uncomfortable. You'll also want to beware of complications, which can crop up.
- Bring along a mild painkiller, such as paracetamol, to reduce fever and ease discomfort.
- Calamine lotion will help to reduce itching spots.
- Lavender oil, in a mild carrier oil, can be rubbed into spots to reduce itching and encourage healing, as well as rubbed into the glands, to encourage healing. It's particularly comforting in the case of mumps.
- For fevers, try the homeopathic remedy Belladonna, particularly if your child is red-faced and uncomfortable. The homeopathic remedy Chamomilla will help with pain, such as earaches, headaches and sore throats, which may accompany the illness.

Alert!

If your toddler has a particular allergy or intolerance (Tom for example, has an intolerance to wheat and diary products), consider getting them to wear an allergy identification bracelet or necklace. These are available from Medic-Alert Foundation, 21 Bridge Wharf, 156 Caledonian Road, London N1 9UU, Tel: 020 7833 3034. These are essential if your child is allergic to any form of health treatment, such as antibiotics, which may be administered in an emergency.

Prickly heat

Prickly heat typically occurs in the groin, on the trunk and neck, and is due to the sweat glands becoming blocked, possibly because of un-evaporated sweat. The skin becomes inflamed and itchy and may be compounded by fungal infections.

What to do

- Keep skin clean and dry.
- Wear loose-fitting cotton clothes.
- Take a cool wash as soon as the first prickliness is felt, and at the beginning and end of each day.
- After washing pat dry thoroughly, but don't rub. A little dusting powder may help to soak up excess moisture.
- An antifungal essential oil, such as tea tree, can be gently applied to the skin in the form of a cream, to prevent secondary infection.

Overheating

See page 142.

Travel sickness

Travel or motion sickness is actually fairly rare in under twos, and seems to strike from around three to 12 years, more often in girls than boys. It also appears to be worse in the morning rather than later in the day. The cause is conflicting signals between what the eye sees, and what the inner ear, which detects changes in movement, feels.

What to do

- Avoid the conflicting signals between eye and inner ear by lying down (thus avoiding vertical movement as much as possible) with eyes shut, or by looking at the horizon. Or try anchoring the head with a neck pillow or bracing against a chair or wall.
- Any form of transport that allows you to move around, a train or a large plane, for example, can be helpful.
- In cars and coaches, ensure your toddler can look ahead rather than out of the side, ideally at a fixed point, such as the horizon. This means ensuring that the child's seat is high enough.
- Sit a potential sufferer in a place in the plane/car/coach/ship that

moves slightly less if this is at all possible. On small planes, for example, it can be helpful to sit between the wings. On trains or coaches, the best place is the centre, not over the wheels. On a ship, aim for somewhere near the middle on a low deck.

- On trains, try to ensure any potential sufferers sit facing the direction of travel and away from smoking carriages and the buffet car.
- Consider avoiding meals and fatty foods for up to two hours before travel and, on a short journey, all food in transit. For snacks pick something easily digestible. Try bananas, apples, boiled sweets and dry biscuits.
- Don't allow your toddler to read and draw. Encourage distractions like group word and travel games.
- Ensure plenty of fresh air, for example turning on the air jets above the seats on a plane.
- On ships, outside decks, away from engine fumes, are good places to park an unwell toddler.
- Refresh your toddler's face with a damp flannel.
- Holding a bag to the mouth may be helpful. This removes the fear of where to be sick if it happens.
- Various drug-based treatments, including Junior Kwells, which contain Hyoscine, can make the mouth and eyes dry. If you want to use these you may have to try various types before finding one which works for you. Drugs have be given before travel. Kwells, for example, should be given 30 minutes before travel, and antihistamines three to four hours before.
- Traditional remedies that may help include ginger (chew the raw roots, or take in capsule, tea or candied form). Eating fresh mint leaves, peppermint sweets or lemon drops, or inhaling peppermint essential oil from a tissue may also help.
- Homeopathic remedies should also be considered. The best one seems to be Tabacum, which can be taken as required throughout the journey.
- Take strong, lockable plastic bags in case your toddler is actually sick. Or use disposable nappy sacks, which, if you can stand their 'perfume', can disguise the original problem. Always carry wet wipes, which will prove very useful if your toddler is sick.

Less common ailments

Deep vein thrombosis (DVT)

A recently raised concern is the link between long flights and deep vein thrombosis (DVT). It is known that long haul flights and sitting still anywhere for long periods increases the risk of a blood clot forming in a deep vein in either leg. A clot moving to either lung causes a pulmonary embolus, which can be fatal. The symptoms of a DVT are a swollen, hot, painful and sometimes red calf.

DVT is not, however, a risk for toddlers or young children, but it's worth being aware of the problem when you are travelling alongside them.

In adults the normal risk of getting a DVT is 5 in 100,000. Long haul flights increase the risk because of:

- Decreased movement of the legs causing impaired circulation in the veins, especially if sleeping in odd positions.
- Decrease in cabin pressure.
- Dehydration caused by dry air, inadequate fluid intake and alcohol and caffeine drinks.

Certain people are more at risk, including those who: are over 40; are overweight; suffer from extensive varicose veins; have had a recent leg injury or surgery (or a leg in a plaster cast); are pregnant; are taking oral contraceptive pill or HRT (the risks are not high enough to recommend stopping taking these before flying); have family history of clotting disorder; suffer from heart disease; have had a stroke, thrombosis or malignancy; or suffer from paralysis of the lower limbs.

What to do
- In order to prevent DVT, try to move around the cabin every so often, and change your position in the seat.
- While sitting, try to exercise the calf muscles and flex and rotate the ankles every 20 to 30 minutes.
- Avoid alcohol and caffeinated drinks, and drink plenty of water.
- Consider wearing support stockings during the flight. These are

241

available from pharmacists, who will measure your legs and give advice for correct fitting.

Rabies

A child recently died of rabies after having been bitten by a dog in Thailand, proving that vigilance is important. Rabies is found in mammals in Europe, Greenland, North and South America, Africa, Asia and The Middle East in developed, as well as less developed countries. It is absent in Great Britain, Ireland, Australia, New Zealand and several other islands. For this reason, the official blanket recommendation is not to touch mammals in areas where rabies is present.

The incubation period between a bite and the appearance of symptoms is between nine days and many months. The average time is four to eight weeks. The first symptoms are slight fever, headache and loss of appetite, leading to restlessness, hyperactivity, disorientation and in some cases seizures. Often the victim is intensely thirsty, but attempts to drink cause painful, violent spasms in the throat.

What to do
- Try to make your toddler aware of the issue, without going into too much detail.
- Encourage them not to approach or touch any animal while travelling.
- Rabies may be spread by licks and scratches as well as bites, and it is carried by cats, monkeys, dogs, bats and many other mammals.
- Consult your doctor before travelling. He or she may be able to provide some useful advice or precautions.
- Pre-travel immunisation is strongly recommended, particularly if travelling to areas remote from medical care.

Is there a doctor in the house?

How regularly do you go to the doctor with your toddler? How important is on-call medical provision on holiday? Would having a doctor nearby or in the hotel give you peace of mind to enjoy your holiday?

If you are concerned, choose a destination where you know there is an on-site English-speaking doctor on call, or a major hospital nearby. Concern about being close to hospitals or medical care may also render less developed destinations no-go areas.

So if you want to be certain of access to an English-speaking doctor pick a travel operator that will provide details of one. Or choose a cruise (see page 126) that has a doctor on board and probably nurses as well (Tom prefers the nurses).

Get the doctor's contact details before you arrive so you have them if needed. Visits to the doctor will need to be paid for and, unless the condition is serious, will probably not cost enough to exceed the excess on your travel insurance policy.

- Use common sense as well. If your child is prone to any particular childhood ailment, choose a holiday on which illness wouldn't be disastrous. If they suffer from ear infections, for example, avoid high altitudes (skiing in high altitude resorts) or flying. Cancelling the holiday if you can't leave home is bad, but it's worse if your toddler gets an infection at the end of the holiday and you are unable to return. If colds are common, look for somewhere where there is more in the way of entertainment than sun and swimming, which might not be suitable for a few days.

Better safe . . .

Not all countries operate to the same safety standards as the UK, and even within the UK, many places are simply not equipped to deal with the potential hazards that a toddler can find and/or create. The best advice is to establish your own safety standards, and to be rigorous about checking and upholding them while travelling. The checklists throughout the book will help to keep your toddler safe from harm (see pages 97, 112, 179 and 207), but bear in mind the following, no matter where you are travelling:

General safety on holiday

Holidays shouldn't be dangerous, but they can turn out to be, because everyone relaxes and your environment and the culture may be un-familiar. Tourists may be targeted by criminals because they are known to be carrying money and passports, and because they are a little distracted. Having toddlers with you can make you an easier target so it's important to remember the usual rules.

- Don't look like a tourist. Plan your route in advance, rather than hovering looking lost.
- Don't flash your guidebook, whether on the seat of the car or in your hand – a plain cover can help.
- If hiring a car, specify that you want one without the company markings and with local number plates.
- Dress so you don't stand out – whether in clothes which are too smart or too casual.
- Travel light so you can move easily. A backpack is very useful, but don't keep valuables in it. Use a pouch or moneybelt at the front where you can see it.
- Think about taking a mobile phone so you can always get in touch with help.
- Take photocopies of the relevant pages of your passport, driver's licence, airline tickets, credit cards, in case they are lost, and keep the copies separate from originals.
- Avoid taking food or drink from strangers and warn your children to do the same. If you wish not to appear rude you could offer to take it 'to eat later'. These items are sometimes drugged, particularly on long trips by train or coach.

Watch your valuables

You will have more luggage to handle so make sure you keep track of your valuables. Invest in a money belt or similar for tickets, passport, money and other documents. One tip is to go to www.yellowtag.com – they tag your luggage with a code so it can be traced by email.

I've lost my mummy

This is undoubtedly a parent's worst nightmare. Getting lost is terrifying for both toddlers and parents, but if it does happen, having a pre-agreed plan is essential. The best way to avoid your toddler getting lost in the first place is to make sure that you always have at least one adult bringing up the rear of the group. Having them strapped in a buggy, or on a leash is another good way to make sure you don't lose your most prized possession. Tom has this infuriating habit of trying to get his wrist out of the leash strap without me noticing. So watch for this. The favourite game of most toddlers – especially two and three year olds – is 'hide and seek'. Terrifying in a crowd.

Remember, your toddler won't always know where they are going. This can make for slow progress if there is only one parent, but it's not as slow or as upsetting as getting lost.

Top tips for keeping tabs

- Dress your toddler in at least one really bright piece of clothing (fluorescent is great), which can help you locate them in a crowd. Alternatively, make sure that their backpack is really brightly coloured.
- Instruct your toddler to shriek as loudly as possible if lost. It is a good idea to suggest that he or she yells your name as there may be a number of other mums or dads there.
- While it is not considered a good idea to put the toddler's name on the outside of their clothes, it might be useful to provide them with a kind of ID card inside their pack or possibly sewn into clothing. This could include a parent's name as well as the child's, and possibly a phone number – ideally a mobile phone number if you have one with you.
- It may also be useful to give the toddler a card with the local holiday address – say a hotel business card – and the telephone number of the property or a local rep.
- Alternatively you could get them to memorise a family friend's phone number, which they can call. They may know their home number but, of course, you won't be there to answer.
- It can be very helpful to make sure every member of the party has their own pre-paid phone card for use in the local phones.
- Kid ID bands are also an idea. There are also personal alarms with which toddlers could be provided to sound if they get into any kind of difficulty.

- It is extremely helpful to have an accessible, good and up-to-date photograph of your toddler, just in case he does go astray. A shoe print is useful as well.
- Bear in mind, however, that whatever the stories in the news, harm to children is no more common that it was 100 years ago and the vast majority of lost children will be treated with great care.
- If you are concerned, discuss the issues with your toddler. Motorway stops can feel particularly dangerous because of the ease of getaway, and you might prefer not to allow one child to go to the lavatory alone, for example. Disappearing children in theme parks are not something the establishments concerned would like to publicise if it did happen but, without scaring the toddler, you might like to offer at least the standard pointers on not taking food from or following strangers. Let them know that if they need help, they should also find staff, a policeman or woman, or a clerk in a shop.
- The obvious way to locate a lost toddler is to yell 'I've lost my child', so all adults in the vicinity know what has happened and can help. If you don't speak the local language, you need to find an adult who does who can pass on the information. Either way you need to tell people what the child looks like and what they are wearing.
- With older children you might like to provide a local phone card or even a mobile phone so that they can ring someone if they do get lost. This is no use to a toddler who is liable to lose things. In this case, miss out the mobile but think of sewing a relevant phone number somewhere it is less likely to go missing.
- Explain the dangers of wandering off alone, particularly where the weather may suddenly turn nasty, as in the UK, Ireland or other islands.
- It is useful to point out that if there is a noise at night it is best to yell at it. If it is an animal it will go. If it is a searcher, they will be able to find the lost child more easily.
- One of the best arguments for buying a decent guide is that it will provide information on local emergency numbers (see page 421) and how to find English-speaking medical services.

12. More than One?

Whether you are expecting a baby or travelling with more than one toddler in tow, you'll need to take some extra precautions and undertake a little more advance planning. There's no question that two can be more than twice the work (and pleasure, of course), but it's perfectly possible to travel with a brace of toddlers (or more), and with one on the way.

Travelling with a bump

At five months, I was white-water rafting on the Alsek Tashashini River in the Yukon. I don't particularly recommend this activity for pregnancy, but if you are fit and healthy, and your baby is well, it certainly is possible.

I continued to travel around the world for my job up until I was eight months' pregnant, stopping only when it became too uncomfortable, and many women continue well into the latter months of pregnancy. It's worth considering a few points, however:

- Try to travel during your second trimester (months 4 to 6). You'll likely have passed the morning sickness stage, and not be big enough to be seriously uncomfortable in the smaller seats. Consider travelling business class, which allows a great deal more room. You can often be bumped up (pardon the pun) free of charge, if the flight is not full.
- There are no real dangers caused by flying in early pregnancy, and certainly no increased risk of miscarriage or premature labour – unless you are predisposed to this.

- One potential problem could be an increased exposure to radiation, which is more than 100 times ground level at higher altitudes. For the record, that's the equivalent of a single chest X-ray on a return trip from London to New York. Although this may have very little effect on your baby in the latter stages of pregnancy, in the early months it is not recommended. The advice? Avoid unnecessary long-distance flights.

- Remember that many airlines (particularly the charters) will be unlikely to allow you to travel after about 32 weeks, and certainly not after 36. Some are even stricter, so check before you go. Whatever you do, get a certificate from your doctor stating how many weeks' pregnant you are, and that you are fit to fly. You may well need confirmation to reassure check-in staff and crew.

- Later in pregnancy, cabin pressure (particularly on long-haul flights) can encourage fluid retention, which creates extra pressure on the abdomen and potentially exacerbates blood pressure problems. This is one reason why airlines are not keen for heavily pregnant women to fly, although cynics claim that it has more to do with the cost of re-routing, should labour begin on board, than it does with health risks to mothers.

Safety notes

• High fever and dehydration caused by diarrhoea have been implicated in miscarriage. For this reason some practitioners feel it best to restrict travel during pregnancy to countries with a developed medical system and, even more importantly, to those where you are less likely to encounter infections.

• Avoid travelling to countries requiring vaccinations. Immunisation is not generally recommended during pregnancy.

• If you wish to visit somewhere where a vaccination is either mandatory or advisable (not the same thing) you should discuss the matter with your GP at least two months before departure.

• The World Health Organisation (WHO) has advised against pregnant women and small children visiting areas where cholera

---

and malaria are endemic. Many anti-malarial drugs are also contraindicated during pregnancy.

• Avoid European and Scandinavian forests in late spring and summer because of the risk of tick-borne encephalitis.

• Mosquito repellents containing DEET (see page 162) are not recommended for use in pregnancy. You may wish to avoid countries with a high mosquito population; it seems that pregnant women are more likely to be bitten (and the reasons for this are various, including increased blood flow to the skin and body size).

Comfortable travelling

Depending on your size and symptoms, travelling while pregnant can be a breeze or an experience you'd rather forget. Before setting out, I suggest that you get a copy of 'Travelling in Pregnancy', produced by the Royal College of Obstetricians and Gynaecologists (available from 27 Sussex Place, Regent's Park NW1 4RG, Tel: 020 7772 7200).

Before you go:
• Pack your antenatal notes (or a copy of them) for easy access in the event of an emergency. Make a note of any medication you may be taking.
• Obtain the local numbers for the British Embassy or Consulate, just in case you need them in an emergency – and find out their 'opening hours'. You may also want to have the number of a good, recommended obstetrician. Your hotel might be able to help with this, or the British Embassy.
• Prebook if you can, asking for either an aisle seat, or one of the bulkhead seats, which offer more leg room.
• Wear loose, comfortable clothing and shoes that you can slip on and off easily.

On board:
- Keep the circulation flowing when you're flying. Continually move your limbs and walk up and down the aisle. Poor circulation can cause lower back pain, abdominal discomfort and muscle cramps, but it can also lead to deep vein thrombosis (DVT; where blood clots form in the deep veins of the legs, see page 241). These clots may travel to the heart or lungs, with occasionally fatal results. The best advice is to prevent the condition by drinking lots of water and moving the muscles of the legs as often as possible (see page 241).
- Place the seatbelt under, not across, your bump.
- Drink plenty of non-alcoholic fluids to prevent fluid retention. Water is the best natural diuretic, so drink as much as you can (after all, those trips to the loo act as good stimulation for your muscles).
- If you are worried about thrombosis one of the tips is to fly business class as the larger seats offer more room to move and among other things less sustained pressure on the calves.

At your destination:
- Stick to comfortable clothes if you plan to walk a lot at your destination. My bump felt like a hot water bottle strapped to my tummy, and many women feel hotter than usual in pregnancy. Choose loose clothing in natural fibres. While support tights might ease discomfort, they can be too hot. Look for lightweight brands.
- If you have any health problems while travelling, be sure to let any healthcare provider or even pharmacist know that you are pregnant. Avoid taking any drugs, particularly tetracycline antibiotics, unless there is an emergency. If in doubt, arrange a call to your own doctor to double check a diagnosis and form of treatment.
- Eat only freshly cooked food, and stick to bottled water. If you anticipate a problem getting safe, healthy food, consider bringing some of your own. Certainly a supply of fresh fruit carried on board would not go amiss, along with some rye crackers, hard cheese and chopped vegetables for nibbling. Keep them cool with a cold pack.

- Legislation insists pregnant women use a seat belt when travelling by car. However, a car seat belt placed across the abdomen can be dangerous in the event of an accident, so keep the shoulder strap high above your bump, and place the lap belt across your thighs. If you are planning on doing a lot of travel by car, you may wish to invest in specially adapted seat belts.

Are you covered?

Even where there is a reciprocal healthcare agreement with the UK, it may not be comprehensive, or cover some months of pregnancy. In fact, in some places it may be impossible to find a doctor who is willing to treat under the scheme. Go for travel insurance, and check the restrictions on the policy. Some insurers will cover everything up to 26 weeks, but nothing afterwards. Check carefully and ensure that you are covered.

Some fail to provide cover for a condition relating to pregnancy. Others require that there be no pre-existing or hereditary problem relating to pregnancy. You may also find that annual policies are inadequate – take time to read the small print. You may not, for example, be able to claim for cancellation if your due date falls within 10 weeks of the end of the cover. Remember that you are unlikely to be covered if you travel against the advice of your doctor; this situation may be different if you were advised not to travel after booking, but it's worth looking into.

Make sure that your policy offers:
- Cover in pregnancy.
- An English-language phone service.
- Repatriation, if necessary.
- Extra accommodation and travel expenses for anyone who has to stay on to help.

With more . . .

> Having two toddlers is more than twice the work of one. Maybe 10 times harder.
>
> Mother of two toddlers, from Southampton

It goes without saying that two or more toddlers can increase the potential for disaster; however, with a little foresight and careful planning, it's perfectly possible to travel with more than one. Keep things as simple as possible, and be prepared for any eventuality.

Top tips

- Ask for advanced seat assignments for air travel whenever possible. This is important when travelling with two lap babies, as airlines often have restrictions on the number of lap children that can sit in the same row. If travelling alone with your toddlers, having pre-assigned seats means that flight attendants won't have to shuffle other passengers around to make room for you and your crew.
- Choose bulkhead seating. Some airlines have bassinets (sky cots) for very young babies (see page 52), normally attached to the bulkhead wall. Furthermore, the floor space in front of the seats may be a much-needed playground or sleeping area for bored toddlers . . . without the opportunity to kick the seats in front.
- Tell the airline or your travel agent you are travelling with several infants or toddlers. Even if your ticket says 'no advance seating', some airlines will go ahead and give you a seat assignment to avoid disrupting boarding procedures at the airport.
- Buy a seat for each of your babies or toddlers. Yes, it's more expensive, but most airlines offer good discounts for toddlers under two (check with the airline to see if they have a limit on the number of infant fares one family can have).
- Use a combination of umbrella buggies and backpacks to make travel easier. With one or two babies in a buggy and another on your back, you'll be able to move in and out of crowded airports a lot faster. Alternatively, snap-and-go buggies with detachable infant

car seats are a wise choice if you want to cut down on carry-on baggage.

- Ask if you can check in your buggy at the gate and pick it up at the gate on the other end. This way, you'll have a place to put your little one if your flight gets delayed or if you have a long way to walk to the gate or baggage claim. You don't want to have to juggle a toddler on each hip as you race through the airport to make a flight.
- Arrange for an airport cart to meet you at your arrival gate if you are changing planes. Toddlers (and I speak from experience here) love the novelty of the ride and you'll be thankful for the lift to the next gate.
- Pack a change of clothes for each toddler in a resealable bag for fast changes on the road. You'll save time not digging around for a sock or undershirt at the bottom of a carry-on, you can keep all your toddler' clothes separate, and you can toss the dirty clothes bags into your other luggage.
- Research your destination well ahead of time to find toddler-friendly restaurants, hotels, and parks. Knowing ahead of time which restaurants don't mind breakfast cereal on the floor or finding a tot park near where you're staying will substantially cut down on the chances of a meltdown after a long day of travel!
- Bring along some help if you can afford it. An extra pair of hands not only gives you a much-deserved break, but it gives you the opportunity to spend a little one-on-one time with each toddler, and your partner!

13. Eco-friendly Travel

With or without toddler, it's possible to have an eco-friendly experience. This may seem nigh on impossible with a family in tow, but anyone who genuinely cares about the environment can have a satisfying holiday with the minimum of fuss. Tearfund (www.tearfund.org), an organisation that specialises in offering advice to the travel industry, suggests the following advice for holidaying without detriment to the environment.

A holiday is an experience that is based on the character of the destination, the environment and the people there. A holiday is also a time to relax and refresh, not just to switch off and pretend you are in the UK. You have chosen a certain destination based on its characteristics, and while it's a great idea to take time to recharge, it's also important to leave the hotel to see the unique cultural and environmental side of the destination. That doesn't mean cramming in the sights (stressful for toddlers) or the opposite, just switching off (not a possibility with investigative toddlers).

Many of the problems in modern-day tourism are caused by a breakdown in communication, whether that be based on misunderstanding, co-modification of culture, exclusion from certain areas (hotels and beaches, for example), jealousy/resentment from local people due to tourist wealth or attitude (when they treat somewhere like they own the place).

So how can you ensure a happy eco holiday? Consider the following advice:

- Avoid conspicuous displays of wealth (things like showy prams or flash toddler clothing).
- Pay a fair price for goods; don't haggle to the lowest possible. With

toddlers it's not normally possible to shop at full tilt for hours, so slow down and enjoy the experience. Allow time for a cup of tea or a chat with the stallholders.

- Don't just go to the 'safe' places in the hotels. Venture out to the markets. See the whole thing as an adventure and take the time to explain some things to toddlers, particularly if everything is new.
- Use your kids as a way in to ask some of the most obvious questions – it will endear you to others and may provide entry points into the local culture.
- Choose souvenirs that support local artisans.
- In developing countries, in particular, avoid areas that are segregated (some beaches in Goa, India, for example, exclude the locals)
- Be careful in public places, but don't develop an unhealthy, overcautious approach. Suspicion is insulting to locals, and in most countries, they welcome tourists and look forward to getting to know you.
- Reduce packaging to avoid waste when you are there, and consider bringing home anything that cannot be adequately disposed of. This is a particular problem in underdeveloped countries.
- Reduce water usage in water scarce areas. It might be heavy, but it might pay to bring your own.

14. A Final Checklist

The final checklist.

All of those parents with toddlers I interviewed confessed that they take too much luggage on holiday. They use less than half of their provisions, and wear less than half the clothing they pack. In fact, the low-cost airline Buzz last year offered travellers £10 discounts (in a fare that is often as low as £50) for limiting their luggage to on-board bags.

That's great for the business user, or on a weekend break, but it's nearly impossible to cut down on luggage to that extent if you are travelling with toddlers. Particularly if you are going a bit further afield, or on a skiing or other activity break that requires specialist equipment.

That said, there are ways to reduce your luggage load, which will make things easier to manage in terms of packing and unpacking, and, of course, carrying. There are a few ways to achieve this.

First of all, begin packing several weeks in advance, according to a pre-planned list. You can use your own, or adapt the one I've supplied (see page 257) to your needs. If you plan early, you'll be much less likely to panic and throw in a whole lot of things you simply don't need.

Remember that you don't need to buy everything (toiletries, snacks, medicines, even clothing) in advance. For one thing, you can buy a lot at the airport (you need to do something while waiting for that plane) and also on location. You'll probably be less tempted to blow your holiday budget on things you don't need than you would at home, with a trusty card in hand.

The following checklist is set up to give you an idea of the types of things you need to pack, both for you and your toddler, with a view to keeping luggage down, and being practical! This list is set up for a summer holiday of about a week.

For you

- A sarong (as a beach towel, beach bag, and, well, sarong). Men can wear them too!
- Flip-flops (wear other shoes in transit).
- Swimwear.
- One T-shirt (wear the other inflight, wash in the shower overnight).
- Two or three changes of underwear.
- A comb.
- One dress/pair of trousers/shirt.
- Travel wash powder or liquid, and a laundry line. Useful even in environmentally sensitive areas is Mountain Suds, a bio-degradable cleaner that is designed for use on clothes, dishes, hair and you.
- Camera and film (over 50 percent of parents I spoke to confessed to have forgotten this; a disposable camera is one option).

The rest you can buy, discounted, at the airport or at your destination. Check with your local hotel or tour operator to make sure that there are shops near (and open) to where you are going. If, of course, you're going somewhere smart, this may be impractical advice. But still keep it to a minimum.

For your toddler

- Nappies (even if potty trained, just in case of emergencies or delays). You can always buy more overseas.
- One/two small comfort blankets (one to lie on, one to cover toddler).
- Zip-lock bags (for storing soiled nappies, clothes and shoes).
- Wet wipes.
- Sample-size containers of toiletry items, such as baby bath or shampoo.
- Tissues.
- One favourite toy (ideally a Beanie Baby) and small-sized books (see page 431) to read at bedtime.
- A few sturdy toys that don't have easy-to-lose parts.
- Clothes should include three T-shirts and three pairs of shorts, in

cotton and matching colours; two jumpers/cardigans; one pair of sandals and one pair of socks.

- One/two bathing suits.
- One washable bib.
- One sunhat (with neck and ears covered).
- One spouted cup.
- Snack food (see page 220).
- Nightlight (for nighttime nappy changes without turning on the lights).
- Masking tape for the base of the bath if you fear slipping (or use a towel).
- Socket protectors.
- Potty (if applicable).
- Car seat (see page 79).
- Lightweight, collapsible buggy (check to make sure you can't hire one on location. Forget the three-wheeled ones, which are better over difficult terrain and sandy beaches but are cumbersome and heavy to manoeuvre). Most airlines now allow you to take a buggy either to the gate or to the door of the plane itself and store it in the overhead bin of the plane).
- A monitor if you are happy to leave the child in a bedroom. See Baby Monitors for potential technical problems. (forget if hotel/resort may provide baby listening or sitting).
- Prescribed medication. Prevent leaks by packing medicines and toiletries in re-sealable plastic bags.
- Bring a 2-foot square of plastic, vinyl, or even washable wallpaper to put under your baby during diaper changes (you can buy commercial changing pads for this purpose, too).
- Keep toddler's outfits in hand luggage and change of T-shirt for you.
- Travel size baby/child shampoo and wash in one.
- A baby front carrier (sling is ideal for younger babies, keeping them at the carrier's body temperature, high enough to see around and join in any conversation, while offering the security of parental closeness in an unfamiliar environment).
- A First Aid kit (see page 225).
- Put even potty trained toddlers in nappies at night. Alternatively, for toddlers liable to wet the bed – a waterproof sheet of some

kind, thus avoiding the potential embarrassment of negotiating a cleaning or replacement cost. The larger the flat sheet the better as children may well move off smaller sheets if they have a large bed to move around in.

Buy on location

- Drawing materials. If you are planning any museum visits in particular buy drawing material. Toddlers can be entertained (sometimes only briefly) by drawing what they can see.
- Materials for putting together a diary of the trip including possibly Sellotape, glue stick, scissors plus a large scrap book, perhaps extra paper for creating pockets to hold items. Allow in the budget for postcards to be purchased for the diary.
- Toys. It's a souvenir and plaything. And ideally disposable at the end of the holiday.
- Bucket and spade and beach ball.
- A large beach umbrella. Hire or buy. Many beaches in the more crowded parts of Europe would never contemplate permitting you to use your own.
- A cool bag and cool pack for food and drink out and about and on the beach. If you need hot or cold drinks consider a lightweight thermos.
- Shoes for the beach to protect against hot sand and anything nasty lurking in it.
- Large bag suitable for beach/day trip stuff.

Last minute shopping before you go

Tesco is an excellent toddler-friendly place to find almost everything you need. Check out their website (www.tesco.co.uk), which includes a section on the baby and toddler club. The club allows privileged parking space, discount vouchers on numerous items and an excellent magazine offering common sense advice through pregnancy until your child reaches school age. Tesco's *You and Your Child* catalogue was the winner of the Mother and Baby Catalogue of the Year 2000–2001 and 1999–2000, and the Tommy Parent Friendly Award for the Best Catalogue 2001.

PART THREE
The Parents' Guide to Popular Destinations

Introduction

Mahatma Gandhi said, 'Be the change you want to see in the world'. In other words, if you want the world to be a more toddler-friendly place, do something about it. Tell the airline, tour operator, hotel manager, travel agent or whoever suggested the holiday that you are either incredibly displeased or extremely delighted with their service or product; that your expectations have been exceeded or that you feel misled by their 'fun for all the family' waffle.

Direct feedback from parents is the only way the travel industry will learn the importance of targeting the toddler market effectively. If they believe they will lose custom and therefore income by not listening to you, they will do something about it. An Andy Warhol comment is apt in this context: 'They always say time changes things, but you actually have to change them yourself.'

Martin Hayward, Director of Consumer Consultancy at the Henley Centre (www.henleycentre.com) claims:

There is a growing opportunity for the marketers of products and services to exploit the previously rather ignored sector of parents with toddlers. A number of major demographic shifts lie behind their growing appeal as a target audience. Firstly, as the average household continues to grow in affluence there is clearly a lot more money about. As households become better off, they start to spend a higher proportion of their income on leisure goods and services (spending on which overtook spending on food for the first time in 1999). Secondly, parenthood used to be a passport to poverty but today's parents are older and more affluent before they start a family and are having fewer children. This means that firstly they are better off, but secondly they are already used to the nice things in life and are not going to let children get in the way of them having a nice time. It also means that the children themselves have considerable spending power.

So, we have the power now.

Of course, you can't do much to change the prevailing culture in individual countries, but fortunately most resorts – especially in southern Europe and South America – are happy to welcome children at this formative, creative (some might say destructive) and challenging age. Their minds are like little sponges and they absorb all the sights and sounds around them. Toddlers love the diversity and excitement of travel in all its forms. Usually.

If they don't enjoy flying or sailing, why not try a holiday in Britain? There are excellent facilities and beaches, although English attitudes to children – and toddlers in particular – can still be a trifle Victorian. This attitude is changing but only very slowly, according to the parents I interviewed.

Continental Europe has much to offer families with toddlers, thanks to the wide variety of affordable and accessible self-catering accommodation available. Log cabins in Sweden, farmhouses in the Mediterranean region, white-washed apartments on the Greek Islands or simple chalets in Alpine forests are all viable options if you are happy to do the cooking and cleaning.

And further afield, if you (and your toddler) are prepared to travel for seven hours or more, you will find a warm welcome and excellent facilities in Dubai, New Zealand, Australia, Canada and the Caribbean, to name but a few.

This second section of the book is designed to give you an idea of what is on offer in some of the most toddler-friendly countries in the world, alongside information on how to get there and when to go.

The information contained here is based on the recommendations and advice offered by the many, many parents of toddlers that I interviewed for this book. It is, by no means, an exhaustive look at the best places to travel with toddlers, and it certainly isn't a comprehensive guide to a particular country or city. What it does, however, is offer you a taste of the types of entertainment, hotels, transportation and attractions that families with toddlers enjoyed on their travels.

For anyone thinking of travelling to the locations mentioned here, I strongly recommend a good travel guide (see page 423), and plenty of advance planning in the form of telephone calls, faxes and emails, to ensure that you are getting what you want. But if you are considering one of the popular destinations listed in this book, this section may help to give you a clear idea of what's available, and whether or not it is a holiday suited to your family.

A combination of factors was taken into account when preparing this section, including budget, climate, health issues, and the needs of toddlers as well as parents. The countries chosen were all strongly recommended by the parents I spoke to (as well as their toddlers).

Since there is nothing toddlers enjoy more than messing around on beaches, I have recommended resorts on the coast that have excellent, clean beaches.

I have only included attractions that would appeal to toddlers, so this excludes most museums and theme parks that are geared towards older children. In the list, you will find steam trains, playgrounds, petting farms and zoos, aquariums, and many other innovative and inventive attractions, such as theatres for toddlers, worlds in miniature and eccentric theme parks. Check out, for example, the fabulous 'The Big Sheep' in Devon (see page 283).

In some countries it is better to stay in self-catering accommodation rather than hotels or camp sites. In others, it is the reverse. I have indicated this where applicable.

The time it takes to reach each destination is important, and if you are flying into a time zone that is considerably different from Greenwich Mean Time, jet lag could disorientate young children. It helps if toddler-friendly airlines fly to your chosen destination, and if they are able to fly from a regional (and possibly more toddler-friendly) airport (see pages 33–47).

I have made suggestions to suit all budgets, and recommended the best months to travel to each country (usually during spring and autumn when the climate is milder). This does not necessarily mean you will be travelling in an off-peak season, but for popular destinations in Europe this could be the case.

You might be surprised to see only Florida mentioned for the USA, and I should point out now that this is not an oversight! The US is an enormous country, with a wealth of wonderful attractions and holidays for families of young children, but it is simply beyond the scope of this book to focus on anything more than what parents rated to be the best value, most fun and most toddler-friendly. If you are planning a trip to the US, I suggest a camping (motorhome) holiday (see page 181), which allows you to take in the breadth and diversity of the landscape, as well as the very different small and large communities en route. Every state has its own toddler-friendly resorts, attractions and hotels, so take time to investigate local tourist boards before you travel.

The most popular destinations

Short Haul
- England, Scotland, Wales and Ireland (see pages 266–317)
- Spain and the Spanish islands (see pages 331–336)
- France and Corsica (see pages 337–345)
- Italy and Sardinia (see pages 346–350)
- Portugal (see pages 351–354)

Long Haul
- Florida (see pages 379–385)
- Caribbean (see pages 386–389)
- Cape Town (see pages 390–395)
- Canada (see pages 396–409)
- Australia (see pages 410–420)

The following destinations also have a lot to offer for young families:

- Turkey (see pages 375–378)
- Denmark (see pages 367–374)
- Netherlands (see pages 355–359)
- Belgium (see pages 360–366)
- Guernsey and Jersey (see pages 318–325)
- Isle of Wight (see pages 277–280)
- Isle of Man (see pages 326–330)

England

There's no place like home. I have nothing but praise for this country. Why do we need to fly anywhere when everything our toddlers need is at home? My brood don't care if the beach is in Cornwall, Corsica or Costa Rica. To them, a beach is a beach is a beach. Whatever the weather. And at this age, that is all they are really interested in. Last year I spent thousands on a trip to the Caribbean. The journey was long, it cost me a fortune but the weather was great and I think our lot enjoyed it. About a week after we got back we went down to Cornwall for the weekend and all my four-and three-year-old could talk about was what they had found on the beach in Cornwall, and that it was much more fun than the other place – the name of which neither could remember.

Father of six, two of whom are toddlers, from Southampton

The basics

The best way to get about with toddlers? Let the train take the strain. Believe it or not, toddlers love travelling by train. They hate travelling by car. One toddler told me: 'Mummy and daddy always get very cross in the car when we stop. They don't on a train.'

Culture – Toddler-friendly in the places recommended below
Toddler-friendly rating –
   attitude 3/10
   facilities/countryside/climate 8/10
'Best bits' for toddlers – The beaches, steam trains, petting zoos, friends made

266

'Best bit' for parents – Accessibility
When to go – Always out of school holidays

Useful websites
Book train tickets online www.thetrainline.com
Helpful site unravelling the rail network www.rail.co.uk
Use the route planner for driving in Europe as well as the UK
    www.rac.co.uk
Information on airports in the UK and Ireland www.a2bairports.com
All about the capital www.thisislondon.co.uk

Why holiday in England?

- No air travel. Most toddlers don't mind planes but they hate airports (with a few notable exceptions). According to my research, this was one of the main reasons for spending a holiday in England.
- Although England doesn't have as much sunshine as more southerly resorts, there are masses of wonderful attractions to entertain toddlers. All the parents I spoke to who had travelled around England with their young families had unanimous praise for the country. The skill is to choose the accommodation and attractions you visit wisely and not waste time with so-called 'family-friendly resorts', which tend to provide theme parks, museums and adventure playgrounds that are only suitable for children aged 10 or over. The outstanding attractions on offer include:
- The best petting zoos in the world.
- The best steam trains (all of which claim to be Thomas the Tank Engine or directly related to him). The original is in the Isle of Man, where the film was made (see page 329). Remember that toddlers can't differentiate between a ride on the Orient Express, a ride on the Rocky Mountaineer or a ride on a steam train in Cornwall. It is simply a ride on a train to them.
- Legoland in Windsor is perhaps the most famous 'land in miniature' but there are hundreds more round the country (see below).

- For other attractions, go to www.sightseeing.co.uk – it will give you further ideas to entertain your toddler. But remember that museums, historical monuments, art galleries and most theme parks will not be suitable.
- Our coastlines may not supply white sands and azure sea like the beaches in the Seychelles, but as far as toddlers are concerned the sand here makes better sandcastles and there are fascinating rock pools to explore, full of starfish, crabs and other sea creatures. In general, toddlers seem to be less concerned about the weather than their parents. They are happy to play on the beach even when it is windy and spitting with rain.

Where to stay

- If you seek a little luxury, go for a weekend break at any hotel in the Luxury Family Hotels Group (Website: www.luxury-family-hotels.com); or Radfords Hotel in Dawlish (Tel: 01626 863 322, Website: www.radfordshotel.co.uk).
- Visit www.childfriendly.co.uk, www.babycentre.co.uk or any of the hotel groups listed on pages 119 to 123.
- Self-catering cottages offer excellent accommodation. Be sure to specify that you have toddlers when booking. Check out Rural Retreats (Tel: 01386 701 177, Website: www.ruralretreats.co.uk); Toad Hall Cottages (Tel: 08700 777 234, Website: www.toadhallcottages.com); Norfolk Country Cottages (Tel: 01603 871 872, Website: www.norfolkcottages.co.uk); Beverley Holidays (Tel: 01803 843 887, Website: www.beverley-holidays.co.uk); Shoreline Cottages (Tel: 0113 289 3539, Website: www.shoreline-cottages.com); Hoseasons Country Cottages (Tel: 01502 500 500, Website: www.hoseasons.co.uk); Landmark Trust (Tel: 01628 825 925, Website: www.landmarktrust.co.uk); Forgotten Houses (Tel: 01326 340 153, Website: www.forgottenhouses.co.uk); Classic Cottages (Tel: 01326 555 555); Premier Cottages Direct (Tel: 01271 336 050, Website: www.premiercottages.co.uk); or Helpful Holidays (Tel: 01647 433 593, Website: www.helpfulholidays.com). It is also worth looking at

www.easycottages.com and www.cottages4you.co.uk.

- Choose accommodation on or near a beach, and ensure that the beach has passed EU standards for cleanliness (see below). Self-catering firms with a good range include Country Holidays (Tel: 01282 445 400, Website: www.country-holidays.co.uk); English Country Cottages (Tel: 0870 585 1100); and National Trust (Enterprises) Ltd (Tel: 01225 791 199).

- Centreparcs in Sherwood Forest (Rufford Newark, Nottinghamshire, Tel: 01623 827 400); Elveden Forest (Brandon, Suffolk, Tel: 01842 894 000); and Longleat Forest (Warminster, Wiltshire, Tel: 01985 848 000) all offer children's clubs from 3 years plus, children's play area and babysitting services as well as a toddlers' pool. For reservations, contact 08705 200 300, Website: www.centreparcs.co.uk (see Holiday Villages, page 94). Oasis Forest Holiday Villages (Tel: 08705 086 000, Website: www.oasishols.co.uk) in the Lake District National Park has a fully registered kindergarten for babies from three months to five years, which includes tumble tots, a toddlers' pool and soft play area.

- See also the advice given for each of the regions below.

Beaches

- To find out which beaches in the UK are the cleanest visit www.goodbeachguide.co.uk. Some toddler favourites around the country include Holkham (tourist information, Tel: 01328 710 885); Walberswick (Tel: 01502 724 729); West Wittering (Tel: 01243 775 888); Compton Bay (Tel: 01983 760 015); Studland Bay (Tel: 01929 422 885); Bude (Tel: 01288 354 240); Formby (Tel: 0906 680 6886); and Bamburgh (Tel: 01289 330 733).

- Beaches in the southwest are often cleaner. Among the best are Newquay and St Ives in Cornwall, Weymouth and Bournemouth in Dorset, and Cowes on the Isle of Wight.

- In the southeast, Bognor Regis in West Sussex and Hove in East Sussex are recommended. Sandgate Beach at Deal and Sandwich in Kent, Brightlingsea and Felixstowe in Essex and Cromer in Norfolk are also considered safe for swimming.

- In the northeast, Anderby in Lincolnshire, Reighton in North Yorkshire and Seaton Carew in Hartlepool are considered safe.

- In the northwest, the safest beaches for swimming are Bigger Bank at Walney Island in Cumbria and West Kirby in the Wirral.

What the regions offer

I've listed only the attractions, accommodation and eateries that have been tried and tested by families with toddlers and recommended as either very good or excellent. Please note that this is not always the same as the places that tourist offices claim to be 'fun for all the family'. Just because an attraction has buggies for hire, children's menus and baby-changing facilities doesn't mean the attraction itself is of interest to a toddler. Toddlers enjoy beaches, aquariums, petting zoos and play-grounds – in that order, it seems. All of which England has (excuse the pun) in spadefuls.

The English Tourism Council offer an extremely informative and well laid out website www.englandgetaway.com. Use it! It's one of the best resources I found.

London

Tel: 09068 663 344 – calls cost 60 pence per minute; Website: www.londontown.com, or www.londontouristboard.com

Where to stay
- The best toddler-friendly hotels in London tend to be the smaller ones. Two of the best and most characterful and friendly are: Browns in W1 (Tel: 020 7493 6020), which is very friendly and old-fashioned with squeaky floorboards; and The Goring Hotel (Tel: 020 7396 9000) in Victoria, where all the rooms overlook a pretty garden. Both wonderful. Both central.

The best bits
- Pick up the London Pass (www.londonpass.com), which gives free access to over 50 London attractions – some of which are toddler-friendly. Don't spend any more than four hours at a

270

time sightseeing. You and your toddlers will get tired very quickly.

Fish

- The London Aquarium (County Hall, Riverside Building, Westminster Bridge Road, Tel: 020 7967 8000) is one of the best in the world.

Picnic in the park

- When the sun shines, take a picnic to the park. Best park for picnics is Green Park, which has bands playing in the summer, jugglers and street entertainers. Why not visit the new Thames Barrier eco park in the London Borough of Newham, and Princess Diana's Memorial Garden in Kensington Gardens. Open air concerts are excellent for small children, and there is always a summer programme of events at Kenwood (Hampstead), Kew Gardens (Richmond) and Crystal Palace Park (South London). Take your toddler and a picnic and enjoy!

Zoo

- Try out Battersea Park Children's Zoo (Tel: 020 8871 7540), which is good for toddlers. And, of course, London Zoo (Regent's Park, Tel: 020 7722 3333) is a favourite with toddlers even though they aren't allowed to touch most of the animals. If you get held up at Gatwick, try Gatwick Zoo (Rectory Lane Charlwood, West Sussex, Tel: 01293 862 312) which was founded over 30 years ago and has over 280 different species of animal from marmosets to spider monkeys, wallabies and penguins. It also accommodates the cats, dogs and giant snakes impounded at airport customs.

Don't bother

- Leave the Tate (Britain and Modern), Westminster Abbey, the Tower of London and London Dungeon for another five years or so. They won't be interested at this age.

Where to eat

- Smollensky's (The Strand, WC2, Tel: 020 7497 2101); Pizza

271

Express (Tel: 01895 618 618 for branches). Also try Yo Sushi (Tel: 020 7841 0700 for branches); the cute metal waiter that serves canned drinks will fascinate them more than the food. Avoid the larger theme restaurants which are usually crowded and of more interest to older children. Bread and Roses (68 Clapham Manor Street, SW4, Tel: 020 7498 1779) is known for its family appeal – on Sunday's there's an African buffet with music and entertainment designed especially for children. Fish County Hall (3b Belvedere Road, SE1, Tel: 020 7234 3333) has a knockabout atmosphere that makes it okay for children to whizz around and feel welcome – they also have their own menu and kid's pack.

South East England

(East Sussex, Kent, Surrey, West Sussex) Tel: 01892 540 766, Website: www.gosouth.co.uk

Where to stay
• The Hurtwood Inn Hotel was hotel of the year in 2000, and it's found in Guildford, Surrey (Peaslake, Guildford, Surrey GU5 9RR, Tel: 01306 730 851, Fax: 01306 731 390, Website: www.hurtwoodinhotel.com. If B&Bs are more your style, Hatpin, in West Sussex, also welcomes toddlers (Bosham Lane, Old Bosham, Chichester, West Sussex PO18 8HG, Tel: 01243 572 644, Website: www.hatpins.co.uk). In Kent, you'll find the Caravan Holiday Park of the Year in Folkestone. Varne Ridge Holiday Park is highly recommended for toddlers. Check out their website for details (145 Old Dover Road, Capel le Ferne, Folkestone, Kent CT18 7HX, Tel: 01303 251 765, Website: www.varne-ridge.co.uk).

The best bits

PARKS
• Princes Park, Gildredge Park, Hampden Park and Helen Gardens Park in Eastbourne have swings for toddlers and older children. All four have adjacent kiosks selling ice creams and drinks. Princes

272

Park, opposite the beach, has a paddling pool in the play area.
Beware the unfenced boating lake but enjoy feeding the swans.
Hampden Park has a large pond, which is only partly fenced.
Toddlers feeding ducks and walking around the pond need close
supervision. There are some nice picnic areas.

- At Groombridge Place (Tel: 01892 863 999) there are adventure
  playgrounds, imaginative natural sculptures, and a Raptor Centre
  which puts on birds-of-prey shows every day. More than just
  flowerbeds.
- Knockhatch Adventure Park (Hempsted Lane, Hailsham, East
  Sussex BN27 3PR, Tel: 01323 442 051, Fax: 01323 843 878,
  Website: wwwknockhatch.com) has an indoor play area suitable
  for toddlers and older children, with an under fives area. Although
  part of a large adventure park, you can simply pay to visit the
  indoor area. Coffee area adjacent to play area.

PETTING ZOO

- Drusilla's Park, Alfriston (Polegate, East Sussex, Tel: 01323 874
  100, Fax: 01323 874 101, Website: www.drusillas.co.uk) is an
  excellent small zoo with toddlers' indoor and outdoor play areas.
  At Seven Sisters Sheep Centre, on the Downs (Tel: 01323 423
  207) toddlers can see and feed baby lambs in lambing season
  (spring).

STEAM TRAINS

- The Bluebell Railway (Sheffield Park Station, East Sussex, Tel:
  01825 723 777) will be a favourite of any Thomas the Tank
  Engine fan, as will the Didcot Railway Centre (Didcot,
  Oxfordshire, Tel: 01235 817 200) where on certain 'steam days'
  you can ride on the trains.
- Eastbourne Miniature Steam Railway (Lottbridge Drove,
  Eastbourne, Tel: 01323 520 229, Website: www.emsr.co.uk) has
  steam train rides around a wildfowl lake, play park and café.
  Adjoining golf course.

TODDLER THEATRE

- Eastbourne Theatres are well worth visiting. Kids under 2 years go free and they have toddler shows during traditional family holiday times (Rupert the Bear, Postman Pat, Noddy, etc). One of the few places anywhere that invites children to the New Years Eve Party.

- Wish Tower Puppet Museum (King Edward's Parade, Eastbourne, Tel: 01323 417 776, Fax 01323 644 440, Website: www.puppets.co.uk) is great for children of all ages. They have a selection of all kinds of puppets from different eras and cultures plus puppet shows.

Where to eat

- Beachy Head pub (Tel: 01323 728 060) in Eastbourne has an area for toddlers to play and eat. Children's meals available. Lunchtimes are very busy, so better to go as early or late as poss. Open all day.
- ESK Warehouse (Courtlands Road, Eastbourne, Tel: 01323 416 916) has a play area for young children but toddlers would need supervision. Ideal if you want to shop. There is a coffee area adjacent to the play area, which costs 50 pence for half an hour.

Southern England

(Berkshire, Buckinghamshire, Hampshire, Oxfordshire, Dorset and Isle of Wight) Tel: 02380 625 518, Website: www.gosouth.go.uk)

Where to stay

- Heathlands Hotel (12 Grove Road, East Cliff, Tel: 01202 553 336), Suncliff Hotel (29 East Overcliff Drive, East Cliff, Tel: 01202 291 711) and Riviera Hotel (Burnaby Road, Alum Chine, Tel: 01202 763 653) all have babysitting and are within walking distance of the beach, which is where toddlers really want to be when the sun shines.

The best bits

FISH
- The Aquarium (Clarence Esplanade, Southsea, Tel: 023 9287 5222) has jellyfish, rock pools, creatures, a fish hospital, and an interactive area plus outdoor play area.

- Bournemouth has a good Oceanarium (Pier Approach, Tel: 01202 311 993).

LEGOLAND

- The world of Lego (Winkfield Road, Windsor, Berkshire, Tel: 01753 626 100) is set in over 150 acres of attractive parkland with over 50 different rides, shows and attractions. It's a fabulous day out for toddlers, but they're bound to want you to buy them some, and it doesn't come cheap! New attractions include the Wave Rider, the Creation Centre, Lego Racers 8c and The Lego Millennium Dome. Located on the B3022 Bracknel/Ascot road 2 miles from Windsor town centre. Well signposted from the M4 and M3. By rail, just under 30 mins from London Paddington or Waterloo, with dedicated shuttle bus services to the Park from both Windsor stations.

MODEL VILLAGE

- Seek out Bekonscot Model Village (Beaconsfield, Tel: 01494 672 919), one of the oldest model villages in the world. The circa 1930s village even has a four-track outdoor model railway, as well as castles and churches and miniature shrubs set in beautifully landscaped gardens.

PLAY AREAS

- Action Zone at the Farmhouse (Burrfields Road, Portsmouth, Tel: 023 9265 0510) is an indoor action-adventure centre for children under 4ft 9in. Double-decker freefall slide, spook tunnel, rope bridge, boulder canyon and ball pit and soft play for children under 4. Parents must remain on the premises. Or check out the Kidzone Safety Beaches, Wacky Warehouse (Tel: 01202 294 307) for an indoor soft play area.
- The Playzone (Unit A4, Oak Park Industrial Estate, Harbour Road, Cosham, Tel: 023 9237 9999) has activities for all ages – mazes, ballpits, slides, ropes and climbing walls.
- Pirate Pete's (Clarence Pier, Southsea, Tel: 023 9286 4789) has an indoor play area suitable for toddlers and children must be under 5ft tall.

WINDSOR

- This place has loads more than just the Castle (check it out on www.windsor.gov.uk.). Much of the town centre is now pedestrianized and all roads have raised crossing areas for buggies. There are large undercover 'outdoor' areas in the Windsor Royal Station – with toddler-friendly cafés and wide walkways. Toddler-orientated shops abound (Baby Gap, John Lewis's excellent baby and toddler department, Early Learning Centre, Beatrix Potter shop), and restaurants have intelligent children's menus (as well as beans, burgers and ice-cream) served all day. Batchelor's Acre is an open space just off the High Street, with a child's play area and water feature. Windsor Leisure Centre has a children's pool with waves, slides and water features – a favoured treat after a day at Legoland.

ZOO

- Marwell Zoological Park (Colden Common, Winchester, Hampshire, Tel: 01962 777 407) has over 200 species of animals, including Siberian tigers, snow leopards, rhino, meerkats, hippos and zebra. There's Penguin World, Encounter Village, Tropical World, Giraffe House, new Owl Aviaries and Nocturnal House. With rail trains, special events, creature close-up sessions and adventure playgrounds, this is one of the best toddler-friendly theme parks you'll find in the country.
- Visit the Staunton Country Park (Middle Park Way, Leigh Park, Havant, Tel: 023 9245 3405) where you can meet and feed the animals, featuring shire horses, sheep and pigmy goats.

Where to eat

- In Bournemouth, eat at Uncle Sam's American Style Diner (48 Old Christchurch Road, Tel: 01202 293 355); Harry Ramsdens (by Bournemouth Pier, Tel: 01202 295 818) or Big Steak Pub and Wacky Warehouse (Pier Approach, Tel: 01202 294 307).
- In Southsea, try the Clarence (Clarence Esplanade, Tel: 023 9273 4622) which has a Charlie Chalk Play area and children's menu. Sur la Mer (69 Palmerston Road, Tel: 023 9287 6678) has toys to play with as well as a children's menu.

276

- In Portsmouth, The Farmhouse (Burrfields Road, Tel: 023 9267 1111) has a family room plus play area. Sovereigns (Big Steak Pub, Kingston Crescent, Tel: 023 9263 9673) has a Wacky Warehouse play area. Thatched House (Locksway Road, Tel: 023 9282 1527) has a family room with indoor and outdoor play areas and a children's menu.
- At Bat & Ball (Hayden Farm Lane, Clanfield, Tel: 023 9263 2692) children are welcome until 9pm and balloons, funbooks and crayons are provided.

Isle of Wight

A small island that punches bigger than its weight, as far as my toddlers are concerned. My two loved the dinosaur connection. It also appears very safe.

Father of two toddlers, Northampton

The basics
Time difference from UK – None
Best way to get there – Ferry (Wightlink and Red Funnel Ferries)
  Tel: 023 8033 3042, Website: www.redfunnel.co.uk
  (Southampton to East Cowes),
  Tel: 0870 582 7744, Website: www.wightlink.co.uk
  (Portsmouth to Fishbourne, Lymington to Yarmouth)
Culture – Toddler-friendly
Toddler-friendly rating – 9/10
'Best bits' for toddlers – Dinosaurs and beaches.
'Best bits' for parents – Close to home, accessibility. Very safe. Excellent walks. Lots to entertain the toddlers.
When to go – Late spring, early autumn
Where to go – Touring island – not an island to stay in one place
Accommodation – Hotels (although there are holiday parks and self-catering apartments)
Tour operators – Both Wightlink and Red Funnel (see above) offer good-value holiday packages

The journey to the Island itself is enjoyable for toddlers. Good motorway networks ensure a fast and smooth drive to the ferry ports of Portsmouth, Lymington, Southampton and Southsea.

Alternatively, rail connections from London take less than an hour and a half. Then the sea crossing to the Island, on a choice of hover-craft, catermaran or car ferry, allows your holiday to begin.

For further information call 01983 813 818 or visit www.island breaks.co.uk.

Where to stay

- Places to stay that are toddler-friendly include The Priory Bay Hotel (St Helens, Tel: 01983 613 146), which has babysitting and childcare. It's in an idyllic location, just a short stroll from the sea.
- Alternatively the Orchards Holiday Caravan and Camping Park (Tel: 01983 531 331, Website: www.orchards-holiday-park.co.uk) is an option.

The best bits

BEACHES

- Over half of the Isle of Wight is recognised as an Area of Outstanding Natural Beauty, while much of the coastline is designated Heritage Coast, a title awarded only to the coastlines of the highest quality in England and Wales. The beaches are excellent for toddlers and Compton Beach on the south-west coast is considered one of the best family beaches in the world. Award-winning Sandown and Shanklin have long, sandy beaches and excellent facilities for families. Colwell Bay, a small sand and shingle beach is tucked away on the quieter west coast of the Island with panoramic views of the western beaches of the Solent. Totland Bay is a delightful small beach with a short esplanade and privately owned pier.

DINOSAURS AND THE REST

- The Isle of Wight is one of the top ten sites for finding dinosaur fossils in the world, hence there is a strong 'dinosaur' theme running through many of the attractions on the island. Most

278

toddlers will be fascinated by dinosaurs – and those parents I interviewed (and their toddlers) were enthralled. Check out the recently opened Dinosaur Museum (Tel: 01982 404 344) in Sandown. The best of the rest are listed below.

- Blackgang Chine (Tel: 01983 730 233, Website: www.blackgang chine.com), Amazon World (Tel: 01983 867 122, Website: www.amazonworld.co.uk); Robin Hill (Tel: 01983 730 052, Website: www.robin-hill.com); Brickfields Horsecountry (Tel: 01983 566 801, Website: www.brickfields.net); Calbourne Mill and Museum (Tel: 01983 531 227, Website: www.calbournewatermill.com); Carisbrooke Castle (Tel: 01983 522 107, Website: www.english-heritage.org.uk); Colemans Animal Farm (Tel: 01983 522 831); Dinosaur Farm (Tel: 01983 740 844, Website: www.dinosaur-farm.co.uk); Dinosaur Isle and Flamingo Park Wildlife Encounter (Kirby, misperton, Malton, Yorkshire Y017 6UX, Tel: 01983 612 153, Website: www.flamingoparkiw.com).

Events

- There are many events that would appeal to toddlers. These include the Yarmouth Easter Duck Race (Tel: 01983 760 108) and 'Steam Up' at Compton Farm (01983 740 215) – steam engines and fire engines – both of which happen in May.
- Other events include sheep shearing and spinning demonstrations (last weekend in May) at the IW Rare Breeds park (see below) – which is also a children's fun day with lots of face painting and dressing up.
- East Cowes Victorian Festival (second weekend in July; Tel: 01983 281 524) is a wonderful family day with arena events which include children's fairground, music and stall-holders dressed in Victorian costume.
- Carnivals and festivals include Ryde Festival and Fireworks (third weekend in July; Tel: 01983 823 828); Sandown Carnival (during third week in July; Tel: 01983 563 207). A main carnival event with procession of floats around the town, fancy dress parade, children's day, bands, competitions.

Fish

- Fort Victoria Marine Aquarium (Tel: 01983 760 283, Website: www.isleofwightaquarium.co.uk).

Parks and Playgrounds

- The Needles Park (Tel: 0870 458 0022, Website: www.theneedles. co.uk).
- Peter Pan's Playground (Tel: 01983 566 339) on the Esplanade in Ryde.
- Puckpool Park (Tel: 01983 562 086) in Seaview near Ryde.

Toddler Theatre

- Shanklin Theatre (Tel: 01983 868 000) performs a modern pantomime with audience participation every Wednesday.

Wildlife

- Isle of Wight Donkey Sanctuary (Tel: 01983 852 693, Website: www.donksanc.demon.co.uk).
- Isle of Wight Rare Breeds and Waterfowl Park (Tel: 01983 855 144/852 649).
- Tiger and Big Cat Sanctuary (Tel: 01983 403 883/405 562).
- Every toddler will love hand-feeding the penguins at Flamingo Park (as well as the macaws and parrots). For feeding times and more information, contact 01983 612 153.

Where to eat

- Toddler-friendly places include Chequers Inn (Rookley, Tel: 01983 840 314), a rural pub with large play area, voted 'family pub of the year 1999'.
- The Wight Mouse (Chale, Tel: 01983 730 431), which has live entertainment nightly, pony rides, pet's corner and garden play area.
- Nestling in the woods overlooking the Priory Bay Hotel (see above), the Priory Oyster offers freshly barbecued Bembridge lobster, salads and pastas.

South West England

(Somerset, Bristol, Cornwall, Devon, Dorset (Western), Isle of Scilly, South Gloucestershire, Wiltshire)
Tel: 0870 442 0880, Website: www.westcountrynow.com

Where to stay
There are loads of good places in this area. Here are a few recommendations:

- Bedruthan Steps Hotel, Cornwall (Tel: 01637 860 555, Website: www.bedruthanstepshotel.co.uk)
- Fowey Hall Hotel, Cornwall (Tel: 01726 833 866, Website: www.luxury-family-hotels.co.uk)
- Watergate Bay Hotel, Cornwall (Tel: 01637 860 543, Website: www.watergate.co.uk)
- The Gara Rock, Devon (Tel: 01548 842 342, Website: www.gara.co.uk)
- Polurrian Hotel, Lizard Peninsula, Cornwall (Tel: 01326 240 421, Website: www.polurrianhotel.com)
- Radfords Country Hotel, Devon (Tel: 01626 863 322, Website: www.radfordshotel.co.uk)
- Saunton Sands Hotel, Devon (Tel: 01271 890 212, Website: www.sauntonsands.co.uk)
- The Knoll House Hotel, Dorset (Tel: 01929 450 450, Website: www.knollhouse.co.uk)
- Moonfleet Manor, Weymouth, Dorset (Tel: 01305 786 948, Website: www.luxury-family-hotels.co.uk)
- The Sandbanks Hotel, Poole, Dorset (Tel: 01202 707 377, Website: www.sandbankshotel.co.uk)
- Calcot Manor, Nr Tetbury, Glos (Tel: 01666 890 391, Website: www.calcotmanor.co.uk)
- Woolley Grange Hotel, Bradford on Avon, Wiltshire (Tel: 01225 864 705, Website: www.luxury-family-hotels.co.uk)
- Stay at the Braddon Cottages (Tel: 01409 211 350) in Ashwater Devon, west of Okehampton off the A30 at Roadford Lake. There is a children's games room, swing, slide and sandpit for toddlers.

Set in 100 acres of meadow overlooking a beautiful valley with views south to Dartmoor.

- For a larger hotel, pick Berkeleys of St James in The Hoe, Cornwall (Tel: 01752 221 654) which is a non-smoking hotel and offers babysitting as well as pushchair-friendly lifts. Alternatively the Grand Hotel in the Hoe (Tel: 01752 661 195, Website: www.plymouthgrand.com) is central, has babysitting and staff who made Tom feel like a king.

- Try the Halfway House Inn, Cawsand Bay (Tel: 01752 822 279) or the Gabber Farm, Down Thomas, Nr Plymouth (Tel: 01752 862 269) which has babysitting and family rooms as well as animals to watch.

- Guest houses are plentiful in the area and these can be preferable to the larger impersonal hotels if the owners are toddler-friendly. Contact the guest house before you arrive to make sure they have cots. Highbury in Lipson (Tel: 01752 665 957), Drakes View in West Hoe (Tel: 01752 221 500) and Crown Yealm in Newton Ferrers (Tel: 01752 872 365) offer babysitting and gardens that are toddler safe.

- In Devon, Downe Cottages (just outside the village of Hartland, Tel: 01237 441 881 or visit www.downecottages.com) have been converted from Victorian stone barns into luxury holiday accommodation. Comprising one-, two- and three-bedroom properties, they provide a real home from home in a beautiful rural setting, just a short walk from the beaches and coves of the North Devon coast.

The best bits

ADVENTURE PARKS

- The region around Plymouth and Dartmouth has many purpose-built plastic 'family-friendly attractions' but these are more relevant to older children who are able to go on the rides and appreciate the surroundings. One of the best, safest and most fun I've discovered for toddlers in the UK is Woodlands (Tel: 01803 712 598) in Blackawton, Totnes, South Devon. It's an all-weather leisure park, which has rides suitable for toddlers, 16 excellent playzones, and a falconry and animal complex.

- Another good one is Dobwalls Family Adventure Park, near Liskeard, Cornwall (Tel: 01579 320 325), which also has its own steam railway.
- The Big Sheep (Abbotsham, Tel: 01237 472 366) in Devon is a must (it's a working farm turned wacky tourist attraction. Combining traditional rural crafts, such as cheese making and shearing, with hilarious novelties such as sheep racing and duck trailing, it also has massive Ewetopia adventure play zones for kids and fun live shows for adults).
- Also pay a visit to Once Upon a Time (Woolacoombe, Devon, Tel: 01271 870 999).

BEACHES

- The counties of Devon and Cornwall are surrounded by the sea so they have lots of good beaches. This is really all Tom wanted to know when we made our way by train to this part of the country.

BUTTERFLIES, OTTERS AND DONKEYS

- The Buckfast Butterflies and Dartmoor Otter Sanctuary (North Petherwin near Launceston, Cornwall PL15 8LW, Tel: 01364 642 916, Email otters@paston.co.uk, Website: www.ottertrust.org.uk) is fascinating.
- So is the Miniature Pony Centre in the unfortunately named Wormhill Farm in North Bovey, nr Newton Abbot, Devon (Tel: 01647 432 400), where your toddler almost certainly will ask for his own pony to take home.
- For more donkeys there's the Tamar Valley Donkey Park in St Anns Chapel, Gunnislake, Cornwall (Tel: 01822 834 072), which has donkey rides, baby animals, toddler playgrounds, a good picnic area and is worth a day's visit.
- For more otters, the Otter Sanctuary at Tamar (Tel: 01566 785 646), in North Petherwin, nr Launceston, Cornwall, is also excellent for toddlers and has helpful toddler-friendly guides.

Fish

- Plymouth has the national marine aquarium (Tel: 01752 220 084, Website: www.national-aquarium.co.uk), which claims to be one of the UK's most popular attractions. It's fascinating, well thought-out and, most importantly, toddlers can see what is happening and don't have to be picked up all the time in order to get a better view. One warning: I suggest only going out of school time when you can actually get to see the fish and not piggy-back your toddler over the top of other adult and older children heads. This aquarium has everything from seahorses to sharks, and there are excellent guides who are used to speaking to rather than speaking down to toddlers. The play areas are all based on a marine theme. Good changing facilities and eateries which have more unusual toddler fare as well as nuggets, burgers and fries. Closed Christmas Day, but open from Easter until end of October each year. It's a day's adventure so give it that.
- The Blue Reef Aquarium in Newquay Cornwall is also worth visiting (Tel: 01637 878 134).

Hedgehogs

- Tom's favourite was the South West Hedgehog Hospital at Prickly Ball Farm, in Denbury Road, Newton Abbot, Devon (Tel: 01626 362 319, Website: www.hedgehog.org.uk) which was absolutely delightful. Watching the toddlers watching the hedgehogs watching the toddlers kept me amused all day.

Little Monkeys

- A protected colony of woolly monkeys are kept at the Monkey Sanctuary in Looe, Cornwall (Tel: 01503 262 532). Beautiful gardens and a large play area suitable for toddlers. There is only limited access with pushchairs, but you will be able to navigate the paths – just go out of school holidays.

Parks

- Bath, though beautiful, has more to interest grown-ups than toddlers. Many of the attractions are museum-based but toddlers enjoy the parks, especially Royal Victoria Park with its extensive play area, which is popular all year around.

PIXIES

- Pixieland in Dartmeet, Princetown, Devon (Tel: 01364 631 412, Website: www.pixieland.co.uk) is definitely worth a visit for families with toddlers – especially if your toddler still believes in fairies and little people. I still do.

STEAM TRAINS

- In the immediate area you will find the Avon Valley Steam Railway (Website: www.avonvalleyrailway.co.uk) at Bitton (regularly visited by Thomas the Tank Engine and his Friends), and the Brokerswood Country Park (Tel: 01373 822 238, Fax: 01373 858 474, Email: woodland.park@virgin.net).
- The Bodmin & Wenford Railway in Bodmin, Cornwall (Tel: 01208 73666) is a 6-mile branch line linking Bodmin town to the mainline station at Bodmin Parkway and Soscarne connecting with Camel Trail. It's operated with steam locomotives (Thomas the Tank engine to you and me) except Saturdays and gives access on foot to Lanhydrock House (which Tom didn't like) and Cardinham Woods (which he did). Best route is via the town centre along Lostwithiel Road and the whole journey takes about 1½ hours return. Take a picnic lunch.
- Alternatively try South Devon Railway (Tel: 01364 642 338), again steam and just over 7 miles running beside the River Dart and offering a useful route between the tourist centres of Totnes and Buckfastleigh; or Launceston Steam Railway (St Thomas Road, Tel: 01566 775 665), from medieval Launceston to the picturesque hamlet of New Mills. Charming.

TODDLER THEATRE

- Bath's Theatre Royal (Tel: 01225 448 844, Website: www.theatreroyal.co.uk) has a number of child-friendly events, including kids' shows and workshops called 'Springboard' for the 3+ age group on Saturdays. The Theatre Royal also runs occasional art workshops for pre-school children and their parents. And of course there's the Pantomime in December and January every year.

WILDLIFE PARK

- The excellent Dartmoor Wildlife Park and Conservation Centre (Sparkwell, nr Plymouth, Tel: 01752 837 209) has a wide selection of endangered animals from around the world, including big cats, bears, wolves and birds of prey. Open all year 10 am to dusk, it has that added attraction of telling toddlers about conservation in a very simplistic and entertaining way. They say you can see everything in 1½ hours. Not with a toddler you can't. Give it a half day at least.

Heart of England

(Derbyshire, Shropshire, Gloucestershire, Herefordshire, Leicestershire, Lincolnshire, Northamptonshire, Nottinghamshire, Warwickshire, West Midlands, Worcestershire) Tel: 0800 044 440, Website: www.visit heartofengland.com

Where to stay
- The Village Hotel & Leisure Club (Castlegate Park, Birmingham Road Dudley, DY1 4TB, Tel: 01384 216 600, Email: village.dudley@village-hotels.com) has lots of child-friendly facilities, including swimming pool, crêche and children's activities, and they run family-fun days with small animals, face painters and costume characters. They have family rooms and there is a babysitting service.
- Moreton Park Lodge (Moreton Park, Gledrid, Chirk, Wrexham LL14 5DG, Tel: 01691 776 666, Fax: 01691 776 655, Website: www.moretonparklodge.com). Facilities include free use of cots subject to availability and Billy Badger's Playden.
- Egypt Mill (Nailsworth GL6 0AE, Tel: 01453 833 449) has cots and high-chairs, and staff will heat and store babies' bottles as required. There is a baby-listening service via intercom to reception. Normal beans, spaghetti and pizza-type menus for children – but the chef is happy to provide small portions of adult meals on request. This hotel is entered across a bridge over a river

with a mill-race, which is exciting for children to look at but they would need to hold an adult's hand!

- The following have all received good reviews from families:
- Evesham Hotel (Coppers Lane, Evesham, Tel: 01386 765 566, Website: www.eveshamhotel.com)
- Terrick Hall Hotel (Terrick Road, Whitchurch, Shropshire, Tel: 01948 66303)
- Doddington Lodge Hotel (Doddington, Whitchurch, Shropshire, Tel: 01948 662 539)
- Hanmer Arms Hotel (Hanmer, nr Whitchurch, Shropshire, Tel: 01948 830 532)
- Combermere Arms (Burleydam, Whitchurch, Shropshire, Tel: 01948 871 223)
- In Shrewsbury, the Radbrook Hall Hotel (Radbrook Road, Tel: 01743 236 676) has an indoor and outdoor play area for toddlers and babysitting services.

The best bits

FAIRY TALES

- In Telford, visit Wonderland (Tel: 01952 591 633 Fax: 01952 591 633, Website: www.wonderland.uk.ws). It's in a woodland setting, and a genuinely magical place where toddlers can discover their nursery rhyme and fairy tale favourites

IN MINIATURE

- There is a wonderful Model Village at Bourton on the Water, Gloucestershire (Tel: 01451 820 467).

MAZES

- Spend time at Symonds Yat, in Herefordshire's Wye Valley (Tel: 01600 890 360, Website: www.mazes.co.uk). Eccentrics Lindsey and Edward Heyes have built the Amazing Hedge Puzzle, an eight-sided maze, which confounds grown-ups as much as the toddlers. Visit the UK's only Museum of Mazes, where you learn about the mystical and symbolic aspects of the subject. The maze is called a labyrinth of love: you enter it with your friend, then split up and try to find each other again (don't try this with your toddler). There's a raised viewing platform on the outside of the maze, so you're able to watch without going inside.

On your bike

- My favourite is the Pedalabikaway Cycle Centre at Cannop Valley, near Coleford, Forest of Dean (Tel: 01594 860 065, Website: www.pedalabikeaway.com). Tom was able to sit in the child seat in the back of the bike while I rode along on cycle tracks though 24,000 acres of beautiful forest. The best way to reach the Forest of Dean is by train.

Parks

- Stratford Park, close to Stroud town centre, has excellent squirrel-spotting opportunities, a good tree collection and a lake with ducks, as well as unusual tiered rings that toddlers love to climb. There is a Museum in the Park, which was designed with plenty of input from children. It includes low-level hands-on displays, galleries and a 'boat' area with books and toys. There are hidden objects to hunt for and various other special events for children.
- Birdland Park and Gardens, Bourton on the Water (Tel: 01451 820 480) has 7 acres of woodland, river and gardens inhabited by over 500 birds (including penguins and flamingos, parrots and toucans), plus a play area with more than the usual swings and slides to keep toddlers occupied.
- For glorious walks, try the Beechenhurst Lodge and Picnic Site at Beechenhurst, Forest of Dean (Tel: 01594 827 357) or the 120-acre Slimbridge Wildfowl and Wetlands Centre, at Slimbridge (Tel: 01453 890 333, Website: www.wwt.org.uk). Both are award-winning and include well-designed children's activity and play areas. Slimbridge boasts the world's largest collection of exotic, rare and endangered wildfowl. Slimbridge is between Bristol and Gloucester. Follow the signs from the M5 (junctions 13 or 14).

Petting farms

- The Countryside Experience at Park Hall, Oswestry, Shropshire

(Tel: 01691 671 123, Website: www.parkhallfarm.co.uk) is a
Victorian farm with huge horses, friendly pets and farm animals as
well as an indoor area with toy tractor, bouncy castle, games and
computers.

- Hoo Farm Animal Kingdom (Tel: 01952 677 917, Website:
  www.hoofarm.com) is a real children's paradise. Bottle-feed the
  lambs, collect the eggs, ride the mini quad bikes and visit the
  mini-farmyard tractor area.
- Rays Farm Country Matters (Tel: 01299 841 255, Website:
  www.stargate-uk.co.uk/adverts/rays.html) has wild animals and
  birds and over 40 woodcarvings in the myth and magic
  woodlands. Over 300 farm animals including deer, ponies, goats,
  owls and llama.
- Gobbett Rare Breeds Farm and Nursery in Ludlow (Tel: 01746
  718 276) has a fascinating collection of rare and unusual poultry,
  waterfowl and other farm animals. In the same area, visit the
  Wernlas Collection (Onibury, nr Ludlow, Tel: 01584 856 318)
  which is a conservation centre specializing in the breeding of rare
  and traditional poultry. Rare breeds of goats, sheep, pigs and
  donkeys entertain the youngsters.

Play areas
- Other attractions to interest toddlers include the Playbarn
  (Bridgebuilder, Wrekin Retail Park, Telford, Shropshire, Tel: 01952
  243 741) and Charlie Chalk (Clock Tower, Donnington, Telford,
  Shropshire, Tel: 01952 677 568).

Pots
- Visit the Gladstone Pottery Museum (Uttoxeter Road, Longton,
  Stoke-on-Trent, Tel: 01782 319 232), where your toddler can
  make a china flower – or at least try to. Under 5's get in free. At
  The Wedgewood Story (Barlaston, Stoke-on-Trent), toddlers are
  allowed to paint a plate and have it fired then the finished product
  is sent on to your home address. At the Bridgewater Pottery Café
  (Lichfield Street, Hanley, Stoke on Trent ST1 3EJ, Tel: 01782 269
  682) toddlers can decorate plates and cups, and you pay according
  to type of ware decorated.

SIMULATED BALLOON RIDES

- The Secret Hills at the Shropshire Hills Discovery Centre (School Lane, Craven Arms, Shropshire, SY7 9RS, Tel: 01588 676 000, Website: www.shropshire-cc.gov.uk/discovers.nsf) is an all-weather, glass-roofed building, where you can have fun in the simulated hot-air balloon ride and see the famous Shropshire Mammoth. Discover archaeology, nature and lovely scenery. This is millennium money well spent!

STEAM TRAINS

- Both Dean Forest Railway in Lydney, Forest of Dean (Tel: 01594 843 423) and the Warwickshire Railway in Toddington (Tel: 01242 621 405, Website: www.gwsr.plc.uk) are excellent steam railways run by enthusiastic volunteers. Special events at both include 'Thomas the Tank Engine' events in summer and Santa specials in December. Open weekends and school holidays March–October, plus weekends in December.
- For another Thomas the Tank experience, visit the Severn Valley Railway (The Railway Station, Bewdley, Worcs, DY12 1BG, Tel: 01299 403 816, Website: www.svr.co.uk) and see the beauty of the River Severn on a steam-driven train.
- The Foxfield Steam Railway (Tel: 01782 233 144) is also a big attraction thanks to Thomas the Tank Engine. Other toddler-friendly activities include the Dimensions fantasy fun pool and the excellent petting farm on the Shugborough Estate in Milford (Tel: 01889 881 388).

TRAMS

- The National Tramway Museum (Crich Matlock, Derbyshire, Tel: 01773 852 565, Website: www.tramway.co.uk) has an indoor play area with a soft model tramcar to play in plus softball sections and padded toys and games suitable for toddlers. The tram ride is fun, especially if you go on top or in one of the balcony tram cars. The line is 1 mile long with street scenes and a view over Derwent Valley.

Zoos

- West Midlands, Dudley Zoo and Castle (2 The Broadway, Dudley, West Midlands, DY1 4QB, Tel: 01384 215 300, Website: www.dudleyzoo.org.uk) open daily from 10am-3pm in winter, 10am-4.30pm in summer. Dudley Zoo has geared itself to the needs of families with toddlers, but leave the castle for another five years if you have a two- or three-year-olds. The animals on show can easily be seen at toddler level, without the adults resorting to piggy-backing them all over the place. Children up to four get in free, and there's a good selection of activities, from face painting to animal feeds and talks, to discovery centres where they can stroke a snake, fondle a frog or cuddle a cockroach. There's a land train, picnic area and adventure playground – all of which your toddler will love. It gets crowded during school holidays so visit at other times.

- Twycross Zoo (Atherstone, Warwickshire, CV9 3PX, Tel: 01827 880 250). There are over 1000 species from around the world in the 50 acres of parkland. The notable primate collection ranges from tiny Pygmy Marmosets (toddlers will love these) to impressive silverback Western Lowland Gorillas. Twycross is the only UK zoo to house our closest living relative – the Bonobo. Other animals to see include chimpanzees, lions, tigers, giraffe, pythons, alligators, elephants and flamingos. The sealions, penguins and seals are fed mid-afternoon most days. Popular with toddlers are Pet's Corner (where zoo babies mix with farm animals) and the Children's Adventure Playground, which has an undercover soft play area for younger children.

Where to eat

- For food, visit the Wacky Warehouse (Red House, Lilleshall, Telford, Shropshire, Tel: 01952 603 768) or eat at Captain Coconut (Tayleur Arms, Bratton, Telford, Shropshire, Tel: 01952 770 335). Both of these offer more than the usual burger, nuggets and chips.

- The Cookhouse (Shrewsbury Road, Bromfield, Ludlow, Tel: 01584 856 565) is a café, restaurant and bar offering the best fast-food fine cuisine, and toddlers are welcome. Or try Aragon's (Church

Street, Ludlow, Tel: 01584 873 282) for freshly cooked food at reasonable prices.

- In Whitchurch try out the Gingerbread Man Pub (Market Drayton, Tel: 01630 652 771), which has an indoor Tom Cobleigh Playbarn.
- Woodruffs Organic Cafe (High Street, Stroud, Glos., Tel: 01453 750 898) has a totally organic menu. There is a first-floor family room with high-chairs or a small table with small chairs, children's play-area and space for buggies. The menu offers small portions of adult meals.
- Fromebridge Mill (off the A38 at Whitminster, Tel: 01452 741 796) has high-chairs and an excellent 'healthy' children's menu, including steak, pasta, chicken, gammon, scampi, plaice, korma (yes, korma!) and vegetarian options. You enter across water with a view to the mill-race but this is well-protected.

East England

(Bedfordshire, Cambridgeshire, Essex, Hertfordshire, Norfolk, Suffolk) Tel: 01473 822922, Website: www.eastofenglandtouristboard.com

Where to stay
- Stay at the Bedford Arms Hotel (George Street, Woburn, Tel: 01525 290 441) and eat at the Market Place Restaurant (Tel: 01525 290 877), which both welcome and cater for toddlers, rather than just tolerate them. The Swan at Woburn Sands (part of the Beefeater group) is also toddler-friendly.

The best bits

ADVENTURE PLAYGROUNDS
- Funstop (Cromer, Tel: 01206 514 976) is a children's indoor adventure centre with a giant slide, ball pond, tubes, scrambling nets, a special under 3's area and a super snack bar, plus lots more.
- Another must do is a visit to the Dinosaur Adventure Park (in Lenwade, near Norwich, Tel: 01603 870 245). Lots of exciting

attractions including the Dinosaur Trail, Woodland Maze, new Secret Animal Garden, Climb-a-Saurus, adventure play areas and education centre. There is a picnic area or visit 'Dippy's Diner'.

- Jungle Wonderland (in Hunstanton, Norfolk, Tel: 01485 535 505) is an adventure playground catering for children from 2 to 12, with a soft play area, a giant ball pool, Kenny the Croc Slide, and many more soft play items, plus an 80-seater diner.
- Childsplay Adventureland (Colchester, Tel: 01206 366 566) is a premier indoor play facility for under 9's. ROSPA-inspected for safety, ball pools, slides and a special area for babies and toddler's, with a coffee shop and restaurant.
- Go Bananas (Colchester, Tel: 01206 761 762) is a children's adventure playground with an under 5's village with adventure play, soft play and full service cafeteria.
- Toddler World (Hatfield, Tel: 01707 257 480) is aptly named and worth a visit. It has a large soft play area, with wendy house, ball pits and takes about 40 toddlers at a time! Fabulous.
- Alternatively try Activity World (Peterborough, Tel: 01733 314 446), which has a toddler-friendly indoor Adventure Playground, with sandpit, houses and play area; or the Big Sky Adventure Park (Peterborough, Tel: 01733 390 810) where you can find a full range of soft play activities for 0- to 10-year-olds, including slides, climbs, inflatables and ball pools, all in a completely safe environment.

ANIMAL PARKS

- At Whipsnade Wild Animal Park (Dunstable, Bedfordshire, Tel: 08705 200 123, Website: www.whipsnade.co.uk) you can see 2500 animals in 600 acres of countryside. Whipsnade is one of Europe's largest conservation parks. Check out the tigers, giraffes, bears, chimpanzees, hippos, and more. Californian sealions, elephant walk, free flying birds and penguin feeding, children's farm, adventure playground, steam railway and free Safari Tour Bus, plus wonderful creatures up close in the Discovery Centre. Tom was dragged out kicking and screaming at closing time.
- Woburn Safari Park (Woburn Park, Bedfordshire, Tel: 01525 290 407, Website: www.woburnsafari.co.uk) has two play areas

specifically for toddlers – the Tiny Tots Safari Trail and the Badger Valley outdoor play area. The drive through the Safari is exciting – without any walking (or pushchair pushing), and in the leisure area there are lots more animal attractions suited to toddlers. Also excellent is the Australian walkabout, where visitors walk among tame wallabies. Your toddler will want to take one home.

- Cambridgeshire's Wildlife Breeding Centre (Hadstock Road, Linton, Cambridgeshire, Tel: 01223 891 308) is a fairly good place for toddlers. Tom was happy wandering around the landscaped grounds and saw zebra, tapir, tigers, leopards, tamarin monkeys, parrots, hornbills, giant tortoises, snakes and other animals, set in 16 acres of lovely gardens with picnic spots and a children's play area suitable for toddlers.

Steam trains

- Knebworth Country House and Park (Knebworth, Herfordshire, Tel: 01438 812 661) is only of interest to toddlers for the miniature railway which runs in a loop around the grounds. There's also a chance to buy Thomas the Tank Engine flags. They won't be interested in the Country House.
- An alternative for train addicts is the Nene Valley Railways in Peterborough (Tel: 01780 784 444) which also claims to be (like everywhere else in the country) the home of Thomas the Tank Engine. Thomas events held throughout the season.

Zoos

- Banham Zoo (Banham, Norfolk, Tel: 01953 887 771) is set among 30 acres of parkland. The zoo features over 1000 animals from around the world, a free safari road train (loads of fun for toddlers), and all-weather activities centre. The wildlife spectacular takes visitors on a journey to experience at close quarters some of the world's most exotic, rare and endangered animals.
- Colchester also has an excellent zoo (Maldon Road, Stanway, Colchester, Essex, Tel: 01206 331 292) that hosts nearly 200 species of animals in 60 acres of natural parkland. Winner of Best Essex Visitor Attractions for 4 year olds. There are around 200 species in 40 acres of parkland. Award winning enclosures include

Spirit of Africa, the Elephant Kingdom, Wilds of Asia, Penguin Shores and Out of Africa. Get closer to the animals with 14 displays including feeding the elephants, snake handling, falconry, sealions and parrots. Excellent for toddlers.

- Or visit Hamerton Zoo Park (Huntingdon, Tel: 01832 293 362), a wildlife park with over 100 species. There is a gift shop, covered picnic area and Children's Zoo, keeper talks and animal contact/handling sessions.

Where to eat

- Waterfront Inn, Chelmsford (Tel: 01245 252 000) is a bistro downstairs, posh restaurant upstairs. Excellent and value-for-money food, high chairs and play area upstairs (unsupervised). Staff very toddler-experienced and tolerant. Kiddies portions and menu plus outdoor area to eat. By the river so plenty of ducks and moorhens to watch – so keep an eye on them as the guard rail is insufficient to prevent them from falling in.
- Another excellent find is The Punch Bowl, High Easter (Tel: 01245 231 222). David and Penny Kelsey run this fabulous restaurant in the backwaters of Essex. Gardens and adjacent church yard in which to play. Fab food and entertaining hosts, they occasionally have magicians to entertain the adults as well as children. Sunday lunchtime is best. High chairs and kiddies portions – 10/10.
- Or try Paris House (Woburn Park, Woburn, Bedfordshire, Tel: 01525 290 692) set in a Mock Tudor building in the grounds of Woburn Abbey (and therefore near Woburn Safari Park).

Northumbria

(Co. Durham, Northumberland, Tees Valley, Tyne & Wear) Tel: 0906 683 3000 – calls cost 25 pence per minute – Website: www.visit-northumbria.com

(East Riding of Yorkshire, North East Lincolnshire, North Lincolnshire, North, South and West Yorkshire) Tel: 01904 707 070, Website: www.yorkshirevisitor.com

Where to stay

- Try the Millhouse Inn and Brentwood Hotel (114 Moorgate Road, Rotherham, Tel: 01709 382 772)
- Hanover International Hotel and Club Skipton (Keighley Road, Skipton, North Yorkshire BD23 2TA, Tel: 01756 700 100, Fax: 01756 700 107, Website: www.yorkshirenet.co.uk/ hanoverskipton). This modern hotel is situated on the outskirts of Skipton and on the banks of the Trans-Pennine Waterway. Parents can relax while children (from ages 1 month to 7 years) are offered two hours of free childcare in the fully equipped and staffed day nursery. Babysitting facilities are available.

The best bits

BEACHES

- Try Roker and Seaburn beaches (Sunderland boasts some of the most beautiful beaches in the country). When the tide is out, you can walk to St Mary's Island and lighthouse, half an hour from Whitley Bay, and trips up the lighthouse can be arranged. Whitley Bay and Tynemouth beaches have superb golden sand, with shops, toilets and restaurants nearby.

BUTTERFLIES

- There is an interesting Butterfly Farm at Tow Law Nursery (High Stoop, near Tow Law on south side of A68, Tel: 01388 730 980). Visitors are encouraged to interact with tropical and native butterflies in the greenhouse.

IN MINIATURE

- Bondville Miniature Village (Tel: 01262 401 736).

LEISURE CENTRES

- Gateshead and Newcastle leisure centres have regular activity sessions for the under fives, such as gym tots, baby ballet and soft play. Swimming pools in Gateshead, Birtley, Felling and Dunston offer sessions for parents and tots.

Otters

- Every toddler seems to enjoy the Otter Trusts North Pennines Reserve (Vasle House Farm, near Bowes, Tel: 01833 628 339, Website: www.ottertrust.org.uk). It is a 230-acre wildlife reserve with British and Asian otters, red and fallow deer, rare breeds of farm animals and bird hides, overlooking wetland areas. Picnic site, walks, visitor centre, tearoom and gift shop.

Petting Zoos

- Discover the area's fauna and flora at the Low Barns Nature Reserve (Witton-Le-Wear, nr. Bishop Auckland, Durham. DL14 0AG, Tel: 01388 488 729).
- Whitworth Hall Country Park (Spennymoor, County Durham, Tel: 01388 811 772, Website: www.whitworthhall.co.uk) has a deer herd and walled garden.
- The Reptile Trust charity (1-3 Busty Bank, Burnopfield, Tel: 01207 271 766) cares for abandoned and unwanted snakes, lizards and other reptiles.
- Hall Hill Farm (on the Wolsingham road, near Lanchester, Tel: 01388 730 300, Website: www.hallhillfarm.co.uk) is a family farm set in attractive countryside with an opportunity for toddlers to see and touch animals at close quarters. Farm trailer rides, woodland and riverside walks. Farm teashop and children's play area. Special lambing events during April.
- Toddlers also enjoy Bede's World, Jarrow, about 20 minutes away from the city centre. Celebrating the life of Venerable Bede and Anglo-Saxon times. There's a farm with bulls, sheep and goats, plus demonstrations of Anglo-Saxon housebuilding skills. Indoor and outdoor.
- Odds Farm Park (Woodburn Common, Tel: 01628 520 188) and Paradise Wildlife Park (Broxbourne, Tel: 01992 468 001) provide wonderful opportunities to see and, in most cases, touch the animals (something toddlers like to do).
- At Mablethorpe visit the Seal Sanctuary (Tel: 01507 473 346).

PLAY AREAS

- The Smugglers Cave soft play area (Seaburn Centre, Whitburn Road, Sunderland, Tel: 0191 529 4872) caters for younger children (6 months to 6 years) but toddlers will require supervision.

STEAM TRAINS

- Thomas The Tank has come to Sunderland. Monkwearmouth Station Museum (Tel: 0191 567 7075) is a real Victorian railway station. Visit the ticket office, watch the trains pass by and 'drive' a full-sized bus.
- Alternatively, follow the track of the world's first passenger steam train at Shildon's Timothy Hackworth Victorian and Railway Museum (Museum Shildon County Durham DL4 1PQ, Tel: 01388 777 999, Fax: 01388 777 999). Enjoy a picnic at Harwick Hall Country Park or one of the county's many other attractive picnic areas and country parks. Visit the world's oldest existing railway, originally opened in 1725 at Tanfield (Old Marley Hill near Stanley, Tel: 0191 388 7545 www.tanfield-railway.co.uk). This is a three-mile steam passenger railway. Or visit the Tanfield Railway in Sunniside and the Bowes Railway Centre in Springwell Village, or the Bill Quay Farm, which has panoramic views of the Tyne, rare livestock, artworks and wildlife.

TEDDY BEARS

- Visit Bears Plus Crafts (95 High Street, Carrville, Durham, Tel: 0191 383 9615), a work studio and shop where visitors see a full-time resident bear-maker do his stuff . . . literally. You can purchase the crafts, finished bears and even the kit to make your own bears if you feel so inclined. For further information check out www.bearspluscrafts.com
- An alternative is the more interesting-sounding Bear Bottoms (87b Elvet Bridge, Durham, Tel: 0191 383 2922, Website: www.bearbottoms.co.uk). There are daily bear-making or bear-reconstruction demonstrations in the afternoon from the artist in residence. Advice on bear designing and making. Exhibitions and events and bears for sale.

THEME PARKS

- Flamingo Theme Park and Zoo (Tel: 01653 668 287) is the UK's fourth most visited theme park. It boasts the North's largest privately owned zoo, and there's a Kiddies' Kingdom which kept Tom amused for hours. There's lots for older children with white-knuckle rides, but sufficient interest for toddlers to merit a mention in this book.
- You could also try out Alphabet Zoo (Wigan, Tel: 01942 494 922) and the Fun Farm (Weston, Tel: 01406 373 444).

WILDLIFE

- Visit the Wildfowl & Wetlands Trust (Fish Lane, Burcough, Ormskirk, Lancashire L40 0TA, Tel: 01704 895 181) an excellent centre for young families. Hands-on attractions and interaction with exotic birds, visitor centre and café. Toddlers love it.

Where to Eat

- Stop at Est Est Est (Tel: 0113 267 2100) to make your own pizzas – they are great with children.
- Try out Brewers Fayre, which has kiddies menus and sizeable play areas. Restaurants available at Anchor Inn, Settle Road, Gargrave (Tel: 01756 749 666); Arena Court, Attercliffe (Tel: 0114 243 2320) and St Andrews Road, Apsley (Tel: 01484 511 250).

North West England

(Cheshire, High Peak District of Derbyshire, Greater Manchester, Lancashire, Merseyside) Tel: 01942 764 116, Website: www.visitnorth west.com)

(County of Cumbria including English Lakeland) Tel: 01539 444 444, Website; www.gocumbria.co.uk

Where to stay

- Hanover International Hotel & Club (Keighley Road, Skipton, North Yorkshire BD23 2TA, Tel: 01756 700 100, Website: www.hanover-international.com) has excellent day nursery run by fully qualified staff and babysitting facilities.

- In Cumbria, try Slakes Farm, Milburn, Appleby-in-Westmorland, Cumbria CA16 6DP (Contact: Mrs Braithwaite, Tel: 01768 361 385) This is a 400-acre 18th-century farm rearing cattle and sheep. Open Easter-November, it offers room for six people (children encouraged!) Or go for Butterflowers Holiday Homes, Port Haverigg, Millom, Cumbria LA18 4HB, Tel: 01229 772 880, Fax: 01229 774 445.

The best bits

ADVENTURE PARK

- Gulliver's World (Warrington, Cheshire, Tel: 01925 230 088) offers over 45 rides and attractions, about half of which Tom could go on. A landscaped setting of lake and woodland, rides and attractions includes soft play areas for toddlers.
- Camol Theme Park (Park hall Road, Charnock Richard, Chorley, Lancashire, Tel: 01257 453 044, Website: www.camelotthemepark.co.uk) has a huge range of thrilling rides and family fun, in the 'magical kingdom' of Camelot. Lots for toddlers to enjoy.

FISH

- The Secret Life of the Lakes is revealed at the Aquarium of the Lakes at the southern end of Lake Windermere (Tel: 01539 530 153, Website: www.aquariumofthelakes.co.uk). Superb displays include Arctic char, England's rarest fish, left behind in Windermere after the Ice Age.
- The Blue Planet Aquarium (Longlooms Road, Cheshire Oaks, Ellesmere Port, Cheshire, Tel: 0151 357 8800, Website: www.blueplanetaquarium.co.uk) is the UK's largest aquarium. Experience an exhilarating journey through the waters of the world. Free face-painting for kids, as well as an underwater carnival.

In Miniature

* Toddlers will love Lakeland Miniature Village at Flookburgh (Coach House, Winder Lane, Flookburgh, Grange-over-Sands, Cumbria LA11 7LE, Tel: 01539 558 500). Excellent little farmyard for toddlers to play farmer in. With mini tractors and plastic cows and sheep, chickens and ducks, they'll have a whale of a time.

Model Railway

* For steam trains try Ravenglass and Eskdale Railway (Tel: 01229 717 171) or Lakeside and Haverthwaite Railway (Tel: 01539 531 594). Hard working steam engines haul trains on this steeply-graded railway. Trains run from April through to the end of October.

Wildlife

* Try Knowsley Safari Park (Prescot, Merseyside, Tel: 0151 430 9009), Blackpool Sea Life Centre (Tel: 01253 622 445), Blackpool Zoo Park (Tel: 01253 830 830) or Leigh Animal Sanctuary (Tel: 01942 671 215).
* Check out Amazonia (Bowness-On-Windermere, Tel: 01539 448 002), Lakeland Bird of Prey Centre (Lowther, Tel: 01931 712 746), Trotters World of Animals (Bassenthwaite, Tel: 01768 776 239) or Kendal Reptiles (Tel: 01539 721 240).
* Chester Zoo has the UK's largest zoological gardens, with spacious animal enclosures. There's a children's farm, brass rubbing and a 'let's make' centre. (Upton-by-Chester, Chester, Cheshire, Tel: 01244 380 280, Website: www.demon.co.uk/chesterzoo.)
* Also fun for little ones is the Docker park Farm Visitor Centre (Arkholm, Carnforth, Lancashire, Tel: 01524 221 331), a small working livestock farm with piglets and lambs to feed. There are hatchery sections, as well as cows, horses, small animals, rabit world, lakes, ferret racing and a tearoom.

Where to eat

* Try out the Moon Restaurant (129 Highgate, Kendal, LA9 4EN, Tel: 01539 729 254) which offers healthy toddler meals a world away from bangers, beans and nuggets.

- Or World of Beatrix Potter Café (Craig Brown, Bowness in Windermere, Tel: 01539 488 444) where toddlers can help themselves to an ice cream machine (not necessarily a good thing) and colouring competitions are organised.
- At Brockhall Visitor's Centre (Tel: 01539 446 601) there is a large adventure playground; children's menus and high chairs are available.
- Wilf's Café (Old Mill Yard, Back Lane, Staveley, Nr Kendal, Tel: 01539 822 329) offers baby-changing facilities and an excellent playroom upstairs (unsupervised).

Scotland

The attitude of the Scottish is so different from that of the English.
I live close to the border and as soon as you cross it you see the
difference. Something in the air perhaps? They actually have –
make – time for children here. I've moved from Canada and this
is just like having a mini Canada on the doorstep.

Mother of two from Carlisle.

The basics

Best way to get there – By train or fly direct
Flight time from London – Approx. 1 hour, 15 mins to
    Edinburgh/Glasgow
Train time from London – 4 hours, 30 mins to Edinburgh, 5 hours,
    20 mins to Glasgow
Culture – Toddler-friendly
Toddler-friendly rating – 7/10
'Best bits' for toddlers – The beaches, the kiddies' clubs in hotels,
    the restaurants.
'Best bits' for grown ups – Attitude toward toddlers. Excellent
    restaurants and great resort hotels
When to go – Any time
Where to go – Around Glasgow and Edinburgh
Accommodation – Resort hotels and guest houses

Major airlines

British Midland (Tel: 0870 607 0555, Website: www.flybmi.co.uk)

British Airways (Tel: 0845 773 3377,
  Website: www.britishairways.co.uk)

Easyjet (Tel: 0870 6000 000, Website: www.easyjet.co.uk)

Train companies

Scotrail (couchettes), Tel: 08457 550 033

GNER, Tel: 08457 225 225

Virgin, Tel: 08457 222 333

Greater Glasgow and Clyde Valley is a central hub in Scotland's transport network. Over 40 airlines service Glasgow International and the area is easily reached from a variety of rail, road and ferry routes. At Glasgow Airport Central and Prestwick you will find toilets and baby-changing facilities throughout the terminal building, including four special babycare rooms. There are also two children's play areas. The service offered by all the major airlines from London to Edinburgh and Glasgow is usually excellent and punctual, receiving nothing but praise from those families who travelled by air. Flying from Stansted airport was considered to be the most 'civilised experience' relative to the other major London airports (so if you live in Essex – go to Stansted).

Toddlers will probably get over-excited by the night time couchette experience on the Scotrail route. For daytime journeys by train, you would have to take plenty of activities to distract them.

Where to stay

- The focus for all families with toddlers who have visited Scotland appears to be based very much on the success of the resort or hotel in which they stayed. The luxurious Gleneagles (Tel: 01764 662 231, Website: www.gleneagles.com) and the value-for-money Polmaily House Hotel (Tel: 01456 450 343, Website: www.bedruthanstepshotel.co.uk/polmailyhouse) near Loch Ness are both outstanding for families with toddlers. Polmaily is a family-run hotel set in 18 acres of gardens, with plenty of room for toddlers to run around. Babysitting, baby-listening and crêche facilities, organized activities, scarecrow making, swimming galas, treasure hunts, videos in all family suites with excellent toddler-friendly videos, indoor and outdoor play areas, pony rides and horse riding – and lots for the grown ups. Fabulous. Gleneagles is not cheap, but toddlers even have their own website to visit and from the age of two upwards are cared for by qualified staff, in play rooms.

- In Edinburgh, try Jury's Inn (Tel: 0131 200 3300, Fax: 0131 200 0400), a three-star inn in central Edinburgh. The Crone Plaze Hotel (Tel: 0131 557 9797, Fax: 0131 557 9789) is a four-star hotel situated on the Royal Mile, close to all attractions, and has a swimming pool and leisure centre. Edinburgh Holiday Inn is about 10 minutes from the city centre, and recommended for toddlers (Tel: 0131 332 2442; Fax: 0131 332 3408).

- The Crieff Hydro (Crieff, Perthshire, Tel: 01764 655 555, Website: www.crieffhydro.com) is a large family resort opened 130 years ago and set in over 900 acres of stunning countryside. The children's club takes toddlers from two upwards for limited sessions during the day and cots, highchairs and organized activities are provided. Others to check out include Murrayshell House Country House Hotel (Scone, Perthshire, Tel: 01738 551 171); or Greywalls Hotel (Gullane, East Lothian, Tel: 01620 842 144), which is set in walled gardens adjacent to the Muirfield golf course.

- Hotels in Glasgow that actively encourage families with toddlers include Novotel (181 Pitt Street, Tel: 0141 222 2775). This is quite a stylish new hotel, conveniently located for shopping, restaurants and theatres, and offering flexible accommodation with many extras. Each room has a double bed and large sofa bed, so they can comfortably accommodate up to 2 adults and 2 children. Children up to 16 years sharing with parents enjoy free accommodation and complimentary breakfast. Bewleys Hotel (110 Bath Street, Tel: 0141 353 0800, Website: www.bewleyshotel.com) is situated in the heart of the city and within easy walking distance of Glasgow's main attractions, rail and coach stations. Offers

47 family rooms (19 double and 37 triple) and babysitting/ listening facilities. Bewleys' ground-floor restaurant Loop has a 'Babies' Menu'. Jurys Glasgow Hotel (Great Western Road, Tel: 0141 334 8161, Website: www.jurysdoyle.com) is a good three-star West End hotel with a pool, children's pool (toddler-friendly), cots and high-chairs in the restaurant. They will arrange babysitting on request.

The best bits

Edinburgh

- Edinburgh is well known for the colour and energy of its festivals. The city celebrates everything from the best in jazz and blues, to the famous Fringe, to books to international film and of course, the Military Tattoo. Families – though welcome at these events – should be aware that during these times Edinburgh may become extremely busy and toddlers could be intimidated by the crowds. This is a pity, as there is a lot to entertain young children (jugglers, clowns and musicians in the streets).
- The Museum of Childhood (Royal Mile, Tel: 0131 529 4142) was ironically created for adults by a city counsellor who was known to dislike children (he was rumoured to 'eat them for breakfast'). It has a nickelodeon, slot machines and a wide collection of toys – can be extremely noisy, so it is more for older children than toddlers.
- The Edinburgh Zoo is world famous, and has the world's largest penguin enclosure, as well as a 'magic forest' for mini-monkeys. (Tel: 0131 334 9171; Website: www.edinburgh-zoo.org.uk).
- Edinburgh Butterfly and Insect World is approximately 15 minutes from the city centre, and well worth a visit. (Tel: 0131 663 4932). Vogrie Country Park and Dalkeith Country Park both offer excellent adventure playgrounds for little ones, and are located near the Butterfly and Insect world. A good day away from the bustle of the city!

Glasgow

- There are family travel passes available for all modes of transport, including Underground, bus and train services, allowing unlimited travel throughout the city. Glasgow is a very walkable city with a high concentration of visitor attractions, shops and restaurants set out on a grid system, some of which is pedestrianized. The prestigious Buchanan Galleries Shopping Centre (220 Buchanan Street, Tel: 0141 333 9898) is great for toddlers as it offers baby-changing and crêche facilities and a large food gallery. It also has a John Lewis Department Store, which has excellent baby-changing facilities (with bottle warmers and separate breastfeeding area) and a good selection of baby food and toddler favourites on the restaurant menu. The mosaic-patterned basement level of Princes Square Shopping Centre (48 Buchanan Street, Tel: 0141 221 0324) is another very popular venue for local and visiting pre-school children, as they can play while the grown-ups have coffee/lunch in one of the surrounding cafés/restaurants. St Enoch Shopping Centre (55 St Enoch Square, Tel: 0141 204 3900) and Braehead Shopping Centre (Kings Inch Road, Tel: 0141 885 1441) both have 'baby taxi' facilities where parents can push the toddler around, keeping the child both amused and within reach. Both centres have large food courts with high-chair facilities. Braehead hosts an outdoor play area with a pirate ship and toddlers (aged three and up) can climb the rigging quite safely. There is also an indoor ice rink, overlooked by the food court, which helps to keep young children amused while eating.

- There are over 70 parks and gardens in and around Glasgow, many of which have children's play facilities. Those to head for include Bellahouston Park (Dumbreck Road) and Calderglen Country Park Visitor Centre (1 Strathaven Road, East Kilbride, South Lanarkshire, Tel: 01355 236 644). The country park has a petting zoo, conservatory, ornamental gardens, play areas, toddler-friendly nature trails and café, and is about 20 minutes drive from Glasgow.

In Miniature

- The Wee People's City (The Lighthouse, Scotland's Centre for Architecture, Design and the City, 11 Mitchell Lane, Glasgow, Tel: 0141 225 8414, Website: www.thelighthouse.co.uk) is aimed at 3- to 8-year-olds and challenges them to think about design through play and the exploration of Glasgow in miniature. The centre has already won two awards for its design and appealing to children is central to its development strategy. Baby changing facilities, high-chairs and a children's menu are available in the wonderful Doocot cafe.

Playground

Freeport Designer Outlet and Leisure Village (Five Sisters, Westwood, West Calder, West Lothian 01501 763 488 www.freeportplc.com) has great shopping for grown-ups, while for children there is Cheeky Chimp's indoor play area, Frontierland, an outdoor adventure play area and Tropical World – a glasshouse containing exotic and rare species of animals and birds.

Puppets

Purves World of Puppets (Bigger Puppet Theatre, Broughton Road, Biggar, South Lanarkshire, Tel: 01899 220 631, Website: www.purves puppets.com) is a Victorian-style puppet theatre showing large-scale puppet shows in UV light. Facilities include conservatory tearoom, world puppetry museum, garden picnic area, children's play area and pets' corner. Open from Easter to end August. It's about 45 minutes drive from Glasgow, but worth it.

Where to eat

It appears that what Scotland lacks in sunshine, it makes up for in the toddler-friendliness of its restaurants – which one mother of three described as 'pure theatre'.

- In Edinburgh, the restaurants most praised by parents were Café Florentin (8 St Giles Street, Tel: 0131 225 6272); The Grain Store

(30 Victoria Street, Tel: 0131 225 7635); The Witchery (within the Secret Garden) and the Secret Garden Restaurant (Castlehill, Royal Mile, Tel: 0131 225 5613) and Daniel's (88 Commercial Street, Leith, Tel: 0131 553 5933). Each was described as having a 'special magic' – either because of the way the staff looked after the children, or the fact there was a garden to play in. The Garden Café founded by Clarissa Dickson-Wright (Lennoxlove House, Haddington, East Lothian, Tel: 01620 870 300) also received praise, as did the Waterfront (1C Dock Place, Leith, Tel: 0131 554 7427) for excellent service.

- In Glasgow, head for Nairn's (13 Woodside Crescent, Tel: 0141 353 0707), owned by Nick Nairn (who is a bit of a dish himself!). It is surprisingly very toddler-friendly, providing high chairs and toddler-sized portions of his excellent recipes. If you are looking for a toddler-friendly chain restaurant, try Di Maggio's Pizzeria (21 Royal Exchange Square, Tel: 0141 248 2111). This is a popular family restaurant serving the best in Italian and European cuisine in a friendly atmosphere and you'll find other branches throughout the city. Also head for D'Arcy's Wine Bar & Restaurant (The Basement Courtyard, Princes Square, Tel: 0141 226 4309); it has a non-smoking room and has outside tables in a central courtyard, ideal for families, as toddlers can play on the mosaic-patterned floor space.

Wales

I didn't realise we had a little Austria on our doorstep until I visited friends in Llandudno. Its beautiful there and the beaches are excellent. The Welsh have a wonderful way with toddlers and I had never realised how beautiful this country was until I went there with my family. Lovely part of the world.

Mother of three toddlers, aged one,
two and three, from Suffolk

The basics

Best way to get there – drive, roads are never congested, or come by rail
English spoken – Yes
Culture – Very toddler-friendly
Toddler-friendly rating – 7/10
'Best bits' for toddlers – Friends, steam engines, beaches
'Best bits' for parents – Easy access, cleanliness and safety
When to go – All year but autumn good
Where to go – Llandudno and Colwyn Bay
Accommodation – Cottage/farmhouse/selected hotels

For the Tourist Information Centre at Llandudno contact 01492 876 413 and at Colwyn Bay, Tel: 01492 530 478. It is worth considering the Flexipass, which consists of one rail and bus ticket that gives you the freedom to enjoy unlimited travel and two for one offers to many attractions. Look for other benefits at www.travelwales-flexi pass.co.uk. Regional Freephone booking numbers: North Wales 0800 834 820,

Mid and South Wales 0800 273 747. Wales Tourist Board www.visit-wales.com

Where to stay

- Stay at St Tudno Hotel (The Promenade, opposite the pier, Tel: 01492 874 411), an excellent seaside hotel that serves high teas and is close to the Welsh Mountain Zoo and Gwydir Forest.
- Alternatively stay in a chalet, cottage or coach house in Colwyn Bay (Nant y Glyn Holiday Park, Tel: 01492 512 282) which has a children's play area. Also consider Treffeddian Hotel (Aberdovey, Tel: 01654 767 213) which is set on the edge of the estuary with views over Cardigan Bay, and is within Snowdonia National Park. An indoor playroom, baby listening service and babysitting are available, as well as children's menus and early suppers.

The best bits

Beaches

- Wales has many seaside resorts but the most popular with young families are in North Wales, around Colwyn Bay, Rhyl, Prestatyn and Llandudno, and smaller ones in Llyn and Anglesey (Llanddona beach is a Blue Flag beach). This is mainly due to the other attractions in the area and the proximity to Snowdonia National Park. For those who believe Switzerland and Austria have a monopoly on dramatic scenery, come here: it's closer to home and much less expensive. The region resembles the very best of everything Austria and Switzerland have to offer, with its mountains, valleys and waterfalls.
- The beaches in Wales are some of the cleanest in the UK. The cleanest (Blue Flag) beaches are Whitesands (Pembrokeshire), Llanddwn (Anglesey), Lydstep (Pembrokeshire), Rest Bay, Porthcawl and New Quay Traeth Yr Harbwr (Ceredigion), and Barmouth in Gwynedd. Over 80 Welsh beaches have received the Seaside Award.

- Llandudno is famous for its Victorian style and Edwardian elegance. It has two beaches, North Shore and West Shore. North Shore has won the Tidy Britain Seaside Award for seven consecutive years. It is 3 miles long and sheltered by Great and Little Orme. There is a children's paddling pool at Craig y Don (Little Orme end). Punch and Judy shows still captivate kids on the sweeping promenade. The West Shore beach overlooks Snowdonia and the Isle of Anglesey. A children's play area is located at the centre of the promenade. Alice Liddell (made famous in the Alice in Wonderland stories) spent her childhood summers at the resort.
- Colwyn Bay is also an excellent resort for toddlers, with 3 miles of golden sands.

Zoo, Dinosaurs, Puppets, Theatre, Trams

- Attractions that toddlers will enjoy include the Welsh Mountain Zoo (Colwyn Bay, Tel: 01492 532 938), Dinosaur World (Colwyn Bay, Tel: 01492 518 111), Harlequin Puppet Theatre (Colwyn Bay, Tel: 01492 548 166) and the Alice in Wonderland Visitor Centre (Llandudno, Tel: 01492 860 082).
- North Wales Theatre (Llandudno, Tel: 01492 872 000) performs national productions including children's' theatre/pantomime; Theatre Colwyn (Colwyn Bay, Tel: 01492 532 668) has cinema and theatre productions with occasional shows for children.
- The Great Orme (Llandudno, Tel: 01492 874 151), Great Orme Country Park Visitor Centre (Tel: 01492 574 237) and Great Orme Tramway (Tel: 01492 877 205). The Great Orme is a large headland on the North Wales coast, in Llandudno. Much like a country park, you can wander across its open spaces, take a tram to the summit of the Great Orme, and visit the prehistoric copper mine. The summer hosts a café and play areas, while the Happy Valley has a toboggan run and ski slope.

Ireland

Wonderful country. Eccentric people, a lot of whom behave like toddlers themselves, whatever age they happen to be. A place with a real sense of fun and zest for life which is infectious. Great for toddlers who don't mind the rain. Which invariably they don't if there's a beach.

Father of three from Southampton, two of whom are toddlers

The basics

Time difference from UK – None
Best way to get there with toddlers – Fly (quicker)
Flight time – (Dublin – London) One hour
English spoken – Yes
Culture – Excessively toddler-friendly. Don't take them into pubs (too smokey)
Toddler-friendly rating – 8/10
'Best bits' for toddlers – Beaches, friends they made, the 'grown ups' they met
'Best bits' for parents – Friendliness and laid back attitude of Irish toward toddlers, didn't like the rain
When to go – Autumn and spring
Where to go – Dublin and coastal resorts
Accommodation – Hotels, camping, self-catering, farm houses – lots of alternatives. Also consider B&B. They are a category unto themselves (same as farmhouses – only without the farms), and are spread all over Ireland

Toddler-friendly tour operators

Swansea Cork Ferries, Tel: 01792 456 116,
   Website: www.swansea-cork.ie
The Caravan Club, Tel: 01342 316 101,
   Website: www.caravanclub.co.uk
Thomas Cook Holidays, Tel: 01733 418 188,
   Website: www.tcholidays.com
Cottage Club Ireland, Tel: 01654 711 735,
   Website: www.cottageclub.co.uk
Crystal Holidays, Tel: 0870 888 0022,
   Website: www.crystalholidays.co.uk
Cresta Holidays, Tel: 0870 161 0910,
   Website: www.crestaholidays.co.uk
Drive Ireland, Tel: 0151 231 1480,
   Website: www.drive-ireland.co.uk
Enjoy Ireland Holidays, Tel: 01254 692 899,
   Website: www.enjoy-ireland.co.uk
Irish Country Cottages, Tel: 01502 560 688
Leisure Breaks, Tel: 0151 734 5200, Website:
   www.irelandbreaks.co.uk

Major airlines

Aer Lingus, Tel: 0845 9737 747, Website: www.aerlingus.com
Air Wales, Tel: 0870 0133 151, Website: www.trravel.com
British European, Tel: 0870 5676 676,
   Website: www.british-european.com
Celtic Airways, Tel: 01752 766 111
Easyjet, Tel: 0870 600 0000, Website: www.easyjet.com
Manx Airways, Tel: 0845 725 6256,
   Website: www.manx-airlines.com
British Airways, Tel: 0845 773 3377,
   Website: www.britishairways.com
Bmi British Midland, Tel: 0870 607 0555, Website: www.british
   midland.com
Ryanair, Tel: 0870 156 9569, Website: www.ryanair.com
Virgin Express, Tel: 020 7744 0004,
   Website: www.virgin-express.com

Where to stay

- Perhaps a better option than hotels would be to opt for country houses and guesthouses in and around Dublin, which are friendlier, more informal and usually family owned. Guest House, the elegant Georgian Harrington Hall (70 Harcourt Street, Dublin, Tel; 00353 1475 3497), is run with the emphasis very much on the personal touch. Babysitting offered and 10 minutes drive from Dublin Zoo. Alternatively, Dawn House (Balheary, Swords, Co. Duline, Tel: 00353 1840 3111), a superb country home with 5 bedrooms en suite, is only 6 minutes from Dublin airport, 15 minutes from the city centre and 20 minutes from the ferry. An ideal touring base, it also offers babysitting and adjoins farmland and a golf course. Dawn House is situated in North County, home to many fine sandy beaches and country walks.
- Ireland's Blue Book comprises a listing of some of Ireland's most exclusive country houses, castles and restaurants with accommodation. For the discerning traveller with toddler in search of traditional hospitality, elegant accommodation and fine cuisine or visit www.ireland-blue-book.com Self-catering is also an excellent idea if travelling with toddlers, in houses, apartments, cottages, even castles. Many cottages are available in rural and remote areas or in towns and cities. Contact 00353 1475 1932 or visit www.irishcottageholidays.com
- To reserve accommodation anywhere in Ireland, call Resireland freephone (from the UK) 00 800 668 668 66. Reservations can also be made on line on the Irish Tourist Board website www.ireland.travel.ie or by email reservations@gulliver.ie.
- For further information about Dublin visit www.visitdublin.com or email information@dublintourism.ie.

The best bits

Beaches
- Ireland has a coastline of 5630 km and a wide variety of small quiet beaches or more lively holiday resorts ideal for toddlers.

315

There are numerous Blue Flag beaches around the country and two Blue Flag marinas (Kinsale Yacht Club and Kilrush Creek marina). Three of these beaches are inland – Lough Lene, Lough Ennell and Loughrea bathing place.

Fort
- Fort Lucan (off Strawberry Beds Road, Westmanstown, Lucan, Co Dublin, Tel: 00353 1628 0166) features an assault course, high tower walks, 40-foot slides, trampolines and suspension bridges – none of which Tom could go on. There is also a maze and tots' area – which he could. Opening can be dependent on weather, so call ahead.

Ingenious Attractions
- Hey! Doodle Doodle, in Temple Bar (Tel: 00353 1672 7382, Website: www.heydoodledoodle.com), allows your toddler and you to explore the creative side. Choose a ready-to-paint ceramic item – plate, mug, bowl, stamp, stencil – and paint it your own way. Tom had hours of fun and I have a brilliant souvenir of his earliest masterpiece. You can also book a party here.

Petting farms
- Dublin has many working farms suitable for toddlers. Arnold's Fruit Farm (Tel: 00353 1843 6554 open June – August) and Newgrange Farm (Tel: 00353 41 9824119 www.newgrangefarm.com) are the best of the bunch. Each has nappy changing facilities and good car/bus parking.

Playgrounds
- The best playground in and around Dublin is at Malahide Demesne, Malahide, Co Dublin. Situated 10 miles north of the city centre, this is 268 acres with the central feature being Malahide Castle. Also includes the Fry Model Railway, a par 3 golf course, football pitches, cricket grounds, tennis courts, children's playground and extensive woodland.
- Marley Park, Rathfarnham, Dublin 14, is situated in the foothills of the Dublin Mountains. The 205-acre park contains a 9 hole

par 3 golf course, tennis courts, woodland walks, two lakes and an excellent children's playground. There is also a miniature train ride for children, which is operated on Saturday afternoons only.

- St Stephen's Green, Dublin 2, is one of the nicest places in the city to spend some time. It opened in the early 19th century and contains a lake, fountains, flowerbeds and trees as well as a scented garden for the blind, an excellent playground for toddlers and numerous statues and memorials. Bring your own bread and feed the ducks. There are always plenty to go round.

Zoo

- Dublin Zoo (Tel: 00353 1677 1425, Website: www.dublinzoo.com) just 3 km from the city centre in the grounds of Phoenix Park, is set in 60 acres of landscaped grounds around ornamental lakes where over 700 animals and tropical birds from around the world can be seen. Like most zoos, Dublin Zoo is heavily involved in conservation work. A daily 'meet the keeper' programme operates, which gives you the opportunity to learn about the many rare and endangered species that live in Dublin Zoo. In addition, there are always new babies or animals on breeding loan from other zoos and wildlife parks. Be sure to visit the 'African Plains', 'World of Primates', 'Fringes of the Arctic' and 'World of Cats'. Afterwards take a train ride around the Zoo. Other facilities include a toddler play area, the pet care area, discovery centre, restaurants (which are fairly toddler-friendly) and gift shop. Take the number 10 bus from O'Connell Street, 25 and 26 from Middle Abbey Street.

Where to eat

- Eat at 101 Talbot (101 Talbot Street, Dublin 1, Tel: 00353 1874 5011) or Cornucopia Vegetarian Restaurant (19 Wicklow Street, Dublin 2, Tel: 00353 1679 7340). Or try Wagamama in town. Toddlers love noodles (look just like worms and make lots of mess). Ideal toddler food. There are three in Dublin – Hume Street (Tel: 00353 1662 8150), Grafton Street (Tel: 00353 1677 1222) and St Stephen's Green Shopping Centre (Tel: 00353 1478 2152).

317

Guernsey

'Wonderful little island for toddlers to explore. Weather can be a bit unreliable, but its milder here than in England and our two didn't seem to care if it was pouring it down. They still wanted to be on the beach.

Mother of two – 3 and 5, London

The basics

Time difference from UK – None
Best way to get there – Fly or ferry
Flight time from London – 1 hour
English spoken – Yes
Culture – Relaxed
Toddler-friendly rating – 9/10
'Best bits' for toddlers – Beaches and playgrounds
'Best bits' for parents – Friendly people and general facilities in
   hotels and restaurants very good. 'Gentle.'
When to go – Late spring/early autumn
Where to go – Anywhere close to the coast
Accommodation – Hotels or self-catering

Toddler-friendly tour operators
Channel Islands Travel Service, Tel: 01481 235 471
ABC Channel Islands Travelcentre, Tel: 01481 235 551

Major airlines
London Gatwick British Airways Express, Tel: 0845 773 3377, Website:
   www.britishairways.com

British European, Tel: 08705 676 676, Website: www.british-european.com

London Stansted, Aurigny Air Services, Tel: 01481 822 886, Website: www.aurigny.com

Manchester British Airways Express, Tel: 0845 773 3377

By sea

Ferry (from Poole, Portsmouth or Weymouth) Condor Ferries, Tel: 0845 345 2000

For further information contact The Guernsey Tourist Board, PO Box 23, St Peter Port, Guernsey, GY1 3AN, Website: www.guernsey-touristboard.com.

Where to stay

- There are excellent hotels which have great facilities for toddlers, and the majority of Guernsey hotels welcome toddlers and offer special children's rates. Many also offer a baby-listening service. There are lots of establishments with swimming pools, including small paddling pools suitable for toddlers.
- Alternatively, Guernsey has a selection of high-quality self-catering accommodation, of which a good number offer children's playgrounds. La Grande Mare Holiday Apartments (Vazon Bay, Castel, Tel: 01481 256 576) cater for families with a baby-listening service, swimming pool and children's playground. Beau Vallon Self-catering Maisonettes (Les Adams, St Peters, Tel: 01481 265 888) also offer these facilities and is a non-smoking establishment.
- Other toddler-friendly self-catering includes La Grange & La Petite Grange (c/o Le Petit Manoir, Pleinmount Road, Torteval, Tel: 01481 249 633); Swallows Apartments (La Cloture, L'Ancresse, Vale, Guernsey, Tel: 01481 249 633); and Le Petit Manoir (La Cloture, L'Ancresse, Vale, Tel: 01482 263 090)
- For an adventurous holiday, La Bailloterie Campsite (La Bailloteire Lane, Vale, Tel: 01481 243 636) has a baby corner, children's play

area and TV room, and is set in a rural area which is shaded during the day.

- The accommodation on Herm is very child friendly, ranging from The White House Hotel (Tel: 01481 722 159) with baby-listening services and a children's menu, to campsites or self-catering.
- The Aval de Creux Hotel (Harbour Hill, Tel: 01481 832 036) in Sark welcomes toddlers, providing a children's splash pool and play area.

The best bits

FISH AND BIRDS

- There is an Aquarium at La Vallette (St Peter Port, Tel: 01481 723 301) and Bird Gardens at La Villiaze (St Andrews, Tel: 01481 236 690).

GUERNSEY

- The safe atmosphere in Guernsey provides an ideal destination for families with young children. During the summer months, children can enjoy the clean, sandy beaches, exploring the rock pools and paddling in the sea.

HERM

- Herm is a child's paradise, offering safe, clean beaches and plenty of nature and wildlife to explore and enjoy.

MODEL RAILWAY

- The Model Railway Exhibition (Camp du Roi, Vale, Tel: 01481 252 929).

ON YOUR BIKE

- For a more active family, Guernsey has created a network of cycle routes, taking the visitor away from busy main roads, to discover the quiet country lanes.

PLAYGROUNDS

- At Saumarez Park, Castel (Tel: 01481 235 904), families will find a delightful playground, a duck pond and plenty of space for games.
- Other playgrounds are located at Cambridge Park, St Peter Port, which has a special fenced in area for toddlers, and Les Amarreurs, Vale, situated next to the beach.
- Beau Sejour Leisure Centre (Amherst, St Peter Port, Tel: 01481 727 211) has an indoor swimming pool, with flumes for the older children and a small children's pool. The centre also has a soft play area, games arcade and café, which caters especially for toddlers.
- Try also The Jungle House (Oatlands Village, Les Gigands, St Sampsons, Tel: 01481 241 643).

Where to eat

- Most restaurant in Guernsey are more than happy to cater for toddlers, providing high chairs, children's menus, play areas and smoke-free areas.
- Try La Quinta Hotel (Rue Maze, St Martins, Tel: 01481 234 100), L'Atlantique (Perelle Bay, St Saviours, Tel: 01481 264 056) and St Margaret's Lodge Hotel (Forest Road, St Martins, Tel: 01481 235 757).
- Some restaurants also provide a special soft play area/room where toddlers can play while their parents relax over their meal. You'll find playrooms at The Pony Inn (Les Capelles, St Sampsons, Tel: 01481 244 374), The Longfrie (St Peters, Tel: 01481 263 107) and The Bowl (Victoria Avenue, St Sampsons, Tel: 01481 710 444).

Jersey

I didn't expect to like this island as much as I did. It's just on our doorstep. Last year we took our two toddlers (three and two) to the Caribbean for the beaches, which they loved – but it's this holiday they keep talking about now. Think it was the locals that did it. They're so different from the mainland. They actually like children here.

Father of two, from Southampton

The basics

Time difference from UK – None

Best way to get there – By car ferry from Weymouth or Poole or by air

Flight time from London – 50 minutes

English spoken – Yes

Toddler-friendly rating – 9/10

'Best bits' for toddlers – The beaches, the other children, the 'lots of creepy crawlies we found on the beach'

'Best bits' for grown ups – The friendliness toward children, accessibility, value for money

When to go – June to avoid crowds and get good weather

Where to go – St Brelade Bay, excellent safe beach

Major airlines

British Airways (Tel: 0845 773 3377, Website: www.britishairways.com)

British Midland (Tel: 0870 6070 555,
　　Website: www.britishmidlands.com)
British European (Tel: 0870 5676 676,
　　Website: www.british-european.com)
British Regional (Website: www.british-regional.com)

By sea
Condor Ferries (Tel: 0845 345 2000,
　　Website: www.condorferries.co.uk)

Toddler-friendly tour operators
Jersey Travel service (Website: www.jerseytravelservice.com)
Pepi penguin beach clubs for kids (Tel: 0870 848 7001)
Premier (Tel: 0870 789 6700, Website: www.premierholidays.co.uk)
　　have a whole page in their brochure on family holidays – free insur-
　　ance and kids stay free programme.
Thomas Cook encourage kids-free programmes (Tel: 0870 443 4453,
　　Website: www.tcholidays.com) and includes kids pack and infor-
　　mation on family holidays.

Jersey is the most southerly part of the British Isles and situated nearer
to France than England. Cared for by the States of Jersey, the Island's
Government, Jersey was the first tourism destination in the world to
gain the Green Globe destination status for its environmental conservation. A natural year-round holiday choice, it is ideal for short or
longer stays perhaps using the island as a jumping off point for visits
to the other Channel Islands and France.

Where to stay

- The best hotels on the islands, with crêche and babysitting
  facilities, include the Apollo Hotel (Tel: 01534 725 441, Website:
  www.apollohotel.co.uk), Beau Couperon (Tel: 01534 865 522,
  Website: www.beaucouperonhotel.co.uk) and Merton Hotel (Tel:
  01534 724 231, Website: www.mertonhotel.co.uk).

- Egon Ronay Family Hotel of the Year winner St Brelade's Bay Hotel (Tel: 01534 746 141, Website: www.stbreladesbay.co.uk) also has the benefit of being close to one of the best beaches on the island.
- Self-catering is available on Jersey but you must book well in advance as there is limited availability. Samares Manor (Tel: 01534 870 551, Website: www.samaresmanor.co.uk) is the best facility available. Situated in excellent grounds with an arts and crafts centre and soft play area for children, as well as opportunities to ride a horse and carriage. It is essential to book well in advance.
- The cost of travel to Jersey is generally inexpensive. There are a large number of scheduled and charter air services from airports throughout the United Kingdom and Ireland. In addition Jersey is also served by modern car-ferries operating from the south coast of England. Travellers choose between fast car-carrying catamarans or the more leisurely conventional car ferry. Car hire in Jersey is easily arranged and very good value. Petrol costs less than on the mainland. Visitors must hold and bring with them a valid driving licence. The maximum speed limit is 40 mph (64 kph). In addition lower speed limits apply in built up areas with a 15 mph limit on 'Green Lanes' (see below).

The best bits

Beaches
- St Brelade's Bay, Green Island and Grouville are the most suitable for toddlers. They are easily accessible, calm with excellent sand ('good for building sand castles') and sheltered from strong winds.

Parks and Playgrounds
- The island has excellent parks and playgrounds – the best being Coronation Park at Millbrook.
- Another attraction worth visiting is Living Legend (Tel: 01534 485 496, Website: www.jerseyslivinglegend.co.je) which tells visitors about the folk law and history of the island, but more importantly has mini golf and an excellent playground and two soft play areas – one inside and one outdoors.

Walks

- Jersey is beautiful. Measuring just 9 by 5 miles, it benefits from a network of quiet country lanes.
- A network of over 40 miles of 'Green Lanes' has been developed, about seven-eighths of which are 'buggy friendly' – but your toddler will be more interested in the beaches!

Zoo

- Jersey Zoo (Tel: 01534 860 000, Website: www.jerseyzoo.co.uk).
- Dinosaur Museum (Tel: 01534 500 700) recently opened.

Where to Eat

- Most restaurants are toddler-friendly, even if they don't have high chairs. The best ones are Big Verns Diner (St Ouen, Tel: 01534 481 705); Partners Restaurant (Jersey Recreation Grounds, St Clement, Tel: 01534 619 202); Les Fontaines Tavern (Route du Nord, St John, Tel: 01534 862 707).
- Get a copy of the Eating Out guide from Jersey Tourism (Tel: 01534 500 700) or available on line, Website: www.jersey.com/eatingout

Isle of Man

Wonderful gentle place. This is the place where Thomas the Tank Engine lives. The film was made here and my toddlers are telling everyone they meet about the experience – whether they ask or not.

Father of three, from Shrewsbury.

The basics

Time difference from UK – None
Best way to get there – Fly
Flight time from London – One hour
English spoken – Yes
Culture – Toddler focused
Toddler-friendly rating – 10/10
'Best bits' for toddler – Everything, beaches, friends made, steam engines, petting zoos
'Best bits' for parents – The fact their children loved it
When to go – Spring and early autumn
Where to go – Stay on the coast
Accommodation – Farmhouses

Toddler-friendly tour operators
Vicki Osborne Travel (Tel: 01983 524 221,
	Website: www.vikkiosborne.com)
Special short breaks by rail and sea, with children half price
Premier Holidays (Tel: 0870 789 6266, Website: www.premier
	holidays.co.uk)

Magic Holidays self-catering (Tel: 08457 585 833,
   Website: www.steam-packet.com/magic)
Cherry Orchard Travel (Tel: 01624 833 811,
   Website: www.cherry.orchard.com)
Discovery Travel (Tel: 01624 625 391)
Everymann Holidays (Tel: 0870 789 6777,
   Website: www.everymann.co.uk)
Goldstar Travel (Tel: 01624 833 558,
   Website: www.porterinhotels.com)

Major airlines

Manx Airlines (Tel: 01624 824 313, Website: www.manx-airlines.com) link the Island with 10 major UK and Ireland centres (Birmingham, Dublin, Glasgow, Jersey, Leeds-Bradford, Liverpool, London Heathrow, London Luton, Manchester and Southampton).
British European (Tel: 08705 676 676, Website: www.british-european.com) fly from Belfast, Bristol and London City.

General Information

Isle of Man Ronaldsway Airport (Tel: 01624 821 600)
For more information contact the Tourist Board (Tel: 01624 686 766,
   Website: www.gov.im/tourism).
To find out about the weather (Tel: 0900 624 3300).

Where to stay

- The Cherry Orchard apartments (Bridson Street, Port Erin, Tel: 01624 833 811, Website: www.cherry-orchard.com) offer bonded travel packages by air or sea. Pool, sauna, gym and games room free to residents. The Mannin Hotel (Broadway, just off Douglas Promenade, Tel: 01624 675 335) has family suites available as does the Douglas Imperial Hotel (Central Promenade, Douglas, Tel: 01624 675 335).
- It is a good idea to rent cottages on the island; these are usually set in stunning locations with park or gardens. Some to consider are: Balladuke Farmhouse (Ballabeg, Arbory, Tel: 01624 822 250); The

327

Brambles (Cranstal Road, Point of Ayre, Tel: 01624 624 461), which has its own private beach; Tholt-y-Will Country Apartments (Tel: 01624 897 831), set in a lovely Swiss cottage.

- Alternatively, stay on a farm, which is probably one of the best ways to really get to know the island and islanders. Ballavell (Ballasalla, Tel: 01624 824 306); Kerrowgarrow (Greeba, Tel: 01624 801 871); Ballasholague (Maughold, Tel: 01624 861 750); Balladhoo Heights (Baldrine, Tel: 01624 863 007); Kionslieu Farm (Foxdale, Tel: 01624 801 349); and Ballacallow (near the railways, Tel: 01624 835 646) are all toddler-friendly with high chairs, cots and play areas. For further information contact www.iomholidaycottages.sageweb.co.uk.

- Another choice is Peach Tree Cottage (off Orchard Road, Port Erin, Tel: 01624 833 502) which has three bedrooms, a lounge, and is very close to shops and amenities. Cherry Tree House (Beach Road, Port St Mary, Tel: 01624 833 502) has a very large garden and excellent views.

- For further information contact www.isleofmantravel.com.

The best bits

Beaches
- No matter where you go on the Isle of Man, you're not far from the sea. The historic fishing port of Peel, in the west, is popular for its fine sands. Port Erin is a wonderful combination of golden sands and rocky inlets, with excellent walks to Bradda Head. Ramsey, in the north, is close to a bustling harbour and sandy beach.

Fairies
- Seventeen National Glens are scattered around the island. These have wooded walks with waterfalls where you can sense the fairies playing in shady glades and under bridges. Many lead to a beach. Admission is free throughout the year.

Teddy bear festivals

- Festivals for toddlers include the Teddy Bears Picnic held last weekend in June when there are side shows, face painting, a bouncy castle and teddy bear competitions in the Villa Marina Gardens (directly behind the Villa Marina, on Harris Promenade) from 1.30pm – 4.30pm.

Thomas, Trains and Trams

- The $15^{1}/_{2}$-mile Isle of Man steam railway runs between Douglas and Port Erin and is open daily from the beginning of January to the end of October. Toddlers will be more impressed by the fact the film *Thomas the Tank Engine* was made here than anything else. You can visit the actual engine and stations used in the making of the film, starring Alec Baldwin and Peter Fonda.
- Snaeffell Mountain Railway between Laxey and Snaefell is $4^{1}/_{2}$ miles long and rises to 2000 ft above sea level (open daily from April to September). Manx Electric Railway is Britain's longest narrow gauge steam railway at over 17 miles long (open from beginning of January to end of October).
- Toddlers will love the electric and horse drawn trams for which the island is famous. A trip along Douglas Promenade in the world's oldest horse-drawn trams is a must.

Wildlife

- Attractions to tempt toddlers include Ballaugh Curraghs Wildlife Park (Ballaugh, Tel: 01624 897 323), a haven for all sorts of wetland wildlife (curraghs is a Manx word for the wet, boggy, willow woodland typical of the area). Although the exact species may vary, the Park always has flamingos, cranes, storks and ibis, while wetland mammals include antelope, tapir, sea lions and various deer. The wildlife park is situated north of the island on the A3, halfway between Ramsey and Kirk Michael. Its flat pathways are mostly accessible for buggies (some off-beat nature trails may be unsuitable).
- Ballalheannagh Gardens has 5 miles of paths leading around a horticultural haven high in the hills above Laxey, east of the capital

Douglas. More than 15,000 different plants put on a spectacular show all year round.

- The Manx Wildlife Trust (Tel: 01624 801 985) has 20 reserves across the island. Other nature trails include Ayres Nature Reserve and Poyll Dooey Wetlands and Nature trails. Your toddler may also be intrigued or terrified (depending on their temperament) to hear there are basking sharks around the island (the Basking Shark Society Tel: 01624 801 207 – can arrange trips to see these creatures at close quarters).

Where to eat

- Restaurants to try include La Piazza (Loch Promenade, Douglas, Tel: 01624 672 136), which is a fashionable Italian restaurant with views overlooking Douglas Bay; the Highlander Inn (Tel: 01624 852 609) on the main road; and Haworths (Tel: 01624 822 940) on the main road.
- Seaview Inn and beer garden (Tel: 01624 812 455) has a putting green, games room with pool, and stunning views over the Bay. Children's menus are available at The Promenade Peel Safeway Café (Chester Street, Douglas, Tel: 01624 673 039).
- The Cat That Café (Tynwald Mills, St Johns, Tel: 01624 801 018) is a popular themed café that serves hot and cold shakes, chocolates handmade on the island by Roly's Chocolate Factory and excellent home-made ice creams in unusual varieties.
- Neb Café (The Tynwald Craft Centre, St Johns, Tel: 01624 801 600) is modern and airy and has a children's menu, with island bar and carvery on Sunday. Also head for the Café Royale, a coffee shop opposite M&S (Duke Street, Douglas, Tel: 01624 675 955) or the Trafalgar Hotel (Tel: 01624 814 601) where they serve a children's menu. Last but not least, The Creek Inn (Tel: 01624 842 216) on the harbourside is a cosy pub serving fresh seafood.

Spain and the Spanish Islands

Don't think about the brochure picture of busy beaches. Yes, Spain's got a 24-hour buzzing culture which suits some and not others. But we picked smaller, quieter resorts more inland and found wonderful, stunning beaches – less crowded and away from the main tourist resorts. These resorts also have village squares with little playgrounds where my two can play with the local children. It's here you'll find little shaded tavernas which serve tapas, and where the owner tries to teach our three-year-old to say 'My name is . . .' in Spanish. My lot never want us to leave.

Mother of three – baby, 2- and 4-year-old, Norwich

The basics

Time difference from UK – 1hour ahead of GMT, 2 in summer. Canary Islands on GMT in winter and 1hour ahead in summer

Flight time from London – Malaga, Barcelona or Seville, 2 hours; Valencia 2 hours, Canary Islands 4 hours

English spoken – In the main resorts, more in coastal areas

Culture – Toddler-friendly

Toddler-friendly rating – 9/10

'Best bits' for toddlers – The beaches, the Spanish toddlers, the restaurants with 'food on little plates' (tapas bars)

'Best bits' for parents – The weather, the food, the attitude of restaurant staff toward toddlers

When to go – May, June and September, avoid high season

Where to go – The quieter, smaller coastal resorts on the Costas Brava, del Sol, Blanca, the best are Calella de Palafrugell,

Llafranc, Tamariu, Aiguablava, L'Escala, Cadaques and S'Agaro.
Avoid Lloret de Mar and Estartit

Accommodation – Self-catering apartments, camping, resort hotels

Toddler-friendly tour operators

Eurocamp (Tel: 01606 787 736, Website: www.eurocamp.com)
Magic of Spain (Tel: 020 8939 5452, Website:
www.magicofspain.co.uk)
Keycamp (Tel: 0870 700 0733, Website: www.keycamp.co.uk)
Spain at Heart (Tel: 01373 814 222, Website:
www.spainatheart.co.uk)
The Individual Travellers Spain (Tel: 08700 780 187, Website:
www.indiv-travellers.com
Villaworld (Tel: 01223 506 554, Website: www.villaworld.co.uk)

Major airlines

British Airways (Tel: 0845 773 3377,
Website: www.britishairways.com)
GB Airways (Tel: 0245 773 3377, Website: www.gbairways.com)
Iberia Airlines (Tel: 0845 601 2854, Website:
www.iberiaairlines.co.uk)

For further information contact the Spanish Tourist Office, Tel: 020
7486 8077 or visit their website at www.tourspain.es, www.tour
spain.co.uk

Where to stay

- Villas and holiday flats let by the week are plentiful. Contact
  Individual Travellers (Tel: 01798 869 485) or Secret Spain (Tel:
  01449 737 850), who have an extensive range of villas and
  apartments – some of which will be suitable for toddlers. Magic of
  Spain are also excellent and have a loyal following of repeat
  customers with young families (always a good sign).
- Camping is also an excellent cost-effective option. Eurocamps have
  many toddler-friendly camps. Check to ensure the resort is either

on or near the beach and that it is within an hour's drive of the airport on arrival. Most have electricity and running water, some have launderettes, restaurants, shops, play areas and pools for toddlers. Take a camping carnet (card) as it is used to check in at sites and also gives you third-party insurance. Carnets are issued by the AA and RAC and by camping and caravanning clubs. For further information contact the Camping and Caravanning Club (Tel: 0247 669 4995).

- Principe Felipe in La Manga del Mar Menor (Tel: 0034 968 137 234) is part of an exclusive resort complex built in the style of a Spanish village. Surrounded by palm and olive groves, there is golf and tennis for the grown ups and a playground and pools for toddlers.
- In Andalusia, try Riu Canel (Tel: 0034 959 477 124). With its three pools, one for toddlers, the beachside Riu Palace is more a summer holiday centre than hotel.
- Club de Mar, at Puerto de Mogan on Gran Canaria (Tel: 0034 928 565 066), is a group of attractive buildings in lovely grounds with rooms and apartments gathered round a small bay with a sandy beach and marina.
- Jardin Tecina at La Gomera, Playa de Santiago (Tel: 0034 922 145 850) is almost like a self-contained resort, such is its range of facilities. Situated on the beach, a cliffside lift takes guests down to the beach club.

The Best Bits

Beaches
- The Spanish coastline has some of the most stunning beaches in Europe, and guaranteed sunshine to add value to the experience (for the grown ups if not the toddlers).
- On the Costa Brava, head for Lafranc, a white-washed resort with a promenade leading to neighbouring Calella – one of the coast's loveliest resorts. Estepona is fabulous for families with toddlers. It has many old squares shaded by orange trees, and is very charming especially out of season. Cabopino is a not-too-crowded

coast and has a wide sandy beach beside a marina.
...sia, the Costa del Sol boasts the quieter beach resort of
...ro de Alcantara, the lovely beaches of Rincon de la Victoria
...alaga, and Playa de Don Carlos near Marbella (the best of
...) beaches on this Costa). The region also boasts the Parque
Natural de Cazorla – over 529,000 acres of stunning nature
reserve.

- On the Costa Blanca, the quieter resorts of Denia and Javea have
  great beaches and are free of high rise hotels. This region also
  hosts the tourist town of Benidorm. Tom was fascinated by the
  huge shadow cast by the skyscraper-high cut-out black bull that
  stares at you from the side of the motorway as you speed your way
  past it en route to less headier resorts. If you think the Costa
  Blanca is all high-rise and kiss-me-quick, head for Guaranar del
  Segura, which is the least crowded of the beaches and surrounded
  by pine forests. You will change your opinion.

Balearics

- The Spanish Balearics attract young families in their thousands.
  The quieter beaches and resorts are the most suitable for young
  families and Menorca is the most popular for those with toddlers.
  It maintains an unspoilt coastline as well as interesting towns,
  including the capital Mao, which is rich in history. The best
  beaches are: Mallorca: Playa de Palma (Palma de Mallorca); Playa
  de Plamanova (Calviá), Playa de Sonserrat de Marina (Arta), Playa
  D'nbossa (Ibiza), Menorca: Cala Galdana (Ferreries).

Canaries

- The most popular of the Canary Islands is Gran Canaria (which
  hosts over 1.5 million visitors a year) and Fuerteventura, which is
  attractive, unspoilt, untouristy, but is subject to water shortages.
  Best beaches are Playa del Inglés, Playa de Maspalomas and Playa
  de Las Canteras. In Tenerife, – Playa de Las Teresitas, Playa de
  Puerto de la Cruz, Playa de Megano.

Valencia

- In Valencia you'll receive one of the warmest welcomes in Spain. You are close to the beach, to the countryside, it is safe, there are lots of great restaurants and hotels that welcome families, and the public transport system is accessible and cheap. The climate is wonderful so long as you avoid the heat and crowds of July and August. Attractions include:
- The City of Arts and Sciences – a new four-part centre for leisure and learning designed by local architect, Santiago Calatrava. The architecture is amazingly innovative. The Hemisferic is an eye-shaped building where the eyelid actually opens and closes. Great for kids, as it houses a huge IMAX cinema and laserdrome. Also part of the City of Arts and Sciences is the Science Museum, in a building designed to look like a huge animal carcass. It features lots of interactive displays and exhibitions that are designed to educate and entertain inquisitive minds.
- The Old Turia Riverbed Gardens set in the bed of the River Turia whose path was diverted outside the city, leaving perfect fertile land. There is a model of literary giant Gulliver on which children can play – inside they will find a model of Valencia City centre.
- The Malvarossa beach has a toddler's playground on the sand.

Where to eat

- Most parents I interviewed found eating out with toddlers in Spain a joy rather than a challenge. Tapas bars are a good place to eat, as they provide little 'toddler sized' dishes of different foods to try out. Ventas, country or roadside restaurants, are particularly good with children and toddlers and they serve excellent, cheap local dishes like fresh grilled sardines and fried rabbit with garlic.
- In Santander, for excellent regional cooking try Bodega del Riojano (Tel: 0034 942 216 750) or Zacarias (Tel: 0034 942 212 333), both of which serve an excellent selection of tapas and local specialities and are great with toddlers.
- Meson Los Patos at Alcudia on Mallorca (Tel: 0034 971 890 265) has a garden and children's playground for toddlers, while you can enjoy traditional Mallorcan dishes including arroz brut (soupy rice served with meat). Sounds awful – tastes fab.

- Las Grutas dè Artiles, Santa Brigida on Gran Canaria is another restaurant with gardens for the children. Set in a cave, it serves authentic Canary Island specialities and grilled meats.
- The markets in Seville and all the coastal resorts along the Costa del Sol are wonderful theatrical places where you can buy local specialities such as the many sausages, cheeses and cured ham. Most markets tend to sell a little of everything and most of the best are held on Sunday mornings.
- In Valencia, good restaurants which provide high chairs, entertainment and child portions are Restaurante Navarro (Calle Arzobispo Mayoral, 5, Tel: 0034 96 529 623) and La Riua (Calle Mar 27, Tel: 0034 963 914 571).

France

I don't think there is anywhere in France that toddlers aren't welcome. The camp sites here are the best in Europe – we're tried them in Spain and Italy but these are particularly good and the French have a way with toddlers. We've also tried villas but the kids love camping best.

Mother of three, from London

The basics

Time difference from UK – 1 hour ahead GMT

Flight time from London – 1 hour to Paris, 2 hours to Nice

Best way to get there with toddlers – Eurostar/Eurotunnel (www.eurostar.co.uk/www.eurotunnel.co.uk)

English spoken – Only major resorts, try to speak at least one sentence in French, they appreciate it

Culture – Toddler focused

Toddler-friendly rating – 9/10

'Best bits' for toddlers – The beaches, the friends

'Best bits' for parents – The weather, the food, the 'journey' ('short and sweet')

When to go – Spring and autumn

Where to go – Lesser known resorts where the French families go, such as Narbonne, La Baule and Corsica

Accommodation – Camping or self-catering

Toddler-friendly tour operators

NB Ask for villas/campsites ON the beach – not NEAR THE beach

Eurocamp (Tel: 01606 787 878, Website: www.eurocamp.com)

Canvas Holidays (Tel: 01383 644 000, Website: www.fr-holiday store.co.uk)

Mark Hammerton Travel (Tel: 01892 525 456, Website: www.markhammerton.com)

Powder Byrne (Tel: 020 8246 5310, Website: www.powderbyrne.com)

Direct Travel (Tel: 020 8641 6060)

Select France (Tel: 01865 331 350, Website: www.selectfrance.co.uk)

Simply Travel (Tel: 020 8541 2223, Website: www.simply-travel.com)

Moriban Travel (Tel: 01920 412 013, Website: www.brittany.co.uk)

VFB Cottage Holidays (Tel: 01242 240 310, Website: www.vfb holidays.co.uk) – especially for Corsica

Brittany Ferries (Tel: 0870 0010 6350, Website: www.brittany-ferries.com)

Bowhills (Tel: 01489 872 727, Website: www.bowhills.co.uk)

Blue Blanc Rouge (Tel: 01924 524 824)

Allez France (Tel: 01903 748 100, Website: www.greatescapes.co.uk)

Major airlines

Air France (Tel: 0845 0845 111, Website: www.airfrance.co.uk) fly from Heathrow, Gatwick and London City

Buzz (Tel: 0870 240 7070, Website: www.buzzaway.com) fly from London Stansted

British Airways (Tel: 0845 773 3377, Website: www.britishairways.com) fly from Gatwick, Heathrow, Manchester, Aberdeen, Belfast, Birmingham, Bristol, Cardiff, Edinburgh, Glasgow, Inverness, Jersey, Newcastle, Newquay and Plymouth

British Midland (Tel: 0870 6070 555, Website: www.british midland.com) fly from Heathrow, East Midlands, Aberdeen, Belfast, Edinburgh, Glasgow, Leeds/Bradford, Manchester and Teeside

Easyjet (Tel: 0870 6000 000, Website: www.easyjet.com) fly from Luton, Liverpool, Gatwick and Stansted

Go (Tel: 0845 605 4321, Website: www.go-fly.com) fly from
Stansted

Scotairways (Tel: 0870 606 0707, Website: www.scotairways.co.uk)
fly from Luton

Ryanair (Tel: 08701 569 569, Website: www.rynair.com) fly from
Stansted, Glasgow Prestwick and Dublin

By train

As toddlers love trains, the Eurostar has become extremely popular
with young families, although the most popular way of travelling
through France remains by car – preferably the owner's own rather
than hire car. Eurostar's (Website: www.theeuroguide.com) ultra
modern, high-speed service is the fastest and most comfortable way
to travel from London Waterloo International or Ashford International
in Kent direct to Paris, Brussels or Lille. Eurostar also offers direct
services to Disneyland Paris and the French Alps. Certain services also
stop at Calais Frethun and Lille. Consider Eurostar Plus which takes
Eurostar to Paris or Lille and connect onto TGV, France's high speed
rail network, and go further into France. Eurodomino Pass is good
value allowing you unlimited travel on France's extensive rail network.
French Motorail is the easiest way to take your car to the South of
France, although not the cheapest. Travel by Motorail from Calais and
enjoy the experience of taking your own car on holiday without the
bother of driving there (if you consider it a bother that is). Your car
will be loaded onto special transporter carriages while you relax in
passenger carriages with a choice of couchette or sleeper accommodation. Services operate to Brive, Toulouse, Narbonne, Avignon and
Nice. Eurostar check-in is at least 20 minutes prior to departure.
Beyond that time, passengers are not allowed to board the train. On
the rest of the SNCF network, the relevant ticket and reservation must
be validated before boarding the train by date stamping them in one
of the orange automatic date stamping machines on the station
concourse. For bookings and information contact 08705 848 848,
Website: www.raileurope.co.uk. For Motorail bookings, call 08702 415
415 or visit www.frenchmotorail.com

By Car

Eurotunnel's car-carrying service runs via the Channel Tunnel from Folkestone to Calais/Coquelles. Taking as little as 35 minutes platform to platform, it's the fast and exciting way to France and beyond. The service operates 24 hours a day, 365 days a year with up to 4 departures an hour at peak periods.

France is well stocked with car hire agencies. Avis Rent a Car (Tel: 0870 6060 100, Website: www.avis.co.uk) and Hertz Rent A Car (Tel: 08705 996 699, Website: www.hertz.co.uk) are but two. The autoroute – fast, efficient and ever so dull – remains the most popular way to reach the south coast of France. In season there are circuses and clowns at certain motor route stops. Check out www.autoroutes.fr

By Sea

An excellent one-stop ship site is www.ferrysavers.com This site lists all ferries (Brittany, Condor, Hoverspeed, P&O) out of the UK. You can't book Eurotunnel but can view the actual crossings. For further information contact www.eurotunnel.com or your travel agent or Tel: 08705 353535.

Skiing

There are excellent ski resorts in France, and many tour operators offer excellent crêche and kids' club facilities suitable for families with toddlers (see Skiing, page 146). Many of these resorts make excellent summer holiday destinations for young families.

Useful websites www.iti.fr (route planner) www.autoroutes.fr (information on motorways) www.equipment.gouv.fr (roads and traffic info) wwwsytadin.tm.fr (traffic reports around Paris) www.saprr.fr (eastern motorway networks) www.intofrance.co.uk (all types of news – strikes, traffic, ferries) www.sncf.com (train timetables and fares) www.bison-fute.equipment.gouv.fr (for traffic – click onto the English version). For further information contact the French Government Tourist Office (calls cost 60 pence per minute), Tel: 09068 244 123 or Website: www.franceguide.com

Where to stay

Paris

- A scheme called Residences de Tourisme provides apartments in specially-run self-catering blocks. Some hotel-type facilities are available, but you pay extra for them.
- Either contact Paris-Sejour-Reservation (90 Avenue des Champs Elysees 75008, Tel: 0033 152 891050, Fax: 0033 153 891059) or get in touch with each residence directly. The Paris Office du Tourisme (127 Ave des Champs Elysees 75008, Tel: 0033 149 525354) provides a full list of residences.
- Other companies specializing in self-catering accommodation include A Home In Paris (16 Rue Mederic 75017, Tel: 0033 142 720006), Paris Apartments Services (69 Rue d'Argout 75002, Tel: 0033 140 280128) and Allo Logement Temporarier (62 rue du Temple 75003, Tel: 0033 142 720006).
- All provide high-quality furnished apartments for stays of one week to six months, sometimes in the apartment of a Parisian who is abroad.

Camping

- Campsites in France are generally excellent and have a variety of activities and facilities ranging from playgrounds to full-blown day to day children's entertainment. I have already mentioned some of these tour operators in previous sections.
- Select France (Tel: 01865 331 350) and Keycamp (Tel: 0208 395 4000) are camping/mobile home specialists that provide good service for families with toddlers.
- Mark Hammerton Travel (Tel: 01892 525 456, Website: www.markhammerton.com/familycamping) is also one to consider.
- In fact, camping is an excellent option at this age if you discovery the right site and location. For family camping in France visit www.camping-in-france.com or ring 01892 525 456.
- Alternatively, if you are looking for a shorter break with the toddlers, visit www.off4theweekend.com, which is a toddler-friendly site.

- Eurocamp (Tel: 01606 787 878, Website: www.eurocamp.com) have several excellent sites and have won the Tommy Award for most child-friendly tour operator several times running. Specify you want a campsite on a beach, which has a toddler-friendly policy. These have kiddies' clubs which take toddlers, and are also smaller in size (usually only 300 sites compared to the normal 750) and have hireable buggies for your stay. Canet-Plage on the western Mediterranean is one of their best, flying direct into Perpignan and only 30 miles from the airport.

Gites

- The top family choice for gîtes is still the Dordogne. Try a week in a gîte with specialist Brittany Ferries (Tel: 08705 360 360) which has an excellent brochure identifying how close each gîte is to the nearest supermarket, doctor, town etc. All useful stuff when you have a toddler.
- Other companies offering rural Gaelic bliss include French Life (Tel: 0113 239 0077), Allez France (Tel: 01903 742 345), Gascony Secret (Tel: 01284 827 253) and Vacances en Campagne (08700 771 771).
- Check out www.brittany.co.uk, properties in Brittany, which have some excellent facilities for toddlers (Domaine de Moustoir, FN94; Kerpenhire Plage CM247, Kerodet PA42 and Le Queric CM302 being the best of the bunch).
- The tour operator Simply Travel is also excellent, providing crèche facilities in the form of 'Shrimps Crèche' open to 6 months to 5 years. Fully qualified nannies and cots are available.

The best bits

Beaches

- France has very toddler-friendly coastal resorts and benefits from many campsites and resorts actually being on the beach – so no need to pack or unpack cars every time your toddler wants to get to the sand. There is an immense choice.
- The South of France is idyllic and expensive but has great beaches.

Camping makes it marginally more accessible during the height of the season. Fly direct to Nice or to Carcassonne for a holiday further west at the lesser known resort of Narbonne.

- Corsica has wonderful views, good beaches and is an excellent choice in the spring and autumn, but busy in summer.
- Brittany has fabulous beaches great for kids, but weather can be temperamental in the spring and autumn. Your toddler will not care – you will. La Baule is an upmarket seaside resort Parisiens usually visit for the weekend. The wealthier ones have second homes there and its close to the Loire for a spot of wine tasting.

Montpelier

- Can get extremely hot in summer, so it's best visited in spring. It's a charming city with lots of leafy squares and playgrounds. The best bits are Le Zoo de Lunaret (avenue d'agropolis, Tel: 0033 467 544523) which is large and buggy friendly. An excellent petting zoo, Le Petit Paradis, is 15 minutes from Montpellier on the N113 or N110 in Vendargues (Tel: 0033 467 919933). Le Jardin des Plantes (Boulevard Henri V, Tel: 0033 467 634322) is a park with playgrounds, duck pond, and easy to navigate with a buggy. Le Domaine de Meric (avenue de la Justice de Castelnau, Tel: 0033 467 724005) is the largest green area in Montpellier where most of the local families congregate at weekends for picnics. You will find entertainers (puppeteers, musicians and magicians performing here during the year).

Nice

- Among the many toddler-friendly places are Parc Phoenix (Tel: 0033 493 180333), where you can see pelicans, butterflies and musical fountains. It's a half-day's entertainment when you can pull your toddler away from the beach. Castel des Deux Roi (Avenue du Mont Alban, Corniche Andre de Joly) is an excellent play area with a mini train and water sprays, which toddlers can play in. There is a tourist train which runs from April till August from 10 am till 8pm every day. Costing under £4 and lasting 45 minutes, it takes you round Nice without the hassle of worrying about navigation or traffic. Aquascope (Quai Lunel,

Tel: 0033 492 004230) is an underwater walk to explore the Riviera's sea shore. Departs every hour with a break for lunch. Toddlers will love it.

Oise
- La Mer de Sable, Oise (Centre Attractif Jean Richard, 60950 Emernonville, Tel: 0033 344 540096) is a park offering attractions, shows and games on the main theme of 'Cowboys and Indians'. Open from early April to late September. Restaurants and picnic area on site. Information on site only available in French.

Paris
- Paris is worth a day or two – no more – when you have toddlers. Spend the rest of your holiday on the coast. While you are there, there is an English-speaking babysitting company. Contact The Babysitting Service (Tel: 0033 146 375124). All the largest hotels also organize babysitting.

Puppets
- Most toddlers like puppet shows so take them to see Ches Cabotans d'Amiens (Théatre d' Animation, Picard 31, rue Edouard David 80000, Amiens, Tel: 0033 322 223090). Cabotans puppet shows are the essence of Picardie's folklore. There are four characters in this traditional farce: the hero is Lafleur, the Picardie peasant, recognizable by his striped red stockings and tricorne hat and is reminiscent of the British Mr Punch.

Steam train
- Chemin de Fer de la Baie de Somme (80230 Saint Valery sur Somme 6, Email: cfbs@neuronexion.fr) is a real steam train which runs between Le Crotoy, Noyelles-sur-Mer, Saint-Valery-sur-Somme and Cayeux-sur-Mer. As you ride along the willow-lined streams, crossing fields and marshlands, you will explore all the leafy charms of the Bay de Somme. Train runs from mid-April until mid-October.

Theme parks
- I wouldn't recommend Disneyland for toddlers. It's great for older children, but toddlers get too tired and flustered. Nigloland is good for little ones, though (on the RN 19 in Dolancourt, Aube en Champagne, Tel: 0033 325 279452, Website: www.nigloland.fr). Stay at the 2-star hotel de Troyes (168 avenue due General Leclerc, 10000 Troyes, Tel: 0033 325 712345).
- Parc Asterix is also recommended (60128 Plailly, on the autoroute A1, Paris-Lille 30 km from Paris, Tel: 0033 344 623131, Website: www.parcasterix.fr.)

Wildlife
- Réserve Naturelle des Marais d'Isle (Aisne) is situated in the centre of Saint-Quentin. It contains a range of interesting flora and fauna and is a stopping point for many migratory birds. Many of the children's games on site are suitable for toddlers. (Contact: Office de Tourisme de Saint-Quentin Haute Picardie, Tel: 0033 323 050650/670 500, Email: saintquentin.haute.picardie.@ wanadoo.fr)

Where to eat

- Try out bakeries with seating areas such as Paul and Le Pain quotidien in Paris because they have high chairs and are prompt to serve. Also, the menus are usually tempting.
- The restaurant Chez Clement (Champs Elysées, Tel: 0033 140 738700) has very good-value kid's menus including dishes with salmon or chicken.

Italy

My three-year-old made so many friends last year. He remembers all their names. A campsite is the best way for your toddler to make friends, especially in Italy, where everyone's so much more tactile and talkative. Queuing for showers in the afternoons, or the bread and milk in the morning – you always get into conversation. Can't understand a word they're saying, of course.

Mother of Thomas, aged 3, Brentwood

The basics

Time difference from UK – 1 hour ahead of GMT
Flight time from London – 2 hours to Pisa, Rome and Milan
Best way to get there with toddlers – Fly, ideally from regional airport if possible
English spoken – Mainly in tourist regions
Culture – Toddler-friendly
Toddler-friendly rating – 9/10
'Best bits' for toddlers – The beaches, the Italian toddlers, the food
'Best bits' for parents – The weather, the attitude toward toddlers, the scenery, the food
When to go – Spring and autumn, avoid crowds and heat of summer
Where to go – The coast. Viareggio, Tuscany and Umbria. Sardinia – holiday villages
Where not to go – Florence, Venice, Rome, Milan in summer
Accommodation – Self-catering villas or camping only if tent/caravan is already provided on site.

346

Toddler-friendly tour operators

Eurocamp (award-winning toddler-friendly tour operator 2000), KeyCamps. Usually cheaper to book a package holiday than travel independently. There may be a minimum stay requirement and tour operators offering the widest and best variety include Italian Chapters (Tel: 020 7722 9560), Tailor MadeTours (Tel: 020 8291 9736), Vacanze in Italia (Tel: 01798 869 426).

Major airlines

British Airways, 2 daily flights to Pisa, (Tel: 0845 773 3377,
    Website: www. britishairways.com)
Ryanair, 3 daily flights to Pisa, (Tel: 08701 569 569,
    Website: www.ryan air.com)
Gandalf Airlines (Website: www.gandalfair.it)
British Midland (Tel: 0870 6070 555,
    Website: www.britishmidland.co.uk)
Buzz (Tel: 0870 240 7070, Website: www.buzzaway.com)
Alitalia (Website: www.alitalia.it)

By train

Although not as efficient as the French TGV's, trains are good in Italy and one of the best ways to explore the countryside. Italian State Railway information line (Tel: 0906 550 8925)
For further information contact the Italian State Tourist Board (Tel: 0207 408 1254).

Where to stay

- In Viareggio there are two hotels facing the promenade which offer babysitting: Hotel Excelsior has its own private beach (Viale Carducci 54, Viareggio, Tel: 0039 0584 50726/7, Fax 0039 0584 50729 2) and the Grand Hotel e Royal has a private garden, outdoor pool and private beach (Viale Carducci 44, Viareggio, Tel: 0039 0584 45151, Fax 0039 0584 31438). Only 2 kms from Viareggio, in the resort of Lido di Camaiore facing the promenade is the four-star Grand Hotel Riviera with private garden and outdoor pool (Viale Lungomare Pistelli n.59, Lido di Camaiore, Tel: 0039 0584 617571, Fax 0039 0584 619533). It offers babysitting and has a toddler's club three times a week in July and August.

Camping

- There are some excellent campsites in the mountains and around the coastal regions. The Amalfi as well as the Adriatic coast has many and there are some very toddler-friendly sites in both areas.
- Lido Di Pomposa, a 2-hour drive from Verona or Venice airports, is one of the best for toddlers as it is situated on the beach, so no need to pack and unpack cars.
- Another is Sarteano, just south of Pisa and a few minutes from the beach.
- Cicina near Pisa is also worth considering. It has a toddler's club, but is about a 10-minute drive from the beach, which makes it more impractical. All are available through Eurocamps (Tel: 01606 787 878, Website: www.eurocamp.com). Specify when choosing a campsite that you want one on the beach with a toddler kiddies' club facility.

Self-catering

- If you choose a self-catering holiday, you have the choice of over 2000 farms, villas and mountain chalets offering reasonably priced self-catering or hotel-style accommodation as part of the Agriturismo scheme (Agriturisimo information line, Tel: 0039 0564 417418, Website: www.agriturist.it). Facilities range from first-class hotel accommodation in beautifully kept villas and ancient castles to basic rooms sharing the home with the family working on the farm. Some have restaurants which serve farm and local produce, while others offer riding, fishing and other activities.
- There are also 'residence', found in the ENIT accommodation lists. These are halfway between a hotel and self-catering flat and often offer cooking facilities and some sort of restaurant service.

The best bits

The attitude

- According to those parents I spoke to when researching this book, Italy is perceived as the place where toddlers and children are most welcome. The only negative experiences were in cities such as Rome, Florence and Venice, where a combination of too much heat, too many tourists, too many bridges and canals with no barriers (in the case of Venice), and (in Rome especially) too much car pollution. Toddlers are nicely placed at car exhaust height. That said, in both urban and rural communities children are welcome in all but the smartest establishments and throughout Italy restaurants are likely to be full of families.
- All of the coast of Tuscany is suitable for toddlers, as well as the western part of Liguria, the so-called 'riviera di Ponente', and many of the resorts along the Adriatic coast (especially those in the Veneto and Emilia Romagna, though some resorts, like Rimini, can be very crowded in July and August).

Viareggio

- The most popular resort in Italy for toddlers, according to comments from the families I spoke to, is the town of Viareggio. The beach is clean, white sand, the tides are low and the surf is gentle while there are always coastguards to monitor the swimmers. It's just a stone's throw from the wonderful medieval, magical walled city of Lucca which has colourful markets, interesting shops, many cafés and toddler-friendly restaurants.
- Other excellent towns to visit include Fiesole, a hilltop site, originally Etruscan and set among olive orchards in the Tuscan hills. It also has very toddler-friendly cafés and bars.

Where to eat

- High chairs and special menus are rare, but most places provide cushions and smaller portions. Similar to other Mediterranean countries, smoking is very popular. Lunch is usually served between 1 and 2.30pm, dinner between 8 and 11pm. Meals are a big event in the Italian culture and children of all ages – especially toddlers – play a big part. Pick an osteria, trattoria, pizzeria or birreria (serving pasta and snacks). Gelataria serve icecream and paticceria serve pastries and cakes.

- In Viareggio, II Pino sul Tetto (Viale Capponi 11, Tel: 0039 0584 51674; closed on Wed) has a small private garden and is situated in a pine forest. Gran Caffe' Margherita (Piazzale Margherita, Tel: 0039 0584 962553; closed Wed) is also very toddler-friendly, and so is Britannia (Viale Carducci 42, Tel: 0039 0584 47484; closed Mon).
- San Gimignano is a beautiful hill town with cafés and restaurants happy to serve and entertain toddlers – even if they do wander into the kitchen. Try La Terrazze (Tel: 0039 0577 940328), set on a terrace with views overlooking the Tuscan hills. Staff are very good with toddlers and it is reasonably priced considering the priceless views.
- All towns in Italy have excellent and colourful weekly markets. Large towns will have several daily markets and a weekly flea market usually held on a Sunday. Go early – about 6am – as stallholders set up at 5am. To get the most from a self-catering holiday, go to the food markets, and choose from the wide range of foods in season. Grapes and mushrooms are best in autumn, asparagus, strawberries and Roman artichokes are good in spring.

Portugal

Golf for the grown-ups and sand for the children. Unless you head for Lisbon you won't find much else here – but what more do you need? Its safe, the Portuguese are infatuated with toddlers especially and you'll be hard-pressed to find a hotel, restaurant or shop that won't make you feel more than welcome. We stayed at a hotel last year in the Algarve. Not only were the receptionists chatting to my toddlers, the lady who cleaned our room would play with them for a good ten minutes if we were still there; the staff in the restaurant in the morning would show them round kitchen. Everyone from the window cleaner to the front of office manager was great. This must be the friendliest toddler country in the world.

Father of three, from Southampton

The basics

Time difference from UK – 1 hour ahead of GMT in summer
Flight time from London – 3 hours to Faro
English spoken – In major resorts
Culture – 'Fabulously friendly'
Toddler-friendly rating – 10/10
'Best bits' for toddlers – The beaches, the friends made
'Best bits' for parents – The culture, the short journey time
When to go – Spring is quieter and there are wonderful wild flowers but can rain; autumn is also good
Where to go – Specific resorts on the Algarve (see below)
Accommodation – Resorts and self-catering villas/camping

Toddler-friendly tour operators

British Airways Holidays (Tel: 01293 722 727, Website: www.britishairways.com)

Something Special (Tel: 08700 270 508, Website: www.something special.co.uk)

Thomson (Tel: 020 7387 9321, Website: www.thomson.co.uk)

First Choice (Tel: 01293 560 777, Website: www.firstchoice.co.uk)

Major airlines

TAP Air Portugal is the national carrier (Tel: 0845 601 0932).

PGA Portugalia flies from Manchester to Lisbon, Porto and Faro.

British Airways (Tel: 0845 773 3377, Website: www.britishairways. com) flies to all airports in Portugal under the auspices of GB Airways.

GO (Tel: 0845 605 4321, Website: www.go-fly.com) flies to Lisbon and to Faro.

Where to stay

- In the Algarve, Le Meridien Dona Pilippa (www.lemeridien-hotels.com) has an excellent crêche facility (see Hotels, page 120).

The best bits

The attitude

- The Portuguese attitude toward children makes the Italians appear almost reticent in comparison. Restaurants usually have special menus for children and the Portuguese include children in most of their social events – so they won't be surprised if and when you bring yours along too. A child under the age of eight sharing with parents is entitled to 50 percent discount and many hotels will make arrangements for babysitters.

Beaches

- Most people head for the Algarve, but Lisbon also has some lovely beaches as well as being a cultural hotpot of stunning architecture, excellent restaurants and friendly people.
- The beaches at Colares, Cascais, Costa da Caparica, Estoril, Guincho and Sesimbra are all worth visiting if you are travelling to Lisbon – but your most relaxed experience will be on the quieter resorts in southern Portugal.
- The best beaches in southern Portugal are west of Lago, round Cabo de Sao Vicente (Cape St Vincent), and north as far as Sines, and east of Faro. Peaceful and empty, with unspoilt landscapes a few kilometers inland. The busiest is Priai da Rocha, and Vila Nova de Milfontes and Zambujeiro do Mar on the Alentejan coast are some of the quietest.
- The least developed beaches are those that stretch north from Cabo de Sao Vicente, which are fairly inaccessible and windy thanks to the full force of the Atlantic breezes. They also have strong currents so are not suitable for toddlers.
- Quieter resorts to look out for include Burgau, which still retains a fishing village feel despite being developed as a tourist resort. The sandy beach Cabanes Valhal west of Burgau is lovely, with lots of toddler-friendly restaurants.
- If you want to get away from crowded resorts avoid Monte Gordo, Albufeira and choose Faro to fly in and out of – no more.
- Other resorts to consider include Luz, with one of the best beaches on the coast being Praia da Luz. It's a very peaceful, relaxed place to stay.
- Praia da Oura has lovely beaches but noisy nightlife.
- The resort of Praia da Rocha and port of Portimao are best avoided. Crowds. Pollution. Road congestion.

Entertainment

- A lot of the 'child entertainment' other than beach is aimed at older children (water parks, riding, watersports), although – as you might expect in one of the golfing capitals of the world – there are plenty of wannabee Tiger Woods practising their swing.

- The coastal resorts of Albufeira, Vilamoura and Portimao all have mini golf courses.
- Zoo Marine (on the N125 between Guia and Alcantarilha, Tel: 00351 244 560426) is a mini funfair with big wheel, merry-go-round and bouncy castles ideal for toddlers. Plus performing dolphins, seals and parrots.

Gardens
- If you want a break from the beach, try the gardens and small zoo next to the castle at Silves. Silves is a stunning town, full of mosques, bazaars and orchards full of citrus fruits – all of which will appeal more to you than your toddler.

Markets
- Markets are also excellent in Portugal, and especially in and around Lisbon and the Algarve. The biggest and best are held in Lagos, on the first Saturday of each month, and there are special fairs in August, October and November. Quarteira has a large gypsy market every Wednesday, and the resident fish market in Albufeira is worth visiting.

Where to eat

- For restaurants, check out Bella Italia (Rua Dr Fransisco Gomes, Albufeira, Tel: 00351 289 542856) for pizzas and pasta. Or Restaurant Aldeia Cova (Vale de Eguas, Albufeira, Tel: 00351 289 395281), which serves local cuisine and has a very toddler-friendly staff. Tell them you are bringing a 2-, 3- or 4-year-old and they will have something special waiting.

The Netherlands

Amsterdam is a wonderful place for families with young children – take canal boat rides, play in the massive parks that dot the city, visit the floating markets by pedal boat, and eat yummy food that seems made for kids, especially the pancakes.

Mother of two toddlers, from London

The basics

Time difference from UK – GMT + 1 hour (winter) + 2 hours (summer)
Flight time from London – 1 hour
Best way to get there with toddlers – Fly direct
English spoken – Widely
Culture – Toddler tolerant
Toddler-friendly rating – 9/10
'Best bits' for toddlers – Zoos, canal boats, trams and city farms
'Best bits' for parents – As interesting for them as their toddlers
When to go – Summer (up to 8 hours of sunshine)
Where to go – Amsterdam
Accommodation – Resort hotels

Major airlines
VLM (Tel: 020 7476 6677, Website: www.vlm-airlines.com) fly from London City to Rotterdam.
KLM Cityhopper (Tel: 08705 074 074) fly from Bristol, Cardiff and London Heathrow to Amsterdam.

KLM Royal Dutch Airlines (Tel: 08705 074 074,
Website: www.klm.com) fly from London Heathrow to
Amsterdam.

KLM UK (Tel: 08705 074 074, Website: www. Klmuk.com) fly from
Aberdeen, Belfast, Birmingham, Edinburgh, Glasgow,
Humberside, Leeds, Bradford, London City/Gatwick/Stansted,
Manchester, Newcastle, Norwich, Sheffield, Southampton and
Teesside to Amsterdam.

Parents recommended flying from Stansted direct to Amsterdam,
mainly due to Stansted being an excellent airport for toddlers and
the flight being the quickest way to reach the destination. KLM as
an airline is also good with toddlers. However, you can also take
the Eurostar, change at Brussels for an intercity bound for
Amsterdam.

For further information contact 0906 871 7777 or visit
www.holland.com/uk.

By sea

Stena Line, Harwich to Hook of Holland, two daily crossings,
(Tel: 08705 707 070, Website: www.stenaline.co.uk)

P&O North Sea Ferries, Hull to Europoort (Rotterdam) is an
overnight ferry. (Website: www.ponsf.com)

DFDS travels from Newcastle to Ijmuiden (Amsterdam), (Tel: 08705
333 000)

Where to stay

- In Amsterdam, the Bridge Hotel (Amstel 107–111, Tel: 0031 20
  6237068, Fax: 0031 20 6241565) is toddler-friendly with large
  rooms. The Concert Inn (de Lairessestraat, Tel: 0031 20 3057272)
  has spacious rooms and apartments that cater for young families.
  Both are located close to parklands and playgrounds. The Best
  Western (Tesselschadestraat, Tel: 0031 20 6126876) has special
  family rooms.

- In Rotterdam, stay at Alexander, Hotel Central (Kruiskade, Tel:
  0031 20 6243535), which is very toddler-friendly with crèche

facilities. The Gran Dorado Group (Tel: 0031 20 6791370) has a family holiday resort half an hour from Rotterdam with a children's club, play area and petting farm, plus toddler-friendly restaurants.

The best bits

Attitude

- The Dutch are relaxed about toddlers, who are well catered for in hotels (with babysitting services and contact number for outside agencies if they don't have one in house), restaurants and public attractions. Emphasis on wheelchair access means buggies are used more easily, even on public transport – though the cobbled streets aren't the easiest of surfaces to ride or walk on.

Amsterdam

- One of the top five best cities to take toddlers in continental Europe. The big selling point about Amsterdam is that it is flat. This is important if you are carrying a baby, pushing a buggy, or have a family in tow – too many hills and you can feel your visit to a city is downhill all the way. Trams are a brilliant way to explore and I defy any toddler to not be enchanted by them – Tom was. There are more than 270 trams in Amsterdam and around 90 have been painted with special scenes – there is even a 'fare dodger's tram'! You buy a day pass, which is valid on all buses, trams and the underground. Canal boats are equally exciting for youngsters, as are the pedal boats that can be directed around most of the city. Canal boat operators include: Rederij Noord-Zuid (Tel: 0031 20 6791370), Rederij Amsterdam Canal Cruises (Tel: 0031 20 6265636), Rederij Lovers (Tel: 0031 20 5301090) and Canal Bus (Tel: 0031 20 6239886).

VONDELPARK

- Plenty to do for toddlers in this lovely city-centre park, including a little zoo with farm animals and a poffertjes (little Dutch pancakes) restaurant.

357

A LITTLE CULTURE

- Sound boring? Try it Amsterdam style. The Helden & Beoven Cinema (Nieuwmarkt 11, Tel: 0031 20 4274407) is especially for children, and they sit on golden benches with blue velvet pillows. Once inside, they can eat their entrance ticket and enjoy lemonade and popcorn. Every Friday there is a special dinner performance with pancakes. Parents do not need to accompany children.
- The First Museum of Florescent Art was named after Jimi Hendrix's masterpiece. It's great fun for toddlers because it is interactive and bright! Found at Electric Ladyand, 2nd Leliedwarsstraat 5, 1015 TB Amsterdam (Tel: 0031 20 4203776).
- The Circus Ellboog organises performances for children throughout the Netherlands, and they can take part in the performance on certain days (Passeerdersgracht 32, Tel: 0031 20 6269370).

ZOOS AND CITY FARMS

- Artis Zoo incorporates covered and open animal pens, along with a Planetarium, fabulous aquarium and the Geologisch Museum (Tel: 0031 20 5233400), its an all-weather attraction.
- Alternatively go to the Amsterdamse Bos (Tel: 0031 20 6409253), the largest recreational area in Holland, to see the donkeys and llamas in the Vondelpark (Tel: 0031 20 5237790) and highland cattle in the Amstelpark (Europaboulevard).

The Hague

- More famous for its bureaucrats than toddler friendliness, but its worth considering for the puppet theatres (Frankenstraat, Tel: 0031 20 6635703).

Rotterdam

- Try out one of Holland's largest zoos Diergaarde Blijdorp (van Aerssenlaan 49, Tel: 0031 10 4431495); or Plaswijckpark (Ringdijk 20, Tel: 0031 10 4181836), which is a park situated in the green heart of Rotterdam with several large play areas and a children's farm suitable for toddlers.

Theme park

- Efteling theme park pre-dates all the best-known theme parks of Europe and as most parents with young children will testify, out-charms them too. There may be a few white-knuckle rides to entertain older children and adults, but the heart of the park is centred on fairy tales, folklore, myths and legends. Several UK tour operators feature short breaks to Efteling, usually based on crossings from Harwich to the Hook of Holland on the Stena Line HSS high-speed ferry (Amsterdam Travel Service, Tel: 0870 727 5885).

Where to eat

- Must-sees for toddlers (and their parents) include the Kinderkookcafe (Oude Acterburgwal 193, Tel: 0031 20 6253257), where children can try their hand at being a chef and restauranteur for the day.
- The Enfant Terrible (De Genestetstraat 1, Tel: 0031 20 6122032) is a small café designed for parents and under fives. You can either eat here with your child, or eat in peace while a play leader keeps your tot amused. For a small fee, they'll even look after your toddler if you want to pop into town for a quick break.
- Also consider De Ponteneur (le Van Swindenstraat, Tel: 0031 20 6680680) and Caramba (Lindengracht, Tel: 0031 24 2020612). Both open daily and offer special kiddies' menus and play area.

Belgium

An unexpected delight. I thought Belgium would be little more than good chocolate, excellent chips and lousy weather. My two had a whale of a time. It's good any time of year – but my tip is to stick to summer and autumn. More chance of better weather.

Mother of three, from London

The basics

Time difference from UK – 1 hour ahead of GMT
Flight time from London – 1 hour
Best way to get there with toddlers – Take Eurostar: 2 hours 40 minutes straight to Midi Station, Brussels
English spoken – Fairly common, but take a phrase book
Culture – Quietly toddler-friendly
Toddler-friendly rating – 9/10
'Best bits' for toddlers – The beaches, the playgrounds, the petting zoos, the chips, chocolates
'Best bits' for parents – The fact there is a lot for toddlers to see and do
When to go – Summer and early autumn
Where to go – Brussels, Bruges, Namur, Antwerp, Liege
Accommodation – Farmhouses

Toddler-friendly tour operators
Belgian Travel Service Ltd (Tel: 01992 456 101, Website: www.bth.be)

A1 Holiday Breaks (Tel: 020 7431 4560,
　 Website: www.al-holidaybreaks.com)

Major airlines

Sabena (Tel: 0845 6010 933, Website: www.sabena.com)
British Airways (Tel: 0845 773 3377, Website:
　 www.britishairways.com)
British Midland (Tel: 0870 607 0555,
　 Website: www.britishmidland.com)

By train

Eurotunnel (Tel: 0870 240 2995, Website: www.eurotunnel.com)
Eurostar (Tel: 08705 186 186, Website: www.eurostar.com)

General Information

- For further information on Liege and Namur contact the Belgian
  Tourist Office on 020 7531 0390 (free brochure line, Tel: 0800
  9545 245, Email: info@belgium-tourism.org, Website:
  www.belgium-tourism.net). For information on Brussels, Brugge
  and Antwerp go to www.visitflanders.com and brochure line 020
  7867 0311.

Where to stay

- In Brussels, a good hotel for toddlers is l'Amigo (1–3 rue de
  l'Amigo, 1000 Bru, Tel: 0032 5474747, Website:
  www.rfhotels.com). It provides cots, crêches and babysitting
  services, as well as being quite central. Many of the five-star hotels
  on the coast have babysitting services.
- For farmhouses, book through the accommodation reservation
  dept of the Belgium Tourist Office (Website: www.belgium-
  tourism.net).

The best bits

Antwerp
- This city is the famous for its art, diamonds and fashion – none of which your toddler will find of interest. It may be one of the greatest cities in the world, but it only offers one genuine delight for a toddler – one of the oldest and most famous zoos in the world with over 4000 animals (26 Koningin Astridplein, Tel: 0032 3 2024540, Website: www.zooantwerpen.be). Toddlers can do their own thing in the Kid Site. Vriesland (the penguins' quarters) and Hathi-Mahal (the elephants' quarters) are must sees. All Tom wanted to know was if he could touch the penguins. Olmen Zoo (Antwerp, Tel: 0032 3 2024540, Website: www.olmensezoo.be) has one of the largest walk-through aviaries in Europe. They also have white tigers, a circus, a train, playground, children's farm and goat meadow.
- Magic World (Tel: 0032 3 2370329) is Antwerp in miniature. Ipenberg Recreational Parks (Tel: 0032 3 6581919) is an indoor area with rocks, castles, waterfalls, climbing towers, swings and slides, climbing bars, tubes, merry-go-rounds and boating lakes. Bobbejaanland (Tel: 0032 14 557811), 45 km east of Antwerp, has over 50 attractions plus music and dance shows, and clown performances. About 20 percent of the attractions are toddler-friendly.
- Wild Animal Park Planckendael (Tel: 0032 15 414921, Website: www.planckendael.be) is excellent value. The koalas are very funny. Coolongalook, Yarto and Alkina are now on view on a permanent basis. Offers an adventure path for toddlers, an African and Australian continent theme, a children's farm and huge playground suitable for toddlers in the middle of 40 acres of nature.

Brugge
- The countryside is on the doorstep and all the hotels and restaurants provide babysitting and listening and cots without cost and query. High chairs and child portions are also available in

most of the restaurants. Public transport is accessible and easy to
use if you have buggies. Pony and trap rides are available – and
fun. Trains and buses for children under six are free. The city is
small enough to reach all the attractions either by walking or by
bus. The centre of Brugge is traffic free except for public transport
and horse and trap, so it is a relatively safe area for wandering and
children. Parking is easy and the outskirts of the town are only a
10-minute drive away.

- The city is a maze of canals, so water is never far away, and there
  is also the Minnewater Park which is very central and has a
  beautiful lake.
- Visit the excellent Dolphinarium where you can watch sea lions
  and dolphins (Tel: 0032 50 383838).
- Zeebrugge is linked by a 7.5 mile canal, and fun for a day trip as it
  has good sandy beaches and is safe for toddlers.

Brussels

- Brussels has an efficient, cheap and reliable tube network covering
  the city and the main attractions. It operates a hop-on hop-off bus
  system departing from Central station during July and August as
  well as the more conventional bus routes. The city also has trams,
  which your toddler will love but which are slightly difficult to
  navigate with buggies. Brussels Public Transport Museum (Tel:
  0032 25 153108, Website: www.mtub.yucom.be) is worth a visit –
  and your toddler will enjoy the open air tram rides through woods
  in good weather.
- Visit the Theatre du Ratinent (Ferme Rose, avenue De Fre 44, Tel:
  0032 23 751563), a puppet show for children from age two on
  Wednesdays, Saturdays, and Sundays at 3pm. Or try the Theatre
  Royal Le Perruchet (50 av de la Foret, Tel: 0032 26 738730),
  which is an excellent puppet show. None are in English but your
  toddler will like them anyway. Very colourful puppets bashing
  each other on the head!
- Also worth a journey is Mini Europe (Tel: 0032 24 741313,
  Website: www.minieurope.com). Located next to the Atomium
  (Bruparck, 1020 Brussels), Mini Europe is the only park where

you can have a whistlestop tour of Europe in a few short hours.
You can make the models work yourself. The eruption of
Versuvius, the fall of the Berlin Wall, the bullfight in Sevilla. With
over 300 models, it entertained Tom for a few hours.

Liege

• Liege, east of Brussels, also has plenty to offer. Visit the Wild Safari
World Digne (Aywaille, Liege. Tel: 0032 43 609070, Website:
www.mondesauvage.be), a safari and recreational park accessible
by car or small train. Wild animals, and a large playground with
attractions combined with a petting farm for children, full of
domestic animals such as donkeys, goats, sheep, ponies, ducks,
geese, rabbits and peacocks. A self-service café and restaurant are
situated in an aviary which contains a large collection of exotic
birds. The restaurant also has baby changing. It is accessible from
Liege by the motorway E25 exit 46. Also worth visiting is the
Aquarium and Zoological Museum of the University of Liege (Tel:
0032 80 684265, Website: www.ulg.ac.be/aquarium). It's
predominantly a wildlife park with animals of the Ardennes. Tour
by train (duration trip 40 mins). It has a play area and amusement
park (although the latter is more suited to older children).
• There is also a good playground at L'Hirondelle, Oteppe, Liege
(Tel: 0032 85 711131) and Mont Mosan Recreational Park Huy
(Tel: 0032 85 232996) has a parrot show, a sealion show, large
playground, inflatable castle, and minature golf.

Namur

• Check out very pretty and unspoilt Namur and visit the Ostrich
Farm, Sorinnes-Dinnant (Tel: 0032 81 223406, Website:
www.autruches.com, Email: info@autruches.com). Your toddler
will be interested to see these animals, perhaps less so to try the
ostrich sandwich spread, meat and eggs. You can buy all these at
the local shop – including the feathers.
• Also worth visiting is the Animal Farm Penteville Gembloux (near
Namur, Tel: 0032 81 601884), a large collection of animals with
about 100 different Belgian and foreign species. There is a play
garden and cafeteria. Excellent for toddlers.

Playgrounds and parks

- Domaines Provinciaux are large parks with large playgrounds and other hands-on inventive attractions for toddlers – and are designed for visitors to spend the entire day.
- On rainy days, go to Badaboum (Chaussee de Louvain, 491 1300 Wavre, Tel: 0032 10 224500). There is an indoor playground for 1- to 11-year-olds and a café. Kid's Fantasy Club Forest (Chaussee de Ruisbroek, 81 1190 Forest, Tel: 0032 23 321642) is a large indoor adventure playground where for a set fee you can stay all day. Your toddler will want to. You may not. Kid's Factory (Chaussee de Bruxelles, 63 1410 Waterloo, Tel: 0032 23 512345) has giant inflatable obstacle courses and areas for babies and toddlers. You pay a fixed price for unlimited time. For further information about playgrounds in Belgium visit www.expatinbrussels.com.

Theme parks

- Aqualibi (Wavre, Tel: 0032 10 414466/421600) is an aquatic theme park attached to Six Flags Theme Park, which is Belgium's best amusement park with loads of thrill rides – about 10 percent of which are suitable for toddlers.
- Or try Houtopia – a children's world (Place de l'église, 17 6660 Houffalize, Tel: 0032 61 289205). You can walk, crawl and slide through the body of a giant (parents with bad backs take care). Sharpen your senses in an old temple. While the children play in the playground, adults can relax at the restaurant L'Espace Gourmand. You won't want to. Well thought out. Good day's entertainment.
- De Panne (Meli Park, De Pannelaan 68, Adinkerke, Tel: 0032 58 420202) is a theme park that is ideal for toddlers. Tom, like most toddlers, is into spiders, ants, bees, and basically anything that is smaller than him. So he loved this. Honey bees are the theme and rides and exhibits all have this busy bee motive. It kept him amused for a few hours.

Toddler theatre

- The Children's Museum (rue du Bourgmestre 15, Brussels, Tel: 0032 26 400107) has workshops for painting, collage and theatre suitable for toddlers. Theatre du Ratinet (avenue de Fre 44, 1180 Brussels, Tel: 0032 23 751563) is a puppet show for toddlers – open on Wednesdays, Saturdays and Sundays at 3pm. Tom loved it, despite the plays being in Dutch!

Zoo

- Visit Animal Farm at La Crete des Cerfs (Chemin des Chanteraine, 6830, Tel: 0032 61 467152). Walk among bison, lynx, fallow deer, deer and ostriches. Animals live in 'semi freedom'.

Where to eat

- As one of Belgians great delicacies happens to be fantastic chips – a particular favourite of Tom's and most other toddlers – you can't go wrong. I would hold back on the mussels for a few years, as allergic reactions could be violent. There are plenty of chicken, cheese and ham dishes and cafés will be happy to produce an omelette if nothing takes their fancy on the menu. And then there are the chocolates, of course. Neuhaus is the leading Belgian chocolatier. At most shops you can find not only the chocolates but marzipan models of animals and 'little people' that toddlers will prefer to keep rather than eat. There are also wonderful cake shops selling excellent patisseries. At the Chocolate Line Simon (Stevinplein 19, Bruges), watch how they make chocolate in the kitchen; or drink hot chocolate made from hot milk, cream and melted chocolate at De Provoeri, a tearoom opposite an excellent chocolate shop Sukerbuyc (Katelijnestraat 5), owned by the same family.

Denmark

One of the most toddler-friendly countries we've found in Europe, and we've toured them all. Even the cities are wonderful.
Mother of two toddlers, aged 3 and 4, from Newcastle

The basics

Time difference from UK – 1 hour ahead of GMT
Flight time from London – 1½ hours
English spoken – In main cities and towns mostly
Culture – Quietly toddler-friendly
Toddler-friendly rating – 10/10
'Best bits' for toddlers – So much to do
'Best bits' for parents – So much for toddlers to do, clean and safe
When to go – Spring and autumn
Where to go – Copenhagen, Odense, Arhus
Accommodation – Camping or farmhouses, also consider family hostels, which are good in Denmark

Toddler-friendly tour operators
Bridge-Scandinavia (Tel: 0870 727 5786),
DFDS Seaways Harwich (Tel: 08705 333 000, Website: www.dfdssea ways.co.uk)
Scantours (Tel: 020 7839 2927, Website: www.scantoursuk.com)
Travelling Together (Tel: 01763 262 190, Website: www.travelling together.co.uk)

Major airlines

British Midland (Tel: 0845 6070 555,
  Website: www.britishmidland.co.uk)
Brymon Airways (Tel: 0345 222 111,
  Website: www.britishairways.com)
Go Fly Ltd (Tel: 0845 60 54321, Website: www.go-fly.com)
Varig (Tel: 0845 603 7601, Website: www.varig.com)
British Airways (Tel: 0845 77 33377, Website:
  www.britishairways.com)
Ryanair (Tel: 0870 156 9569, Website: www.ryanair.com)
SAS (Tel: 0845 6072 7727, Website: www.scandinavian.net)

By plane

Most international flights arrive and depart from Copenhagen Airport, which has baby-changing facilities and is one of the major hubs of northern Europe. Copenhagen is served daily by Scandinavian Airlines (SAS), and British Airways, among others. British Airways fly from London Heathrow and Birmingham to Copenhagen. Ryanair operates flights from London Stansted to Aarhus in East Jutland twice daily. If you are flying to Denmark, many airlines have special offers on car hire – so called fly drive offers. These include Europcar (Tel: 08457 222 525), Avis (Tel: 0870 606 0100), Budget (Tel: 0800 181 181) and Hertz (Tel: 08705 996 699).

By train

There is a rail shuttle service from Copenhagen Airport (Website: www.cph.dk) to Copenhagen Central Station and other stations. The journey from the airport to the Central Station takes only 12 minutes, runs every 20 minutes and is cheap. From Billund Airport (Website: www.billund-airport.com) there are bus services to main towns in Jutland, such as Arhus, Vejle, Sikeborg, Struer and Horsens. Rail Europe can also book certain rail journeys within Denmark (Tel: 08705 848 848) and Ultima Travel (Tel: 0151 339 6171). Danish State Railways (DSB) InterCity services link most towns in Denmark, with frequent services on major routes. InterCity trains offer baby changing, and you need to make reservations especially if you want to cross the

Great Belt Bridge. Many railway stations offer luggage trolley services although some services require a deposit.

By sea

If you are travelling by sea from Harwich to Esbjerg, there are 3 or 4 weekly departures by DFDS Seaways. (Tel: 0870 533 3000, Website: www.dfdsseaways.co.uk)

By road

Travel with Eurolines from London, Victoria Coach Station, directly to destinations in Denmark, including Copenhagen and Arhus. You can book your Eurolines journey at any National Express Agent nation-wide (Tel: 0870 580 8080, Website: www.gobycoach.com). Travellers wishing to bring their own car can do so by travelling on the DFDS Seaways ferry directly to Denmark from Harwich to Esbjerg or by trav-elling via the Channel Tunnel and driving up to Denmark. The distances from London using the Channel Tunnel are 786 miles to Copenhagen (using Puttgarden(D) to Rodby (DK) ferry route) 788 miles to Arhus and 771 miles to Odense.

General information

For further information visit www.visitdenmark.com or call 020 7259 5959.

Where to stay

• Camping and caravaning are very popular in Denmark, which has over 520 well-equipped star-rated camping and caravan sites (Website: www.campingraadet.dk). To be able to stay at Danish camping/caravan sites you need to have a valid camping carnet – you can either buy it at the first site you stay at or use the Camping Card International. The camping/caravan sites in Denmark are star rated with one to five stars, five stars being the highest.

• Holiday centres are found throughout Denmark. They offer a wide range of indoor and outdoor activities, although not all necessarily suitable for toddlers. Good ones include include DanParcs Sohojlandet (Tel: 0045 75455757, Website: www.danparc.dk) and Danland Tel: (0045 33630200, Website: www.danland.dk)

- Farm holidays are excellent here. Ferie Pa Landet (Tel: 0045 86373900, Website: www.bondegaardsferie.dk) publishes a brochure with around 140 farms.
- Families with toddlers will enjoy home-exchange holidays. The co-ordinator will try to match families with children of the same age, so that suitable toys are available. Bicycles, boats etc. may also be at the guest's disposal. Further information from Dansk Boligbytte (Tel: 0045 39610405, Website: www.homelink.org.uk).
- A Green Key has been introduced that is given to environmentally friendly hotels/holiday centres and family hostels. There are 116 certificates awarded at present. To find out more about it visit www.dengroennenoegle.dk. For more information on hotels contact www.danishhotels.dk or visit 'Wonderful Copenhagen Hotel Booking on Tel: 0045 70222442, Website: www.visitcopenhagen.dk or Easybook, Tel:0045 35380037.
- Country Cottages are an excellent way to holiday with toddlers and discover more about Denmark. All cottages are well furnished, with some even including an indoor swimming pool, sauna or whirlpool. Most country cottages are let through the local tourist offices or letting agencies (DanCenter, Tel: 0045 70130000, Website: www.dancenter.com)
- Camping is excellent in Aarhus: try Aarhus Nord Camping (Randersvej 400, Lisjerrg 8200 Aarhus N, Tel: 0045 86231133; Website: www.dk-camp.dk/aarhusnord); Ajstrup Strand Camping Tel: (0045 86933535, Website: www.dk-camp.dk/aistrup); Blommehaven Camping (Website: www.blommehaven.dk). They are all set in woods and the facilities are excellent. Babysitting can be arranged and they each have kiddies' clubs suitable for toddlers.
- If you prefer staying in a chalet, pick Lilleadalens Camp (Tastrupvej 16, 8382 Hinnerup, Tel: 0045 86985847), which is perfect for families with toddlers.

- In Odense, Hotel Windsor (Vindegade 45, Tel: 0045 66120652) has a play room. Hotel Ansgar is also toddler-friendly (Ostre Staionsvej, Tel: 0045 66119693).

The best bits

Aarhus
- The Aarhus Pass, which is valid for 1, 2 or 7 days, provides you with free transport on the Aarhus City Transport system as well as free entry to all sights. The Pass is available at the tourist office (Tel: 0045 89406700, Website: www.aarhus-tourist.dk), hotels and major newsagents.
- Aarhus has the countryside on its doorstep. There are lots of green parks and squares in town, with toddler playgrounds and soft play areas with the all-important sand pit. The sandy beaches and clean water are ideal for families, especially Balleghage, Moesgard, Ajstrup, Den Permanente and Bellevue beaches. Marselisborg woods feature playgrounds. Pony Express is popular with the toddlers and an excellent way to see the sites of Aarhus.

Copenhagen
- According to my research, this is the most toddler-friendly city in Europe. Tiny in comparison to the other cities on this list (just 88.3 square kilometres), you can stroll around everywhere on foot without using public transport and all buses take huge old-fashioned prams, so they don't have a problem with buggies. That also goes for trains and most stations have lifts, so it's very easy to travel with a toddler – no matter how large your buggy is.
- The city is very 'green' with three large parks (four including the famous Tivoli Gardens), all with playgrounds, and many smaller ones. The countryside is only minutes away by train and it is easy to get to Klampenborg, where you can take a horse and carriage ride in the Royal Deer Park. You will also find Bakken, the world's oldest amusement park, as well as the closest sandy beach to the city centre, Bellevue.

- In Copenhagen (Tel: 0045 70222442, Website: www.visitcopenhagen.dk), your first investment should be a Copenhagen Card. It's your pass to over 60 museums and attractions (a third of which are toddler-friendly), and your ticket to unlimited travel by bus and train in the greater Copenhagen area. The Copenhagen Card is valid for 24, 48 or 72 hours, and is sold from tourist offices, travel agents, hotels, railway stations and from the 'Wonderful Copenhagen Tourist Information'.

- No trip to Copenhagen would be complete without a visit to the famous Tivoli fun fair (Tivoliland Aalborg, Tel: 0045 33116526, Website: www.tivoliland.dk) in the middle of town. Tivoli offers the fun of the fair, the peace of a park and the ambience of open-air cafés, restaurants and bars. There's also a marooned pirate ship and an authentic-looking castle – the Valhala Castle, home of the Nordic God, Odin, who welcomes toddlers to his Valhala restaurant complete with high chairs and baby-changing facilities. Tivoli is situated on the wooded outskirts of Dyrehaven.

- For the more scientifically minded, there's the Experimentarium (7 Tuborg Havnevej, Tel: 0045 39273333), a collection of hands-on exhibits demonstrating the wonders of natural science. Crazy mirrors, water wheels, computer rooms, logic puzzles, as well as a kid's pavilion which is suitable for toddlers.

- Copenhagen is also the proud owner of a major zoo (Zoologisk Have, 32 Roskildevej, Tel: 0045 36302001) with lions, giraffes and seals that will keep your toddler quiet for an hour. Most popular with toddlers are the Monkey House, Children's Zoo and the Night Zoo, where day is turned into night. Just outside the city lies Denmark's Aquarium (Danmarks Akvarium, Kavalergarden I, DK 2920, Charlottenlund, Tel: 0045 39623283) with its spectacular tropical and seawater landscape tanks filled with fish and aquatic mammals from all over the world.

- The Tojhus Museum (Tojhusmuseet 3, Tojhusgade, Tel: 0045 33116037) or Danish Defense Museum is also an unexpected hit with toddlers. Perhaps the Dungeons and Dragons iconography of double-handed swords and suits of armour has something to do with it. There's also the Changing of the Guard at Amalienborg at noon every day, which they won't understand but they will find of

interest. Or try a trip on one of the canal boats (Gammel Strand/Nyhavn, Tel: 0045 33133105), which takes you through canals across the harbour to Christianshavn.
- Parks with good playgrounds include Kongens Have, Frederiksberg Have, Botanisk Have and Kastellet, which are located in the centre of Copenhagen.

Legoland
- You can't go to Denmark without visiting the original Legoland (lego is like sand – toddlers will 'get it'). Legoland West Jutland (Tel: 0045 75331333, Website: www.legoland.dk) is a must see and you will find different exhibits from the one in Windsor, so go along and marvel!

Odense
- The Odense Adventure Pass gives you free entry to some attractions as well as a discount on others. The pass gives you free transportation on the local buses and some trains. It is available from the tourist office (Tel: 0045 66127520, Website: www.odenseturist.dk) as well as most hotels.
- Attractions include Lovens hule (Roersvej 33, DK 5000, Odense C, Tel: 0045 66121307, Website: www.lovenshule.dk), which is an indoor adventure playground for toddlers.
- Egeskov Castle (DK-5772 Kvaerndrug, Tel: 0045 62271016) has a large playground (close to Odense).
- Odense Zoo (Sonder Boulevard 306, Tel: 0045 66111360, Website: www.odensezoo.dk).

Where to eat

- In Copenhagen, try Amokka (38 Dag Hammerskjolds Alle, Tel: 0045 35253535), which is a coffee house cum restaurant cum shop serving gourmet toddler food. Frigate Sct Georg III (Tivoli 3 Vesterbrogade, Tel: 0045 33159204) also serves gourmet toddler food (i.e. no nuggets and no burgers). Base Camp Holmen (12 Halvtolv, Tel: 0045 70232318) has an excellent playroom where

they can play while you eat and keep your eyes on them.
Langelinie Pavilion (Langelinie, Tel: 0045 33121214) has great
views of the harbour and has a choice of café, restaurant or
brasserie to eat in. The brasserie has the best views and is the most
toddler-friendly.

- The most toddler-friendly restaurants in Aarhus are Jensens Bof
  Hus (Tel: 0045 86124488), Italia (Tel: 0045 86198022) and China
  Wok House (Tel: 0045 86126923).
- In Odense, try Bone's Restaurant (American Vindegade, Tel: 0045
  66181116).

Turkey

You go into a shop, and they immediately focus on the children. The grown-ups completely disappear. Mine get offered Turkish delight, apple tea, introduced to their children. Incredible. The Turkish are also great 'picker-uppers' – so beware. They usually do it without asking. One tip is it gets blistering hot in the summer months (as in dangerously so) so don't, under any circumstances take your children here then.

Father of two, from Windsor

The basics

Time difference from the UK – 2 hours ahead of GMT
Flight time from London – 3 hours approximately
Best way to get there – Fly to Antalya
English spoken – In the major resorts only
Culture – 'children are a blessing not a nuisance'
Toddler-friendly rating – 8/10
'Best bits' for toddlers – The beaches, Aegean and Mediterranean coasts, friends made
'Best bits' for parents – The beaches are excellent, people friendly
When to go – April, May and October
Where to go – Coastal resorts around the beaches mentioned below
Accommodation – Hotel resorts, or villas in the region of Pamplylia along the Turquoise Coast

Toddler-friendly tour operators

Club Med (Tel: 020 7348 3333, Website: www.clubmed.co.uk)

Mark Warner (Tel: 0207 761 7000, Website: www.markwarner.co.uk)

Crystal Holidays (Tel: 020 8241 5040,
   Website: www.crystalholidays.co.uk)

Prestige Holidays (Tel: 01425 480 400, Website: www.prestige
   holidays.co.uk)

Major airlines

Turkish Airlines (THY, Tel: 020 7766 9300) offer standard IATA child reductions – 90 percent for under twos and 50 percent for two to twelve.

You pay £10 for a visa when you arrive in Turkey. The queue is long (wait up to 15 minutes at height of season). Pay in Turkish lira.

General information

Most of the major tour operators have product in Turkey along the coast. According to Travel Choice, it is the only other country which appears in the top ten of British resorts, outside the Spanish and Greek Islands. Toddlers are welcome in hotels and restaurants although they may not have the high chairs or the cots. Visit in April, May and October to avoid crowds, heat and mosquitoes. The roads along the coastal resorts are adequate, but the focus of your holiday here is to stay put, and on the beach, using the most of what the resort you have chosen has to offer.

For further information contact www.ExploreTurkey.com or call 020 7629 7771 (information) or 09001 887 755 (brochure).

Where to stay

- At Club Med (Tel: 0700 258 2633) more than half of the 'gentils membres' are families – although not all 'villages' are suitable. Palmiye village looks after children of all ages and offers a circus school, windsurfing, waterskiing, sailing and tennis (with tuition in most of these).

- Also try the Robinson Club Lykia, Oludeniz Kidirak Mevkii, Fethiye, Turkey (Tel: 0090 2526166010) which is ideal for families. Toddlers under two years of age with a baby bed are free of charge.

The best bits

The attitude
- The Turkish do, indeed, love children and you will find lots of support if you need buggies carried for instance.

Beaches
- The best, sandiest beaches are at Alanya, Cesme, Icmeler, Kemer, Olu Deniz (busiest beach on the coast), Patar, Altinkum and the popular holiday resort of Side. All these beaches have a wide range of watersports for the grown ups to take part in. The beaches at Kas and Kalkan are rocky and there are strong currents on the Black Sea beaches near Istanbul. Kemer is busy and popular, with sand and shingle beaches, and still has that small town feel to it, due to all the buildings being low rise. It's also less than half an hour from Antalya airport.

Antalya
- There is a zoo at Antalya (Kepez, 0090 2423323232) at the clifftop Karaali Park, and the Insuyu Caves on the main road from Antalya are also worth a brief visit for toddlers to marvel at the underwater lake and stalactites. For details of their locations, visit www.antala-ws.com.

Istanbul
- The capital Istanbul is full of parks – the lovely Yildiz Park which has amazing view of the Bosphorus, and Gulhane Park which is also home to the Istanbul zoo and aquarium, playgrounds and funfairs as well as horse drawn carriage rides.

Where to eat

- Restaurants in Turkey, with a few exceptions, are extremely friendly towards children. Do let them know you are bringing a small child.
- Try out Korfez restaurant in Cesme (Yali Caddesi, Tel: 0090 2327126718) which serves simple food at low prices and welcomes children. Sahil restaurant (Cumhuriyet Meydani, Tel: 0090 2327126646) serves excellent fish and is also in Cesme.
- In Bodrum, try Han restaurant during the day (Kale Caddesi, Tel: 0090 2523161615) which has dancing and live music in the central courtyard. Also Mausolus restaurant (Neyzen Tevfik Caddsi, Tel: 0090 2523164176).

Florida

If you have a toddler who can manage the nine-hour flight to Florida, it's worth it. Virgin were great with our lot. The beaches are wonderful, absolutely fantastic, and the grown-ups have fun too. Disney World they found too tiring and couldn't go on a lot of the rides. I think toddlers don't appreciate the magic at that age. I had more fun than they did.

Father of two toddlers, from Durham

The basics

Time difference from UK – 5 hours behind GMT (west of the Apalachicola River is 6 hours behind GMT)
Flight time from UK – Approximately $8^{1}/_{2}$ to 9 hours to Miami, Orlando, Tampa
English spoken – Yes, and Spanish widely spoken
Culture – Toddler-friendly in the resorts
Toddler-friendly rating – 7/10
'Best bits' for toddlers – Beaches and friends and aquariums
'Best bits' for parents – The service, the weather, the beaches
When to go – Winter (summer too hot; spring too crowded; autumn risk of hurricanes)
Where to go – Gulf, Gold Coast
Accommodation – Resort hotels/self-catering apartments

Toddler-friendly tour operators
An endless list offering packages, self-catering villas and apartments, and motor-home rentals. These are the companies recommended by

families with toddlers who have visited Florida.

Airtours PLC (Tel: 020 8559 7720, Website: www.airtours.co.uk)

British Airways Holidays (Tel: 01293 722 727, Website:
www.britishairways.co.uk)

First Choice (Tel: 0870 750 0001, Website: www.firstchoice.co.uk)

Florida Vacations (Tel: 01582 469 888, Website:
www.vacationsgroup.co.uk) for villas)

Virgin Holidays (Tel: 01293 562 944, Website:
www.virginholidays.co.uk)

Major airlines

British Airways (Tel: 0845 7733377, Website:
www.britishairways.co.uk)

Virgin Atlantic (Tel: 01293 747 747, Website: www.virgin.co.uk)

General information

Avoid Miami Airport, which is one of the busiest in the world, as there are long queues for immigration. Pick Orlando for customer convenience. Moving walkways and automated monorail system make moving around the two terminals easy. Multilingual tourist information centres by the security checkpoints are open from 7am till 11pm. Many hotels have their own courtesy buses, and the Mears Transportation Group (Tel: 001 407 4235566) serves most destinations in the area. Sanford Airport is much quieter than the main Orlando airport. There are taxis and several car rental outlets just outside the building terminal.

In Florida you will be able to rent buggies at the major theme parks and car hire firms are obliged to supply car seats, while many restaurants have special menus. On planes, buses and trains, children under 12 pay only half fare, less if they are toddlers. The main thing to worry about is too much sun. Just a few minutes' exposure at midday can burn the skin.

Where to stay

- If you are not on a package tour, stay at the Westin Resort on Miami Beach (4833 Collins Ave 33140, Tel: 001 305 5323600)

380

which is quiet but has a lot to entertain toddlers. For luxury, the
Boca Raton Resort and Club (501 E Camino Real, Boca Raton
33431, Tel: 001 561 3953000), will please both the grown-ups
and toddlers, as will the Four Seasons Palm Beach (2800 S Ocean
Boulevard, Palm Beach 33480, Tel: 001 561 5822800). Both come
at a price. The Sheraton Bal Harbour Resort (9701 Collins Ave, Bal
Harbour 33154, Tel: 001 305 8642610) is close to the beach and
has a 10-acre tropical garden for toddlers to run (riot) in.

- The Holiday Inn Sunspree Resort (1617 North First Street
  Jacksonville Beach, FL 32250, Tel: 001 904 2499071, Fax: 001
  904 2414321) has a kids-eat free-policy and is on the beach.
- At Saddlebrook Resort (5700 Saddlebrook Way Wesley Chapel,
  Florida 33543–4499, Tel: 001 813 9731111, Fax: 001 813
  9738933, Website: www.saddlebrookresort.com) every day is
  different for toddlers. Monday is Outer Space Day, Tuesday is
  Outdoor Adventure Day, Wednesday is Under the Sea Day,
  Thursday is Around the World Day, Friday is Blast from the Past
  Day, Saturday is Our Own Earth Day and Sunday is Anything Can
  Happen Day. As a member of the resort's S'kids Club, toddlers
  enjoy a variety of themed activities and off-property excursions to
  area attractions.

Don't bother

- Disney World is wonderful for children of a slightly older age (five
  plus), although their press office tried to convince me otherwise.
  Over 300 parents of toddlers who visited said with a few
  exceptions they felt their children would have appreciated it more
  when they were slightly older. The children simply didn't 'get' it
  but your toddler may. Water parks are all designed for older
  children.

The best bits

Beaches

- Florida remains the most toddler-friendly state because it has
  excellent beaches that please both the parents as well as the

toddlers. There are life guards on the beaches and ramps everywhere for buggies. Most families who had a happy experience with their toddlers recommended heading for the Gold or Gulf Coast, which has the best beaches. The beaches in St Petersburg and Clearwater have won family-friendly awards.

Clothes for toddlers
- Sawgrass Mills (Greater Fort Lauderdale, Tel: 001 954 8462350, Website: www.sawgrassmillsmall.com) has the world's largest designer outlet mall including Ralph Lauren Kids' Factory Store, Osh Kosh B'gosh, Baby Gap outlets, Disney's Character Premier, K-B Toys, GameWorks and Toy Works.

Fish
- Miami Seaquarium (4400 Rickenbacker Cswy, Key Biscayne, Tel: 001 305 3615705, Website: www.miamiseaquarium.com) is home to Lolita the Killer Whale and TV superstar Flipper. You can bring your toddler to meet Salty the Sea Lion and the dolphins performing with Lolita.
- The Florida Aquarium (701 Channelside Drive in Tampa (formerly 13th Street), Tel: 001 813 2734000, Website: www.flaquarium.net) is also interesting to toddlers. This world-class aquarium includes hands-on exhibits from the shorelines to the deep sea. Highlights include a touch tank full of slimy sting rays, shark exhibit 'Awes & Jaws' and daily dive shows.

Gardens and butterflies
- Flamingo Gardens (Tel: 001 954 4732955, Website: www.flamingogardens.org) has a free-flight aviary and Birds of Prey exhibit.
- The famous Butterfly World (Tel: 001 954 9774400, Website: www.butterfly world.com) showcases thousands of butterflies as well as hummingbirds, waterfalls, orchids and roses.

In miniature
- A must-see for toddlers is Kid City! This miniature city features streets, sidewalks, park benches, shade trees, picnic tables and 14

buildings representing various business in a typical city. The city's library, restaurant, school, courthouse, doctors' surgery, town hall, police station and fire station can be explored by little hands and curious minds.

Museums

- Museums in Florida offer excellent hands-on exhibits. The $3 million 3D blockbuster IMAX Theatre at the Museum of Discovery & Science Fort Lauderdale (Tel: 001 954 4676637, Website: www.mods.org) is a treasure of exhibits that challenge, educate and delight youngsters. It was built to promote the understanding and appreciation of science through entertaining interaction with educational exhibits, programmes and films. The Discovery Centre is specially designed for toddlers and pre-schoolers to meet new friends and have fun while developing motor skills and learning basic science.
- The Buehler Planetarium (At Broward Community College, 3501 SW Davie Rd, Davie, Tel: 001 954 4756680) allows children to explore uncharted territories in the deep beyond, with exhibits and educational programmes. Kids can also gaze at the stars through powerful telescopes in the evenings.
- The Young at Art Children's Museum (Young At Art of Broward, Inc., 11584 West State Road 84, Davie, FL 33325, Tel: 001 954 4240085, Website: www.youngatartmuseum.org) has art, activities and interactive exhibits specifically for children to discover the world in which they live. One of their new exhibits, Global Village, features interactive activities enabling children to journey around the globe and experience various cultures.
- At Miami Museum of Science and Space Transit Planetarium (3280 S Miami Ave, Coconut Grove, Tel: 001 305 6464200, Website: www.miamisci.org) you can see rare birds and reptiles. There is an excellent 'gravity' playground for babies and toddlers.

Water taxis

- These whisk families along Florida's inland waterways – no car seats needed (Tel: 001 954 4676677, Website: www.watertaxi.com). The Venice of America offers glass-bottom boat tours, sightseeing cruises

and airboat tours of the river of grass at Everglades Holiday Park.
The Jungle Queen (Tel: 001 954 4625596, Website:
www.junglequeen.com) gives a step back into history onboard a
paddle wheeler. Riverfront Cruises (Tel: 001 954 4633372, Website:
www.riverfrontcruises.com) are also recommended.

Zoos and wildlife

- Parrot Jungle and Gardens (11000 SW 57 Ave, South Miami, Tel:
  001 305 6667834, Website: www.parrotjungle.com) is 'Where Fun
  Comes to Life'. This is a world-famous bird sanctuary, wildlife
  habitat and botanical garden where parrots fly free, feed from your
  hands and pose for pictures.
- Miami MetroZoo (12400 SW 152 St, South Miami, Tel: 001 305
  2510400, Website: www.zsf.org) is a zoo for endangered and
  threatened wildlife, voted among the top 10 zoos in the country
  for service.
- Everglades Safari (26700 SW 8 St Miami, Tel: 001 305 2266923,
  Website: www.evergladesafaripark.com) – Home of the Worlds
  Best Airboat Ride – features an alligator farm and show, a jungle
  rail and a thrilling airboat ride through winding trails in the
  Everglades.
- Award-winning Busch Gardens (Tampa Bay, Tel: 001 813 9875660,
  Website: www.buschgardens.com) appeals to toddlers, mainly
  because of its animals. You literally come face to face with a lion,
  hand-feed a giraffe and get up close and personal with the dozens
  of African species that roam the Serengeti Plain. This family
  entertainment park features eight distinctly themed sections, which
  capture the spirit of the African continent. Busch Gardens also
  features an excellent interactive children's adventure area called
  Land of the Dragons, with child-sized rides and a theatre.

Where to eat

- Good places to eat that cater for toddlers include Miami Beach
  11st Street Diner (1065 Washington Avenue, Tel: 001 305
  8670950). It is set in a 1948 steel dining car and fun staff serve

both traditional food and modern dishes.

- Miami Beach Woolfies (2038 Collins Avenue, Tel: 001 305 5386626) is a well-known deli where colourful waitresses dispense huge portions of New York Jewish food 24 hours a day.
- Miami Beach Blue Door Delano Hotel (1685 Collins Avenue, Tel: 001 305 6746400) is an expensive restaurant part-owned by Madonna (this will impress older toddlers who know who Madonna is), where colourful waiters serve colourful food in a colourful hotel to colourful people. Weird and interesting.
- Downtown East Coast (360W Flagler Street, Riverside, Tel: 001 305 3724291) has a huge choice of fresh fish and seafood, cooked any way you like.
- On Cocoa Beach try Herbie K's (2080 N Atlantic Avenue, Tel: 001 407 7836740). It's a 50s-style diner, complete with jukebox, bubbly waitresses and good meals – a very American menu most toddlers will love.
- Try the Gold and Treasure Coasts. Martha's Suppler Club (6024 N Ocean Drive, Dania, Tel: 001 954 9235444) known for its good seafood and views of the Intercoastal Waterway. Or Pal Charley's Crab (1755 SE 3rd Street, Deerfield). This restaurant has different menus for lunch and dinner – mostly seafood. A special sunset menu is available from 4–6pm and is ideal for families with toddlers.
- Aptly titled Scallywags (555 NE Ocean Blvd, Hutchinson Island, Tel: 001 561 2253700) has seafood buffets on Wednesdays and early bird specials.
- At the Ashley (61 SW Osceola Street, Tel: 001 561 2219476) there is a varied breakfast menu, and Down the Hatch (4894 Front Street, Ponce Inlet, Daytona Beach, Tel: 001 904 7614831) serves excellent fish and meat dishes.
- Lastly, The Treasure Ship (3605 S Thomas Drive, Panama City Beach) is housed in a replica sixteenth-century galleon. It has open air decks, water views and good seafood. They will love it.

Caribbean

The people are incredibly friendly. Go low season as it gets far too hot for toddlers if you go during the winter and they spend most of their time indoors. Go with a tour operator who knows what they're doing. I wouldn't try this on an independent package. Plus we had some difficulties on the flight with our two. Eight hours is a long time confined in a small space – for the grown-ups as well as the children.

Mother of two toddlers, from Lincoln
on trip to Dominican Republic

The basics

Time difference from UK – 5 hours behind GMT in Eastern Caribbean up to 6 hours behind GMT in Jamaica
Best way to go with toddlers – Virgin and BA fly to St Lucia, Antigua and Barbados direct
Flight time from UK – 8 hours to major airports (direct)
English spoken – Yes, widely
Culture – Extremely friendly – more on some islands than others (see below)
Toddler-friendly rating – 10/10
'Best bits' for toddlers – Beaches, friends, resort staff, food
'Best bits' for parents – Beaches, kiddies' clubs, weather, laid-back atmosphere
When to go – Spring (low season) and just before Christmas
Where to go – St Lucia, Barbados, Turks & Caicos, Jamaica
Accommodation – Resort – either villa or resort hotel

Toddler-friendly tour operators
Caribtours (Tel: 020 7751 0660, Website: www.caribtours.co.uk)
Virgin Holidays (Tel: 01293 562 944, Website:
    www.virginholidays.co.uk)
British Airways Holidays (Tel: 01293 722727,
    Website: www.britishairways.com)

Major airlines
British Airways (Tel: 0845 773 3377, Website:
    www.britishairways.co.uk)
Virgin Atlantic (Tel: 01293 747 747,
    Website: www.virgin.co.uk)

Best resorts for toddlers

Antigua
- Antigua, has excellent beaches and resorts closer to the airport.
  The landscape is less interesting than some other islands, but a few
  resorts are good for toddlers:
- The Royal Antiguan (Tel: 001 954 4818787) provides a
  playground that keeps children of all ages occupied. Activities
  include seashell arts and crafts, dialect class and T-shirt painting.
- Stay at the St James' Club (Tel: 001 954 4818787 or Caribtours,
  Tel: 020 7751 0660) and rent a villa with kitchen – and have
  access to the extensive facilities of the Club. St James Club offers a
  year round 'Club Kidz', a complete supervised activity programme
  for children ages 2 to 12. Activities for ages 2 to 6 include block
  building, ball games, painting, bead stringing, reading, treasure
  hunts, movies, nature walks, cookie and cake baking, measuring
  and pouring and other various arts and crafts.

Barbados
- Superclub's Almond Beach Club in Barbados is worth considering
  (Tel: 001 246 4327840).
- Alternatively Coconut Creek (book through British Airways
  Holidays, Tel: 0870 242 4245) is an all-inclusive resort that offers

'children stay free' deals and has a kiddies' club suitable for toddlers.
- See also Turtle Beach, below.

Dominican Republic
- The Dominican Republic offers the best value for money, with many all-inclusive resorts, non-stop charters and good beaches, although even in low season, feedback was that it gets very crowded and 'You don't get to see much of the island. You could be anywhere'. Having said that, I've also heard firsthand reports from people who have enjoyed fabulous holidays with toddlers at some of the five-star resorts. Most have kiddies clubs, kids' menus, pools for the little ones, and lots to entertain mum and dad in between!

Grenada
- Just Grenada (Tel: 01373 814 214) features a number of toddler-friendly properties including Blue Horizons, set in 60 acres of tropical gardens, just 300 yards from the two-mile stretch of white sand beach at Grand Anse Bay, and Lance aux Epines at Prickly Bay where guests enjoy comfortable, spacious accommodation just 20 yards from the Caribbean Sea and within walking distance of shops, restaurants and bars. Accommodation is in self-catering cottages with maid service, plus free watersports and a housekeeper who will cook local dishes on request for just a small gratuity.

Jamaica
- Franklin D Roosevelt (book via Caribtours, Tel: 020 7751 0660) is an all-inclusive resort west of Ocho Rios, not far from the famous Dunn's River Falls. Each family is assigned its own 'nanny' between 9am and 4pm daily for the duration of their stay. There is a children's centre with a daily programme, and the hotel offers a selection of activities for adults as well.

St Lucia
- St Lucia has good beaches, interesting scenery and many resorts which have toddler-friendly programmes. But most resorts are over

an hour and half drive from the airport and toddlers became very impatient to see the beach.

Turks & Caicos

- Turks & Caicos was a good all-round favourite, mainly due to the Beaches resort on the island. It has an excellent crêche facility and 'Kids Kamp' as well as nine restaurants, four pools and excellent beaches.

Turtle beach

- The Turtle Beach Resorts on the Islands of Barbados and Tobago boast the Tommy Turtle Kids Club which caters for children aged 3 to 11 years of age. Supervised and run by fully trained, experienced staff, activities include pool and beach games, calypso and reggae dancing lessons, tie-dye classes, hand-painting T-shirts, clay play, jewellery making, face painting, magicians, computer and educational games, children's videos and movies. Safari-style outings are also arranged to places of interest like Farley Hill Wildlife Reserve, Cherry Tree Hill lookout, Harrisons Caves, and mini golf courses. Turtle Beach provides special kids' menus. Babysitting and nanny service are available for a modest fee and cots, cribs and high chairs are all available. Suites can take 2 adults and up to 3 children.

Cape Town

Cape Town is one of those places that is brilliant for toddlers but no one knows about it. You can get sun, sand and excellent value for money.

>Father of three, two of whom are toddlers, from York

The basics

Time difference from UK – 2 hours ahead of GMT
Flight time from London – 11 hours
English spoken – Widely
Culture – Laid back
Toddler-friendly rating – 9/10
'Best bits' for toddlers – The beaches, the aquariums, the animals
'Best bits' for parents – The beautiful scenery, the excellent food, value for money
When to go – Feb to Easter and September
Accommodation – Hotel or self-catering apartment

Toddler-friendly tour operators
Kuoni Worldwide (Tel: 01306 743 000, Website: www.kuoni.co.uk)
Virgin Holidays (Tel: 01293 617 181, Website: www.virginholidays.co.uk/sa)
Thomas Cook Holidays (Tel: 01733 418 650, Website: www.tch.thomascook.com)

Major airlines

South African Airways (Tel: 020 7312 5000, Website: www.saa.co.za)
Virgin Atlantic (Tel: 01293 747 747, Website:
   www.virginatlantic.com)

General information

Best Website www.capetown.at
Local Tour Guide Roddy Bray (Email: roddyb@mweb.co.za, Tel:
   0027 21 4342295)
Cape Town International Airport has excellent baby-changing facilities and a play area.

According to those families who have been here with their toddlers, Cape Town has lots to offer a young family – excellent beaches, great attractions, good accommodation and great restaurants. It is also much safer than many guide books would have you believe, as long as you don't look like a tourist, and wear lots of expensive-looking jewellery out to town. Common sense really. The city has an excellent climate throughout the year but the best time to visit is Mid-Feb to Easter. November/ December are also good and have the advantage of whales (season: August – December).

Where to stay

- For self-catering, stay at Harbour View Cottages (1 Loader Street, Tel: 0027 21 4186081) less than 1km from V&A Waterfront and city centre. Pick a cottage with its own swimming pool and harbour view. No charge for toddlers not occupying a bed.
- Alternatively try Elephant Eye Lodge (9 Sunwood Drive, Tel: 0027 21 7152432) in Constantia, one of Cape Town's most salubrious suburbs only 20 minutes drive to the coast or the V&A Waterfront. Well out of the city centre, it's close to a beach, forest walks and stunning scenery.
- Or try Houtkapperspoort (Hout Bay Road, Tel: 0027 21 7945216) or the Oatlands Holiday Village (Froggy Pond, Simon's Town, Tel: 0027 21 7861410) which is 1km from the safe Boulders Beach. It has over 20 self-catering chalets and a playground, pool and trampoline.

The best bits

Beaches

- Cape Town has excellent beaches, but the best is Boulders Beach (39km south of central Cape Town). It has a resident penguin breeding colony and large granite boulders create a stunning protected setting. A popular beach, especially in December, so arrive as early as you can.
- An alternative is Fish Hoek (30km south of central Cape Town). This beach has gentle waves, excellent sand, and a playground and café on the beach. There is a paved parkway to navigate a buggy and protection from the wind on windy days.
- Camps Bay (8km southwest of central Cape Town) is an excellent sandy beach, with palm trees to give shade and some grass. There's a tidal pool and small rock pools which toddlers will love to explore, and it's easily reached from the centre of Cape Town by car or bus.
- The four lovely bays in the neighbouring suburb of Clifton are more sheltered but there are steps down to the beaches.
- Muizenberg has a 32km beach, with play areas for children. The water is quite calm and much warmer than the Atlantic side.

Cable car

- The cable car up Table Mountain (Tel: 0027 21 4245148) is fascinating for both toddlers and grown-ups. You'll encounter 'dassies', which are outsized fluffy guinea pigs, at the top of the Mountain, which your toddler will want to feed and take home. You can't do either, as they bite – and believe it or not, their closest relatives are elephants!

Fish

- The Two Oceans Aquarium (V&A Waterfront, Tel: 0027 21 4183823) is one of the best in the world. Exhibits include seals and sharks. The aquarium allows grown-ups to swim with the sharks for a fee for 20 minutes if they have passed their PADI diving course! There is also an Alpha Activity Centre with free organized activities such as puppet shows, face painting and computers. In

the Touch Pool, adjacent to the Diversity Hall, toddlers are allowed
to stroke crabs, starfish and prickly sea urchins.

Gardens

- Kirstenbosch National Botanical Gardens (Tel: 0027 21 7621166)
  is excellent for picnics. It boasts enormous Shona sculptures of
  animals, which are wonderful for toddlers. The gardens are
  exceptionally beautiful and there are great walks among the 9000
  different species of plants from all over Southern Africa, including
  giant fig trees, banana trees and proteas. The glass house has a
  display of strange desert plants and ferns. The shop is one of the
  best curio shops in Cape Town and there is a good restaurant in
  the gardens with a play lawn for toddlers.
- Groot Constantia (Tel: 0027 21 7945128) is a stunning 17th-
  century Cape Dutch manor house with large grounds, outdoor
  restaurant and a large toddler-friendly playground. Groot
  Constantia is the most toddler-friendly of the wine estates in the
  Constantia region of Cape Town.

Penguins

- At the World of Birds (Valley Road, Hout Bay, Tel: 0027 21
  7902730), see more than 3000 birds and small animals in walk-
  through aviaries. You can watch the penguins, pelicans and owls
  being fed at different times of the day. Restaurant with baby-
  changing on site. Hout Bay also has a harbour and a pretty beach
  with calm water. There are regular trips to see the seals from the
  Harbour, an enjoyable 45-minute round trip.

Theme parks

- Ratanga Junction (Tel: 0027 21 5507000, Fax: 0027 21 5507080)
  is a theme park, with steam trains and gentler family rides, and
  while it is mostly for older children, there is plenty to keep a
  toddler occupied. Ratanga is like a small Disney World and could
  occupy a full day. There are shows, lots of places to eat and a
  range of rollercoasters, water rides and fun rides for small ones.
- Another option is Scratch Patch and Mineral World in Simons
  Town (Tel: 0027 21 7862020) where over threes enjoy taking a

bag and filling it with the semi-precious polished gemstones that cover the floor. You can cross the catwalk to see one of the world's largest gemstone tumbling plants in operation. The train journey from Muizenberg to Simon's Town along the coast is very picturesque.

Waterfront

- The Waterfront is a very toddler-friendly and safe environment with a stunning backdrop of sea and Table Mountain. There are two indoor craft markets, boat rides in the harbour and out to sea, lots of toddler-friendly places to eat and shop, and in summer there are street performers such as mime artists.

Wildlife

- Spier Estate (50km from Cape Town, Tel: 0027 21 8091100, Email: info@spier.co.za) offers one of the best family days out in Cape Town. There's a huge picnic area, children's playground and guided pony rides. There is also a cheetah park, part of a breeding programme, where you can enter the enclosure to pet a purring cheetah. There is an excellent farm shop and deli which bakes excellent cakes and fresh bread, and sells salads, soft cheeses, cold meats and dips. There are also four restaurants – Spier Café, the Taphuis Grill, Riverside Pub or the excellent Cape Malay Jonkershuis Restaurant. Up the road is the Fairview wine farm, which has peacocks and a delightful goat house. It offers goats cheese tastings. Watch the baboons and ostriches at Cape Point Nature Reserve (the Cape of Good Hope); just at the entrance is the Cape Point Ostrich Farm where you can see the birds close up, watch chicks hatch and youngsters in pens.
- Excellent picnic spots include the Barnyard Farmstall (Steenberg Road, next to Steenberg Estate) which has ducks and chickens wandering about, and an excellent and inventive children's playground suitable for toddlers. The farm stall sells breads, dips and salads. Also check out the Imhoff Farm (Kommetjie Road, opposite Ocean view turn-off, Tel: 0027 21 2781704) which has camel rides, where toddlers can ride in the same saddle as their

parents. You can also see ostriches, stroke farm animals and be afraid of the snakes in boxes!

Where to eat

- Toddlers are welcome in most restaurants in Cape Town – even the serious ones. Best bets for a peaceful meal are: Bayfront Blu (Tel: 0027 21 4199068) at the Two Oceans Aquarium (see above) which has all-day breakfasts; and Zerbans (Tel: 0027 21 6717718), on Victoria Wharf, which has wonderful cakes, bread and coffee.

Canada

I had been to Vancouver with my husband on honeymoon, and thought it would be a good place to take young children as well as older ones. It was.

Mother of three – 8, 5 and 3 – from Harwich

Although Canada is a vast country, you never get a sense of its immensity; instead, it's a haven for toddlers, with lots of forests to explore, beautiful, clean lakes and beaches, gorgeous mountains (and toddler-sized hills), all of which seem perfectly designed for picnics, days out, and even long car journeys. And Canadians are unbelievably friendly and accommodating. A perfect holiday, really.

Mother of two toddlers, from London

The basics

Time difference from UK
    Vancouver – 8 hours behind GMT
    Prince Edward Island – 4 hours behind GMT
    Montreal – 5 hours behind GMT
    Toronto – 5 hours behind GMT
Flight times from UK
    Toronto – 7 hours 15 minutes
    Vancouver – 10 hours 5 minutes
    Edmonton – 8 hours 50 minutes
    Calgary – 9 hours 20 minutes (for Banff)
English spoken – Yes, but in Quebec French is the first language
Culture – Very laid back, toddler-friendly

Toddler-friendly rating – 9/10

'Best bits' for toddlers – Excellent beaches in Vancouver, PEI and Ontario (north of Toronto); plenty of amusement parks, picnic sites, playgrounds, fishing sites (with toddler-sized rods), boating expeditions, skiing, water sports and snow fun (in the winter months) across the provinces; Toronto is a particular favourite

'Best bits' for parents – Interesting for them as well as being good for toddlers

When to go – Summer, autumn and Christmas

Where to go

On the east coast Quebec City, Montreal, Prince Edward Island

Centrally, Toronto and the skiing and 'cottage country' north of the city

On the west coast Edmonton, Vancouver, Victoria

Accommodation – Resort hotels or touring in a motorhome; cottage or chalet hire

Toddler-friendly tour operators

Frontier Canada (Tel: 020 8659 5636, Website: www.frontier-canada.co.uk)

All Canada Travel & Holidays (Tel: 01502 585 825, Website: www.all-canada.co.uk)

First Choice (Tel: 0161 745 7000, Website: www.firstchoice.co.uk)

Hemmingways (Tel: 01737 842 735, Website: www.hemmingways.co.uk)

Major airlines

Air Canada (Tel: 0870 524 7226, Website: www.aircanada.ca)

Virgin Atlantic (Tel: 01293 747 747, Website: www.virgin.com) flies direct from Gatwick to Toronto

British Airways (Tel: 0845 773 3377, Website: www.britishairways.com) fly direct from London Heathrow to Toronto, Montreal and Vancouver daily

General information

Best websites: www.tourismvictoria.com, www.tourism.ede.org

The major airports in Toronto, Montreal and Quebec have good baby-changing facilities and a good range of retail outlets as well as play areas. On the west coast, the airports are excellent. Vancouver has a huge range of retail outlets, play areas, and baby-changing facilities. Calgary, the gateway to the Rockies and the national parks of Banff and Jasper, is also excellent, and has lots of soft toy shops where toddlers will be happy to play for hours, and huge models of cows and horses which your toddler will want to touch, if not ride. If you can, fly direct without stopovers. Edmonton International Airport has toddler play areas and changing areas, plus a nursery complete with cot.

On the coasts, the weather is not dissimilar to the UK's but more extreme – winters are colder; summers hotter. Central Canada is considerably colder in winter, and very, very hot in summer. To avoid the extremes, the best time to travel with a toddler is in the autumn, when the colours are at their best, the climate is warm and mild, and older children are back at school. This is not necessarily a 'low season' for Canada, as their 'Fall Colours' are a big attraction, so tour operators have little reason to drop prices. Spring is also a nice time to travel, but remember that Canadian schools finish in early June, so their summer holidays officially begin a lot earlier than ours.

Where to stay

- The Fairmont Group of hotels (see Hotels, page 118) are based all over Canada and the US (with a collection of 38 distinctive city centre and resort hotels) and have excellent kiddies programmes – some of which cater for toddlers.
- In Montreal the Château Bonne Entente (3 400, chemin Sainte-Foy. Sainte-Foy, Quebec G1X 1S6, Tel: 001 418 6535221/1 800 4634390, Fax: 001 418 6533098,
  Email: hotel@chateaubonneentente.com,
  Website: www.chateaubonneentente.com) is the place to stay with young children. It has family suites called 'Operation Enfant Soleil' (in honour of a Charity for sick children) with one parent's bedroom and one children's bedroom complete with bunk beds, TV and VCR with Walt Disney home videos, colouring books and

toys. There is also an excellent playground and a daycare centre.

- In Quebec City, Le Château Frontenac (1, rue des Carrières, Tel: 001 418 6923861) is in a lovely location overlooking the river. It provides a welcome package for children, an indoor pool with wading area, in-room video games, cribs, cots, children's menu and babysitting. Children under 17 stay free if sharing with their parents.

- In Vancouver, best place to stay is the Best Western Chateau Granville (1100 Granville Street. Tel: 001 604 6697070, Website: www.bwcg.com), which has its own kiddies' club, crêche and babysitting and is central yet close to the beach. In Victoria, most of the hotels are toddler-friendly and offer babysitting services. Stay at Best Western Carlton Plaza (642 Johnson Street, Tel: 001 250 3885513, Website: www.bestwesterncarltonplaza.com), which offers a family package including a bag of toys for the children and milk and cookies. Playpens are available and suites usefully have microwaves. Other toddler-friendly hotels include the Howard Johnson (310 Gorge Road East, Tel: 001 250 3822151, Website: www.hojo-canada.com), which is very family-oriented and children under 17 stay for free. Travel Lodge (229 Gorge Road East, Tel: 001 250 3886611, Website: www.travellodgevictoria.com) offers microwaves in room and even has a 'sleepy bear room' with VCR, children's movies and activity books. This is common to most Travel Lodges. If you want to self-cater, an excellent option is Maple Moose Farm Inn by the Sea (6786 East Sooke Road, Tel: 001 250 6423261, Website: www.maplemoose.ca).

- In Ontario, choose to stay at one of the lodges north of Toronto; many have kids clubs and life guards on duty at all times. Better still, head to Niagara Falls, a spectacular sight for children of all ages (make sure you take a trip on the Maid of the Mist boat, beneath the falls), and Marineland nearby. For details of accommodation in Ontario, see the website for worldweb travel guide, on www.ontario.worldweb.com.

- Canada has magnificent wide open spaces, and you can see as much as possible if you rent a motorhome and drive along scenic routes (see Camping, page 181).

The best bits

Alberta

- The Province of Alberta is great for young families. There are plenty of attractions, activities, festivals and events where you can indulge the children in the fun and new adventures that they crave, without breaking the bank. Most Edmonton and area attractions have family rates and often children under three are free. Here are a few of your best bets for even the youngest tourists to Edmonton:

DANCE

- The finery of one of North America's most colourful First Nations exhibitions, along with the beat of the drummers, has children dancing along as they visit the Syncrude Gallery of Aboriginal Culture (Tel: 001 780 4539100, Website: www.pma.edmonton.ab.ca).

DISCOVERY

- Take the tots to Discoveryland at the Edmonton Space & Science Centre (Tel: 001 780 4529100, Website: www.edmontonscience.com). Designed for kids ages 2 to 8 years of age, highlights include waterworks, construction zone, discovery den, potter's corner, and a walk-on piano. Children watch, learn, touch and have fun by participating with the other children.
- There is also an IMAX theatre, Canada's largest planetarium, a Space Gallery, an Environment Gallery, Forensics Gallery, and the Health Gallery.

FESTIVALS

- If you happen to be there at the time, Alberta has a wide variety of festivals suitable for toddlers. From late May to June, the Northern Alberta International Children's Festival is held. songs, dances, plays and music from around the world, as well as storytelling and painting and drawing. For tickets, call the Arden Theatre Box Office (Tel: 001 780 4591542/1692, Website: www.discoveralberta.com/childFest).

- In July Edmonton hosts the International Street Performers Festival. Downtown Edmonton is alive for ten fun-filled days of free performances by internationally-known street acts including magicians, clowns, jugglers, mime artists, musicians and comics for the young and young-at-heart. For tickets call 001 780 4255162, Website: www.discoveredmonton.com/streetperformers.

THEME PARK

- Galaxyland amusement park features a variety of rides and attractions designed especially for toddlers while the World Waterpark features special morning hours for toddler and parents swimming sessions. The 'Little Caribbean' water spray area is especially popular with beachcombers at this year-round indoor attraction. Daily dolphin presentations, the Sea Life Caverns, Professor Wem's Adventure Golf and lots of great shops with children's apparel and toys will keep even the most active family busy for a few hours or a full day. Both Galaxyland and World Waterpark are part of the West Edmonton Mall (Edmonton, Alberta, T5T 4M2, Tel: 001 780 4441700). The on-site Fantasyland Hotel (Tel: 001 780 4443000, Website: www.westedmontonmall. com) is convenient for that quick afternoon nap. Among the 350 rooms are 120 special family theme rooms including Western Rooms, Igloo Rooms, Polynesian Rooms, and even Truck Rooms, to name just a few of the accommodation adventures.

WILDLIFE

- Visit the indoor display of free-flying butterflies at the Devonian Botanic Garden, 15 minutes drive from West Edmonton Mall. Or take a 45-minute drive to Elk Island National Park for incredible wildlife viewing. This 'safari-type' nature preserve is home to more than 40 species of mammals, including plains and wood bison (buffalo), moose, elk, deer, beavers, and more than 200 species of birds.

ZOO

- Affordable and fun for children of all ages, the Valley Zoo (Tel: 001 780 4966911) is located 10 minutes drive from West Edmonton

Mall in the picturesque North Saskatchewan River valley parkland.
A special treat for the very young, the Little Children's Zoo with its
storybook themes, such as 'Mary had a little lamb', offers hands-
on activities and a petting area. There is a miniature train ride,
elephant encounter, sea lions feeding, and a chance to ride a
camel. Over 350 domestic and exotic species are displayed indoors
and outside in a park that can be comfortably walked in an hour
or two.

Calgary

- Fly direct into Calgary and take a short drive to the National Parks
  of Banff and Jasper and the Rockies. Go at Christmas or just after.
  It's a fairy-tale land with guaranteed snow, but it gets extremely
  cold.

Horses

- Canadians respect the 'earth' and know how to treat their wildlife
  and, in Calgary in particular, their horses. It's one of the few places
  you can teach your toddler (aged 3 plus) to understand horses,
  and even ride one. Led by Mac Mckenny who owns Homeplace
  Ranch (Site 2, Box 6 RR1 Tel: 001 877 9313245, Website:
  www.homeplaceranch.com), a team teach toddlers to feel
  comfortable and confident around a horse from this early age. The
  instruction enables them to learn to ride more easily when they
  are older. They will thank you in later life.

Ski resorts

- The ski area Marmot Basin has an extensive children's programme
  in place, including the 'Little Rascals Nursery' for toddlers. The ski
  resorts of Whistler and Big White offer particularly good facilities
  for toddlers. In Whistler the ski school caters for 18- to 36 month-
  olds with outdoor and indoor activities, crafts and story time, and
  there is ski instruction from 3 years plus. Big White's ski school
  also caters for 18 months plus with play time and ski instruction
  plus free safety helmets. For more information see Skiing,
  page 150.

Prince Edward Island

- One of the most beautiful parts of Canada, and a region that is
  frequently overlooked by travellers – who think of Canada as the
  Rockies and Vancouver and little else – is Atlantic Canada.
  Newfoundland, Prince Edward Island, Nova Scotia and New
  Brunswick have a lot more to offer than some of the larger cities in
  Canada. The accents of the locals, and the glorious landscape are
  reminiscent of the very best you will find in the Scottish
  Highlands, the West coast of Ireland and the South West of
  England. At the annual Cape Breton Celtic Colours festival,
  bagpipes and fiddles play a big part in the celebrations. More Irish
  music is heard in the capital of Nova Scotia, Halifax, than is heard
  in Dublin. Although Halifax is a very interesting town which
  grown-ups will find of interest, there is more to offer toddlers on
  Prince Edward Island, which is safe, clean and flat, and has
  fabulous beaches (the sand squeaks on Red Point Beach – your
  toddler will love it). The flight from Halifax to Prince Edward
  Island takes 40 minutes.

ANNE OF GREEN GABLES

- Charlottetown is about as laid back as it gets, and the island's
  adopted patron saint 'Anne of Green Gables' peers out at you from
  every shop window. Lucy Maude Montgomery, who wrote the
  Anne books, lived and wrote here and the island is a living
  museum to her work. There's Green Gables House in PEI National
  Park, Lucy's birthplace at Clifton Corner, Anne of Green Gables
  Museum at Silver Bush – in fact it's very difficult to get away from
  the little girl. Your toddler will not know who Anne is but,
  especially if you have a little girl, she will like the dolls. Contact
  Green Gables House Heritage Place, Ardgowan National Historic
  Site, 2 Palmers Lane, Charlottetown, PEI C1A 5V6, Tel: 001 902
  5667050, Fax: 001 902 5667226, Email: atlantic-
  parksinfo@pch.gc.ca.

NATURE PARKS

- Cabot Beach Provincial Park, PEI National Park, Cedar Dunes
  Provincial Park and Brudenell River Provincial Park. Prince

Edward Island National Park is in Charlottetown; details available
from 2 Palmers Lane, Charlottetown, PEI, Canada C1A 5V6,
Tel: 001 902 6726350, Fax: 001 902 6726370;
Email: peinp_pnipe@pch.gc.ca.

Quebec

- The Province of Quebec on the East Coast also has lots to
  recommend it to young families:

Bugs

- The Montreal Insectarium (4581 Sherbrooke Street East Viau, Tel:
  001 514 8721400, Website:
  www.ville.montreal.qc.ca/insectarium), in the grounds of the
  Montreal Botanical Garden, is home to some 2000 creatures of the
  insect world. Visitors can stroll among Quebec's most beautiful
  butterflies, which flit about freely in an airy Butterfly House.

Zoo

- Alternatively seek out the larger animals at Parc Safari (850 Route
  202, Hemmingford, Tel: 001 450 2472727, Website:
  www.parcsafari.com). This is the only zoo in Quebec where you
  can touch, pat and feed the animals!
- In the Montérégie, only 30 minutes from Montreal, you will find
  animals from around the globe, a water park, rides, shows,
  activities and fun for the whole family!

Vancouver

Vancouver has Kid Friendly! Services Inc (www.kidfriendly.org) which
lists all the things children – not just toddlers – can do in the city.
Not all the ideas are toddler-friendly, so consider what your toddler
will tolerate and understand. Here are some selected attractions:

Farm

- Maplewood Farm (Tel: 001 604 9295610) is a working farm just
  20 minutes from downtown Vancouver with resident horses,
  donkeys, pigs, ducks and birds – and they will be able to touch
  and stroke and feed the lot.

FISH

- In the New Canada Pavillion in the Vancouver Aquarium (Tel: 001 604 6593474) you can watch killer whales, dolphins and beluga whales in daily shows or feed a sea otter and view the sharks.

OPEN SPACES

- Granville Island (Tel: 001 604 6665784) has a water park and a merry-go-round in the Kids' Only Market. They can feed the seagulls or watch the turtles in the lagoon. You'll also find freshly made doughnuts (the smell is incredible) and there are lots of street entertainers and musicians – and occasionally magicians.
- Grouse Mountain is also worth visiting. The Skytram (Tel: 001 604 9813103) to the top is exciting, and there is a children's adventure playground, as well as a forest walk. Best in the early autumn rather than the winter, when snow will be heavy on the ground.
- Stanley Park (Tel: 001 604 4437443) is also an option. Ride the miniature railway, build sand castles on one of the many beaches, splash around in the toddlers' pool, pet the animals at the kids' farmyard or check out the whales at the Vancouver Aquarium Marine Science Centre. (Tel: 001 604 2578400).

STEAM TRAIN

- One thing they will understand thanks to Thomas the Tank Engine is steam trains. The Royal Hudson Steam Train/MV Britannia Boat Trip (Tel: 001 604 6887246) is worth a visit. Head up to Squarmish on the historic Royal Hudson Steam Train and return by boat on the MV Britannia (which has no baby-changing). The trip takes you through some of the world's most breathtaking scenery – none of which will impress your toddler as much as the steam train does.

VICTORIA

- Victoria on Vancouver Island is a family-friendly city with a large number of attractions and amenities to suit. The downtown core is relatively small, making it a very walkable city. The Victoria Bug Zoo (1107 Wharf Street. Tel: 001 250 3842847, Website:

www.bugzoo.bc.ca) will be the most popular attraction during your stay. A disturbingly large variety of bugs are on view, including scorpions, tarantulas, praying mantis, centipedes, giant stick insects, colourful beetles, huge grasshoppers and more. They will make you wince and your toddler happy. Guides will allow your toddler to hold some of the bugs. Dare you to not leave the premises feeling itchy!

- Try out Beacon Hill Childrens Farm (Tel: 001 250 3812532, Website: www.greatervictoria.com). Located in Beacon Hill Park and open in spring and summer, the park contains alpacas, zebus, tropical birds, potbellied pigs, goats and rabbits.
- Or visit Goldstream Provincial Park and Visitor Centre (3400 Trans-Canada Highway, Tel: 001 250 4789414, Website: www.crd.bc/parks), which features the natural history of the area and is geared towards toddlers.
- Miniature World (Humboldt Street, Tel: 001 250 3859731, Website: www.miniatureworld.com) has scaled-down versions of the world's largest railroads, circus scenes and doll houses.

Toronto

This is one city holiday that works well for toddlers. Toronto is a big city (although not by UK standards), with an excellent public transportation system, good shopping, and plenty to amuse toddlers. Keep an eye out for the 'mooses' – brightly coloured and individually decorated full-sized fun animals that can be found all over the city. Go on a moose hunt!

OUTDOOR ACTIVITIES

- For whole-day fun, try Ontario Place, a wonderful whole-family-friendly park with shops, rides, attractions, an IMAX cinema and restaurants, all in a setting of canals, lakes and lagoons on Lake Ontario (955 Lakeshore Blvd West, Toronto, Tel: 001 416 3149900).
- Or visit Centreville Amusement Park on Toronto Islands. This family-orientated facility features turn of the century rides and entertainment geared mostly to younger children and toddlers,

with a petting zoo and mini golf (Toronto Islands, Tel: 001 416 2030405).

- Just north of Toronto is the province's answer to Disneyland – Paramount Canada's Wonderland – with lots of rides, entertainment and fun for any toddler who has ever seen a cartoon! (Tel: 001 905 8327000, Fax: 001 905 8327419).

WORLD'S TALLEST BUILDING

- The CN Tower will enthral older toddlers and parents alike, with dining, shops and games as part of the package. Worth a visit (301 Front Street West, Toronto, Tel: 001 416 6014707).

OVER THE FALLS

- No trip to Ontario would be complete without a trip to Niagara Falls, a stunning natural feature with a host of activities. Just two hours' drive from Toronto, it's worth a visit. Take a trip on the Maid of the Mist boat, which travels under the falls (Tel: 001 905 3585781; Fax: 001 905 3588527, Website: www.maidofthemist.com), and visit nearby Marineland, an aquatic theme park with plenty for little ones, including a petting zoo (Tel: 001 905 3569565; Fax: 001 905 3566305).

ZOO

- The Toronto Zoo is situated to the east of Toronto, in Scarborough, and hosts a huge variety of animals, in a wonderful setting, complete with monorail and buggies for hire (Tel: 001 416 3925900). The pandas are a special treat!
- For more information about Ontario and, specifically, Toronto, attractions, accommodation, adventures, shopping and dining, see www.travelinx.com.

Where to eat

- In Toronto, try The Old Spaghetti Factory, which is always a hit with toddlers (54 The Esplanade, Toronto, Tel: 001 416 8649761).

Mr Greenjeans is also a good choice, with plenty of fun and healthy food for kids, alongside the old favourites. Better still, there are colouring books and entertainment to keep things going (The Toronto Eaton Centre, 220 Yonge Street, Tel: 001 416 9791212). Medieval Times offers a show and banquet that will tempt toddlers and parents alike (Exhibition Place, Tel: 001 416 2601234, Fax: 001 416 2601179). And don't miss Chuck E Cheese's, which is literally an emporium of toddler food and fun. There are several outlets in Canada, two of which are in Toronto. (Tel: 001 905 6024090).

- Prince Edward Island is famous for its potatoes and you can even buy Anne of Green Gables chips (which taste like any other). The island is also famous for its fish and seafood. Lobster dinners, which are held in church halls and cultural centres from May to September, are huge buffets of food produced on the island, which visitors can attend. The food served at restaurants – be it fast food or cordon bleu – is excellent, fresh and simple.

- In Victoria, toddler-friendly restaurants include White Spot (710 Caledonia Avenue, Tel: 001 250 3829911, Website: www.whitespot.com). Booster seats and highchairs available – as are burger and chips! Also try The Key (550 Fort Street, Tel: 001 250 3867789, Website: www.kegsteakhouse.com) where they offer a children's menu, crayons, change table, booster seats and high chairs. The Old Spaghetti Factory (703 Government Street, Tel: 001 250 3818445, Website: www.oldspaghettifactory.ca); Uncle Willy's Buffet (801 Vernon, Tel: 001 250 4751914) and Pizza Hut (Tel: 001 250 3822044, Website: www.pizzahut.com) are also worth a visit.

- Montreal is a city that lives on its stomach and thanks to the French influence, the regional cooking is of a very high standard – and most restaurants welcome toddlers, even if they don't have the high chairs. The best include Nickels (1384 Sainte-Catherine Street West, Tel: 001 514 3927771); Guy-Concordia (Tel: 001 514 3927771); Champ-de-Mars (Tel: 001 514 8615731) and Le Jardin Nelson (407 Place Jacques-Cartier, Tel: 001 514 8489575, Website: www.jardinnelson.com), which has musicians playing while they serve pancakes, pizzas, paninis and excellent salads.

Ristorante Giorgio (200 Saint-Laurent Blvd, Champ-de-Mars/Place d'Armes, Tel: 001 514 8423821). My favourite is Schwartz's (3895 Saint-Laurent Blvd, Tel: 001 514 8424813, Website: www.schwartzsdeli.com). It serves excellent smoked meat – and everyone from President Clinton to Celine Dion has eaten here, not that your toddler will care. Now Bob the Builder, that would be different. In Quebec, but outside Montreal, try Petit Coin Breton (2600 Laurier, Ste Foy, Tel: 001 418 6536061), a highly recommended creperie, and the following pizzerias have both gardens and soft-play areas: Pizza Magazine (955 Jean Gauvin, Quebec City, Tel: 001 418 8774747), Chez Hercule (234 Proulx, Vanier, Tel: 001 418 5278384) and Pizza Delice (146 Route Kennedy, Levis, Tel: 001 418 8332221).

- In Calgary, head for Ocean's Restaurant (a fish restaurant with a difference – namely a good approach to toddlers! (1316 33 St NE, Coast Plaza Hotel, Calgary, Tel: 001 403 2078117). Kelsey's Bar and Grill (a chain found throughout Canada, and notably good for kids) is found at 3545 32nd Avenue SE in Calgary (and many other locations) (Tel: 001 403 2913145).

Australia

We went to see relatives the first time round, dreading the journey with two toddlers. But we came prepared with games, books, the lot, and the crew were great. Australian cities have lots of parks with great playgrounds for kids. You'll also find a lot of communial BBQs to add another dimension to your Sunday picnic. Top tips for Australia – always make sure your toddler wears a hat which has a flap at the back to cover the neck. Australian sun is strong even through the cloud. And secondly, if anyone is seriously contemplating taking toddlers to Australia – which I can totally recommend – don't go for anything less than three weeks.

Mother of toddling twins, from Banbury

The basics

Time difference from UK – 10 hours ahead of GMT
Flight time from London
    Adelaide – 20 hours
    Sydney – 22 hours
    Melbourne – 22 hours
Culture – Laid-back
Toddler-friendly rating – Once you've got there 9/10
'Best bits' for toddlers – Beaches, friends made, koalas, lots to do on
    flight!
'Best bits' for parents – Laid-back culture, al fresco lifestyle
When to go – Melbourne and Sydney – Dec to Feb; northern
    Australia Nov to Mar

Where to go – Adelaide, Melbourne, Sydney and Hamilton Island
Accommodation – Hotel or self-catering

Toddler-friendly tour operators
British Airways Holidays (Tel: 01293 722 727, Website: www.britishairways.com)
Austravel (Tel: 020 7734 7755, Website: www.austravel.com)
Travel Australia (Tel: 01603 402 323, Website: www.travelaustralia.com)

Major airlines
Qantas (Tel: 08457 747 767, Website: www.qantas.com.au)
Air New Zealand (Tel: 0800 737 000, Website: www.airnz.co.nz)
Singapore Airlines (Tel: 0870 608 8886, Website: www.singaporeair.co.uk)

General information
A surprising number of parents had travelled with young children to Australia (over 10 percent, making it one of the most popular long-haul destinations for young families). Many of them went to visit relatives and found the experience – for the most part – extremely positive. Singapore Airlines proved to be the best way to fly due to a combination of excellent cabin crew, interesting goodie bag, good food and individual TVs on each seat. Qantas and Air New Zealand also received very positive comments about their service and facilities. You need a very toddler-friendly airline when taking such a journey.

Southeastern Australia (Melbourne and Sydney) rarely experiences cold weather but can be rainy at any time of the year. Northern Australia (Adelaide) has a Mediterranean-type climate with moderate rainfall falling mainly in the winter (April to September).

Don't read this chapter unless a) you are planning to spend more than three weeks in Australia and b) you have a toddler who is not hyperactive. If your toddler can survive (or you can survive) the long haul 20 to 22 hour journey, possibly with no stops, then certain parts of Australia are excellent places to visit – where both you and your young family will be entertained.

For information on South Australia visit www.southaustralia.com and while in Adelaide pick up a copy of 'Kids in Adelaide', a monthly publication available from local pharmacies, cafes, and theatres featuring a 'What's On' calendar especially for kids. (Tel: 0061 882 729433)

Where to stay

- Australian Farmhost holidays (PO Box 41, Walla Walla, NSW 2660, Tel: 0061 260 298621, Fax: 0061 260 298770, Email: farmhost@albury.net.au) provide accommodation and activities for the entire family. It is a safe environment for toddlers to have contact with farm animals and become involved in their feeding and care.
- While in Adelaide stay at Adelaide Heritage Cottages (Friendly Meeting Chapel, Tynte Street, North Adelaide, Tel: 0061 882 721355); Country Comfort Inn (226 South Terrace, Adelaide, Tel: 0061 882 234355); or Bayview Holiday Apartments, only 1 min from the beach at Glenelg (Tel: 0061 882 949666). All of these offer some services for the children, such as cots, babysitting services and gardens or terraces to play in.
- Further afield in South Australia, enjoy the real country atmosphere by staying on a farm – the kids will love it. SA Farm and Country Holidays (Tel: 0061 1300 655276, Website: www.weblogic.com.au/farmhols) has a full listing of properties.
- There are four hotels on Hamilton Island: Hamilton Island Apartments and Villas (self contained holiday apartments); Palm Bungalows & Terrace; the Reef View Hotel, which has some amazing views of the Coral Sea; and Palm Terrace, a three-star property that targets families. Families tend to opt for the apartments, Palm Terrace or the four-star Reef View Hotel. Most of the holiday packages to Hamilton Island include the unique 'Kids stay, play and eat for free' feature. The 'Clownfish Club' offers excellent facilities for little ones from 6 weeks to 5 years. It's operated by fully qualified nannies and is open 7 days from

8.30am to 5.30pm. The usual art and craft activities take place as well as dressing up (as a possum rather than a cow!). (For all information, Tel: 0061 749 469999 or visit www.hamiltonisland.com.au).

- Accommodation in Melburne tends all to be very toddler/child friendly. Check out the apartments of Melbourne, which include 15 properties located throughout inner Melbourne (400 St Kilda Road, Melbourne, Tel: 0061 398 201000). Or try the Pacific International Suites near the heart of Melbourne's shopping districts (471 Little Bourke Street, Tel: 0061 396 073000). Punt Hill Serviced Apartments are in six locations across Melbourne – including Flinders Lane in the city, South Yarra, St Kilda Road, North Melbourne, Armadale and East Melbourne (267 Flinders Lane, Tel: 0061 396 501299).

- In Sydney, try Aaron's (37 Ultimo Road, Tel: 0061 292 815555) which offers apartments, rooms with en suite bathrooms and cot, and baby sitting – as well as being central to toddler-friendly attractions in the city. Old Sydney Park Royal (55 George Street, Tel: 0061 292 520524) offers personal attention and is situated within the historic Rocks area, close to the Circular Quay and the Opera House. Baby sitting and cots provided. Stafford (75 Harrington Street, Tel: 0061 292 516711) is housed either in the central property or one of the seven charmingly restored 1870 terrace houses nearby.

The best bits

Adelaide

- Bordered by wide terraces and parklands, Adelaide is compact and easy to explore on foot. It is relatively flat, with a wide pedestrian-only shopping mall and many excellent parks, gardens and playgrounds for the kids to run around in. Attractions for toddlers include:

BOATS

- Perfect for kids is a boat ride aboard 'Popeye' along Adelaide's River Torrens, or alternatively the 20-minute tram ride to the seaside at Glenelg.

TOY FACTORY

- Kids will love the Toy Factory (Tel: 0061 883 891085) in the Adelaide Hills, where they can climb the biggest rocking horse in the world standing 20 metres high with three observation galleries. The Toy Factory provides sweeping views of the Gumeracha Valley and sells a large range of wooden toys, homeware, novelties and gifts at factory-direct prices.

TRAINS

- A great way for families with toddlers to reach the scenic, wine-producing Barossa Valley north of Adelaide is by the Barossa Wine Train (Website: www.barossawinetrain.com.au), with fully refurbished Bluebird Rail carriages. In the Barossa itself, don't miss the Whispering Wall, where a trick of acoustics allows sound to travel long distances along the Barossa Reservoir.
- The Fleurieu Peninsula, about an hour's drive south of Adelaide, offers the Cockle Train – an historic steam train that trundles along Australia's first public iron railway, built in the 1850s. Enjoy spectacular views of the Southern Ocean as you take the 30-minute journey between Victor Harbor and Goolwa. Catch Australia's only horse-drawn tram, pulled by huge Clydesdales, along the restored wooden causeway to Granite Island, where the colony of penguins nesting in the rocks is always popular with kids.

WILDLIFE PARK

- In the Adelaide Hills, a 20-minute drive east of Adelaide, Cleland Wildlife Park (Tel: 0061 883 392444, Website: www.cleland.sa.gov.au) allows small and big kids to come face to face with koalas, hand-feed kangaroos and meet the wallabies and emus that roam freely in the park. There are also forest and swamp aviaries to walk through with an abundance of birdlife, wombats to get acquainted with, Tasmanian Devils to astound and the perennial favourite of all kids, a reptile display to visit.

Hamilton Island

- This is idyllic for both your toddlers and you. Of all the places in Australia, this received more positive comments than any other from families with young children. It is situated in the heart of the Whitsundays, the group of 74 tropical islands lying in the Coral Sea between the Queensland coast and the Great Barrier Reef, and is the only island in the group with a variety of hotels and apartments to suit all tastes and budgets, including families travelling with toddlers. Hamilton Island Airport services regular flights from Sydney, Melbourne, Brisbane and Cairns with both Ansett Australia and Qantas. The hotels (see above) have pools and facilities for toddlers. It can get very hot in summer though (Dec to Feb).

Melbourne

- The city has loads to offer families with toddlers and is well worth considering as a stopover for a week or long weekend. There are very safe roads with a newly introduced 50 km/hour speed limit in residential areas. Public transport includes trams, trains and buses, making it very easy for individuals and families to see the city and its attractions. The City Circle tram is a free service. Toddler-friendly highlights include:

FISH

- In Melbourne Aquarium (Tel: 0061 399 235917, Website: www.melbourneaquarium.com.au) you travel through mangrove swamps, rock pools, billabongs and transparent tunnels where giant sharks and stingrays will surround you (don't watch Jaws III before doing this). Then slowly descend into a massive Oceanarium and finish with a wild, underwater roller-coaster ride on the simulator. Totally involving and interactive, the aquarium is located on the Yarra River, opposite Crown Entertainment Complex in the heart of Melbourne. Located on the free city-circle tram, baby changing rooms and buggy friendly.

GARDENS

- The Royal Botanic Gardens (Tel: 0061 392 522300, Website: www.rbgmelb.org.au) has over 51,000 plant species from Australia and around the globe. The internationally renowned 19th-century landscape design with its stunning views and Ornamental Lake makes the gardens good value for entertaining toddlers and adults alike. Take a tour, wine and dine at the Observatory Café or the tea rooms – which are very relaxed about toddlers who want to run around as well as eat. Good changing facilities and excellent visitor centre located at the Observatory Café, where information officers can help you with any question you care to ask about the plants or the nearest toilet.

MUSEUM

- Melbourne Museum (Tel: 0061 383 417172, Website: www.museum.vic.gov.au). I know, I know, it's a museum, but it's great for toddlers! Loads of real, hands-on, virtual and innovative fun. You can walk through a living Forest Gallery, discover the vibrant story of Melbourne, experience Aboriginal performances (bit scary for toddlers), and marvel at Australia's unique wildlife. Explore the secrets of your mind and body and visit the dinosaurs. 'Why couldn't the London Dome have been more like this?' was one comment from a satisfied mum who visited this year with her family. Performances, activities and interactive displays bring Melbourne's innovative museum to life. Excellent. It also incorporates a Children's Museum, catering specifically for 3-to 8-year-olds, an ideal hands-on, indoor and outdoor learning environment, with an emphasis on discovery through exploring with the senses. Facilities include Imax theatre, InfoZone, restaurant and café (with baby changing) and it is easy to navigate around most areas with a buggy.

WILDLIFE

- Healesville Sanctuary (Tel: 0061 395 72826, Website: www.zoo.org.au) is located in the picturesque Yarra Valley, and provides visitors with a unique Australian wildlife experience. You can stroll among kangaroos, koalas and other indigenous animals.

Winner of the Australian and Victorian Environmental Awards. Baby-changing, playground and safe picnic area.

- At Ballarat Wildlife Park (Tel: 0061 353 335933, Website: www.ballarat.com/wildlife.thm) experience the excitement and activity of close contact with Australian wildife in natural bushland surroundings. Meet wombats and crocodiles as well as kangaroos and koalas. BBQ, coffee shop with changing facilities.

Zoo

- Melbourne Zoo (Tel: 0061 392 859300, Website: www.zoo.org.au) just minutes away from the city centre exhibits more than 350 animal species from around the world, including all the Australian favourites – little penguins, platypus and kangaroos. Innovative African and Asian Rainforest zones, featuring gorillas, agile otters and majestic and ever-so-scary Sumatran tigers. You can meet the keeper as well.

Sydney

- Sydney has much to offer toddlers. To find your way around, I recommend *Kidz Stuff*, an excellent book by Naomi Beames and Wendy Docherty. It has about 2500 entries on children's activities, attractions, events, entertainment, toy shops and toy libraries, kids' clothing outlets, hotels, restaurants, services and more. The listings note suitable ages and there are many options for toddlers. (Order a copy from Tel: 0061 299 543299 or website: www.kidzstuff.com.au). *Sydney's Child* is a free magazine available throughout the city and contains feature stories, events calendar and services. It has recently gone online at www.sydneyschild.com.au. Check out also www.sydneyforchildren.com.au and www.timeout.com/sydney/kids

Adventure park

- Wonderland (Tel: 0061 800 252198 – toll free – or 0061 298 309100, Website: www.wonderland.com.au) is a children's adventure park with seven themes, each with rides, entertainment, shows and eateries. Entry fee gives unlimited access to all the fun.

BEACHES

- Sydney has more than 30 beaches to choose from – some of which are sheltered and ideal for toddlers. Avoid the surf beaches of the Pacific Ocean and pure pose beaches such as Bondi. The surf can be dangerous, but all the beaches are manned by trained lifeguards. Best beaches for toddlers are Manly beach on the North Shore and Manly Cove which is on the harbour side (you have to catch a ferry or sea cat over from Circular Quay). Both have calm water and the ferry port is only a few minutes walk from the cove which means there are toilets, shops and restaurants on hand.

MUSEUMS

- The Australian Museum (Tel: 0061 293 206000, Website: www.austmus.gov.au) has an area designed specifically for children up to 5 years old – Kids' Island is a special 'hands on' place. Powerhouse Museum (Tel: 0061 292 170111, Website: www.phm.gov.au) has designed kids' interactive discovery spaces that stimulate children's interest in movement, machines, music and much more. It's one of those places where parents can sit and watch their toddlers on a discovery tour.

OPERA HOUSE FOR TODDLERS

- Sydney Opera House (Tel: 0061 292 507111, Website: www.soh.nsw.gov.au, Email: bookings@soh.nsw.gov.au) has a wonderful programme for children called *Kids@theHouse*. The calendar of events includes Baby Proms.

PIRATE SHIP

- Bounty Cruises (Tel: 0061 292 471780, Website: www.thebounty.com) is a replica of Capt. Bligh's tall ship that sails the harbour daily from The Rocks. Kids' Show Afloat (Tel: 0061 298 176704, Website: www.seapecruises.com.au) caters for 2- to 10-year-olds. Each Saturday, there are three cruise options depending on age. The $2\frac{1}{2}$ hours of cruising around Sydney Harbour includes lunch, fun, games and a goodies pack. There's a circus show for 2- to 8-year-olds, a party band for 2- to 6-year-olds and a fun disco for 3- to 10-year-olds. Bookings are essential.

TODDLER THEATRE

- The Rocks Puppet Theatre (Tel: 0061 292 412902) has a wonderful collection of handmade marionettes, shadow, arm and rod & glove puppets that perform in half-hour shows on the weekends – it's pure delight for young audiences. Fox Studios Backlot (Fox Studios Australia, Lang Road, Moore Park, NSW 1363, Tel: 0061 293 834000, Website:www.foxstudios.com.au) has lots of entertainment, shows as well as a playground, Lollipops, with interactive play zones and supervised activities. There's also the Babe set to run around, The Simpsons Experience, and more.

ZOO/AQUARIUM

- Like most major cities Sydney has its own aquarium and zoo. The aquarium (Tel: 0061 292 622300, Website: www.sydneyaquarium.com.au) has thousands of species of marine life – from tropical fish and turtles to sharks and seals. Visitors walk through underwater tunnels so that they are surrounded by sea life – quite mesmerising! Taronga Zoo (Tel: 0061 299 692777, Website: www.zoo.nsw.gov.au) has a wide range of animal life – for the little ones, there's a petting farm, seals on show and a lot more.
- Take a trip to Featherdale Wildlife Park (Tel: 0061 962 21644), which is in a natural bush location with more than 2000 native animals, or visit the Koala Park (Tel: 0061 294 843141, Website: www.koalaparksanctuary.com.au) where koalas roam freely.

Where to eat

- Adelaide is renowned for its excellent local produce and fine wines, which has given rise to a wealth of streetside cafes and restaurants to suit every fussy little eater. For lunch or dinner in Adelaide, some ideal spots are Café Paesano (100 O'Connell Street, Tel: 0061 882 390655) and Stanley's Great Aussie Fish Café (76 Gouger Street, Tel: 0061 884 100909).
- The most toddler-friendly restaurant in Sydney, according to those I spoke to, include Ash's Table (93–94 North Steyne, Manly, Tel: 0061 299 763382). This restaurant is excellent for toddlers and a

favourite with locals. Big glass sliding doors open onto ocean views, an inexpensive menu, and there are magazines and a box stuffed full of toys to keep you and your toddler entertained. Café Sydney (Level 5, Customs House, 31 Alfred Street, Tel: 0061 292 518683) is also recommended.

- In Melbourne, try the Dragon Boat Palace – which is noisy and bustling with efficient waiters pushing trolleys with delicious morsels. For meat eaters there is a huge choice. (149 Lonsdale Street, Tel: 0061 396 390888). Or Marios with arguably the best coffee, where oldies can get their caffeine fix while toddlers enjoy the delicious freshly-squeezed orange juice. (303 Brunswick Street, Fitzroy, Tel: 0061 394 173343). Or Soul Food Café, which is a spacious vegetarian eatery with loads of room for toddlers to play. (273 Smith Street, Collingwood, Tel: 0061 394 192949.)

Appendix

International emergency telephone numbers

Country	Ambulance	Fire	Police
Australia	000	000	000
Austria	144	122	133
Belgium	100	100	101
Canada	911	911	911
Cayman Islands	911	911	911
Cyprus	112	112	112
Denmark	112	112	112
Dominican Rep.	911	911	911
Finland	112	112	10022
France	15	18	17
Germany	112	112	110
Greece	166	100	100
Ireland	112/999	112/999	112/999
Israel	101	102	100
Italy	118	115	112
Jamaica	110	110	119
Kenya	999	999	999
Luxembourg	112	112	112
Malta	196	191	191
Monaco	112	112	112
Netherlands (Holland)	112	112	112
New Zealand	111	111	111

Norway	113	110	112
Portugal	112/115	112/115	112/115
Saudi Arabia	997	998	999
Sth. Africa	10177	10111	10111
Spain	061	080	091
Turkey	112	110	155
United Kingdom	112/999	112/999	112/999
United States	911	911	911

Sources and advice

www.travel-news.org – Excellent site offering up to date travel information and news

www.abta.com – Site of the Association of British Travel Agents with search facility

www.aito.co.uk – Site of the Association of Independent Tour Operators

www.a2btravel.com – Good one stop source of travel information

www.expedia.co.uk – One of the first online travel agents who have got their act together

www.otc-uk.com – Site of the online travel company, with good ideas

www.holidaywizard.co.uk – View and order brochures on line

www.realholiday.co.uk – Site of the Campaign for Real Travel Agents with a special offers section

www.traveldonkey.com – An addictive database of travelogues and reviews from public about their holiday ups and downs.

www.fco.gov.uk/travel – Reassuring government advice on where not to visit, what not to do while you are there and who to call if you do

www.timeout.com – Time Out covers cities world-wide, with an emphasis on contemporary culture and streetlife

www.holidaytravelwatch.com – What to do if your holiday goes wrong

www.bol.com – Online booksellers with an excellent travel section

www.thetravelbookshop.co.uk – Travel books specialist

www.stanfords.co.uk – Online branch of Stanfords with catalogues

Travelling by road, rail, air and sea

www.thetrainline.com – Book train tickets online

www.rail.co.uk – Site that unravels the rail network

www.a2beurope.com – One stop site for information on ferry services

www.cruise2.com – Everything about cruising

www.a2bairports.com – Information on airports in the UK and Ireland

www.pit.org.uk – UK transport timetables including bus and coach services

www.rac.co.uk – Useful route planner for driving in Europe

http://weather.yahoo.com – Gives a five-day forecast for your next trip

www.ukpa.gov.uk – Site of the UK passport agency

www.kropla.com – Site that tells you the electric plug you need for each country

www.oanda.com – Online currency converter

www.travelwithcare.co.uk – Order travels goods from sleeping bags to night lights

www.doh.gov.uk/traveladvice – Health advice for travellers from the Government including details of Form E111

www.medisearch.co.uk – Medical site with details of what immunisations you need for each destination

On location

www.antor.com – Site of the Association of National Tourist Offices

www.fieldingtravel.com – About the world's trouble spots

www.goodbeachguide.co.uk – Guide to the UK beaches from the Marine Conservation Society

www.zagat.com – Restaurant guide covering London, Paris and major cities in North America

Recommended Guidebooks

Some guidebooks take payment for inclusion. Those who do not follow this practice, will undoubtedly be more reliable!

The Good Hotel Guide, Continental Europe,
by C. Raphael, Ebury Press, £14.99
An independent and reliable guide. It does not detail limitations on children as these generally do not apply outside the UK.

In general guides if they do mention children do so only as a token and the material is often written by someone living in the city who includes places which are of limited use to those who are only visiting for a few days. However, the following are in themselves good ranges:

Time Out Guides (Tel: 020 7813 3000)
Covering cities, with around 4–6 pages on facilities for children including eating out, child-minder services, shopping, grand days out, animals and parks, theme and safari parks, and activities and sports. This is often written more for residents than visitors. £9.99

Rough Guides (Tel: 020 7556 5000)
Do not generally cover options for children except in their city guides but are highly practical. £8.99 to £14.99.

Lonely Planet (Tel: 020 7428 4800)
Aimed at the practical backpacker, slightly less useful to travellers because so often focused on the minutiae of savings and deals, at the expense of the overall picture. The useful website includes a world guide, themed guides, the Thorn Tree (interactive for posting queries and answering them), Postcards (updates from readers), Propaganda (info on the guides in the series), Scoop (world travel news) and Health.

Food for thought

Vegan Travel Guide to UK and Southern Ireland £5.90 inc p&p from The Vegan Society, Donal Watson House, 7 Battle Road, St Leonards-on-Sea, East Sussex TN37 7AA. Lists more than 700 places to stay and eat and details among other things where children are welcome.
Vegetarian London, by Alex Bourke, Paul Gaynor, and Tony Banks: Vegetarian Guides, £5.99
Vegetarian Europe, by Alex Bourke: Vegetarian Guides, £9.99
Vegetarian Britain, by Alex Bourke: Vegetarian Guides, £7.99
Vegetarian France, by Alex Bourke: Vegetarian Guides, £6.99
These four titles include details on suitable hotels and guesthouses plus restaurants and cafes, but no information on child welcome.

Two of the best books to buy for recipe ideas are Annabel Karmel's *Superfoods for Babies and Children*, published by Ebury Press or the *Organic Baby & Toddler Cookbook*, by Lizzie Vann at Baby Organix.

Useful contacts

Travelling by road, rail, air and sea

The AA (Tel: 08705 448 866, Website: www.theaa.co.uk)
A membership organisation with member only information services such as a European route service but also: AA Roadwatch (Tel: 0900 0340 1100), 60p a minute. Provides traffic information on specific motorways and A roads, general national traffic information, and weather information.

French Autoroute Information on the radio on 107.7FM for traffic conditions. In French Tel: 0033 836 681077 at around 25p a minute.

Britax (Tel: 01264 386 034, Website: http://www.britax.co.uk)
Principally a manufacturer of seats for aircraft and the UK's leading manufacturer of car seats for children. The helpline may not be as helpful as it might be but can provide details of more important stockists and send out brochures, including on polystyrene seats.

Gemmaway Coach Tours (Tel: 01923 286 150)
Probably unique among coach tour operators in that it positively welcomes families. The family-run company makes a big effort to provide a personalised service and for example on visits to the Edinburgh Festival finds accommodation in a number of smaller, central hotels rather than bussing in from the outskirts or further afield.

In sickness and in health

The National Radiological Protection Board (NRPB, Tel: 01235 831 600)
Produces a leaflet Ultraviolet Radiation as well as reports and consultation documents around the issue. Can also provide a leaflet with more detailed information on fabric and sun protection.

Swimrite (Tel: 01384 898 205, Website: www.swimrite.com)
Sells SwimEAR, a US product designed to counter the surface tension, which causes water to stay trapped in the ear canal and potentially LEAD to infections. Apparently on application the product evaporates any remaining water within seconds.

MASTA
Travellers Health Line (Tel: 0906 822 4100;
60p per minute, calls usually averaging two minutes).
The health line, which covers 250 countries, will supply a written personalised travel health brief, all data validated by the London School of Hygiene and Tropical Medicine after you leave a message on the answering service detailing date and destination of travel. If pregnant you should say so when requesting information. Similarly you should give ages of children in the party. The information is keyed into a data-bank from which the health brief is compiled and posted back by first class return. This includes recommended and suggested immunisa-tions, malaria advice, health news and news safety reports from the Foreign Commonwealth office and World Health Organisation. The databank is reportedly updated daily. The website includes a 'Before you go' section (including advice on what consulates can and cannot do to help); and information on immunisations, descriptions of various drugs and illnesses, and advice on procedures while travelling, including information for some special needs travellers. It also sells some basic travel health products online.

Nomad Travellers Store and Medical Centre (Tel: 020 7833 4114)
Healthline (Tel: 09068 633 414; calls 60p per minute direct to a health professional). Run by a couple who have themselves travelled well off the beaten track with their offspring, can provide all kinds of travel health information. There are leaflets like Bite Avoidance & Wound Care in the Tropics, and Diarrhoea – What to Take and When to Take It, though if you want to discuss anything in depth it is best to go into the store in person and see one of the health professionals free of charge. Nomad particularly recommends this if you are travelling with a baby. The company can also provide a tailor-made first aid kit

after discussion with parents, designed to meet the potential problems of different destinations.

Helios (Tel: 01892 537 254, 24-hour answering machine service Tel: 01892 536 393, Website: www.helios.co.uk)
Provides a useful homeopathic travel kit with 36 relevant travel remedies.

Homeway Ltd (Tel: 01980 626 361,
Website: www.travelwithcare.co.uk)
A carefully chosen range of travel accessories including a number of security items. First Aid Kits including a roll up bag, blister kit.

Neals Yard Remedies (Tel: 0161 831 7875,
Website: www.nealsyardremedies.com)
Sells a travel roll ready packed with the most useful alternative first aid remedies including essential oil lavender, hypericum and calendula tincture, arnica ointment, Hypericum and Urtica ointment, citronella essential oil, chamomile tea, a five-flower rescue remedy, and Arnica 30 homeopathic tablets, or empty ones, which you could fill as you wish.

Trailfinders (Tel: 020 7938 3999, Travel Clinic Tel: 020 7938 3999)
A Travel Essentials shop selling a range of travel gadgets alongside the travel clinic. One First Aid kit includes a doctor's letter for customs.

Protec Health (Tel: 0800 838 098, Website: www.protec.health.com)
Non-Deet chemical repellent Protec, available as a lotion or spray, containing Merc 3535 or IR 3535 in a formulation including elements designed to make it easier on the skin but without perfume. Available direct or through limited number of retail outlets.

Suncare

The National Radiological Protection Board
(NRPB, Tel: 01235 831 600)

Produces a leaflet 'Ultraviolet Radiation' as well as reports and consultation documents around the issue. Can also provide a leaflet with more detailed information on fabric and sun protection.

Childcare Products (Tel: 0161 427 8598,
Website: www.childcareproducts.co.uk)
Baby travel warmer for use in winter – a heat pack inside a furry teddy.

Sea Band Ltd (Tel: 01455 639 750, Website: www.sea-band.com)
Sea Bands operate by exerting pressure on the acupressure point on each wrist with a round plastic 'button' set in an elastic wristband. They can be used continuously and are reported by some children to help with motion sickness both on a boat and in a car. Children's wristbands are extra colourful.

Travelwell (Tel: 01264 364 474, Website: www.travelwell.co.uk)
An anti motion sickness product using magnets.

Active Birth Centre (Tel: 020 7482 5554,
Website: www.activebirthcentre.com)
In its shopping section the centre sells two slings including the String baby sling which, when you don't require it, can be folded small enough to fit in your pocket.

Huggababy (Tel: 01874 711 629, Website: www.huggababy.co.uk)
Stockist of the Kelty Elite Backpack, reported as comfortable, easily adjustable once you've mastered the adjustment straps, well padded and with good weight distribution.

National Childbirth Trust Maternity Sales
(Tel: 0141 636 0600, Website: www.nctms.co.uk)
A catalogue that makes a point of trying to provide items not easily found elsewhere, mainly aimed at those with babies and toddlers.

Snow and Rock
(Tel: 0845 100 1000, Website:www.snowandrock.com)
Produces a large catalogue as well as operating stores; larger ones on

the M25, Covent Garden, Bristol, Sheffield, and Hemel Hempstead plus smaller stores at Holborn, Birmingham and Kensington.

Urchin Mail Order Ltd
(Tel: 01672 872 872, Website: www.urchin.co.uk)
One of the more stylish catalogues of infant gear. Including a best selling backpack with a sun canopy rain cover with frame or for extra comfort the Bush Baby.

Safariquip (Tel: 01433 620 320, Website: www.safariquip.co.uk)
Aimed mainly at more adventurous and long-haul travellers. Filters, purifiers and purifying tablets.

Safety

European Union
(Website: www.europa.eu.int/water/water-bathing/index_en)
Run by the EU, covers all beaches in the EC and the standards they have met. Some of the final detail links seem to be missing but this does include a tourist atlas of tourist beaches which provides some useful outline info.

Tidy Britain Group
(Tel: 01603 766 076, Website: www.blueflag.org.uk)
For details of the European Blue Flag beaches and marinas send a 57p A4 SAE or see the website.

Marine Conservation Society
(Tel: 01989 566 017, from 9 to 5pm)
The Good Beach Guide
The Society researches data collected by the Environment Agency in England and Wales and parallel organisations in Scotland, Northern Ireland etc. It identifies where UK water companies discharge sewage and what treatment is provided at these outlets.

The Environment Agency
(Emergency Hotline 0800 80 70 60, Floodline 0845 988 1188)
The website offers up to date reports on bathing water quality at 472 sites around England and Wales, tested on average once a week from 1 May to 30 September. Results are up-dated weekly on the back yard sections which cover specific areas of Britain, including some inland waters like lakes (in 2000 including Cotswold Water Lake Park, Frensham Great Pond, Windermere Fellfoot, Windermere Millerround Landing and Windermere, lakeside YMCA). The agency also runs for example beach surveys in conjunction with members of the public. For details see www.environment-agency.gov.uk/helpus/

In Wales the Green Sea Partnership of around 40 organisations, which includes government agencies, local authorities and the voluntary sector, researches resort beaches, rural beaches and in conjunction with the Tidy Britain Group has developed the Green Coast Award for beaches without infrastructure but high environmental quality. There are also awards to rural beaches which only achieve mandatory bathing water quality.

An annual booklet, 'Award Winning Welsh Beaches and Marinas', describes each beach which has received an award and details its water quality history. The partnership is also working on a website which should be accessible via that of the Wales Tourist Board – www.visit wales.com. A scheme covering rural beaches in a similar way is also planned for England.

Watch out for flags showing the cleanliness of beaches and sea water. The Seaside Awards flag is yellow with a blue corner. The EC Blue Flag beach flag is blue.

PHP Ltd (Perfectly Happy People, Tel: 0870 607 0545,
Website: www.phpbaby.com)
The UK's main stockists of the Canadian Kooshies brand, along with items from other producers. Items can be purchased on line. A babysafe clip to clip to a standard adult seat belt to ensure that the belt accommodates the bump.

Final checklist

If you don't want to take certain bits of equipment with you – hire them.

Baby Equipment Hirers Association (Tel: 01831 310 355)
Can provide details of your nearest member with 100 across the UK. They hire all kinds of baby equipment including cots, buggies, high seats, backpacks and more on a short or long-term basis.

Entertainment

The Children's Book Company
(Tel: 020 8567 4324, Website: www.childrensbookcompany.com)
As well as selling any British children's title in print (delivery in three days) the site offers a newsdesk, monthly advice articles, a chatroom, story tasters, book reviews covering age suitability, reading levels and format style as well as story lines and quality of illustration, and more.

The Swimshop (Tel: 01582 562 111, Email:swimshop@aol.com)
Diving bricks, sticks and more.

Tomy (Tel: 020 8661 4400, Website: www.tomy.co.uk)
Produces a soft activity quilt and play arch gym which folds flat.

Michelin Maps and Guides
(Tel: 01923 415 074, Website:www.michelin-travel.com)
Has re-done the I-Spy books. Useful among the 50-plus subjects subjects include *On a Car Journey*, *Ships and Boats*, *Wild Flowers*, *Channel Tunnel*, *Castles*, *Trees*, *Mini Atlas to Britain*, *On a Ferry*, *Trucks & Trucking*, and *Caravans and Motor Caravans*. They are stocked by large bookshops and for example Stanfords (see More Information) which has a web site.

Early Learning Centre
(Customer Services, Tel: 01782 402 000, ELC Direct 08705 352 352)

More than 200 stand alone stores plus Debenhams department stores and more than 200 Sainsbury's. The range of toys sold varies each season and you are more likely to find items for travel in the summer, however you could look out for items like puzzle travel packs.

Walker Books (Tel: 020 7793 0909)
Princess Puzzles, Number Puzzles, Animal Facts and Puzzles. Gamebooks cater for three different skill levels, with different ways of reading each book and things to find and clues to solve. Also titles like *Monster Puzzles, A Busy Day at the Harbour, A Busy Day at the Railway Station* and *Animal Facts and Puzzles.*

Acoustics (Tel: 0118 926 8615,
Website: www.acousticsrecords.co.uk or www.childrensmusic.co.uk)
Hilary James and Simon Mayor are Acoustics and they have worked for *Play School, Listening Corner* and *Green Claws* and were regular presenters of the *Song Tree* on BBC Radio for Schools. Their tapes, which draw on folk tradition with a C&W touch, offer good original material that will bear plenty of re-listenings.

Kettle Records (Tel: 01337 831 121, Website: www.singingkettle.com)
Scottish children's music specialists Cilla Fisher and Artie Trezise plus Gary Coupland, come from a folk background and do children's shows. There is a range of musical styles with some Scottish-tinged moments. Tapes can be purchased on line.

The Singing Kettle Greatest Hits Volume One includes a number of traditional but less well known songs like 'Bunny Fou Fou' or 'Baby Bumble Bee', others written by themselves and by others including Woody Guthrie's 'Riding In My Car'. The Singing Kettle Greatest Hits Volume Two. As above with different songs. Singing Kettle 1 includes 'Granny Aff A Bu's, 'Apples and Bananas', 'Tatie Soup'; Singing Kettle 2 includes 'Green Grass Grew', 'Buy Me A Banana', 'Leap Frog'; Singing Kettle 3 includes 'Bunny Fou Fou', 'No Pyjamas On', 'Music man and Woman'; Singing Kettle 4 includes 'School Dinners', 'Boa Constrictor' and 'Air Guitar'.

The Big Green Planet Songs and rhymes with a green message.

Meringue Productions
(Tel: 020 8744 2277, Website:www.meringue.co.uk)
Dinosaur Diaries (Radical Rex/Mount Blowyourtop Explodes, Dinosaur
Disco/Bones, Expedition/Above It All, Hank the Tank/Gravity). Simple
tales punctuated by songs of different kinds of dinosaurs – including
Charlotte and Emily Brontesaurus.

Oh No! Not Another Travel Song Tape Upbeat/comic versions of
standard songs. 'The Wheels on the Bus' gets a Latin treatment, with
the wheels falling off and the daddies on the bus ranting and raving.
'Mulberry Bush' is sung with early BBC enunciation and other titles
are 'I've Been Working on the Railroad', 'Row, Row Your Boat', and
'Michael Row the Boat Ashore'.

Are We Nearly There Yet? Similar, but including small in-car exer-
cises.

Oh No! Not another Nursery Rhyme Tape 'Old Macdonald', 'Sing
a Song of Sixpence', 'Horsey Horsey', aiming for street cred with children. Baby Pan Pipes designed for tranquillity, tracks including Brahms
lullaby, 'Ba Ba Black Sheep', 'Little Bo Peep', and 'Scarborough Fair'.
A link with Amazon enables purchasing on-line or by cheque direct.

Ragged Bears (Tel: 01264 772 269, Website: www.ragged-bears.co.uk)
You purchase the tapes with the books online from the publisher and
other imprints it distributes.
- Humpty Audio Cassettes, featuring real instruments, rather
  'sweeter' than most of the others featured here, a style well suited
  to the Golden Slumbers tape.
- Old King Cole and Other Rhymes 37 traditional songs
- 40 Traditional Nursery Rhymes
- Children's Choice, Songs like 'How Much is that Doggy in the
  Window?' 'Teddy Bears' Picnic', and 'Puff the Magic Dragon'.
  Golden Slumbers; Lullabies
- Nonsense and Stuff!; Funny songs including
  'Supercalifragilisticexpialidocious', 'Michael Finnegan', 'The
  Hippopotamus Song', 'Bananas in Pyjamas', and famous nonsense
  rhymes.

Peony Records (Tel: 029 2081 5201)
- They Sang and Were Glad features nursery rhymes and action songs sung plainly but with poise on tapes produced by someone who studied at the Royal College of Music in London and worked as a professional musician and is keenly aware of the role of music in a child's physical and educational development.
- God's Wonderful World – Christian songs like 'All Things Bright and Beautiful'.
- Thank You God for Snails. A further tape is in production and CD versions may be available. Cheques payable to Julia Plaut, money back if not happy.

Playsongs Publications
Tel: 01799 599 054, Website: www.playsongs.co.uk)
- Playsongs features action songs for babies and toddlers with accompanying book giving actions.

No on-line purchases on own site but available from Amazon, eToys and Blooming Marvellous.

Index

Gatwick Airport *see* London Gatwick
Gemmaway Coach Tours 425
geranium 163, 164
Germany
  car first aid kits 82, 225
  motorhomes 182
ginger 240
gîtes 342
Glasgow 307–8
Glasgow Airport 45, 304
Glasgow Prestwick International Airport
    43–4, 304
global warming 12
Gold Medal 187
Granville Island, Vancouver 405
grazes 236
Great Little Trading Company 136
Greece
  carers 215
  toddler-friendly 10
  weather 12
Greek Islands: self-catering 262
Green Coast Award 430
Green Sea Partnership 430
Grenada 388
Grouse Mountain, Vancouver 405
Guernsey 265, 318–21
  the basics 318–19
    major airlines 318–19
    toddler-friendly tour operators 318
  the best bits 320–1
  where to eat 321
  where to stay 319–20
guidebooks 26, 423–4

Hague, The 358
Hamilton Island, Australia 415
Harding, Maria: *Weather to Travel* 14
Hardy, Roger 62
Haven Europe 175
hay fever 14, 65
Hayward, Martin 261–2
'Health Advice for Travellers' booklet
    224
Health Education Authority: Sun Know How
    campaign 133–4
health insurance 224
Healthway Medical 164
heat exhaustion 142, 143
Heathrow Airport *see* London Heathrow
heatstroke (sunstroke) 143, 144
hedgehogs 284
Helios 427
Hemmingways 186
hepatitis A 98
Herm 320

Hertz 75, 82
high chairs 19, 110, 115, 218, 431
Hillwood Holidays 150
hiring equipment 27, 431
Holgates Caravan Park, Lancashire 168
Holiday Autos 82
holiday brochures 4, 5, 7, 12–13
holiday parks *see under* camping
Holiday Resort Unity, Somerset 168
holiday villages 17, 20, 94–106
  domestic 95–7
  drinking water 106–7
  overseas 98–104, 106
  poolside safety 98
  water safety 97
Holland *see* Netherlands
Holland America Line 128
Homeopathic Medical Association 233
homeopathic remedies 229–31, 240, 427
Homeway Ltd 167, 427
Honeypot Caravan & Camping Park, Suffolk
    168
horses: Canada 402
Hospital for Tropical Diseases 231
hotels 107–25
  airport 33, 48
  the best 12
  chains/groups 19, 24, 108, 119–23
  costs 15, 19
  discounts 22, 109
  does your family fit the bill? 111
  getting the room you want 114–15
  independent 19, 108
  indoor space and activities 13
  larger 24
  middle-sized 25
  mini-bars 21, 114, 115
  nearby facilities 13
  room size 19, 22, 114
  safety 112–14, 116–17
  seaside 27
  services 19, 109
  sleep problems 124–5
  smaller 24, 108–10
  smart 11, 108
  television 13
  top-rated 117–23
  websites 119
  what to ask 109–11, 112–13
house swaps 16–7
Huggababy 428
Humberside International Airport 38
humidity 143
Humpty Audio Cassettes 433
Hyatt hotels and resorts 123
Hyoscine 227, 240